Islam and Warfare

The question of how Islamic law regulates the notions of just recourse to and just conduct in war has long been the topic of heated controversy, and is often subject to oversimplification in scholarship and journalism. This book traces the rationale for aggression within the Islamic tradition, and assesses the meaning and evolution of the contentious concept of jihad. The book reveals that there has never been a unified position on what Islamic warfare tangibly entails, due to the complexity of relevant sources and discordant historical dynamics that have shaped the contours of jihad.

Onder Bakircioglu advocates a dynamic reading of Islamic law and military tradition; one which prioritises the demands of contemporary international relations, and considers the meaning and application of jihad as contingent on the socio-political forces of each historical epoch.

This book will be of great interest to scholars and students of international law, Islamic law, war and security studies, and the law of armed conflict.

Onder Bakircioglu is a Senior Lecturer in the School of Law at the University of Leicester.

"This is a scholarly, rigorous, thoroughly documented and intellectually honest account of the ambiguity and complexity of the Islamic doctrine of jihad. By persuasively demonstrating that war and peace are always outcomes of human agency, this book is an eloquent call to moral choice and political action, beyond stale polemics of absolute text or abstract doctrine."

Prof Abdullahi Ahmed An-Na'im

"With admirable scholarly mastery, Onder Bakircioglu, explores the nature of jihad in Islamic thought about war and peace, demonstrating conclusively that there is no authoritative doctrine available to resolve interpretative controversies so central to current debates about Islamic extremism. An indispensable study for legal specialist, and indeed, for anyone concerned with a deep understanding of the bearing of Islam on the regulation of warfare."

Prof Richard Falk

Routledge Research in the Law of Armed Conflict

Available titles in this series include:

Islamic Law and the Law of Armed Conflict
The Armed Conflict in Pakistan
Niaz Shah

Cluster Munitions and International Law
Disarmament with a Human Face?
Alexander Breitegger

Forthcoming titles in this series include:

Accountability for Violations of International Humanitarian Law
Essays in Honour of Tim McCormack
Jadranka Petrovic

International Law and Drone Strikes in Pakistan
The Legal and Socio-Political Aspects
Sikander Ahmed Shah

Islam and Warfare
Context and Compatibility with International Law
Onder Bakircioglu

The Concept of Military Objectives in International Law and Targeting Practice
Agnieszka Jachec-Neale

Islam and Warfare

Context and Compatibility with International Law

Onder Bakircioglu

Routledge
Taylor & Francis Group
LONDON AND NEW YORK

First published 2014
by Routledge
2 Park Square, Milton Park, Abingdon, Oxon, OX14 4RN

and by Routledge
711 Third Avenue, New York, NY 10017

Routledge is an imprint of the Taylor & Francis Group, an informa business

British Library Cataloguing in Publication Data
A catalogue record for this book is available from the British Library

Library of Congress Cataloging-in-Publication Data
Bakircioglu, Onder, author.
Islam and warfare : context and compatibility with international law / Onder Bakircioglu.
pages cm — (Routledge research in the law of armed conflicts)
ISBN 978-0-415-82888-8 (hardback) — ISBN 978-0-203-62760-0 (ebk)
1. War (Islamic law) 2. War--Religious aspects—Islam. 3. Jihad.
4. International law (Islamic law) I. Title.
KBP2416.B35 2015
341.6—dc23

2014021090

ISBN: 978-0-415-82888-8 (hbk)
ISBN: 978-0-203-62760-0 (ebk)

Typeset in Baskerville
by RefineCatch Limited, Bungay, Suffolk

Table of Contents

Acknowledgements

During the writing of the book, I incurred many intellectual and personal debts. I am particularly indebted to Hakeem Yusuf and Brice Dickson, who encouraged me to write this book and provided wise counsel every step of the way. I have benefited greatly from the intellectual and moral support of Caroline Fennell, Ronagh McQuigg, Olufemi Amao, Jean Allain, Kemal Sahin, Daniel Benitez, Fatih Ozturk, Mumin Hakkioglu, Haydar Olmez, Ahmet Yagli, Yasar Aydin, Canan Ugur, Ipek Aydin, and Selman and Zeycan Ozdan. I owe Peter Macalister-Smith for his invaluable feedback on the early versions of the work. I would also like to thank the anonymous reviewers of Routledge, whose detailed and insightful comments have been very helpful in revising the draft. I am grateful to Natasa Mavronicola and Hannah Russell, who graciously eased my teaching load to enable me to finally finish writing this book. I owe a huge debt of thanks to Emine Aydin for helping me prepare the bibliography. My heartfelt thanks are due to Derya Tekin for her excellent breakfasts and thought-provoking arguments.

I would like to thank my siblings, Tulay, Erkan, Hakan, Engin and Serdar for their constant inspiration and encouragement. Finally, my profound thanks go to my parents, Perihan and M. Nuri Bakircioglu, for their unconditional love and unwavering support – this book is dedicated to them.

Introduction

Islam as a religio-political force has, in recent decades, drawn the world's attention through such phenomena as the Iranian Revolution,[1] the unyielding mujahideen resistance against the Soviet invasion of Afghanistan, and the assassination of Egypt's President Sadat by a militant Islamic group. However, it was when al-Qaeda and its affiliates were established to have been behind the 11 September 2001 (9/11) attacks in the US that the age-old images of Islam – the dogmatic, backward and fanatical religion – were significantly revitalised within the Orientalist[2] discourse.[3] The 9/11 attacks also fuelled apprehension about jihad and its potential implications, including massive terrorist attacks on Western nations, the re-establishment of the caliphate,[4] the subjugation and murder of non-Muslims and Islamic world conquest through the use of brutal force.[5]

1 The Islamic takeover of power in Iran was one of the most significant non-communist mass uprisings of the last century, which threatened vital economic and political interests of the Western world in the region. The Iranian revolution also marked Islam's revival as a force to be reckoned with in regional and international politics. See A. Dawisha, 'Islam in Foreign Policy: Some Methodological Issues' in: A. Dawisha (ed.), *Islam in Foreign Policy* (Cambridge: Cambridge University Press, 1983) 1.

2 For an analysis of Western representations of 'the Orient', see E. W. Said, *Orientalism* (London: Penguin Books, 2003).

3 As Minou Reeves points out, Islam's image in the West, over the course of some 13 centuries, has been stubbornly biased and consistently negative, which deeply permeates the European consciousness. An overwhelming majority of European writers frequently portrayed Muhammad as a man with serious moral faults. Likewise, many a churchman, politician, historian, orientalist, dramatist, and philosopher had attributed to Islam in general and Muhammad in particular offensive and even fiendish characteristics. See M. Reeves, *Muhammad in Europe: A Thousand Years of Western Myth-Making* (New York: New York University Press, 2000) 81–82.

4 The institution of the caliphate was abolished in 1924 by the People's Republican Party in Turkey, which, departing from the theocratic Ottoman legacy, aimed to reshape Turkey and its institutions according to a secular system inspired by the West. See K. H. Karpat, 'Modern Turkey' in: P. M. Holt *et al*, *Cambridge History of Islam* (Cambridge: Cambridge University Press, 1992) 527, 533.

5 J. Strawson, 'Holy War in the Media: Images of *Jihad*' in: S. Chermak *et al* (eds.), *Media Representations of September 11* (Westport: Praeger, 2003) 17–18.

The impact of the 9/11 attacks was so great that even balanced portrayals of Islam were eclipsed by stereotypical images of a fundamental, anti-Western, and warmongering religion that bore the hallmarks of medieval prejudices and rhetoric. The popular representation tailored for the Western audience has reflected Islam as monolithic, intrinsically aggressive, and determined to wage interminable wars against the interests and values of the Western civilisation.[6] A cursory analysis of popular news coverage[7] reveals that Islam itself is largely held responsible for the constant threat of violence posed by some militant groups claiming to be acting under the duty of jihad, a term which has long entered into common usage, albeit largely misinterpreted.[8] Regrettably, the misreading and/or misrepresentation of the Islamic attitude to war and peace has strengthened the long-held prejudice that incessant military struggle is an intrinsic feature of Muslim foreign policy. While terrorism in the name of religious belief is not a phenomenon peculiar to Islam, there now exists a prevalent stereotypical Western perception that crudely considers Islamic terrorism a basic component of jihad.

The caricaturisation of Islam as the arch-enemy of the Judaeo-Christian tradition owes its main sources to the extremist discourse and acts of terrorism engaged in by radical non-State actors. Ironically, the exaggeration, and at times demonisation, of the 'Islamic threat' is akin to the 'Communist threat' theme that dominated the Cold War period during which American national security strategists often portrayed communism as an 'international conspiracy . . . directed generally against the inherent dignity, freedom, and sacredness of the individual, . . . [as well as] against the Judaeo-Christian code of morals on which . . . [the] Western civilisation rest[ed]'.[9] The dissipation of the 'spectre of communism' appears to have granted the chance for Western policymakers to turn to scaremongering against Islam.[10]

6 As Peters poignantly reminds us, Islamic warfare 'has always appealed to Western imagination. The image of the dreadful Turk, clad in a long robe and brandishing his scimitar, ready to slaughter any infidel that might come his way and would refuse to be converted to the religion of Mohamet, has been a stereotype in Western literature for a long time. Nowadays this image has been replaced by that of the Arab 'terrorist' in battledress, armed with a Kalashnikov gun and prepared to murder . . . innocent Jewish and Christian women and children'. R. Peters, *Islam and Colonialism: The Doctrine of Jihad in Modern History* (The Hague: Mouton Publishers, 1979) 4.

7 See generally, E. Said, *Covering Islam: How the Media and the Experts Determine How We See the Rest of the World* (London: Vintage, 1997).

8 *Jihad* is commonly mistranslated as holy war; yet neither the Quran nor the *hadith* contains the concept of holy war, which was coined by Europeans in the eleventh century, referring to the Crusades. See G. Marranci, *Jihad: Beyond Islam* (New York: Berg, 2006) 18; L. Napoleoni, 'Modern *Jihad*: The Islamist Crusade' (2003) 23 *Sais Review* 53, 65.

9 NSC-17, 'The Internal Security of the United States' (June 28, 1948) cited in: D. Campbell, *Writing Security: United States Foreign Policy and the Politics of Identity* (Minneapolis: University of Minnesota Press, 1998) 27.

10 While the phenomenon of Islamophobia is not new, many Muslim communities in Europe have lately been subject to increasing levels of hostility, suspicion, prejudice,

The assumption that Islam poses a radical challenge to what the West stands for is strengthened by the scholarship and journalism of oversimplification that largely inform the Western audience of Islam and its military aspect. This oversimplified representation of Islam is further supported by Huntington's 'clash of civilizations' model, formulated in the wake of the post-Cold War era, which mainly advanced the view that ideological or economic reasons would no longer play as prominent a role as the cultural, historical, traditional, and, most importantly, religious factors as the principal sources of divisions and conflicts between nations. Presenting a rather negative image of Islam, Huntington claimed that Islam is simply 'a religion of the sword . . . [which] glorifies military virtues'.[11] Huntington further overstressed the warlike aspect of Islam by noting that 'Muhammad himself . . . [was] a hard fighter and a skilful military commander', and that 'the Koran and other statements of Muslim beliefs contain few prohibitions on violence, and a concept of nonviolence is absent from Muslim doctrine and practice'.[12] The fact that there is no plain or uncontested stance towards war and peace in Islam is largely obscured by this portrayal, which crudely considers hostility to be an inherent feature of Islam.[13] This outlook, in other words, views Islam itself as one of the material sources of potential conflicts, a conclusion based on dubious generalisations and not fully in accord with historical realities.[14]

negative stereotyping, and verbal or physical harassment. It is recognised that irrespective of its daily forms, whether racism, discrimination, or violence, Islamophobia constitutes a clear violation of human rights and a grave threat to social cohesion. In its thought-provoking report, the Runnymede Commission on British Muslims and Islamophobia identified the dominant stereotypical tendencies characterising Islamophobia, such as considering Islam monolithic, static, unresponsive, authoritarian, inferior, or primitive, and viewing Muslims as aggressive, manipulative, backward, and self-righteous in their beliefs and values. The report calls for serious action to eradicate Islamophia in order to reduce discrimination, hatred, and aggression on grounds of religion, colour, ethnicity, or cultural practice. See *Islamophobia: Issues, Challenges and Action*, A Report by the Commission on British Muslims and Islamophobia (London: Trentham Books, 2004) 21ff; also see The Parekh Report, *The Future of Multi-Ethnic Britain: Report of the Commission on the Future* (London: Profile Books, 2002) 245–246; I. Ramberg, *Islamophobia and its Consequences on Young People: Seminar Report* (Strasbourg: Council of Europe Publishing, 2004) 6ff.

11 S. P. Huntington, *The Clash of Civilizations and the Remaking of World Order* (New York: Simon & Schuster, 1996) 263; S. P. Huntington, 'The Clash of Civilizations?' (1993) 72 *Foreign Affairs* 22, 49; J. Rehman, *Islamic State Practices, International Law and the Threat from Terrorism: A Critique of the 'Clash of Civilisations' in the New World Order* (Oxford: Hart Publishing, 2005) 1–2.

12 Huntington (1996), supra note 11, 263.

13 J. Rehman, 'Islam, "War on Terror" and the Future of Muslim Minorities in the United Kingdom: Dilemmas of Multiculturalism in the Aftermath of the London Bombings' (2007) 29 *Human Rights Quarterly* 831, 832ff; F. Halliday, *Islam and the Myth of Confrontation* (London: I.B. Tauris, 2003) 107.

14 To support his conclusions, Huntington, among others, argues that 'Islam is an absolutist faith. It merges religion and politics and draws a sharp line between those in the *Dar al-Islam* [Abode of Islam] and those in the *Dar al-Harb* [Abode of War]. As

Undoubtedly, Islam, since its inception, has confronted other civilisations, including the West, for a variety of economic, political, and religious reasons. As two major world religions, Islam and Christianity not only posed mutual threats to one another's very existence, but also presented ideological and moral challenges to one another's outlook, for both claimed monopoly on truth, with their alternative visions of religious belief and ideal behaviour, and universality in their missions. Whilst the Islamic world had been far ahead of the Christian West during the Middle Ages in economic, military, scientific, and cultural spheres,[15] the balance had tilted towards the West with the industrial and scientific revolution, which later culminated in the subordination of many non-European nations to Western powers through colonial and imperial enterprise. With the end of the classical colonial period in the post-1945 world, international conflicts became less frequent owing to the much greater destructive capacity of conventional warfare, a phenomenon that led some non-State actors to employ asymmetric military means to target nation-States. It is within such a context that some Muslim groups, with the aim of defending their version of Islamic values against their perceived enemies, have resorted to acts of terrorism.

Although such atrocities as the 9/11 and 7/7 attacks were sought to be justified with reference to Islam,[16] the tendency to view Islam mainly through the lens of terrorism, intolerance, and brute force blurs the fact that Islam possesses a rich potential to promote peace; that Islamic warfare is subject to strict limitations, and jihad does not connote terror and aggression; and that militant groups do not represent billions of Muslims who, in the main, denounce indiscriminate violence. Accordingly, the abuses of the doctrine of jihad by self-proclaimed contemporary jihadists should not encourage the use of blatant anti-Islamic rhetoric, claiming that Islam itself contains the seeds for wanton violence; for this would deepen mutual misunderstanding, fear, resentment, hatred, and disaccord between the Western and Islamic worlds.

a result, Confucians, Buddhists, Hindus, Western Christians, and Orthodox Christians have less difficulty adapting to and living with each other than any one of them has in adapting to and living with Muslims.' Huntington (1996), supra note 11, 264. This claim, however, misses two important points: first, the categorical distinction between *Dar al-Islam* and *Dar al-Harb* had been drawn by Muslim scholars during the imperial period of Islam, congruent with the political exigencies of the era, and hence the distinction is man-made, and not based on eternal principles; second, Huntington completely ignores Islam's superior medieval record on tolerating religious minorities belonging to the category of the 'People of the Book'. These points will be revisited later.

15 As Lewis points out, 'in the period which European historians see as a dark interlude between the decline of ancient civilization – Greece and Rome – and the rise of modern civilization – Europe, Islam was the leading civilization in the world, marked as such by its great and powerful kingdoms, its rich and varied industry and commerce, its original and creative sciences and letters'. B. Lewis, *The Crisis of Islam: Holy War and Unholy Terror* (London: Phoenix, 2004) 4.

16 Within the last decade, militant groups also conducted terror attacks in Istanbul (2003), Madrid (2004), and Mumbai (2008) – all ostensibly committed under the duty of jihad.

It is, then, the duty of responsible scholarship to promote an accessible and fair account of Islamic 'just war' tradition in an effort to dispel illusions about jihad, a concept which has long been misused and abused on account of ignorance or ideological prejudice. This book explores issues surrounding Islamic tradition on warfare, aiming to highlight its guiding principles within the historical context in which they took on their defining characteristics. By examining this controversial subject, this book seeks to challenge the mainstream perception[17] that jihad is merely a religiously sanctioned aggressive warfare to propagate Islam, a religion which, according to this crude perception, poses a danger to humanitarian values, and violates the basic principles of modern international law. Refutation of these blanket assertions can plausibly be done by disclosing the complexity of the normative framework of Islamic warfare. It is, however, imperative to note at the outset of such an endeavour that in every religious, ethical, and ideological system there surfaces, at some point, a certain degree of cleavage between the theory and practice. Such variance may particularly arise in the fog of war wherein military necessities and human frailty might engulf religio-ethical principles.

Among the key research questions of this study are: Are the primary sources of Islam open to re-interpretation to effectuate a change in (re)reading the legal parameters of Islamic warfare? Does the concept of jihad necessarily connote aggressive force or acts of terrorism? What are the main intellectual stands on the use of force in Islam? Do Islamic principles on matters of war and peace comply with the principles of modern international law, which envisage unilateral force merely in self-defence? In an attempt to answer these questions, the book first provides a historical and contextual survey of the sources of Islamic law with a view to illustrating their continuing relevance to the debate on jihad and its interpretation. The second part traces the origins and evolution of the Islamic use of force discourse. This overview is divided into two parts: the first examines Islamic *jus in bello* rules, while the second explores Islamic *jus ad bellum* norms, which will be the main focus of the study. This survey clarifies how the sources of Sharia in general, and warlike verses of the Quran in particular,[18] have developed over time, laying the groundwork for the forthcoming analysis of how jihad is to be

17 There is, indeed, a tendency to exaggerate threats posed against the Western world by the militant, religious movements grouped together under the assumed monolithic rubric of 'Islamic totalitarianism'. These radical movements are portrayed to regard such Western notions as individual rights and freedoms as the height of depravity, and to have an agenda of waging jihad against all those who refuse to embrace the dogmas of Islam. Hence, Muslim totalitarians, as the argument runs, single-mindedly seek to eradicate the Western culture and values in order to bring about the global triumph of Islam. See generally, Y. Brook; A. Epstein, '"Just War Theory" vs. American Self-Defence' in: E. Journo (ed.), *Winning the Unwinnable War: America's Self-Crippled Response to Islamic Totalitarianism* (Plymouth: Rowman & Littlefield, 2009) 81–82.

18 For the benefit of non-specialist readers, this book employs a simple form of transliteration whereby common Arabic terms, such as Sharia, Quran, jihad, *ijtihad*, Shia, or Sunni, are restricted to roman letters and no diacriticals are used to stress pronunciation.

interpreted according to the contemporary context of international relations. The third part of the book assesses the opposing doctrinal views on the meaning and implications of Islamic warfare. Finally, the fourth section, accompanied by examples of Islamic State practice, proposes a contextual interpretation of jihad in the United Nations (UN) era. The study will end with a summary of the main conclusions reached.

While modern works on Islam generally produce a single-sided representation of jihad, exclusively highlighting either the peaceful or warlike aspects thereof, this book aims to capture the phenomenon in its overall matrix. This undertaking will reveal that there has never been a unified position on what Islamic warfare actually entails, due to the complexity of relevant sources, and discordant historical dynamics that have shaped the contours of jihad. The main theoretical framework of the study is then predicated upon the major premise that the exact meaning and application of jihad has hitherto been contingent on the socio-political forces of each historical epoch. Linked with this premise, this work advocates a dynamic reading of Islamic military tradition, for blind adherence to antiquated concepts that are not responsive to new challenges fails to bring into play just and practicable responses to the demands of contemporary international relations. Hence, the primary objective of this study is to promote the view that jihad may and should solely be confined to peaceful and defensive measures, a proposition supported by a socio-legal research methodology that benefits from a wide range of perspectives drawn from legal scholarship, history, international relations theory, and theology.[19]

19 It must be noted that the book's scope is essentially limited to the Sunni approach (Sunnis constitute the majority of Muslims worldwide) to just warfare, as the task of adequately treating the relevant Shia perspective requires a separate monograph.

1 Main Sources of Islamic Law

Introduction

Islam possesses some important characteristics of a legal system, which seeks to regulate the behaviour of its adherents in accordance with its ideal paradigm of what constitutes right and wrong, and demands the believer to follow (by means of thought and deed) its precepts, which are believed to have originated from God's will. Classical Islamic jurisprudence rests on a monotheistic outlook that regards God as the ultimate source of law, for He alone is taken to be the ultimate sovereign whose omnipotence over human affairs stems from His status as the sole creator of the entire universe. Humankind accordingly needs no further justification to be subordinate to His will. Unsurprisingly, in relation to the Lord (*rabb*), Islam characterises humans as servants (*abd*).[1] The word 'Islam', likewise, derives from the Arabic term *salam*, which has a two-fold meaning: peace and submission (with the suggestion of total submission to God).[2] A Muslim, then, is a person who unconditionally submits to God to the exclusion of any other revered entity.

The question of how the Islamic law regulates the notions of just recourse to, and just conduct in, war requires a brief examination of the origins, development, and hierarchy of Islamic law. Rejecting a literal and narrow approach, this book advocates the need for a historical and contextual re-reading of the main sources of Islam, whose varied interpretation informs the ongoing debate on the Islamic use of force discourse and its compatibility with contemporary political and legal exigencies. By providing an overview of the sources of Islam, this chapter aims to set the stage for the subsequent analysis of Islamic *jus in bello* and *jus ad bellum* norms.

1 W. M. Watt, *Islam and Christianity Today* (London: Routledge, 1983) 125.
2 For various uses of the word *salam*, see B. Lewis, *The Political Language of Islam* (Chicago: The University of Chicago Press, 1988) 78ff.

I. Primary Sources

A. The Quran

Islamic tradition deals with questions of war and peace in its main sources, which include the Quran, the sacred book of Islam, guiding sayings and deeds of the Prophet (*hadith*), and the individual as well as collective opinions formed by jurists over the centuries since the death of the Prophet Muhammad. It must be made clear at the outset that while there is a consensus over the authenticity of the Quranic text and the traditions and sayings attributed to the Prophet, as recorded by reliable chroniclers,[3] the manner in which these sources has hitherto been interpreted varied considerably. While alive, the Prophet often settled controversies over alternative readings of the Quran, yet his demise compelled the Muslim community to call upon their own resources to determine the true meaning of divine revelations. Hence, Islamic tradition as a whole is a rich composite of binding divine sources and man-made doctrines developed over the course of Islamic history.

The Quran (which literally means recitation or reading) constitutes the most important source of Islam, which is composed of the divine revelations received by Muhammad, whose chief mission was to form an orderly and moral world operating in accordance with sacred messages delivered by God. Consisting of these revelations, the Quran is the primary and most authoritative source of Islamic law.[4] The Quran is the sole Muslim Scripture and it would be misleading to call it the Muslim Bible. This is certainly not to overlook the similarities between Christianity and Islam; these religions have much in common (some of which will be discussed within the context of just war). Both, for instance, emerged from within the same ancient Middle Eastern civilisations; both had adopted the Jewish tradition of ethical monotheism, a prophetic mission of spreading the knowledge of one God and His commandments preserved in sacred texts; and both largely drew upon Greek thought and science, as well as institutions shaped to an important degree by Hellenistic and Roman elements.[5] Nevertheless, unlike the Old and New Testaments, the Quran is not composed of texts written over a long period of time by various authors; it is rather a single text dictated by a single

3 The most credible *hadith* collectors include Sahih al-Bukhari, Sahih Muslim, Ahmad ibn Hanbal, Sahih al-Sijistani, Abu Isa al-Tirmidhi, and al-Nasai. These chroniclers compiled the *hadith* literature about 200 years after the Prophet's demise. See further, N. J. DeLong-Bas, *Wahhabi Islam: From Revival and Reform to Global Jihad* (London: I.B. Tauris, 2004) 52; S. Hasan, 'Islamic Jurisprudence: Sources and Traditions Creating Diversity in Human Relationships' in: S. Hasan (ed.), *The Muslim World in the 21st Century: Space, Power, and Human Development* (London: Springer, 2012) 25ff.

4 F. A. Hassan, 'The Sources of Islamic Law' (1982) 76 *American Society of International Law Proceedings* 65, 66.

5 B. Lewis, *Islam: From the Prophet Muhammad to the Capture of Constantinople*, Vol. II (Oxford: Oxford University Press, 1974) xviii.

author over the course of two decades,[6] with certain distinct messages, injunctions, and truths considered to be universally valid.

Inasmuch as the Quran is believed to contain the literal word of God, it is deemed the most authentic record of Islamic law,[7] incarnating the final, inimitable, and infallible injunctions of everlasting validity. God in the Quran affirms Islam's complete nature, saying that '[t]his day have I perfected your religion for you, completed My favour upon you, and have chosen for you Islam as your religion'.[8] Although the Quran expresses that 'to every people (was sent) a Messenger',[9] and that there is no difference between these Prophets,[10] Muhammad closed the line of Messengers[11] by reintroducing the original, unadulterated teaching of God, which had not been preserved in its pristine form in earlier scriptures.[12] Muslims thus believe that the Quran had been bestowed on humankind though Muhammad, 'the seal of the Prophets',[13] as being God's final effort to repair and reconstruct the original, but distorted and forgotten, message preached by other Prophets since Abraham.[14]

The Quran accordingly presents Islam as the very religion that had been preached by earlier Prophets including Abraham, Noah, Moses, and Jesus,[15] who themselves were thus originally Muslims. Among other prophets, Muslims ascribe

6 The Muslim belief that the Quran represents the unalterable word of God conveyed solely through the medium of Muhammad is unique in that neither the Torah nor the Gospel had been communicated and preserved as such. While some orthodox Jews believe that the Torah had been dictated to Moses on Mount Sinai, the nature of Moses' mediation in recording the divine commandments, the time of the completion of the Torah, and the possible involvement of other authors in the writing of the Old Testament remain controversial. Most scholars, however, believe that both the canonisation and formation of the Old Testament transpired at a date considerably later than what the Bible claims. See further, D. Stern, 'Sacred Text and Canon' in: A. A. Cohen; P. Mendes-Flohr (eds.), *20th Century Jewish Religious Thought* (Philadelphia, The Jewish Publication Society, 1987) 841, 842ff; S. D. Fraade, *Legal Fictions: Studies of Law and Narrative in the Discursive Worlds of Ancient Jewish Sectarians and Sages* (Leiden: Brill, 2011) 478ff.

7 Hassan, supra note 4, 66.

8 Q. 5:3. This study relies upon authoritative scholar Yusuf Ali's translation of the Quran. See A. Y. Ali, *The Meaning of the Holy Qur'an,* 11th ed. (Beltsville: Amana Publications, 2008) 1297. In cases of difficult verses, the reader may refer to the following website for a comparison of various English translations of the Quran: http://www.studyquran.org/EnglishTranslations.htm.

9 Q. 10:47.

10 Q. 2:136.

11 Q. 33:40.

12 Ali, supra note 8, 56.

13 Q. 33:40.

14 Q. 2:127–130.

15 According to the Quran, there are no people who did not receive a messenger (Q: 10.47), hence humankind is not in a position to claim that it has not been warned adequately. See further E. E. Calverley, 'Mohammad, Seal of the Prophets?" 1936 (26) *The Muslim World* 79–82; J. P. Berkey, *The Formation of Islam: Religion and Society in the Near East, 600–1800* (Cambridge: Cambridge University Press, 2003) 48ff.

to Abraham a prominent standing, for he is considered to be a perfect model for the faithful, the harbinger of monotheism, and hence the founding father of Judaism, Christianity, and Islam.[16] Muslim tradition, in other words, rooted Islam within the soil of monotheism, a phenomenon which rendered the appeal of the Quran far more acceptable to those who had already been familiar with the monotheistic conception of the universe. This point is confirmed by some early sources,[17] including *The Armenian History*, written circa 660, which recorded that 'a certain man from among those same sons of Ismael [i.e. Arabs] whose name was Mahmet [Muhammad], a merchant', acting as if by God's command, started preaching the path of truth. 'He taught them to recognize the God of Abraham, especially because he was learned and informed in the history of Moses.' Similar to the Jewish tradition, since 'the command came from on high', the followers 'came together in the unity of religion', abandoning their idols and turning 'to the living God who appeared to their father Abraham'.[18] Muhammad, in this sense, had never rejected the legacy of his predecessors; rather, he saw himself part of a long series of Prophets who had been appointed by God to preach the divine truth. Like Abraham, Muhammad preached monotheism and advised his followers to comport themselves in a manner of righteousness and piety.[19] Again, similar to Christ, he reminded humankind of resurrection, the Day of Judgement, and of the punishments and rewards in the hereafter.[20]

16 Muslims, and some Roman observers and missionaries, believe that Abraham's child Ishmael, whom Sarah's maidservant, Hagar, bore to Abraham, was banished from his home. For when Sarah gave birth to Isaac, she wished him to receive Abraham's inheritance, and thus had Abraham cast Hagar and Ishmael out into the desert near Mecca, where Ishmael eventually became the father of Arabs. See further John L. Esposito *et al* (eds.), *The Islamic World: Past and Present*, Vol. I (New York: Oxford University Press, 2004) 7.

17 For a brief illustration of how monotheism impacted on the spread of Islam, see I. Ishaq; A Guillaume (trans.), *The Life of Muhammad: A Translation of Ibn Ishaq's Sirat Rasul Allah* (Oxford: Oxford University Oxford, 1955) 93.

18 Sebeos; R. W. Thomson (trans.), *The Armenian History Attributed to Sebeos,* Vol. I. (Liverpool: University of Liverpool, 1999) 95–96.

19 See Q. 2:131–133.

20 It is to be noted that while there is no consensus in Christian theology as to whether the atoning sacrifice of Christ has been sufficient to wipe away the sins of Christians, regardless of the merit or repentance of the sinner, Muslims unequivocally reject the doctrine of the all-atoning bodily sacrifice of Jesus through crucifixion and resurrection. According to Islam, faith and deeds performed in the body are the sole determinants of one's fate in the afterlife: 'if any do deeds of righteousness . . . and have faith they will enter heaven', the Quran declared (Q. 4: 124). Thus no Messenger may be relied upon for salvation, for each person is responsible for his own inner and outer attitude. This suggests that what Muslims believe and do in this world would eventually translate themselves into rewards or sufferings in the afterlife. See further D. Thorsen, *Exploration of Christian Theology* (Grand Rapids: Baker Academic, 2010) 28.3.3ff *cf.* J. L. Esposito, *What Everyone Needs to Know About Islam* (Oxford: Oxford University Press, 2011) 31–35.

1. The Compilation of the Quran

Islamic tradition holds that the Quran is revealed to the Prophet Muhammad by God through the medium of angel Gabriel.[21] Muslim theology and jurisprudence consider the entire corpus of the Quran as having sprung from Muhammad's reception of divine revelations (*wahy*). The form of such revelations had been described to be verbal, visual, or otherwise in character.[22] Bukhari relates a tradition on the authority of the Prophet's wife, Aisha, who described the account of the first direct revelation: while in seclusion for peaceful contemplation in a cave near Mecca, Gabriel commanded Muhammad to read the first lines of Sura 96.[23] Puzzled when the unlettered Prophet could not recite, the angel pressed him hard until he yielded and managed to read the first five verses of the Sura. As the Messenger recounted what had taken place, his first wife Khadija and her Christian cousin Waraqa assured him of the sacredness of his mission.[24] Following a brief period of interruption, Muhammad regularly received further revelations, during the process of which he reportedly entered into a trancelike state. These revelations came down in instalments in Mecca and Medina over a 22-year period, until the demise of Muhammad (AD 610–632).[25]

The Quran is revealed in Arabic,[26] containing 114 chapters (*suras*), 6,236 verses (*ayat*), and a total number of 77,934 words.[27] The entire corpus of the Quran was completed during the lifetime of Muhammad, who called upon his scribes to record what had been revealed to him. The Prophet's recitations had initially been written down on whatever material came to hand, including palm leaves, shoulder-blades of camels, wood pieces, and parchment. Under Muhammad's supervision, these fragmented pieces were subsequently collected into *suras* or chapters. However, while the Quran existed in its full, albeit fragmented, form since the first revelation, the written material was not brought together into a single codex during the Prophet's lifetime. The assembly of the whole Quran was a lengthy and arduous task, the completion of which has been attributed to various people among the Prophet's companions, including the four immediate successors as caliphs. Nonetheless, most commentators concur that an official codex had

21 See Q. 53:1–18.

22 According to the tradition, the divine inspiration was revealed to the Prophet sometimes 'like the ringing of a bell', and sometimes the Angel came 'in the form of a man' who conveyed the divine message verbally. *Hadith* Reported by al-Bukhari, *Hadith of Bukhari*, Vol. I, *Hadith* 1:2.

23 See Q. 96:1–5.

24 Al-Bukhari, supra note 22.

25 See generally J. E. Campo (ed.), *Encyclopedia of Islam* (New York: Infobase Publishing, 2009) 590; M. Cook, *The Koran: A Very Short Introduction* (New York: Oxford University Press, 2000) 5.

26 'We have sent it down as an Arabic Quran, in order that ye may learn wisdom', the Quran declares (Q. 12:2).

27 G. Sawma, *The Quran Misinterpreted, Mistranslated, and Misread: The Aramaic Language of the Quran* (New York: Adibooks, 2006) 98.

been collected under the rule of Uthman, the third caliph, within 20 years of Muhammad's demise.[28]

Uthman concerned himself with ascertaining whether or not the texts he assembled had been directly recited by the Prophet. During this process, the main Quranic material was that collated by Muhammad's chief secretary, Zaid ibn Thabit. Uthman is known to have ordered an authorised version of the Quran to be assembled and copied, and commanded his governors to destroy all variant texts.[29] For one of the main challenges lay in the fact that Arabic was the language of desert nomads, and its spoken form was far more sophisticated than its written form at a time when written Arabic lacked vowels or diacritical marks. This led to the acknowledgement of seven variant, but equally authoritative, readings (*qeraat*) of the Quran, which could have caused significant controversy over the meaning. But when the Quran was redacted and an authoritative version was adopted, this conclusively put an end to alternative readings due to assorted spellings. This redacted version, effected by a number of learned *sahaba*, 'has since remained unchanged and unchallenged'.[30]

2. *The Content and Structure of the Quran*

As noted above, Muslims consider the Quran to embody an authentic record of God's eternal and unalterable word.[31] Incorporating an amalgamation of legal and ethical principles, as well as ritualistic and moral exhortations, the Quran provides the fundamental substance of the Islamic law (Sharia),[32] and imposes

28 For a detailed account of the collection process of the Quran, see J. Burton, *The Collection of the Quran* (Cambridge: Cambridge University Press, 1977) 139ff.

29 The dominant view among Muslim scholars is that no alteration had occurred in the Quran, and thus the text that has reached us today was directly revealed to the Prophet. For a discussion about whether any possible alterations (*tahrif*) and/or any additions or omissions have taken place, see A. al-Qaism al-Musawi al-Khui, *Prolegomena to the Quran* (New York: Oxford University Press, 1998) 135ff; *cf.* Burton, supra note 28, 138ff.

30 M. C. Bassiouni, 'Evolving Approaches to Jihad: From Self-Defence to Revolutionary and Regime-Change Political Violence' (2008) 8 *Chicago Journal of International Law* 119, 119.

31 However, the intransigence with which the Muslim scholars defend the integrity of the Quran has been challenged by some Western scholars who questioned the Muslim account by arguing that the Quran, as we know it today, had been assembled at a much later period out of a fragmentary prophetic tradition, and of a large quantity of exegetical material developed during the course of polemics engaged with Jews and Christians. For more on this revisionist theory, see M. Ruthven, *Islam in the World*, 2nd ed. (Oxford: Oxford University Press, 2000) 81ff; *cf.* J. L. Esposito, *The Oxford Encyclopaedia of the Modern Islamic World,* Vol. III. (Oxford: Oxford University Press, 1995) 386.

32 Originally, the term Sharia referred to the practical side of religion and this is how it appears in the Quran: '[t]hen we put thee on the (right) Way of Religion: so follow thou that (Way)' (Q. 45: 18). Muslim lexicographers note that the word Sharia is connected to such concepts as 'path', 'road', 'way', or 'highway'. But, in its broader sense, Sharia came to designate the rules and legal provisions that govern the lives of Muslims.

a clear set of legal and moral obligations on Muslims.[33] The Quran covers the basic components of mundane and spiritual existence, envisaging guidelines for legitimate and ideal behaviour concerning important aspects of life. Lessons of right conduct in daily matters, and wisdom in spiritual matters, may thus be sought from the Quran, which is deemed to have confirmed, subsumed, or restored God's earlier revelations.[34] In view of the fact that God's ordinance is essentially embodied in the Quran, it is only natural that Muslims are required to abide by the moral and legal framework thereof. In fact, according to the Quran's religio-legal matrix, the ideal life in this world is one which is lived according to the relevant Islamic precepts and injunctions (whether ritualistic, moral or legal in character). The Quran, in this sense, consists of a system of duties and responsibilities, which, if duly performed, may not only give the believer an inner satisfaction in the temporal world, but also assure him a place in Heaven.[35]

Muslim scholars usually distinguish between three main categories of ethico-legal injunctions in the Quran. The first pertains to the doctrine of belief in God, His messengers and the Day of Judgement; the next is essentially concerned with ethical human conduct; and the third part is associated with practical or daily actions of believers under Islamic law.[36] These categories are then subdivided into relevant sections, which, among others, deal with rituals, private and public issues, domestic and international politics (including matters of diplomacy, war and peace), and other transactions. Whilst the Quran incorporates a detailed set of practical, legal, and moral rules, when its meaning remains obscure or when it is silent on a particular matter, other sources of Sharia (which will be explored below) may be drawn on to generate answers for the problem at hand. The Quran, in this context, may be compared with a constitution that provides the key material on issues of social, political, legal, and practical nature. It is the role of the scholar, jurist, or legislator to explain or flesh out, while remaining loyal to the letter and spirit of the main text,[37] such general norms to address what is necessitated by concrete circumstances. Naturally, the ever-changing needs of societies require

See F. Griffel, 'Introduction' in: A. Amanat; F. Griffel (eds.), *Islamic Law in the Contemporary Context* (Stanford: Stanford University Press, 2007) 2–3; Ali, supra note 8, 1297.

33 M. H. Kamali, *Principles of Islamic Jurisprudence* (Cambridge: The Islamic Texts Society, 1989) 18; A. An-Naim, 'The Rights of Women and International Law in the Muslim Context' (1988) 9 *Whittier Law Review* 491, 492.

34 Q. 10:37; F. Rahman, *Islam & Modernity: Transformation of an Intellectual Tradition* (Chicago: The University of Chicago Press, 1982) 2.

35 See further, J. Schacht, *An Introduction to Islamic Law* (Oxford: Oxford University Press, 1982) 11; M. Khadduri, 'Nature and Sources of Islamic Law' (1953) 22 *The George Washington Law Review* 3, 7ff.

36 See further M. I. Dien, *Islamic Law: From Historical Foundations to Contemporary Practice* (Edinburgh: Edinburgh University Press, 2004) 37ff.

37 To be sure, when detailed rules are deduced from the Quran, whose commands are deemed to have been issued by the Supreme Legislator, the jurist must strictly remain loyal to the very letter, purpose, and overall framework of the Quran and relevant prophetic traditions to avoid blasphemy.

appropriate refinement and elaboration of Quranic norms through human reasoning.

It is worth mentioning that a notable portion of the Quran's content had essentially been informed by the prevailing socio-political, economic, and religious circumstances of its day; thus, many moral, religious, and social pronouncements of the Quran, even though divinely inspired and transcendental, answer some of the problems faced at the time of Muhammad's ministry. As some of the early verses make clear, the Quran was primarily concerned with the acute problems of its time, which included such issues as polytheism, idolatry, the exploitation and maltreatment of the poor, malpractices in trade, and the overall injustice affecting the society.[38] The Quran addressed these phenomena, whether explicitly or implicitly, mainly when the occasion had arisen. The practical facet of the Quran becomes quite evident when considering that a remarkable part of Quranic revelations was handed down to Muhammad over the course of 22 years in response to pragmatic questions. Not surprisingly, therefore, the Quran contains a rich repository of practical guidance on real-life situations, with injunctions regulating a vast field, from issues of international relations and matters of war and peace down to the habits of everyday life such as relations between spouses, child custody, eating, drinking, and personal hygiene.

In addition to containing moral and spiritual injunctions whose validity cross the borders of time and space, the Quran, then, responded to some of the important socio-political problems of its period. It is thus safe to maintain that the main contours of the Quranic text took shape against a concrete socio-historical background. Some scholars went so far as to maintain that Islam invalidated all previous legal systems since the Quran provided a comprehensive account of everything.[39] Some other scholars, however, particularly Hanafi jurists, claimed that only those pre-Islamic rules and practices which had not been expressly abrogated by the divine will could be recognised as valid.[40] Evidence suggests that Islam did not repudiate the validity of all pre-Islamic doctrines; particularly during the early period of Islam, when Islamic laws were in their nascent stages, there occurred widespread adoption of many legal and administrative institutions and practices of the newly conquered territories. There were, in Hasan's words, 'multiple influences on Muslims in places where they have adopted many social and cultural practices of pre-Islamic origin'.[41] This was natural as the expansion

38 Likewise, issues surrounding Muhammad's prophetic career also find reflection in the Quran, which include the initial Meccan rejection of Muhammad's prophethood and message, and, in the later Medina period, the disagreement with the Jews and controversy with some Christians. See Rahman, supra note 34, 2–5; Khadduri, supra note 35, 8.

39 Q. 16: 89; Q. 6: 38.

40 Khadduri, supra note 35, 3.

41 M. Hasan, *Moderate or Militant Images of India's Muslims* (Oxford: Oxford University Press, 2009) 102.

of the Islamic State[42] necessitated the management of foreign people with their particular traditions, which resulted in the fusion of some raw Islamic legal material with pertinent local customs and traditions. Prominent examples were seen in the law of taxation, the institution of religious foundations (*wakf*), and the way in which tolerated religions were managed.[43] The retention of some pre-Islamic traditions and local institutions was accompanied by the adoption of novel legal concepts, maxims, and methods of reasoning. In this way, as Schacht writes, many rules, concepts, and maxims, which had their origin in Roman and Byzantine law, Canon law of Eastern Churches, Rabbinic law, or Sassanian law, became part of the Islamic law[44] (certainly when integrated within the Islamic law, some such laws must have assumed a character in tune with the overall tenor of Islam). Likewise, when the pre-Islamic law of Arabia (embodied in a system of customary law known as the Sunnah) is examined, certain ancient (particularly Mosaic) practices may be noticed to have been subsumed under the umbrella of Islamic law. Examples include some forms of reprisals or punishments for certain crimes, such as amputation of the hand for thievery, or whipping or lapidation for adultery.[45] Also, certain forms of religious duties, such as the pilgrimage (*haj*), were retained, while their content and form were drastically adjusted to accord with the overall philosophy of Islam. Be that as it may, Islam's rejection of idolatry in favour of God's supremacy resulted in the rejection of many, though not all, pre-Islamic customs and practices that were idolatrous in nature.[46]

42 The interchangeable terms 'Islamic' and 'Muslim State' are used in this book not to designate the nature of a political organisation, but to stress the religious affiliation of the majority of population residing therein. While a State may not be conceived of as possessing a specific religion, in Islamic societies religion may be said to play a more significant role (relative to secular societies) in shaping domestic and international policies. As Esposito points out, although most contemporary Islamic States modelled their political, legal, and bureaucratic structures on their Western counterparts, they generally incorporated some very important Islamic principles into their legal systems and maintained a notable degree of political control over religious matters. See J. L. Esposito, *Islam and Politics*, 2nd ed. (Syracuse: Syracuse University Press, 1987) 94ff. Besides, given that Islam regulates consequential aspects of practical life, it naturally plays a prominent role in determining the contours of private and political human activity.

43 Schacht, supra note 35, 19.

44 Ibid. 21. For further examples of how some key Roman, Jewish, and Sassanian legal concepts and practices impacted upon Islamic legal theory and practice, see ibid. 18–22.

45 It is important to note that the Quran does not envisage lapidation for adultery, but stipulates the punishment of 'a hundred stripes' for the act (Q. 24:2). However, over the course of Islamic history, the practice of stoning for adultery had usually been justified by reference to the tradition. For a discussion see Burton, supra note 28, 102ff; B. G. Weiss (ed.), *Studies in Islamic Law and Society*, Vol. XV (Leiden: Brill, 2002) 85ff.

46 Khadduri, supra note 35, 5.

The importance of highlighting the nexus between certain Islamic injunctions and pre-Islamic customary law is that some primary and secondary sources of Islam may be better understood in the light of the knowledge of the pre-Islamic social setting within which Muslims resided. The same goes for warlike verses and traditions, some of which were formed within the context of pre-Islamic customs.[47] Hence, when an analyst is confronted with some obscure or ostensibly conflicting verses, a detailed evaluation of the relevant socio-historical and cultural backdrop must be conducted with a view to contextualising the issue involved. Given that the Quranic material was communicated to Muhammad piecemeal, it is often possible to comprehend any ambiguity through studying the historical setting or specific challenges faced by Muslims. As discussed below, such contextualisation is essential with respect to the belligerent verses, some of whose application had changed form in line with practical necessities.

3. *The Interpretation of the Quran*

Like other legal systems, Islamic law has been subjected to interpretation in varying degrees, a process which has taken the forms of traditional and customary, or critical and innovative, modes of reading religio-legal precepts. As will be clear, this book advocates the view that any interpretative effort should consider the overall historical context, specific socio-political challenges encountered by Muslims, connected verses, and traditions, as well as the overall logic, object, and purpose of Islam. As subjectivity is an inevitable element of interpretation, regular revisiting and review of primary and secondary principles is essential. Certainly, not every aspect of the religion can be re-read in line with the spirit of the times; for instance, there is very little scope in reinterpreting ritualistic rules or such timeless themes as the unity of God (*tawhid*) and the necessity of doing the right and avoiding the wrong. Another example is the profession of faith, affirming the presence of a unique God and Muhammad's mission as his Messenger, which is not susceptible to divergent readings due to its categorical status.[48]

For the purposes of interpreting the Quran, the aforementioned contextual method calls for the identification of the circumstances within which a verse had been revealed, the specific problem (if any) to which the revelation responded, as well as the overall corpus, objectives, and spirit of the Islamic legal system. The emphasis on context specificity does not, of course, preclude the interpreter from deducing general principles from a specific command or injunction, provided that

47 For instance, the Quranic prohibition of waging offensive wars during the 'sacred months' is a case in point, clearly recognising the pre-Islamic custom of non-violence during this period. See Q. 2:194; Q. 9:5.

48 The Quran states that 'say: "O men! I am sent unto you all, as the Messenger of Allah, to Whom belongeth the dominion of the heavens and the earth: there is no god but He: it is He that giveth both life and death. So believe in Allah and His Messenger."' Q. 7:158.

such deductions accord with the fundamental tenets of Islam and the eternal values it seeks to promote, such as the eradication of immorality and promotion of justice and socio-economic equality.[49]

Islamic law is expounded via the use of *usul al-fiqh,* a method of extracting rules (*fiqh*) from primary sources. Hence, it is through the branch of *usul al-fiqh* that secondary norms may be obtained.[50] The elaboration of Islamic norms is vital, for each era warrants renewed responses. While the Quran explicitly states that it explains 'all things',[51] and that nothing is 'omitted from the Book',[52] this, as Ramadan points out, must refer 'to general principles, to essential and immutable rules', whose practical implementation varies 'according to circumstances and situations'.[53] The Quran, in this sense, contains the most essential elements of legislation and the imperative will of God out of which secondary rules may be deduced.[54]

The modalities and methods of interpreting the Quran present certain challenges on account of its directly revealed character and superiority over other sources. Like other scriptures, the Quran is not always straightforward in its message,[55] which occasionally raises the difficulty of understanding the real sense of a verse while extracting rulings or practices. This resulted in the birth of different methods of interpretation over time within and between various Islamic cultures of different epochs. It must be remembered that the passage of time had significantly impacted on the way some verses have been read, for what was straightforward during the lifetime of Muhammad may have appeared rather obscure to the commentator of subsequent ages. During Muhammad's lifetime, the Prophet expounded the meaning and implications of opaque passages; in fact, according to the Quran, this was one of the duties of Muhammad – to explain 'clearly to men what is sent for them'.[56] Since the prophetic mission could

49 Islam's opposition to excessive disparity in economic resources is manifested, among others, in Q. 11:116; Q. 23:64; Q. 51:19. Tradition also confirms that while Islam does not oppose wealth acquired and used piously, it requires due consideration for the poor and needy. For more on this theme, see M. Mahmud, 'Islam vs. Marxism and Capitalism' in: J. J. Donohue; J. Esposito (eds.), *Islam in Transition: Muslim Perspectives*, 2nd ed. (Oxford: Oxford University Press, 2007) 129, 130.

50 As Kamali points out, 'the main difference between *fiqh* and *usul al-fiqh* is that the former is concerned with the knowledge of the detailed rules of Islamic law in its various branches, and the latter with the methods that are applied in the deduction of such rules from their sources. *Fiqh,* in other words, is the law itself, whereas *usul al-fiqh* is the methodology of the law.' Kamali, supra note 33, 2.

51 Q. 16:89.

52 Q. 6:38.

53 T. Ramadan, *Radical Reform: Islamic Ethics and Liberation* (Oxford: Oxford University Press, 2009) 24.

54 Dien, supra note 36, 35.

55 The Quran itself recognises that some of its verses contain 'hidden meanings', which may be known to God and to 'men of understanding'. Q. 3:7.

56 Q. 16:44. It is noted that Muhammad had not generally engaged in the theoretical or semantic analysis of the verses; he was rather interested in elucidating the practical

not be bequeathed to Muhammad's successors, the so-called caliphs, both divine legislation and their authoritative prophetic interpretation came to a halt, which led to complications particularly when Islam embarked upon expansion outside Arabia. The general development of Islamic law and the interpretation of the Quran could have been much more linear and clear-cut had Muslim rule been confined to Arabia. The newly conquered territories, including Egypt, Syria, Iraq, and Persia, presented such unprecedented challenges that could not be readily met merely through unelaborated principles. This challenge naturally compelled the Muslim community to invoke the prophetic tradition, personal opinion (*ray*) and certain principles of pre-Islamic law with a view to supplementing the divine legislation,[57] and hence addressing the demands of the new societies, with their unique cultural, customary, financial, and religious practices.

In interpreting the Quran, the issue of Quranic orders of rank and priority features as a prominent role in that not all verses, albeit they are all of the same divine origin, enjoin the same degree of normative status. Some verses may be more fundamental and important than others in the way they impose duties on the believer.[58] Likewise, some verses may be more direct in what they demand of humankind; and some may be more explicit or specific on first reading, while others may appear implicit or may refer to general directions from which further clarification may be obtained.[59] Unavoidably, the socio-economic and political context of each historical era has clearly marked out the theoretical framework of the analyst, which determines the way in which the textual material of the Quran is understood, interpreted, and applied to real-life situations.

It follows that the commentator of the Quran has been inclined to approach the text with a mindset that is conditioned by the presuppositions, concerns and expectations of his time. Thus, even when the commentator seeks to identify the rationale of a verse, which may link the cause and consequences of the revelation, he is most likely to approach the verse with a mindset that inquires as to its immediate implications. Such dialectic relationship between the text and its interpreter is not only inescapable, but also necessary to retain the scriptural guidance relevant to the requirements of changing circumstances. This active

implications of the Quranic material. See further A. Saeed, 'Contextualising' in: A. Rippin (ed.), *The Blackwell Companion to the Quran* (Oxford: Wiley, 2006) 36, 49ff.

57 See M. Khadduri, *War and Peace in the Law of Islam* (Baltimore: Johns Hopkins Press, 1955) 27–28.

58 The Quran, among others, envisages a system of duties and responsibilities that aims to direct the individual to the right path (sharia) of salvation. The believer in this system is presented with several choices, divided into categories between the strictly enjoined (*fard*) and strictly proscribed. Apart from these two extreme categories, there are also 'recommended' (*mandub*) and 'objectionable' (*makruh*) actions, which, however, do not impose hard-and-fast rules upon Muslims. There is finally the concept of *ja'iz* to which the law remains indifferent, and hence the individual is left with full discretion in determining his conduct. See further Khadduri, supra note 35, 8–9.

59 I. R. Al-Faruqi; L. I. Al-Faruqi, *The Cultural Atlas of Islam* (London: Macmillan, 1986) 246.

engagement with the text also complies with the notion that the Quran contains sempiternal guidance for humankind of all ages; were the Quran's message merely restricted to the questions faced during the time of its revelation, the universal message of the text could be weakened – i.e. the message might have lost its central pertinence to Muslims of various ages and cultures that seek pragmatic solutions to the problems they confront.

Constant re-engagement with the primary sources is, then, imperative in order to keep Islam's message alive and responsive to the needs of each age. One of the problems surrounding the theme of interpretation is the extent to which elaboration may be carried. The debate among the conservative, radical, liberal, reformist, or revivalist[60] scholars has never been about whether there should be interpretation of the Quranic material or prophetic traditions, but rather the degree to which this could occur. In their attempt to extract further rulings from primary sources, some scholars, including such canonical figures as Abu Hanifah, had faced sharp accusations of neglecting primary sources and of disproportionately relying on their opinions, and thereby of bending the normative status of the Quran and relevant traditions.[61] The primary concern has always been whether commentators remained faithful to the divine law, while codifying secondary rulings to keep pace with times and to address the needs of various societies with distinct habits, customs, and traditions. While, as discussed below, systematic elaboration of primary legislation had largely been interrupted after the age of 'classical' theologians,[62] Muslims have developed numerous schools of thought across various sects of Islam, ranging from literalists, fundamentalists, conservatives, and traditionalists to reformists.[63] Islam, similar to other religious traditions, thus contains within its framework a wide range of different schools that have sought, with varying methods, to contribute to the development of Islamic law.

In their pursuit to extricate further rules and/or extrapolate abstract constructions to concrete circumstances, Islamic theologians and jurists developed sophisticated methods and rules of interpretation with a view to reducing the margin of error. These highly evolved techniques of law-making or interpretation

60 Reformism is generally distinguished from revivalism, for while the former is principally forward-looking, seeking to modify traditional customs or institutions in an effort to keep up with modern times, the latter lays emphasis on the past with intent to return to original, pristine customs and traditions. See further J. R. Willis, 'Jihad Fi Sabil Allah – Its Doctrinal Basis in Islam and Some Aspects of its Evolution in Nineteenth-Century West Africa' (1967) 3 *Journal of African History* 395, 395.

61 For a detailed discussion, see Ramadan, supra note 53, 53–56.

62 Metzemaekers compares such interruption of the interpretative process to the situation in the Roman Catholic Church, where, following the contra-reformation of the Council of Trente in 1518, theologians were for some time no longer permitted to interpret central Christian beliefs by going beyond the theoretical framework drawn by St Thomas Aquinas. For details of the comparison, see L. Metzemaekers, 'How Counter-Developmental is Muslim Fundamentalism? in: C. A. O. Nieuwenhuijze (ed.), *Development Regardless of Culture?* (Leiden: Brill, 1984) 54ff.

63 J. L. Esposito, *The Future of Islam* (Oxford: Oxford University Press, 2010) 88–89.

make use of deductive, inductive, and/or analogical reasoning, and distinguish the general principle (*amm*) from the specific (*khass*), the manifest meaning (*zahir*) from the explicit (*nass*), and the literal sense (*haqiqi*) from the metaphorical (*majazi*). Jurists, among others, may also invoke the doctrine of preference (*istihsan*) to respond to a specific situation in light of such considerations as equity, justice, and fairness.[64] As shown later, the chief purpose of generating secondary norms is to make primary sources applicable to evolving socio-cultural context – while striving to remain loyal to the very motive, effective cause (*al-'illah*), and objective of Quranic injunctions and prophetic example.[65] Nevertheless, as human subjectivity proved to be an inevitable element of the interpretative process, there emerged numerous schools of jurisprudence over the centuries with their distinct approaches to primary sources and problems of day-to-day life – which, as will be detailed later, has also affected the manner in which laws of Islamic warfare in general, and the doctrine of jihad in particular, are interpreted. It is now to the second most important source of Islamic law that the following section will turn.

B. The Sunnah

It was noted above that according to Islam, Muslims may achieve a relatively peaceful, moral, and content life in this world, and secure salvation in the afterlife, by essentially following the commands of God and the example of Muhammad.[66] The prophetic practice, also known as the Sunnah, constitutes the second principal source of Sharia, which includes the anecdotal accounts of the Prophet's sayings, habits, views, acts, or silent approvals. The concept of Sunnah is occasionally used to refer to the practices of Muhammad's companions, too. The written account of these practices is termed as the *hadith*,[67] which contains the documented record of what Muhammad is known to have uttered or done during his lifetime. While the Quran embodies the raw material of the law composed of God's own words, Sunnah is the reflection of God's wisdom with which the Prophet was inspired; and through his exemplary words and behaviour Muhammad sought to transfer such wisdom to humankind.[68] Confirming this point, the Quran demands that

64 For a comprehensive analysis of interpretation techniques developed by Muslim scholars, see Kamali, supra note 33, 3ff.

65 See Ramadan, supra note 53, 57ff; J. P. Piscatori, *Islam in a World of Nation-States* (Cambridge: Cambridge University Press, 1986) 3ff; J. Waardenburg, 'The Early Period: 610–650' in: J. Waardenburg (ed.), *Muslim Perceptions of Other Religions: A Historical Survey* (New York: Oxford University Press, 1999) 3.

66 Lewis, supra note, 5, xviii; C. S. Yaran, *Understanding Islam* (Edinburgh: Dunedin Academic Press, 2007) 1.

67 M. Mir, 'The Sura as a Unity: A Twentieth Century Development in Quran Exegesis' in: G. R. Hawting; A. A. Shareef (eds.), *Approaches to the Quran* (New York: Routledge, 1993) 218; Y. H. Aboul-Enein; S. Zuhur, *Islamic Rulings on Warfare* (Carlisle Barracks: Strategic Studies Institute, 2004) 1–3.

68 The Quran stresses Muhammad's responsibility in guiding Muslims to the right path: 'Allah did confer a great favour on the believers when He sent among them an apostle

believers follow the pattern of behaviour exhibited by the Prophet: 'Ye have indeed in the Messenger of Allah a beautiful pattern (of conduct) for any one whose hope is in Allah and the Final Day, and who engages much in the Praise of Allah.'[69]

For Muslims, the significance of the Sunnah lies in the fact that Muhammad had been the final messenger of God's revelations, and by so being, his practice must be taken into account in order to gain a better theoretical and practical understanding of the Quranic material.[70] As Esposito points out, Muhammad had over the centuries 'served as the ideal model for Muslim life, providing the pattern that all believers are to emulate. He is, as some Muslims say, the "living Quran".'[71] A connected Sunni proposition is that only the Prophet had been divinely protected from committing errors in interpreting and applying the revelations, a doctrine known as the prophetic infallibility.[72] On this view, because Muhammad was the 'seal of the Prophets' and had passed away without an heir of his stature, there remained no intermediary between God and humankind; hence, whilst Muhammad's religio-political position was filled by successors (caliphs), they lacked the necessary mandate to promulgate or authoritatively explain God's law. Although jurists legitimately distinguished the first four 'rightly guided' caliphs[73] from their successors in terms of their motivation, piety, and adherence to the ideal Islamic governance set down in the Quran, it is clear that a gaping gulf between spiritual and mundane power became visible almost immediately after the Prophet's death. The caliphate had basically become a temporal institution whose main role was to interpret and enforce the existing law, guard the religion against internal or external threats, and expand the sphere of Islamic polity.[74]

The legal function of each Caliph did not thus technically differ from that of a jurist whose role was limited to merely interpreting or enforcing the extant law.

from among themselves, rehearsing unto them the Signs of Allah, sanctifying them, and instructing them in Scripture and Wisdom, while, before that, they had been in manifest error.' Q. 3.164. Also see, M. Khadduri 'The *Maslaha* (Public Interest) and *Illa* (Cause) in Islamic Law' (1980) 12 *New York University Journal of International Law and Politics* 213, 213.

69 Q. 33:21.

70 Hassan, supra note 4, 66.

71 J. L. Esposito, *Islam: The Straight Path* (Oxford: Oxford University Press, 1994) 13.

72 The doctrine of prophetic infallibility is controversial, though; some modern critics of Hadith tend to consider Muhammad 'human like the rest of us and [hence] subject to the same experiences as the rest of men'. See further D. W. Brown, *Rethinking Tradition in Modern Islamic Thought* (Cambridge: Cambridge University Press, 1996) 66ff.

73 Many Muslims believe that the pure form of Islamic polity had thriven during the rule of the Prophet and his four successive (righteous) caliphs (chosen from his closest companions: Abu Bakr, Umar, Uthman and Ali). Later caliphs are generally considered to have been driven by self-interest, because they not only had rendered the caliphate a hereditary office, but largely steered their powers towards worldly objectives, and at times adulterated the original message of Islam. For an analysis, see A. Hourani, *A History of the Arab Peoples* (London: Faber and Faber Limited, 2005) 22–37.

74 See further D. F. Eickelman; J. Piscatori, *Muslim Politics* (Princeton: Princeton University Press, 2004) 47ff.

Putting it differently, the death of the Prophet marked the end of divine legislation, which was to be elaborated through interpretive efforts. Remarkably, shortly before his demise in 632, Muhammad recited what many scholars believe to be the final verse of the Quran: 'This day have I perfected your religion for you . . . and have chosen for you Islam as your religion.'[75] This verse not only marked the end of Muhammad's prophetic mission, but also signified that divine law would no longer be sent down. The law was to be fleshed out through human effort henceforth, an endeavour whose results had to be compatible with the basic tenets of Islam. This fact alone made the traditions ascribed to Muhammad all the more important, because they provided a perfect paradigm for the manner in which divine injunctions must be observed and applied in the daily practices of Muslims.

1. The Formation and Function of the Hadiths

A *hadith* is a narration containing a report of what the Prophet said or did, in a form as transmitted by one of his closest companions, who in his turn related it to somebody belonging to the following generation.[76] Every *hadith* has two parts. The first part (*isnad*) contains a list of narrators who handed down accounts of the sayings, teachings, decisions, overt or tacit views, and actions of Muhammad or his immediate companions. This chain traces the sources through whom the Prophetic practice had been reported with a view to attesting the historical authenticity of a particular *hadith*. *Isnad* employs a classical formula along these lines: 'It has been related to me by A on the authority of B on the authority of C on the authority of D that Muhammad said. . .' The second part, on the other hand, consists of the actual content or text (*matn*) of the *hadith*, which communicates what the Prophet reportedly said or did.[77] As said above, this part is mainly composed of Muhammad's actions (*fi'l*), utterances (*qaul*), and his tacit or silent approvals of certain matters (*taqrir*), which shed light on a wide array of important matters in Islam.[78]

Since roughly the second century of Islam, Muhammad's well-attested manner of behaviour has been considered to constitute a normative standard or a uniquely valid rule of conduct for Muslims. Notably, the phenomenon of precedent or normative custom is by no means foreign to the era that preceded Islam; the Arabs

75 Q. 5:3.

76 A. Schimmel, *And Muhammad is His Messenger: The Veneration of the Prophet in Islamic Piety* (London: The University of North Carolina Press, 1985) 26.

77 See I. A. Khan, *Authentication of Hadith: Redefining the Criteria* (London: The International Institute of Islamic Thought, 2010) 28–29.

78 Classical Muslim scholars portray the Prophet's immediate followers as constantly observing, avidly discussing, and meticulously recording everything Muhammad had said or done – covering every conceivable aspect of personal, private, domestic, political, military, fiscal, administrative, public, religious, and moral life. See J. Burton, *An Introduction to the Hadith Tradition* (Edinburgh: Edinburgh University Press, 1994) 19; see generally, E. Dickinson, *The Development of Early Sunnite Hadith Criticism: The Taqdima of Ibn Abi Hatim al-Razi (240/854–327/938)* (Leiden: Brill, 2001).

have felt bound by tradition or precedent since time immemorial. The conventional practice dictated that whatever was customary had to be held as the right and proper form of conduct; hence, the precedent of forefathers was to be revered and imitated. Adherence to ancient traditions and customs often left no noteworthy room for new experiments and innovations that could have upset the *status quo*; entrenched customs had thus presented a significant obstacle to any innovation, so much so that in order to discredit a novel idea, it was often sufficient to label it an 'innovation',[79] a reaction that is still alive among certain Muslim circles. The emergence of Islam naturally proved to be the most radical innovation in Arabia at the time, which had to, and eventually did, overcome the obstacle of such Arab conservatism. And once Islam successfully prevailed over Arabia, the conventional way of adhering to precedence and customs had reasserted itself in the form of following the dictates of Islam.[80]

Over time, jurists sought to develop consensus that secondary rulings were to be derived from the Quran and Sunnah, as opposed to speculative reasoning, which required a greater emphasis on the accurate documentation of the prophetic tradition.[81] Muslim scholars, among whom Ash-Shafi'i played a prominent role, aimed at ensuring the authenticity of transmitted *hadiths* as a means of ensuring unity and predictability in the application of the law. Rejecting the thesis that the authority of the Prophet had been that of an individual who was better placed than any other human person to interpret the Quran, Ash-Shafi'i forcefully defended the moot position that the Prophet's overall practice was divinely inspired. To Ash-Shafi'i, this thinking was the inexorable consequence of the Quranic injunctions to obey God and His Messenger,[82] and the similar injunction to follow the Book and the Wisdom (*hikma*)[83] – the word 'wisdom', Ash-Shafi'i reasoned, could only refer to the deeds and sayings of Muhammad. The eventual prevalence of Ash-Shafi'i's proposition that the acts and sayings of the Prophet had been the reflection of the divine will, complementing the Quran, meant that accepted traditions could no longer be criticised or rebutted through the analysis of their content; for their content was necessarily authoritative unless

79 M. Khadduri; H. J. Liebesny (eds.), *Law in the Middle East* (New Jersey: The Lawbook Exchange, 2008) 34.

80 Schacht, supra note 35, 17ff.

81 Dien, supra note 36, 35–36.

82 The verse reads as 'O ye who believe! Obey Allah and His Messenger, and turn not away from him when ye hear (him speak)' (Q. 8:20). It must be added that this verse is connected with a parallel verse reading thus: 'O ye who believe! Obey Allah, and obey the Messenger, and those charged with authority among you. If ye differ in anything among yourselves, refer it to Allah and His Messenger . . .' Q. 4:59.

83 The verse says 'Our Lord! Send amongst them a Messenger of their own, who shall rehearse Thy signs to them and instruct them in Scripture and Wisdom . . .' (Q. 2:129). Here the traditionalist claim is that the word wisdom (*hikma*) refers to the tradition of Muhammad. See further A. Rippin, *Muslims: Their Religious Beliefs and Practices,* 3rd ed. (New York: Routledge, 2005) 223.

the authenticity of the reports concerned were called into question.[84] The implication of this view was that the veracity of a *hadith* became essentially dependent on the reliability of the chain of narrators transmitting the tradition.[85] The wide acceptance of this thesis raised controversy over the extent to which the reported traditions could be relied upon.

2. Reliability of the Hadiths

As noted above, the Sunnah contains the very views, judgements, and practices of the Prophet, which have hitherto been employed to contextualise and understand the text of the Quran as well as to enrich the extant rules, customs, and principles. Over time, however, the veracity of certain *hadiths* had been questioned on the ground that some of them might well have been fabricated with intent to consolidate a religious or political stance, for a certain position, judgement, or attitude could be deemed correct or acceptable if a reliable chain of transmission testified a corresponding practice of the Prophet.

The possibility of producing seemingly authentic *hadith* had indeed not been an unlikely risk, which loomed larger as spatial and temporal distance grew from the source. Certainly, one of the most significant factors that led certain jurists to doubt the authenticity of some *hadiths* is that, unlike the Quran, which was recorded almost immediately after the Prophet's death, the prophetic traditions were only collected and recorded in the second and third centuries of Islam. This mindfulness also explains why only such authoritative records of Sunnah as those of al-Bukhari (d. 870) and Muslim ibn al-Hajjaj (d. 874) have been accepted by the majority of Muslim scholars as being credible (*sahih*).[86] Such reliable transmitters related traditions through a chain of trustworthy authorities who handed down the relevant information from generation to generation. The companions of Muhammad who witnessed the practice and heard the sayings of the Prophet were undoubtedly the best sources to convey the Prophet's attitude toward a certain situation. After the passing of the Prophet's contemporaries, the following generations had to be content with the information handed down from the earlier generations.[87]

One notable source of distrust emerged out of the occasional inconsistency and variability found among the relevant traditions attributed to Muhammad. This led such scholars as Mu'tazila (d. 748), Sayyid Ahmad Khan (d. 1898), and Ghulam Ahmad Parwez (d. 1986) to doubt the authenticity of some traditions. However, the number of Muslim critics has been small, as the majority of Muslim scholars accept the authority of varied *hadiths* on the basis that there was nothing

84 N. J. Coulson, *A History of Islamic Law* (Edinburgh: Edinburgh University Press, 1964) 56; R. Jackson, *Fifty Key Figures in Islam* (New York: Routledge, 2009) 42.
85 For a detailed analysis, see Khan, supra note 77, xvi.
86 An-Naim, supra note 33, 491.
87 I. Goldziher, *Introduction to Islamic Theology and Law* (Princeton: Princeton University Press, 1981) 37.

wrong with the Prophet having changed tactics in responding to the circumstances, an argument that will feature in contextualising the debate on Islamic laws of warfare in the following chapters.[88] While it may be accepted that flexibility and prudent statesmanship has served the cause of God and made Islam responsive to the particular challenges it faced, the danger of cherry-picking certain traditions (and Quranic verses, by almost always divesting them of their context) in a bid to further a cause has always plagued the Muslim world – and, in the context of Islamic just war tradition, the international community at large.

While the criticism of the *hadith* literature originated within Muslim circles, some Western scholars, including Goldziher, Alfred Guillame, and Joseph Schacht, took issue with the very foundation and validity of prophetic traditions as a source of Islamic jurisprudence.[89] The main arguments to support their critical position are generally built upon these premises: (1) the *hadith* literature is based on oral transmissions that significantly grew larger than those contained in earlier anthologies; (2) *hadiths* transmitted by the younger companions of the Prophet surprisingly exceed those reported by the older ones; (3) the transmission system was applied in such an arbitrary fashion that the genuineness of the traditions could not be proved; (4) there are many contradicting *hadiths* that are equally deemed valid, as Muslim scholars concerned themselves with the validity of the chain of transmission, and not with the content of the *hadith*.[90] On such account, Ignaz Goldziher, one of the most prominent Western critics of the *hadith* literature, went as far as to argue that

> . . .each point of view, each party, each proponent of a doctrine gave the form of *hadith* to his theses, and that consequently the most contradictory tenets had come to wear the garb of such documentation. There is no school in the areas of ritual, theology, or jurisprudence, there is not even any party to political contention, that would lack a *hadith* or a whole family of *hadith*s in its favour, exhibiting all the external signs of correct transmission.[91]

Schacht similarly challenged the credibility of the transmission system, positing that it lacked historical value for largely being invented by those who sought to authenticate their doctrines on the authority of the Prophet. Hardly any legal tradition of the Prophet could therefore be considered accurate, according to

88 See Piscatori, supra note 65, 4.
89 S. S. Ali, 'The Twain Doth Meet! A Preliminary Exploration of the Theory and Practice of *As-Siyar* and International Law in the Contemporary World' in: J. Rehman; S. C. Breau (eds.), *Religion, Human Rights and International Law* (Leiden: Martinus Nijhoff Publishers, 2007) 86–87.
90 M. Z. Siddiqi, *Hadith Literature: Its Origin, Development & Special Features* (Cambridge: The Islamic Texts Society, 2008) 125–127.
91 Goldziher, supra note 87, 39.

the sceptics.[92] Well before the aforementioned Orientalists such as Goldziher, Guillame, and Schacht, however, concerns about the authenticity of traditions had been raised by Muslim scholars, who eventually developed a rigorous method of sifting credible traditions from apocryphal ones whenever contradictions, vagueness, or doubtfulness surfaced. This method divided the *hadiths* into three categories: those transmitted by virtuous people of high knowledge (on religious and moral matters); those reported by people of lesser knowledge, but virtuous in character; and, finally, reports that are suspected of being fabricated as they did not fit within the overall framework of Islam.[93] Authoritative traditionalists, such as al-Bukhari and Muslim, made use of the said method and applied stringent criteria to collect only the most authentic traditions. Bukhari is reported to have interviewed more than one thousand scholars of *hadith* during his lifetime (810–869), and looked for transmitters of exemplary character possessing high literary and academic skills. Bukhari sought evidence to confirm that the transmitters involved actually met and learned from one another – a method which slightly differed from that of Muslim's, who opined that if two transmitters lived in the same locale, one could assume that they learned from each other, and therefore that the chain of transmission could be considered unbroken. Bukhari's search for positive evidence for a real encounter enabled him to acquire wider recognition.[94]

Viewed from this perspective, it seems to be an over-generalisation to claim that the majority of the traditions came from malicious transmitters who, directly or indirectly, served the purpose of supporting a religious or political agenda through forged *hadiths*. True, there exist traditions that are falsely, or with an ulterior motive, attributed to the Prophet, among which some contradict Islam's basic tenets, while some others, albeit fabricated, are yet congruent with Islam's ethical principles including justice, equality, fairness, and honesty.[95] Moreover, as Coulson notes, there were also such reporters who were 'in the *bona fide* belief' that the Prophet would have so acted had he dealt with the same issue.[96] While this is not the place to discuss this matter extensively, suffice it to note that some Western scholars, including Nabia Abbott and James Robson, also criticised Goldziher's and Schacht's sweeping dismissal of the *hadith* literature. These scholars claimed that oral and written transmissions went hand in hand, and the majority of the traditions transmitted by the companions and their successors had been scrupulously scrutinised, particularly by such chroniclers as Muslim and Bukhari.[97] Arguably, a reasonable solution to the difficulty of sifting authentic *hadiths* from

92 M. M. Al-Azami, *On Schacht's Origins of Muhammadan Jurisprudence* (Oxford: Oxford Centre for Islamic Studies, 1996) 2.
93 Goldziher, supra note 87, 39; J. L. Esposito, *The Oxford Dictionary of Islam* (Oxford: Oxford University Press, 2003) 217.
94 A. Saeed, *Islamic Thought: An Introduction* (New York: Routledge, 2006) 42.
95 For such ethical injunctions, see, among others, Q. 16.90; Q. 4:135; Q. 2:178; Q. 7:56.
96 Coulson, supra note 84, 42.
97 Siddiqi, supra note 90, 131–135.

those of the counterfeit ones lies in the following saying attributed to the Prophet: '. . . compare what I am reported to have said or done with the Book of God. If it agrees, I did actually say it; if it disagrees, I did not say it.'[98] It follows that if a *hadith* plainly negates the spirit of the Quran, it should not be taken seriously. Within the context of the Islamic laws of warfare, as will be discussed, a contextual approach may reasonably be adopted with a view to stressing those traditions that accord with the current paradigm of international relations.

II. Secondary Sources

As seen above, the Prophet has metaphorically been described as the corporeal scripture, because his practice was drawn on to flesh out, or throw light on, the divine text. Muhammad clarified and developed the fundamental aspects of Islamic law largely by way of responding to pressing issues. Having contributed to establishing a blueprint for a moral life, his demise imposed a disquieting task on Muslims to keep the Islamic law responsive to unprecedented problems. In the absence of prophetic guidance and authority, the companions of Muhammad did, however, manage to develop the law by devising new juristic tools to answer public needs and meet the demands of rapidly changing socio-political, cultural, and economic milieu.[99]

These tools, known as the 'non-revealed' sources because of their non-divine origin, mainly include: (1) *ijma*: the general consensus of commentators on a point of law; (2) *qiyas*: the method of analogical reasoning; and (3) *ijtihad*: the application of independent personal reasoning in the interpretation of Islamic jurisprudence.[100] Historically, these sources, in particular the *ijma* and *ijtihad*, proved to be crucial in providing answers to questions of law when the primary sources were silent. As alluded to earlier, principles and norms directly originating from the primary sources may not be altered, though they may be subjected to interpretation – whether through *ijma*, *ijtihad*, or *qiyas*,[101] all of which involve derivative legal reasoning. Of course, novel principles whose roots are not strictly embedded

98 See Burton, supra note 28, 54.

99 Remarkably, in the conquered territories of Syria and Iraq, the doctrine of Sunnah was utilised in such a broad manner as to encompass the traditions of the Prophet, his companions (*sahaba*) and their successors (*tabiun*), as well as the local customs. See Khadduri, supra note 35, 12.

100 N. Mohammed, 'Principles of Islamic Contract Law' (1988) 6 *Journal of Law and Religion* 1, 115, 130; M. H. Kamali, 'Methodological Issues in Islamic Jurisprudence' (1996) 11 *Arab Law Quarterly* 3, 3–4.

101 *Qiyas*, which literally means analogical deduction, has been a frequently resorted method of law-making since the earliest periods of Islam. Analogical reasoning or deductions, however, were only invoked when nothing substantial could be found in the primary sources on the disputed point. Obviously, this approach bears significant similarities to that employed by common law judges, who could rely upon relevant previous decisions with a view to solving a controversy at hand. See Hassan, supra note 4, 67.

within primary sources may also be crafted, provided that the results fit the overall Islamic framework.

Secondary sources have thus provided a degree of flexibility to the development of law. In fact, while Islamic law owes its divine origins to the Quran and the prophetic tradition, it has overwhelmingly flourished due to juridical activity,[102] which was particularly intense during the classical period of the Islamic civilisation when socio-political diversity required jurists to expand on the existing norms in line with local customs. Classical jurists had been sensitive to the need for harmonising non-peremptory and derivative principles with prevailing socio-political and cultural dynamics. The classical jurist al-Qarafi (d. 1285), in this context, argued that 'holding to rulings that have been deduced on the basis of custom, even after this custom has changed, is a violation of unanimous consensus and an open display of ignorance of the religion'.[103]

When deriving secondary rulings, however, the Muslim jurists have been restricted relative to their secular counterparts. While non-religious jurists are restrained with such concerns as the hierarchy of the norms and principles of equity, they may depend on their intuitions while making law. The Muslim jurist, on the other hand, must reveal the will of God found in the Quran and traditions, rather than proclaim the dictates of his own intuition in arriving at solutions to legal questions. This, however, did not prevent Muslim scholars of classical ages from developing and expounding a great deal of positive law without being blindly restricted by a literalist approach; although they were certainly much more cautious when they commented on the immutable teachings of the Quran and practices of the Prophet.[104] Hence, early scholars had invoked personal and collective reasoning to devise novel solutions for immediate challenges, while trying to remain loyal to the very objective, rationale, and spirit of primary sources. As discussed below, it was only in the aftermath of this classical period that Islamic scholarship assumed a more constrained, text-oriented approach, which utilised a more literal and stricter implementation of analogical reasoning – at times in disregard of evolving social and human context.

Whilst the supremacy of the holy sources is beyond dispute in Islamic law, equally important is the fact that this law is by no means bestowed upon humans as a panacea for all the ills or problems afflicting them. Instead, contribution to the development of the law to respond to the shifts and tensions of life is encouraged, if not ordained, by Islam. One of the principal requirements of Islamic belief is that the individual must attain a level of consciousness whereby he perceives the world not in a blind, unquestioning manner, but with the eyes of

102 Schacht, supra note 35, 5; Khadduri, supra note 68, 213.

103 Shihab al-Din al-Qarafi, *Kitab al-ihkam fi tamyiz al-fatawa 'an al-ahkam wa tasarrufat al-qadi wa al-imam,* 'Abd al-Fattah Abu Ghuddah (ed.) (Matba'at al-Matbu'at al-Islamiyah, Aleppo, 1967) cited in: S. A. Jackson, 'Jihad and the Modern World' 2002 (7) *Journal of Islamic Law and Culture* 1, 9.

104 See B. G. Weiss, 'Interpretation in Islamic Law: The Theory of Ijtihad' (1978) 26 *The American Journal of Comparative Law* 199, 201; Ramadan, supra note 53, 39–58.

his heart and intellect. Reason in this sense must be employed to comprehend the world and understand the signs that point to the existence of God.[105] Indeed, the Quran invites and demands believers to reflect upon the real meaning of messages delivered to them, and when necessary to expand on divine norms.[106] In Weiss' words:

> The Holy Law is the totality of rules which God has laid down for the governing of Man's behaviour . . . Though ordained by God, few of these rules have been precisely spelled out for man's convenience; rather, man has the duty to *derive* them from their sources. In the standard Islamic metaphor, the rules themselves are 'branches'. . ., which grow out of 'roots'. . ., that is, from the sources. Only the roots are given; the branches, or fruit, are not – they must be made to appear; and for this to happen human involvement . . . is required.[107]

It is in such an effort to respond to the pressing needs and shifting circumstances that classical jurists in particular, have employed their intellectual resources to design novel concepts and legal principles whereby Islamic law underwent a process of development and transformation. However, as Weiss stresses, the prerogative of the Muslim jurist in interpreting primary sources has ultimately been derivative in nature; i.e. contingent upon the authority of God. It follows that there is no automatic validity accorded to the declarations of the jurist. Rather, the jurist may only be confident about his assertion that what he declares to be the law is an acceptable expression of the divine law. Hence, the opinions of the jurists remain moot, and not characterised by absolute definitiveness.[108] Muslim scholarship thus firmly insists that the outcome of the derivative process of the jurists, irrespective of their qualifications, remains as mere opinion (*zann*) rather than definitive knowledge (*ilm*).[109] Regardless of how rigorous the reasoning behind the construction of *zann* could be, it is indefinite knowledge, and hence not *ilm*. The following pages will now turn in more detail to the two most significant secondary sources: *ijtihad* and *ijma*.

A. Ijtihad

The term *ijtihad* literally means 'striving' or 'self-exertion'. In legal usage, it is defined as the total endeavour of a jurist (*mujtahid*) to infer, by exerting himself to the best of his ability and on the basis of credible evidence found in primary sources, a rule of Islamic law. *Ijtihad* thus incorporates an innovative and

105 See generally C. Turner, *Islam: The Basics* (New York: Routledge, 2006) 72.
106 See, among others, Q. 10:24; Q. 30:8; Q. 30:21; Q. 34:46; Q. 39:42; Q. 59:21; Q. 45:13; Q. 3:191.
107 Weiss, supra note 104, 199.
108 Weiss, supra note 104, 203.
109 J. Waardenburg, 'The Early Period 610–650' in: Waardenburg, supra note 65, 4.

comprehensive intellectual effort undertaken by qualified jurists to derive secondary norms from the revealed and prophetic rulings in order to address unprecedented issues in light of the prevailing circumstances of society.[110] Such independent reasoning is, then, exercised to provide answers to a question when the Quran and Sunnah are silent.

It is reported that the permissibility of exercising discretion and deducing secondary rulings through critical thinking had been encouraged by the Prophet himself. According to a well-known tradition, when Muhammad appointed Muadh ibn Jabal as a judge in Yemen, he questioned the latter about the dynamics of decision-making in line with Islamic principles: 'Through which will you judge?' asked the Prophet. 'Through the book of God,' answered Muadh. 'And if you find nothing in the Book of God?' returned Muhammad. 'I shall judge according to the tradition of God's messenger,' said Muadh. 'And if you find nothing in the Messenger's tradition?' again asked the Prophet. 'I shall not fail to make an effort [*ajtahidu*] to reach an opinion.' It is reported that this response pleased the Prophet.[111]

Nonetheless, *ijtihad* by qualified jurists[112] is not only about deriving norms when the primary sources are silent, but it is also about elucidating the revealed or divinely inspired material, particularly when the latter contains general or abstract rulings as opposed to clear injunctions. The main role of independent reasoning has thus been to complement, expound, and flesh out the primary norms in a bid to bridge the theory and practice of Islamic law.[113]

Ijtihad is often dubbed as independent or critical reasoning, because its use requires analytical thinking, and not the blind emulation (*taqlid*) of past rulings delivered by authoritative jurists. *Ijtihad* in this context may be said to be the most significant source of Islamic law after the Quran and Sunnah – with the chief difference that while divine legislation had discontinued after the demise of the Prophet, *ijtihad* has the potential to form part of a continuous process of development. *Ijtihad* is accordingly the main tool for interpreting or re-construing the divine rulings and relating them to the human context so that the Muslim

110 Schacht, supra note 35, 69ff; V. J. Cornell (ed.), *Voices of Islam: Voices of Tradition* (Westport: Praeger Publishers, 2007) 155.

111 See T. Ramadan, *The Messenger: The Meanings of the Life of Muhammad* (London: Penguin Books, 2007) 199.

112 A jurist is generally expected to possess a sound knowledge of Islamic law, with mastery over the language of Arabic, the content of the Quran and relevant commentaries, prophetic tradition (with the ability to distinguish between authentic and forged hadith), *fiqh*, and *usul-al-fiqh*. For more on this, see M. Khan, 'Reason and Individual Reasoning' in: Donohue, supra note 49, 501; see generally W. B. Hallaq, *Authority, Continuity and Change in Islamic Law* (Cambridge: Cambridge University Press, 2001).

113 An-Naim argues that even when a ruling of the Quran or Sunnah may appear to be clear, it may yet need to be subjected to *ijtihad* with a view to demonstrating the application thereof in concrete situations. A. A. An-Na'im, *Toward an Islamic Reformation: Civil Liberties, Human Rights, and International Law* (Syracuse: Syracuse University Press, 1996) 27.

community may keep pace with constant change.[114] Hence, the theory of *ijtihad* acknowledges the signal import of reason in appreciating the law in context, which requires a dialectical engagement with relevant texts and changing practical circumstances.

Islamic law is generally known to be the jurists' law on account of the fact that jurists have been in a position to unearth the hidden meanings or practical implications of the divine law. It is indeed largely owing to the independent reasoning of Muslim jurists that Islamic law developed as a body of positive rules, for an important portion of the sacred law requires hermeneutics and human elaboration due to the abstract or metaphorical manner in which it is formulated. Furthermore, because the law must be expounded and vivified to be applicable to real-life scenarios, juridical work has always been crucial to concretise abstract formulations or craft new solutions that are congruent with the basic Islamic principles. Weiss is thus right in emphasising that 'the Law of God is empirically available [mainly] . . . in the formulations of jurists', simply because the large bulk of positive law has found its concrete manifestations in formulations of the jurists.[115]

It must, however, be stressed that strict adherence to the letter and spirit of authoritative texts has enjoyed pride of place within orthodox Muslim scholarship. The supremacy of the textualist approach, particularly with regard to peremptory rulings, is evident in many Sunni scholars' attempts to steer clear of all appearances of formulating new rules independent of the divinely ordained norms.[116] In actual fact, the success of any critical thinking has essentially been judged by the extent to which consonance is achieved between the primary legislation and secondary law-making process. In Kamali's language, 'since *ijtihad* derives its validity from divine revelation, its propriety is measured by its harmony with the Quran and the Sunnah.'[117] The doctrine of *ijtihad,* then, does not presuppose a full measure of novelty, as the interpreter is charged with the duty to work on the secondary law with precision to render God's fixed law applicable to novel situations – making transcendent rulings to assume adaptability as required by changing circumstances. The basic role of the jurist, who applies independent judgement, is thus to elucidate God's will for humans living in various ages and contexts.[118]

This thinking, then, presupposes that a Muslim jurist does not *invent* rules through reasoning, but merely midwives norms and principles that are already present, albeit in a concealed or gnomic form, in sacred texts. As noted earlier, however, opinions forged through independent reasoning do not constitute definitive knowledge (*ilm*); rather, the knowledge attained through such mental

114 Kamali, supra note 33, 468.
115 See Weiss, supra note 104, 200.
116 B. G. Weiss, *The Spirit of Islamic Law* (London: The University of Georgia Press, 2006) 86–87.
117 Kamali, supra note 33, 468.
118 'A *mujtahid*', writes Smith, 'is a man of faith who endeavours . . . to discern what God's will . . . for today is.' W. C. Smith, *On Understanding Islam: Selected Studies* (The Hague: Mouton Publishers, 1981) 84.

exertion is conjectural (*zann*). This means that a Muslim jurist is not bound by the rulings of other jurists exercising *ijtihad*, unless such an opinion has been issued by a judge regarding a specific case. Nonetheless, as will be examined now, when an individual opinion is widely recognised to the extent that a consensus is formed as to its validity (*ijma*), it may become binding.

B. Ijma

The concept of juristic consensus (*ijma*) as an authoritative source of Islamic law was originally conceived through the exercise of *ijtihad* undertaken by the Prophet's companions and the learned jurists of the classical period,[119] a phenomenon that highlights the dialectical relationship between these secondary sources. While the theological basis of *ijma* is not found in the Quranic text, it is generally said to have been based on a tradition attributed to the Prophet: 'my community will not agree on error'.[120] This has been generally read to mean that after the death of the Prophet, the Muslim community could agree upon doctrines and practices that were not directly expressed in the Quran and Sunnah. Hence, in the absence of prophetic guidance, Muhammad's companions (*sahaba*) invoked the method of general consensus (*ijma)* to enrich the Islamic jurisprudence. New norms extracted through this method formed a substantial portion of Islamic law, supplementing the primary sources.

The deduction of new laws through *ijma* enabled jurists to formulate widely shared principles or practices to tailor solutions to the needs identified. But as the creation of new norms had been a collective effort drawing upon the sacred sources, the prevailing assumption was that new principles formed through consensus could not be deemed ordinary in nature; rather, they belonged to the sacred law. This conclusion was borne out by the aforesaid tradition that the Muslim community was safeguarded against error. Accordingly, the process of *ijma* came to assume an 'aura of holiness', the repudiation of whose outputs 'became sinful in the eyes of some',[121] even though the law obtained though consensus remained derivative in character.

Ijma generally involved lengthy debates conducted by qualified jurists over legal, moral, and practical matters. When such learned scholars reached an agreement on a controversial point of law, *ijma* was declared to have transpired, settling the matter conclusively – until revoked by further *ijma*. The rule or norm created by this process was regarded as binding law.[122] Albeit they are interlaced in gener-

119 An-Na'im, supra note 113, 27.

120 There is another version of the quoted tradition: 'my community does not agree on a mistake'. See I. A. Bello, *Medieval Islamic Controversy between Philosophy and Orthodoxy: Ijma and Ta Wil in the Conflict between al-Ghazali and Ibn Rushd* (Leiden: Brill, 1989) 35.

121 A. Khan, 'The Reopening of the Islamic Code: The Second Era of Ijtihad' (2003) 1 *University of St. Thomas Law Journal* 341, 365.

122 Hassan, supra note 4, 65.

ating novel principles, therein lay the main difference between *ijtihad* and *ijma*: while the former could engender conflicting views over a controversial issue, the latter produced an authoritative response thereto. As Coulson makes clear, although individual opinions resulted in a tentative or moot conclusion known as *zann* (conjecture), even when they draw upon seemingly clear-cut verses or traditions, the exercise of *ijma* led to binding or incontestable expressions of the law for the followers of a particular school of law. Consensus of opinion had thus the advantage of achieving certain knowledge. This, as alluded to earlier, did not mean that when circumstances had changed there could have been no new consensus invalidating the earlier ruling. Indeed, as Esposito and DeLong-Bas put it, in the early Islamic jurisprudence, 'the relationship between *ijtihad* and *ijma* was an ongoing process, moving from individual opinion to community approval to accepted practice to difference of opinion, if conditions changed, and therefore to a fresh reinterpretation of *ijtihad* and *ijma*'.[123]

Certainly, in the absence of consensus, alternative legal views were deemed equally valid.[124] Correspondingly, when there had been competing views advanced by recognised schools of thought, these were also considered authoritative at the same time. Absent unanimity, there had thus been no basis to require Muslims of various schools of law to adhere to one single view[125] – each school could elucidate their reading of the law, while justifying their position by reference to authoritative sources.

The doctrine of consensus therefore tacitly recognised difference over moral and legal issues as inevitable, which naturally allowed the coexistence of various schools of thought.[126] By the mid-tenth century, jurisprudential schools had accordingly developed their distinguishing concepts and doctrines, elaborating upon a considerable body of legal literature. Among these schools, only the principal ones managed to survive into contemporary times. These are the Hanafi school, founded by Abu Hanifa (d. 767); the Maliki school, established by Malik ibn Anas (d. 795); the Shafi'i school, based on the teachings of Idris Ash-Shafi'i (d. 820); the Hanbali school, set up by Ahmed ibn Hanbal (d. 855); and the Jafari School, a Shia school of jurisprudence,[127] following the teachings of the fifth Imam, Abu Jafar Muhammad Al-Baqir (d.731) and the sixth Imam, Jafar Sadiq

123 J. L. Esposito, *Women in Muslim Family Law* (Syracuse: Syracuse University Press, 2001) 148.

124 Coulson, supra note 84, 78.

125 S. A. Jackson, *Islam and the Black American: Looking toward the Third Resurrection* (Oxford: Oxford University Press, 2005) 7–8.

126 Berkey, supra note 15, 147.

127 The Shia schools generally do not dramatically differ from the Sunni schools in their jurisprudential methodology. The Shia emphasis on the prophetic lineage as the essential condition for religio-political leadership represents one of the fundamental points of difference. The Shia schools, when deducing the law, consider the primary sources to be (1) the Quran, (2) the Sunnah of Muhammad, and (3) the *ijtihad* of the Imam, with the last one forming the main distinguishing feature. For more on this theme, see I. Abdal-Haqq, 'Islamic Law: An Overview of its Origins and Elements' in:

(d. 765).[128] Through consensus, these schools transformed a sizeable body of judicial speculations into somewhat categorical rulings. When consensus rendered a certain interpretation or judgement irrevocable, this would set a precedent for future cases of similar facts.[129] The method of *ijma* thus gave substance to many tentative judgements.[130]

Over time, *ijma* had not only reinforced the authority of learned jurists (*ulema*),[131] but also standardised the legal attitude on numerous controversial legal points. Later jurists were consequently discouraged from re-examining judgements or opinions upon which consensus had been reached, as such an exercise appeared superfluous. What is more, in particular from the tenth century onwards, Sunni scholars came to think that classical jurists of such calibre as Hanifa, Malik, Hanbal, and Shafi'i had ceased to flourish, and that henceforth only jurists of established schools could occupy the intellectual scene of Islamic jurisprudence.[132] Muslim jurists were thereafter also required to opine within the bounds of entrenched doctrines set by these schools – a stance that, in effect, marked the end of early juridical tendency to employ critical reason to supplement basic source. This process eventually led to rigid orthodoxy wherein free speculation was replaced by narrow analogical reasoning and crude modelling on precedents.

H. M. Ramadan (ed.), *Understanding Islamic Law: From Classical to Contemporary* (Oxford: AltaMira Press, 2006) 1, 24–29.

128 See S. Laghmani, 'Les Écoles Juridiques du Sunnisme' (2003) 104 *Pouvoirs* 21, 25ff.

129 While jurists who participated in the consensus process became the *de facto* legislators of the community, they had not regarded themselves as being vested with an authority to enact law; rather, they saw themselves merely as 'the recipients of divine grace', a grace that is manifest in the Quranic revelations. See W. B. Hallaq, 'On the Authoritativeness of Sunni Consensus' (1986) *International Journal of Middle East Studies* 427, 428.

130 Nevertheless, some classical scholars, of whom Shafi'i was the prototype, had not considered every type of consensus authoritative – consensus that could lead to certainty had to be strictly based on the Quran and Sunnah. See further, Hallaq, supra note 129, 431.

131 Notwithstanding this, the *ulema* never attained a status akin to that of a Church; neither had Islam developed orthodoxy in the Christian sense of the term – in that there had never been councils, synods, ecclesiastical dignitaries to authoritatively define the truth and error, and to enforce what was deemed the correct attitude. While the learned men of Islam, be they jurists, scholars, or public officers, formulated dogmas and interpreted the scripture, they formed no established ecclesiastical authorities to impose their exclusive interpretations of religion. See B. Lewis, *The Middle East: 2000 Years of History from the Rise of Christianity to the Present Day* (London: Phoenix Press, 2000) 225–226.

132 See W. B. Hallaq, 'On the Origins of the Controversy about the Existence of Mujtahids and the Gate of Ijtihad' (1986) 63 *Studia Islamica* 129, 136; Abdal-Haqq, supra note 127, 1, 17.

III. The Closing of the Door for Critical Thinking

By the end of the ninth century, through independent reasoning and general consensus, a significant corpus of legal rulings and precedents had accumulated. From this point onwards, many scholars, who mainly represented the Sunni majority, came to claim that all the basic questions of law had been resolved by the major schools, and hence personal interpretation of Islamic law was no longer necessary.[133] The early signs of rigidity in the development of the law already became visible as a result of the infallibility of the consensus doctrine. Scholars of this age posited that because all crucial legal questions had been exhaustively settled, the future activity of the jurist needed to be confined to the clarification, application, and interpretation of the law or doctrine as had already been laid down. The task of the jurist was simply to emulate (*taqlid*), follow, or expound the existing precedent.[134]

This position leaned on the assumption that since all essential doctrines had been formulated by classical jurists, it would make no sense in having critical thinking as one of the sources of Islamic law. Besides, those who answered all fundamental legal problems were canonical figures whose academic merits were so superior and rigorous that such qualities were almost impossible to attain for the jurists to come after them.[135] Gradually, therefore, the doctrine of *ijtihad* was replaced by that of emulation, whereby the jurist was expected to master, teach, and apply the official doctrines of his school of thought. This also signified that legal norms could not be extracted directly from the Quran and the Sunnah, but from the authoritative textbooks of established schools.[136] The presumed infallibility of the consensus-based law, and the intellectual barriers to speculation and critical thinking, with its clear disregard for contextual legal interpretation, had progressively rigidified Islamic jurisprudence.

This policy finally assumed an official stance by the declaration of the Iraqi jurists to close the door for the exercise of *ijtihad*,[137] which confined legal reasoning essentially to applying precedents to similar circumstances, and to drawing straight conclusions from the primary sources, in particular from the recognised handbooks of major schools. These handbooks were deemed to contain the authoritative exposition of the law, whose respective approaches to issues of public concern were equally considered valid – notwithstanding the existence of some notable divergences of approach among them. It followed that any

133 Esposito, supra note 71, 195.

134 See B. Lewis; B. E. Churchill, *Islam: The Religion and the People* (Indianapolis: Wharton School Publishing, 2008) 29; K. Bennoune, 'As-Salamu Alaykum? Humanitarian Law in Islamic Jurisprudence' (1994) 15 *Michigan Journal of International Law* 605, 613.

135 W. B. Hallaq, 'Was the Gate of Ijtihad Closed?' (1984) 16 *International Journal of Middle East Studies*, 3, 5.

136 See L. Safi, *Tensions and Transitions in the Muslim World* (Lanham: University of America Press, 2003) 98; also see Khadduri, supra note 79, 72–73.

137 See Abdal-Haqq, supra note 127, 21.

juristic attempt to go beyond the confines of endorsed doctrines could give rise to claims of heresy.

Arguably, another important factor partly responsible for the 'closure of the doors' for critical thinking was the concern to keep the guiding principles of Islam intact and standardise the law in an empire whose borders stretched far and wide. Muslim rulers and orthodox scholars alike dreaded the possibility of the divisive impact of critical thinking and independent reasoning over the unity of Islamic jurisprudence, which was already splintered into numerous schools. Standardisation of the legal tradition through imitation and strict analogy might initially have served as a barrier to the intrusion of anomalous concepts, ideas, or traditions. Likewise, the detrimental effect of excluding constant socio-political changes and novelties of life (such as technology) from the equation of law-making might not have been felt at the early stages of this policy. However, casting the law into rigid formulas and black-letter analyses, and divesting the tradition of its inherent dynamism through imposing strict precedence and analogy, eventually took its toll on the progress and adaptability of Islamic law.

It is worth noting that the main responsibility for the gradual diminishment in formulating fresh legal principles to adapt to new circumstances is often attributed to the influential jurist Ash-Shafi'i, who insisted on the achievement of the consensus of the whole Muslim community in order for the *ijma*-based source of law to be valid and binding. He is recorded as having said to disagreeing scholars: 'You do not have agreement (*ijma*) but disagreement (*iftiraq*).'[138] But it has always been difficult to achieve an overall consensus over most controversial matters, particularly considering the fragmented state of Islamic nations with varying socio-political, cultural, and legal backgrounds. In an effort to secure total consensus over moot issues, Shafi'i maintained that if there existed explicit rulings in the Quran or Sunnah, or unanimous agreement of the scholars, no stray individual opinion was to be allowed. When tackling controversial issues, the argument went, qualified jurists had to seek clarification in, and form opinions through, these sources. On the other hand, if a problem engendered two equally plausible solutions through methodical reasoning, either of them could be valid, although this seldom occurred.[139]

It was Ahmad ibn Hanbal (d. 855), a pupil of Ash-Shafi'i and the founder of the Hanbali school, who made a strong appeal for a literal interpretation of textual sources. Hanbal called for strict restrictions on the exercise of *ijtihad* and analogical reasoning.[140] Such dogmatic views, which advocated restriction over critical reasoning, progressively came to receive wide recognition, which, among other

138 Esposito, supra note 123, 148.

139 J. Schacht, *The Origins of Muhammadan Jurisprudence* (Oxford: Oxford University Press, 1967) 93–97.

140 Elias notes that the Hanbali school has historically given so much weight to literalist methodology that some Hanbali scholars went so far as to postulate that 'an unreliable *hadith* should be preferred over a strong example of reasoning by analogy'. J. J. Elias, *Islam* (London: Routledge, 1999) 48.

things, resulted in increasing juridical efforts to collect the sayings and deeds of the Prophet with a view to generating greater harmony in the interpretation and application of Islamic law. The significance attached to the prophetic tradition as the authoritative law naturally demanded greater attentiveness to the validation of authentic *hadiths*, so that forged traditions, which often crept into the legal literature to reinforce a certain political or religious position, could be weeded out.[141] This, as discussed above, brought about the development of various methods to collect accurate traditions.

Muslim jurists certainly had not altogether abandoned the practice of independent reasoning.[142] For instance, the great philosopher and jurist al-Ghazali (d. 1111) argued that critical thinking based on wider analogy, as opposed to narrow syllogism, and on the general purposes of law was permissible.[143] Ibn Taymiyya (d. 1328) also advocated the indispensability of *ijtihad*. Despite his reliance on the established doctrines of the main Sunni schools, he challenged them whenever he drew disparate conclusions from the Quran and Sunnah. Notably, Taymiyya's writings did not promote the view that ordinary Muslims had to avoid emulating the findings of the existing schools; rather, they stressed that highly qualified jurists needed to pursue their independent judgements where necessary to prevent Islamic thought from stagnating.[144]

Nonetheless, the tide of relying on orthodox interpretation of extant sources progressively rose, and over the centuries far fewer jurists claimed to possess the required qualifications to formulate novel ideas. Hence, although the doors of *ijtihad* remained ajar,[145] Muslim jurists ceased to vigorously and widely exercise it

141 R. H. Salmi; C. A. Majul; G. K. Tanham, *Islam and Conflict Resolution: Theories and Practices* (Lanham: University Press of America, 1998) 55.

142 It is worth noting that in the Shia tradition there were no claims that the doors of the *ijtihad* had been closed. Hence, the use of independent reasoning continued, albeit its practice incrementally lost momentum. Over the centuries, in particular during the Qajar period (1785–1925), Shiite jurists came to permit heavy reliance on the findings of classical works that were authentic and well-preserved. This resulted in incorporating imitation into the practice of *ijtihad* by way of linking ancient texts and rulings with modern works and cases. When classical rules could not be made applicable to new situations, however, the Shiite jurists had to rely on their own mental resources (*aql*) to derive the law. See further, A. A. Sachedina, *The Just Ruler in Shi'ite Islam: The Comprehensive Authority of the Jurist in Imamite Jurisprudence* (Oxford: Oxford University Press, 1988) 159ff; Kamali, supra note 33, 491; J. O. Voll, 'Renewal and Reform in Islamic History: Tajdid and Islah' in: J. L. Esposito, *Voices of Resurgent Islam* (New York: Oxford University Press, 1983) 38.

143 I. A. K. Nyazee, *Theories of Islamic Law: The Methodology of Ijtihad* (Islamabad: The Other Press, 1994) 195ff.

144 B. Haykel, 'On the Nature of Salafi Thought and Action' in: R. Meijer (ed.), *Global Salafism: Islam's New Religious Movement* (New York: Columbia University Press, 2009) 33, 43.

145 Hallaq notes that not until the twelfth century had the phrase 'closing the door of ijtihad' (*insidad bab al-ijtihad*) come into widespread usage. Hallaq, supra note 135, 4.

to resolve new problems.[146] Having complied with this restrictive policy, mainstream Sunni scholars instead studied, systematised, preserved, and transferred the authoritative rulings, a process that eventually caused Islamic law to virtually 'hibernate' for nearly a millennium.[147] Nevertheless, as will be discussed below, there is no hard-and-fast rule in Islam to prevent contemporary scholars from invoking *ijtihad* to invigorate the law, making it responsive to current realities.

IV. The Need for Revival in Critical Discourse

It was noted above that, notwithstanding the sporadic exercise of critical thinking, the practice of juridical imitation pervaded the Islamic world until modern times. An example of condemning critical thinking and advocating emulation is found in a legal opinion issued in Tunisia in the twentieth century:

> It is generally admitted that, ever since the codification of the doctrine of Islam by the four great orthodox imams, this door [of *ijtihad*] is closed and that Muslims must conform their opinions strictly to the opinions enumerated by these imams, without seeking to arrive by means of their own reasoning at a personal opinion about the tenets of Islam.[148]

There is little doubt that blind adherence to orthodox rulings is responsible for the decline of Islamic thought in all intellectual realms, which in turn largely accounts for the Islamic world's centuries-long political, economic, and cultural stagnation. The artificial shackles placed upon Islam's dynamism also paved the way for foreign domination and colonialism over large parts of the Muslim world – which eventually sparked considerable debate over the ways in which Western hegemony could be countered and the once-glorious Islamic culture could be resurrected.[149] Indeed, by the eighteenth century, it became unmistakably clear that many areas of the Islamic world were in decline in the face of Christian Europe's energetic progress that was to mould the socio-political and economic structure of the modern era. The hitherto dominant role played by the Islamic

146 However, as Hashmi observes, the fact that some of the most canonical sources on Islamic law, like al-Shaybani's work on international relations, are centuries old signifies the extent to which Islamic legal and political thought stagnated. See S. H. Hashmi, 'Islamic Ethics in International Society' in: S. H. Hashmi, *Islamic Political Ethics: Civil Society, Pluralism, and Conflict* (Princeton: Princeton University Press, 2002) 148, 151.

147 See Abdal-Haqq, supra note 127, 21; Weiss, supra note 116, 115; H. A. Haleem *et al* (eds.), *The Crescent and the Cross* (London: Macmillan Press Ltd, 1998) 62; Esposito, supra note 71, 196.

148 Quoted in: A. H. Green, *The Tunisian Ulama 1873–1915: Social Structure and Response to Ideological Currents* (Leiden: Brill, 1978) 188–189.

149 It is to be noted that modernists and traditionalists often diverged over what entailed true Islamic values and over the place of the Islamic world in the post-colonial era. See Hasan, supra note 41, 2–3.

civilisation was being overshadowed by the bourgeoning Western political, economic, and military might.[150]

Western material progress was naturally accompanied by seismic intellectual and moral shifts that were to challenge Muslim thinkers who needed to balance entrenched religious standards and the unprecedented demands of modern circumstances. The pressures exerted by such material and conceptual novelties, together with the colonial enterprise over Muslim lands, eventually divided Muslim intellectuals over whether some key modern concepts, ideas, and institutions were to be integrated or rejected – whether wholly or in part.[151] As Esposito puts it, Muslim reactions to Western power and domination ranged from rejection to adaptation, from a policy of cultural isolation and non-cooperation to acculturation and reform.[152]

The first type of reaction manifested itself in various ways, such as the flat denunciation of the European powers as the enemies of Islam, calling for holy war against foreign intrusions, or demanding Muslim repatriation to within the pale of Islam. The majority of such conservative responses equated any form of political cooperation with the Christian West, or modelling on its way of life, with perfidiousness and submission. Yet another sort of Muslim position towards modernity sought to bridge the gap between tradition and innovation through reform.[153] This attitude went beyond merely reacting against the West; rather it sought to produce an Islamic rationale for the modernisation of the political, legal, and social structure of society. Unsurprisingly, such a reformist streak largely sprang from the bitter realisation that the West had long surpassed the Muslim world in such critical areas as warfare, technology, industrial production, trade, and science. By the late nineteenth century, reformist movements incrementally gained momentum within the Islamic world[154] in an attempt to overhaul the principal socio-legal, military, and cultural institutions.[155]

150 Even international law as we know it today has mainly emerged as an extension of Western dominance over world affairs. It is thus no exaggeration to say that the general contours of the current collective security system have come down in unbroken descent from the power structure of the Great Powers. For a general account of how power politics of Western powers shaped the main framework of international law, see F. H. Hinsley, *Power and the Pursuit of Peace: Theory and Practice in the History of Relations between States* (Cambridge: Cambridge University Press, 1963) 153ff; A. Anghie, *Imperialism, Sovereignty and the Making of International Law* (Cambridge: Cambridge University Press, 2005).

151 Rahman, supra note 34, 4.

152 Esposito, supra note 42, 43.

153 Ibid. 44. One of the important factors that, to some degree, informed the modern cultural and political landscape of Muslim States has been the common colonial and post-colonial influences of the Western legal tradition, which contributed to the emergence of a new kind of socio-legal culture and institutional practice. Ali, supra note 89, 95.

154 Esposito, supra note 42, 44.

155 The major examples of such initiatives initially took place in the central Ottoman Empire and Egypt. For a general account, see K. Fahmy, *All the Pasha's Men: Mehmed*

One of the dilemmas confronting the reformers was how modern institutions and technology were to be incorporated without acceding to the secular Western modus operandi, and thereby without damaging core Islamic customs and traditions.[156] The Muslim reformist movement of the nineteenth and early twentieth centuries[157] thus, on the one hand, attempted to modernise the basic tools of the social and political organisation, and on the other, sought to remain loyal to the fundamental tenets of Islam. Irrespective of their intellectual orientations, almost all reformist thinkers challenged the *status quo ante* and searched for ways to transform their societies by, among other ways, criticising dogmatic religious premises and advocating progress with a view to reversing the tide of decline. Islam, they essentially maintained, had to undergo a process of reformation and reinvigoration in respect of mutable principles,[158] so that Muslims could awaken from their debilitating slumber, which rendered Islamic thought bankrupt of any intellectual remedy responsive to modernity.

Reformers saw the artificial restrictions on innovative thinking as hampering the progress of Islamic thought, positing that each generation of Muslims must be permitted to be guided by the works of its predecessors, but believers must also be allowed to resolve the particular problems of their age through critical deliberation. For only in this way would the deleterious effects of unquestioned emulation be prevented from further damaging the cause of Islam. To reformists, Islamic law's inherent dynamism was gradually stultified, and the richness of its texture was in effect fossilised into rigid dogmas by traditional scholars. Reformist thinking hence highlighted the imperative for substantial reinterpretation and reconstruction of many key concepts and principles via free discussion, open-mindedness, and rigorous scholarship.[159]

Ali, His Army and the Making of Modern Egypt (Cairo: The American University in Cairo Press, 1997).

156 For a discussion on this dilemma for the Ottoman society, see B. Toprak, *Islam and Political Development in Turkey* (Leiden: Brill, 1981) 32ff.

157 The movement included such important intellectuals as Mortaza Ansari (1800–64), Jamal al-Din al-Afghani (1838–97), Rashid Rida (1865–1935), Hassan al-Banna (1906–49), Muhammad Abduh (1849–1905), Muhammad Iqbal (1877–1938), and Sayyid Ahmed Khan (1817–1898). See further B. M. Edwards, *Islamic Fundamentalism Since 1945* (London: Routledge, 2005) 20ff.

158 As alluded to above, Muslim reformers distinguished between the timeless principles of Islam and those conditioned by socio-historical conditions, or developed by early scholars. See J. L. Esposito, 'Trailblazers of the Islamic Resurgence' in: Y. Yazbeck Haddad *et al* (eds.), *The Contemporary Islamic Revival: A Critical Survey and Bibliography* (Westport: Greenwood Publishing, 1991) 37, 53.

159 Many of such reformists hold secularist views, arguing that a citizen may act as a believer, but only inwardly, without being subject to coercion exercised by the state or clergy, but also without imposing his purportedly divine views on others. According to this view, absolute faith, free speech, tolerance, and pluralism are not mutually exclusive concepts. See further O. Roy, *Secularism Confronts Islam* (New York: Columbia University Press, 2007) 45ff.

Such denunciation of categorical deference to the determinations of classical texts paid off by encouraging an intellectual revival and prompting anti-colonial aspirations. Indeed, having rejected rigid conservatism, pioneering revivalist movements, like the Sanusiyyah, Wahhabis, and the Aligarh, advocated the contextualisation and reinterpretation of the primary material and urged Muslims to embark upon a rigorous endeavour to refine, revise, and expand the extant knowledge in order to meet the demands of challenging times, and to liberate the oppressed or colonised Muslim population all around the world. This, it was believed, would ultimately enable Muslims to become active subjects of history, and not merely victims of despotism and colonial exploitation.[160]

The impact of such reformist calls has hitherto been notable across the Muslim world, which, particularly since the nineteenth century onwards, has gone through dramatic transformations, including the phenomena of modernity in all spheres of life, socio-political liberalisation, and independence from colonial subjugation.[161] In an effort to allow Islamic law to meet the ever-growing challenges of faith and contemporary circumstances, many contemporary reformers have rightly advocated the revival of *ijtihad*.[162] Among the most pressing problems to have constituted battlegrounds for reformists are the role of science vis-à-vis religion, political participation, secularism, religious freedoms, diversity, human rights, and just war in Islam. Having drawn upon the overall Islamic ethical framework, which places significant emphasis on such notions as justice, equity, non-discrimination, and reciprocity, Muslim scholars have sought to address these thorny problems that require radical rethinking.[163]

Such a task was not inordinately difficult given the flexible nature of Islamic jurisprudence, which could bend antiquated or seemingly unalterable rules – through such supple concepts as 'public interest' and 'juristic preference' – to find just and legitimate solutions to the problems faced. Being part and parcel of the general process of *ijtihad*, such flexible notions have often been invoked by Muslim scholars for the exercise of judicial discretion (*ra'y*). The concept of judicial preference (*istihsan*), for example, has been resorted to when strict

160 See further, N. A. Ziadeh, *Sanusiyyah: A Study of a Revivalist Movement in Islam* (Leiden: Brill, 1968); Saeed, supra note 94, 130ff; Edwards, supra note 157, 21; W. M. Watt, *Islamic Fundamentalism and Modernity* (London: Routledge, 1988) 130ff.

161 Certainly, in many parts of the Islamic world, those calling for the reinterpretation and contextualisation of certain Sharia principles through critical individual or communal reasoning have occasionally been persecuted, denounced, and accused of being subversive, for they threatened the dominant social order. See S. Zubaida, 'Is Iran an Islamic State?' in: J. Beinin; J. Stork (eds.), *Political Islam: Essays from Middle East Report* (London: I.B. Tauris, 1997) 103, 116.

162 See M. A. Faksh, *The Future of Islam in the Middle East: Fundamentalism in Egypt, Algeria, and Saudi Arabia* (Westport: Praeger Publishers, 1997) 42; S. S. Ali, *Gender and Human Rights in Islam and International Law* (London: Kluwer Law International, 2000) 23.

163 See generally, Ramadan, supra note 53, 207–232; A. A. An-Na'im, *Islam and the Secular State: Negotiating the Future of Shari'a* (Cambridge, MA: Harvard University Press, 2008) 111ff; Esposito, supra note 63, 86ff.

analogy produced an inappropriate or unjust outcome. By relaxing strict rules, *istihsan* thus allowed jurists to achieve the fairest outcome possible under the circumstances.[164] *Istislah*, on the other side, is a method of legal reasoning whereby jurists may give precedence to a particular interest over the results of derivative reasoning that is anticipated to cause undesirable consequences. Here the jurist is permitted to put forward an alternative solution, at the expense of deviating from the outcome of conventional reasoning, in a bid to satisfy an important interest, or to attain a beneficial legal ruling.[165] Naturally, such discretionary power equips the jurist with flexibility in reinterpreting or revealing the purposes of the law so that justice is done in a particular situation. Likewise, the concept of public utility (*maslaha*), which was later largely subsumed under the purposive interpretation method (*maqasid*), has also been utilised to mitigate the rigour of certain norms, or to justify a preference between competing interests or rulings with intent to protect a specific value, or to promote the general good.[166] Rather than being mere tools of arbitrary juridical discretion, such concepts have likewise been employed to expose the underlying rationale for, or core meaning behind, each Islamic enactment with a view to promoting justice and the general interests of society. An example in point for the use of purposive approach has been the introduction of modern codes modifying some personal status rules in many Islamic States including Egypt, Iraq, Syria, and Tunisia, where, among others, the practice of polygamy and the possibility for the husband to unilaterally terminate the marriage are either abolished or severely restricted on grounds of equality and fairness.[167]

Today, the aforementioned concepts are frequently invoked so as to bring about socio-legal reforms. The reformist discourse has similarly been active within the context of military force and revolutionary struggles within the Muslim world. As will be seen in subsequent chapters, the common theme that repeatedly stands out has been the need to return to the primary law, as enshrined within the Quran and Sunnah, which is argued to serve as the ultimate yardstick against which the

164 Hence, *istihsan* is a way of reinterpreting the law to achieve equity and to promote the public good. In Shams al-Din al-Sarakhsi's language, *istihsan* 'is abandoning what is difficult and choosing what is easier in matters of religion'. Al-Sarakhsi, *al-Mabsut* X, 145, cited in: H. Gerber, *Islamic Law and Culture 1600–1840* (Leiden: Brill, 1999) 93; also see Hassan, supra note 4, 68.

165 Weiss, supra note 116, 86–87.

166 See generally, Weiss, supra note 104, 199; F. M. M. Opwis, *Maslaha and the Purpose of the Law* (Leiden: Martinus Nijhoff Publishers, 2010); N. M. Goolam, '*Ijtihad* and its Significance for Islamic Legal Interpretation' (2006) *Michigan State Law Review* 1443.

167 The Quran gives permission for plural marriage – restricting the number of wives to a maximum of four – provided that the husband treats his spouses fairly and justly. Q. 4:3. However, the Quran elsewhere clearly says that 'ye are never able to be fair and just as between women' (Q. 4:129), a statement that lays the foundation for the reformist argument that polygamy should not, in principle, be allowed. For a detailed treatment of this point, see M. Badran, *Feminists, Islam, and Nation: Gender and the Making of Modern Egypt* (Princeton: Princeton University Press, 1995) 128ff; Khadduri, supra note 68, 216ff.

validity of traditional views and institutions could be (re)judged. Such an exercise, however, may require a broader assessment of socio-political factors that fashioned the content of temporal norms. The emphasis here is not to catapult Islamic jurisprudence back into seventh-century Arabia, but rather to generate a critical paradigm that deciphers the historical climate within which many concepts were conditioned in order to comprehend the rationale for many time-bound concepts. In actual fact, never in the history of Islamic thought has there been a hard-and-fast separation between religious precepts and dominant socio-political conditions, local customs or societal demands. An interaction between legal doctrines and society has been inevitable given the fact that human agency rarely materialises as an isolated social process.[168]

One critical consequence of this change in perspective is that *non-eternal* rulings may now be understood against the backdrop of their politico-cultural settings, which provided the legal rationale thereof. Hence, except for timeless principles, such a contextualised method of interpreting the law requires the abandonment of outdated doctrines or re-reading of certain norms to meet the exigencies of the times.[169] Within the context of military force in Islam, the rejection of blind adherence to the literalist tradition and antiquated concepts, and the demand for the revival of independent thinking may also be vital for reconsidering some of the discourse-dependent notions of Islamic just war. Indeed, given that both scientific progress and conflict resolution require broad-mindedness and intellectual vigour, *ijtihad* may be put into effect as a means of reasserting the flexibility of Islamic law in the face of novel challenges. This will in all likelihood also enable Muslims to undercut the largely ideological and biased portrayal of Islam as an inherently political and fanatical faith; reopening the door for critical thinking has the potential to demonstrate the complexity of religious attitude towards issues of war and peace – a theme to which the remainder of this book will devote particular attention.

168 See generally, Coulson, supra note 84.

169 Rahman, in this context, maintains that if circumstances no longer justify the applicability of a legal norm, or when circumstances change so much that the law fails to reflect the *ratio legis*, then the law, too, must be modified or be given such meaning that suits new social needs. F. Rahman, *Major Themes of the Quran*, 2nd ed. (London: The University of the Chicago Press, 2009) 47–48.

2 Islamic Tradition on Warfare

Introduction

Islam was established in seventh-century Arabia. During the lifetime of the Prophet, its sphere of influence was merely confined to the Arabian Peninsula, yet in less than a century after its advent, Islam had spread with extraordinary rapidity, growing into an empire, the borders of which stretched from Spain across to North Africa, and from the Middle East to China.[1] As a politico-religious system, Islam is based upon highly detailed rules that govern broad aspects of human behaviour, including a large swathe of private and public matters, moral issues, ritualistic and formal observances, modes of worship, good manners, and hygiene.[2] Islam is deemed to provide a blueprint for an ideal life and society that could be achieved when concrete measures are taken, and religio-moral obligations are fulfilled by believers.

Since Islam seeks to regulate all aspects of social life, not only personal matters (such as marriage, divorce, maintenance, child custody, inheritance, property and so forth), but also public matters (including issues of statecraft and administration of domestic and external affairs) are patterned on the main premises of the religion. This means both private and political affairs are to come under the supervision of the omnipotent God, who said in the Quran: 'nothing have We omitted from the Book'.[3] Islam thus does not distinguish between spiritual and political affairs, nor does it envisage a substantial discrepancy between worldly and heavenly affairs; rather, it establishes a seamless unity between religious and political spheres, and, likewise, between matters of sacred and profane nature. There is accordingly no straightforward separation between religious and political

1 See N. Mohammad, 'The Doctrine of *Jihad*: An Introduction' (1985) 3 *Journal of Law and Religion* 2, 381- 382; A. G. Noorani, *Islam & Jihad: Prejudice versus Reality* (London: Zed Books, 2002) 27–28.

2 Through a casuistic methodology, an approach to religious and moral matters can be inferred from the Sharia and relevant instructions may be obtained as to what is right and wrong under Islam. See S. Bar, *The Fatwas of Radical Islam and the Duty to Jihad* (Oxford: Rowman & Littlefield Publishers, 2006) 1–2.

3 Q. 6:38.

authority, because these two are intertwined in a bid to better implement God's all-encompassing commands.[4]

The ethico-political aspect of Islam regulates and constrains the exercise of force. In the Quran, the divine entity is extensively associated with efforts to discourage the employment of illicit force and to mitigate the intensity of legitimate aggression by the promise of eternal punishment.[5] This is connected with Islam's treatment of life as the supreme and sacred right to which all human beings are entitled, irrespective of any distinction based on religion, race, nationality, colour, gender, and language. The Quran considers any illegitimate infringement upon an individual's right to life to be a grave offence committed against humankind as a whole.[6]

Islam, like some other major systems of belief,[7] offers private and public peace upon the condition that believers observe its precepts faithfully. While the Quran ordains that humankind must strive to achieve all virtues,[8] which include creating conditions for peace, this notion may occasionally be qualified by competing moral and practical demands. Such demands compelled the Prophet himself to engage in armed struggle during his lifetime. Hence, the pertinent question here is not whether warfare is permissible in Islam, but rather under which circumstances it could be waged and conducted.

4 Since Islam cannot be completely detached from public policy and statecraft, the question whether secularism and Islamic faith can ever co-exist has long been subject to controversy. The traditional view holds that in Islam there is only a single law of divine origin, the Sharia, which regulates all aspects of moral, civil, criminal, constitutional, administrative, and commercial matters. Hence, the idea of secularism is relatively foreign to Islam. For a detailed analysis, see B. Lewis, *What Went Wrong? Western Impact and Middle Eastern Response* (London: Phoenix, 2002) 107–129. However, some Muslim reformers, including An-Naim, maintain that Islam and secularism are not two mutually exclusive concepts: 'Secularism does not mean the exclusion of Islam from public life or the relegation of its role to the purely personal and private domain. The appropriate balance can be achieved through the institutional separation of Islam from the state, with regulation of the political role of Islam, whereby Muslims can propose some Sharia principles for adoption as public policy or enactment into legislation, provided that it is done in accordance with civic reason and subject to constitutional and human rights safeguards, which are necessary for Muslim as well as non-Muslim citizens.' For an elaboration of this point, see A. A. An-Na'im, *Islam and the Secular State: Negotiating the Future of Shari'a* (Cambridge, MA: Harvard University Press, 2008) 261.

5 D. Little, '"Holy War" Appeals and Western Christianity: A Reconsideration of Bainton's Approach' in: J. Kelsay; J. T. Johnson (eds.), *Just War and Jihad: Historical and Theoretical Perspectives on War and Peace in Western and Islamic Traditions* (New York: Greenwood Press, 1991) 121.

6 See Q. 5:32; Q. 17:33; Q. 4:29.

7 While their concrete and ideal contours differ, such major traditions as Christianity, Judaism, Hinduism, and Islam have a common calling to reducing aggression and to alleviating the devastating effects of armed conflicts through just war principles. J. C. Super; B. K. Turley, *Religion in World History* (New York: Routledge, 2006) 107ff.

8 Q. 5:48.

The question of whether Islamic force may go beyond self-defensive measures will be explored later; suffice it to note here that Islamic wars must always be fought in accordance with certain norms and restrictions. Contrary to popular misconceptions,[9] therefore, Islamic tradition does not impose an unqualified duty to wage war against those who reject Islam. To be sure, Islam recognised warfare as a legitimate tool to defend the Muslim community, and under certain conditions to expand the sphere of its public order. It is also fair to note that over the centuries, in particular following the rule of the so-called 'first four rightly guided caliphs',[10] many Islamic States, under the pretext of religious cause, engaged in numerous wars principally for political purposes.[11] This phenomenon sometimes blurred the demarcation line between religious wars and wars of conquest or imperial consolidation. Not infrequently, Muslim rulers drew on religious justifications for politically and/or economically motivated wars, largely because this eased the conscience of Muslim warriors, assuring them that the cause for which they fought was righteous.

Parties to an armed conflict tend to claim that they had been in the right, and that their cause was thus justified. No doubt, the Muslim rulers had likewise subjectively believed, or claimed (sincerely or otherwise), that they were justified in waging a given war. The credibility of the 'just cause' argument had unsurprisingly been subject to endless controversy in various just war traditions, for a war may not be considered just on both sides simultaneously, albeit warring parties may both have a certain degree of justness on their sides. As Vitoria rightly highlights, a mere belief of a ruler cannot render an unjust war just; instead, an objective and thorough examination is essential to assess the righteousness of a cause.[12] According to Islamic laws of war, in order for an armed conflict to be considered legitimate, it must be fought in accord with certain principles which regulate the manner in

9 For examples, see H. Zawati, *Is Jihad a Just War: War, Peace, and Human Rights under Islamic and Public International Law* (New York: The Edwin Mellen Press, 2001) 1–5.

10 Most Muslims believe that the pure form of Islam had been experienced during the rule of the Prophet and the first four 'righteous' caliphs – Abu Bakr, Umar, Uthman, and Ali – who were elected from among Muhammad's closest companions. Subsequent caliphs had not commanded such respect, mainly because they turned the caliphate into a hereditary office, and acted upon relatively mundane objectives. See further A. Hourani, *A History of the Arab Peoples* (London: Faber and Faber Limited, 2005) 22–37.

11 See A. A. Engineer, 'Islam and Secularism' in: J. J. Donohue; J. L. Esposito (eds.), *Islam in Transition: Muslim Perspectives,* 2nd ed. (Oxford: Oxford University Press, 2007) 136, 137–138; On the rapidity of Islamic expansion, see Hourani, supra note 10, 22ff; V. J. Parry, 'Warfare' in: P. M. Holt *et al* (eds.), *Cambridge History of Islam,* Vol. II (Cambridge: Cambridge University Press, 1992) 824, 834ff.

12 In Vitoria's words, 'the opinion of the individual [about the justness of a given cause] is not enough to render an act good, but it must come up to the standard of a wise man's judgement.' F. D. Vitoria; J. P. Bate (trans.); E. Nys (ed.), *De Indis Et De Ivre Belli Reflectiones* (New York: Oceana Publications, 1963) bk. II/20.

which wars should be engaged and conducted.[13] These principles seek to ensure that wars are fought for objectively justified reasons, and are conducted in the cause of God with permissible means.

I. Pacifism and War for Just Cause

Whilst it is not the focus of this book to compare Islamic just war doctrine with its Catholic counterpart, it is appropriate at this stage to highlight that in their classical forms, Islamic and Catholic just war thinking share some common traits with respect to such concepts as just recourse to, and just conduct in, warfare.[14] Islam emerged as a younger religion, yet its principles on just war may be said to have reached maturity earlier than Christianity, probably because Islam, from its very inception, had faced material threats posed to its existence by rival powers. This compelled the Prophet to provide both spiritual and practical guidance to ensure the survival of his followers. Indeed, when pacifism did not yield the expected results, warlike measures were taken to reinforce the security and prosperity of the nascent Muslim community, who, soon after being organised within a polity, had to confront the competing forces of the time that sought to maintain the status quo. Christianity, in contrast, came to terms with the necessities of statecraft following its adoption as the official religion of the Roman Empire almost three centuries after its birth.

Although just war doctrine in Christianity was developed by the early fathers of the Latin Church, primarily by St Augustine (354–430) whose teachings were later refined by Thomas Aquinas (1225–1274), its origins may be traced back to Aristotle, and later to Cicero. Aristotle, who coined the term 'just war', argued that the art of war could justly be used against other nations that were naturally inferior to Greeks, and thus meant to be ruled.[15] Unsurprisingly, these ideas were readily invoked to legitimise wars of aggression against the 'barbarians' with a view to subjugating and enslaving them. Cicero, on the other hand, maintained that warfare could be legitimate only when it was fought for defensive or punitive purposes.[16] He posited that war should be waged only as a last resort: 'For since', he noted, 'there are two ways of settling a dispute: first, by discussion;

13 See A. Z. Yamanai, 'Humanitarian International Law in Islam: A General Outlook' in: H. M. Ramadan (ed.), *Understanding Islamic Law: From Classical to Contemporary* (Oxford: Rowman & Littlefield Publishers, 2006) 65, 71ff; K. Bennoune, 'As-Salamu Alaykum? Humanitarian Law in Islamic Jurisprudence' (1994) 15 *Michigan Journal of International Law* 605, 614ff.

14 See J. T. Johnson, 'Introduction' in: J. T. Johnson; J. Kelsay (eds.) *Cross, Crescent, and Sword* (London: Greenwood Press, 1990) xvi.

15 F. D. Miller, *Nature, Justice and Rights in Aristotle's Politics* (Oxford: Clarendon Press, 1997) 28; 84–108; see further M. Davis, *The Politics of Philosophy: A Commentary on Aristotle's Politics* (Lanham: Rowman & Littlefield, 1996) 16–18.

16 Cicero; Nial Rudd (trans.), *The Republic and the Laws* (Oxford: Oxford University Press, 1998) 63.

second, by physical force; and since the former is characteristic of man, the latter of the brute, we must resort to force only in case we may not avail ourselves of discussion.'[17]

Having recognised that wars could be necessary, Christian scholars formed a complex doctrine of just war. However, the relationship between Christianity and belligerency involved puzzling discrepancies, for Christianity originally offered a non-violent belief system, which envisaged individual and collective peace,[18] condemning killing as a heinous sin that separated the wrongdoer from society.[19] Likewise, the notion of universal love was firmly embedded within Christianity, which counselled believers not only to love their neighbours as themselves,[20] but also to love their enemies and to pray for their persecutors.[21] Jesus explicitly advised non-resistance to the evildoer: 'You have heard that it was said: "An eye for an eye and a tooth for a tooth." But I say to you, offer no resistance to one who is evil. When someone strikes you on (your) right cheek, turn the other one to him as well.'[22] Christianity, however, offered divine justice in the afterlife: the central idea was that God possessed the ultimate authority over coercive and punitive measures to be meted out on those who failed in their duties to God. Hence, even when the evil could not be overcome by the good in this world, the ultimate punishment of the evildoer was promised in the afterlife.[23]

The stance of the Church on the concepts of pacifism and non-resistance dramatically changed following the conversion of Constantine to Christianity in 312.[24] Having conceded to Constantine's viewpoint, the leaders of the Church gradually lent their support to the idea that Christians could henceforth serve for the imperial army, and participate in warfare so long as the cause was just.

17 M. T. Cicero; W. Miller (trans.), *Cicero de Officiis* (London: Heinemann, 1928) 37.
18 See Little, supra note 5, 121.
19 See D. S. Bachrach, *Religion and the Conduct of War* (Woodbridge: The Boydell Press, 2003) 24.
20 Mark 12:28–34; 1 John 2:9–10.
21 Matthew 5: 43–44. Similarly, according to Luke, Jesus said: 'But I tell you who hear me: Love your enemies, do good to those who hate you, bless those who curse you, pray for those who mistreat you.' Luke 6: 27–28; also see 1 Peter 3:9, 1 Corinthians 4:12, and Romans 12:14.
22 Matthew 5: 38–39.
23 Christianity put forth an ethic of non-retaliation, for retribution was not deemed to be a task for humans: 'Do not repay anyone evil for evil. . . . Do not take revenge, my friends, but leave room for God's wrath, for it is written: "It is mine to avenge; I will repay", says the Lord.' Romans 12:17–19.
24 When Constantine entered Rome in 312, as the ruler of the Western Roman Empire, he at once favoured the Christian Church, which until then had been subjected to persecution. At the time, it was generally considered that he was taking a serious risk in adopting Christianity, for in contrast to the East, where all provinces were largely Christian, in the Latin West, except in North Africa, Christianity was accepted only by a small minority. See J. N. Hillgarth, *Christianity and Paganism, 350–370: The Conversion of Western Europe* (Philadelphia: University of Pennsylvania Press, 1986) 2.

The principles of non-resistance and pacifism thus progressively lost ground.[25] In 380, during the reign of Theodosius, Christianity was proclaimed to be the official and sole religion of the empire. The progressive reversal from pacifism to the recognition of necessary force transpired particularly when pagans were eventually excluded from military service (in 416), which came to be reserved solely for the Christians as a privilege.[26]

Initially, the difficulties inherent in adopting Christianity as the official religion of an empire were related to the need to survive within a world dominated by a pagan way of thinking, where fighting for one's existence and interests was not only necessary, but honourable.[27] Pacifism was indeed incompatible with the reality of States that relied upon coercion for political control as well as for expansion or preservation of the land. This was particularly true for the declining Roman Empire of the fourth century, the territories of which stretched over vast distances that were increasingly falling under military threat posed by various 'barbarian' tribes of the north and east.[28]

Christian just war thinkers accordingly had to develop an urgent answer to the pressing question of whether a Christian could ever shed blood and yet remain pure before God. It took centuries for such great thinkers as St Augustine, St Thomas Aquinas, Vitoria, and Grotius to develop a coherent Judaeo-Christian concept of just war that sought to reconcile the notions of unconditional love and forbearance with lethal force. Over the centuries, Christian thinkers constructed a theory of war that mediated between the extreme forms of pacifism and boundless war. Under this theory, in order for a war to be righteous, certain conditions had to be satisfied, among which the following are prominent: there must be (1) a just cause (e.g. self-defence against unprovoked assault, or fighting in the path of God); (2) a reasonable probability of success; (3) a righteous intent (e.g. punishment of the wicked); (4) a legitimate authorisation (granted by the competent authority); (5) a purpose of establishing peace; (6) an inevitability of war (i.e. military force should be a measure of last resort); (7) a degree of proportionality in the means used; and (8) an appropriate distinction between civilian and military targets.[29]

25 See A. D. Ritchie, 'The Ethics of Pacifism' (1940) 15 *Philosophy* 227, 232; G. M. Reichberg *et al* (eds.), *The Ethics of War: Classic and Contemporary Readings* (Oxford: Blackwell Publishing, 2006) 60ff.

26 M. T. Karoubi, *Just or Unjust War? International Law and Unilateral Use of Armed Force by States at the Turn of the 20th Century* (Aldershot: Ashgate Publishing, 2005) 29–30; S. D. Bailey, *Prohibitions and Restraints in War* (Oxford: Oxford University Press, 1972) 4; O. Stoll, 'The Religions of the Armies' in: P. Erdkamp (ed.), *A Companion to the Roman Army* (Sussex: Wiley Publishing, 2007) 451, 473.

27 See O. O'Donovan, *The Just War Revisited* (Cambridge: Cambridge University Press, 2003) 9.

28 Hillgarth, supra note 24, 2; see generally W. Goffart, *Barbarians and Romans A.D. 418–584: The Techniques of Accommodation* (Princeton: Princeton University Press, 1980).

29 For a general account of the evolution of the Christian just war doctrine, see generally O. Bakircioglu, *Self-Defence in International and Criminal Law: The Doctrine of Imminence* (London: Routledge, 2011) 107–133; S. C. Neff, *War and the Law of Nations: A General*

While the first six conditions regulate the manner in which wars could be resorted to, the final two conditions, also known as the principles of proportionality and distinction, are concerned with the manner by which legitimately waged warfare should be conducted.

Having rejected the principle of boundless pacifism, yet reminiscent of the Catholic tradition, Islamic just war principles regulate the justificatory bases of warfare (*jus ad bellum*), as well as the manner in which hostilities are to be conducted (*jus in bello*). Indeed, Islamic *jus ad bellum* norms, comparable to those of Catholic teaching, require warfare to be a measure of last resort, waged in response to unjust aggression, persecution, or corruption, declared openly by a legitimate authority, and conducted with the right intention and with limited (but achievable) objectives. At the same time, the requirements that the means employed in warfare must be proportionate to the end sought and that combatants must be distinguished from non-combatants show parallels to 'Western' *jus in bello* norms.[30]

It may be surmised that the substance or content of these principles and the practice of Islamic and Catholic just war traditions varied over the course of history,[31] yet one of the most crucial differences between the Catholic and Islamic teaching on just warfare evolved at a later stage: while the 'Western' tradition, starting from the early modern era, accommodated itself to the secularisation of international politics, Islamic just war thinking was largely governed by religious precepts up until the post-World War II era, which inaugurated the decolonisation process, enabling almost all Islamic States to adopt the rules and processes of modern international law.[32] However, as will be discussed later, Islamic State practice has often demonstrated a degree of pragmatism in international affairs, which attests that religious precepts were not blindly followed; rather, necessities of *realpolitik* were acknowledged when appropriate. For the purposes of this book, this historical reality and Islamic States' eventual embrace of the modern and secular legal framework governing warfare have consequential ramifications for

History (Cambridge: Cambridge University Press, 2005); F. H. Russell, *The Just War in the Middle Ages* (Cambridge: Cambridge University Press, 1975); M. Walzer, *Arguing about War* (London: Yale University Press, 2004); J. V. Elbe, 'The Evolution of the Concept of the Just War in International Law' (1939) 33 *American Journal of International Law* 665; A. Shaw, 'Revival of the Just War Doctrine' (1976) 3 *Auckland University Law Review* 156.

30 See further J. Kelsay, 'Religion, Morality, and the Governance of War: The Case of Classical Islam' (1990) 18 *Journal of Religious Ethics* 123, 123ff; J. B. Elshtain, 'Just War and Humanitarian Intervention' (2001) 17 *American University International Law Review* 1, 5–6; Bennoune, supra note 13, 605–623; St. Augustine; M. Dods (trans.), *The City of God* (New York: Random House Inc., 1950) 693–694; T. Aquinas; T. R. Heath (trans.), *Summa Theologiae,* Vol. 35 (London: Blackfriars, 1972) 81–85; Russell, supra note 29, 16ff.

31 See Kelsay, supra note 30, 124.

32 H. A. Haleem *et al* (eds.), *The Crescent and the Cross: Muslim and Christian Approaches to War and Peace* (New York: Palgrave, 1998) 113; Johnson, supra note 14, xvi.

the endeavour to reinterpret the parameters of military force in Islam – a task to which the following chapters will turn.

II. Siyar and Islamic Laws of War

Islamic just war tradition is part of Islamic International Law (*as-siyar*),[33] which governs such broad themes as the relationship between Muslim and non-Muslim nations, laws of warfare (covering all stages of hostilities, down to truces and peace treaties), rights and responsibilities of minority groups, environmental issues, diplomacy, asylum, jurisdictional matters, law of treaties, and international trade. Having placed emphasis on the Islamic laws of war and peace, Sarakhsi (d. 1011) defined *siyar* thus:

> It describes the conduct of the believers in their relations with the unbelievers of enemy territory as well as with the people with whom the believers had made treaties, who may have been temporarily (*musta'mins*) or permanently (*Dhimmis*) in Islamic lands; with apostates, who . . . abjured after they accepted [Islam]; and with rebels (*baghis*). . . .[34]

Siyar is a branch of Islamic law that is essentially derived from the Quran and the Sunna. The main framework of *siyar* is thus based on the ethico-religious precepts of Islam; and as such it forms an integral part of Islamic law and jurisprudence.[35] Islamic law of nations hence does not constitute a separate system of law, nor does it operate according to a distinct mechanism of sanctions in cases of transgression. Likewise, the Muslim theory of international relations is an extension of Islamic law, albeit – as shown later – evolved in a non-linear fashion within the mould of politico-religious and historical context.

Remarkably, many principles of *siyar* are known to predate contemporary international law.[36] There is a plausible explanation for this: according to Islamic theology, the Muslim community (*ummah*) is none but a single, seamless entity, to

33 The concept of *siyar* has been translated in various ways: 'Islamic law of nations', 'Islamic international law', and 'Muslim law of nations'. For a discussion on terminology, see S. S. Ali, 'Resurrecting *Siyar* Through *Fatwas*? (Re)Constructing Islamic International Law in a Post (Iraq) Invasion World' in: M. C. Bassiouni; A. Guellali (eds.), *Jihad and its Challenges to International and Domestic Law* (The Hague: Hague Academic Press, 2010) 107, 115–116.

34 M. Khadduri, *The Islamic Law of Nations: Shaybani's Siyar* (Baltimore: The Johns Hopkins Press, 1966) 40. Note that while many classical scholars, including Abu Hanifa and Al Shafi'i, wrote on *siyar*, it was Muhammad ibn al-Hasan al-Shaybani (d. 804) who first systematically explored the subject. Ibid. 40–41.

35 S. S. Ali, 'The Twain Doth Meet! A Preliminary Exploration of the Theory and Practice of *As-Siyar* and International Law in the Contemporary World' in: J. Rehman; S. C. Breau (eds.), *Religion, Human Rights and International Law* (Leiden: Martinus Nijhoff Publishers, 2007) 81, 90.

36 Ibid. 89–90.

whom laws apply equally, irrespective of racial, ethnic, cultural, and linguistic differences. Such state of affairs necessitated an Islamic law of nations to distinguish Muslim nations from those of non-Muslims, and to regulate their relations in accordance with their religious status. Having its roots in the soil of primary sources, *siyar* had been refined and systematised mainly during the course of the eighth century by such canonical writers as Imam abu-Hanifa (d. 767) and his followers, abu-Yusuf (d. 798) and, in particular, al-Shaybani (d. 805). While most Western scholars praise Grotius for being the 'father of modern international law',[37] al-Shaybani's monumental work, *al-Siyar al-Kabir*,[38] is largely considered to be the first methodical attempt at exploring the normative rules on the way various nations (separated by religious differences) interacted during times of war and peace. Indeed, Shaybani's comprehensive treatment of international law precedes Grotius' magnum opus on international law and the laws of war and peace, *De Jure Belli ac Pacis*,[39] by some eight centuries. Hence, as Hassan observes, 'a deep examination of the texts of Muslim international law would reveal that a great deal of what is observed today had already been outlined [albeit in a more sketchy fashion] as rules binding on States in their international relations.'[40]

It is, however, worth noting that in distinction to the *ius gentium*, the binding force of which relied on reciprocity and mutual consent, the scope of *siyar* was not contingent upon bilateral agreements between nations. By contrast, obligations enshrined in *siyar* were principally unilateral, and hence pertinent to the stance of Muslims toward the rest of the world. Put another way, *siyar* provided a legal framework by which Muslim nations were obligated to act in a particular manner, regardless of other nations' attitude. Khadduri, in this context, explains that 'the binding force of . . . [*siyar*] was not based on mutual consent or reciprocity, but on the State's own interpretation of its political and religious interests, since Islam regarded its principles or morality and religion as superior to others'.[41] Be that as it may, when a treaty or agreement had been concluded between and among Muslims and non-Muslims, the parties involved were to observe the relevant terms on a reciprocal basis, in congruence with the principle of *pacta sunt servanda*.[42]

Muslims were empowered to terminate their agreements in cases of non-compliance and unilateral denunciation thereof by other signatories, and when

37 See C. A. Stumpf, *The Grotian Theology of International Law: Hugo Grotius and the Moral Foundations of International Relations* (Berlin: Deutsche Nationalbibliothek, 2006) 4ff.

38 This work is translated by Majid Khadduri under the title of *The Islamic Law of Nations,* supra note 34.

39 See H. Grotius; A. C. Campbell (trans.) *The Rights of War and Peace* (London: M. Walter Dunne Publisher, 1901).

40 F. A. Hassan, 'The Sources of Islamic Law' (1982) 76 *American Society of International Law Proceedings* 65, 71.

41 M. Khadduri, 'Islam and the Modern Law of Nations' (1956) 50 *The American Journal of International Law* 358, 358.

42 Khadduri, supra note 34, 40; M. Hamidullah, *Muslim Conduct of State,* 5th ed. (Lahore: Ashraf Press, 1968) 10ff.

the terms stipulated were deemed to have opposed the basic tenets of Islam (in order to avoid abuse, there should arguably be a genuine, and initially unforeseen, situation to justify this ground). Muslims were thus not entitled to denounce their contracts on grounds of unfounded suspicion that other parties would not honour their contractual promises. Also, in cases of material breaches (willingly or otherwise) committed by other parties, Muslims were ordinarily obliged to inform the former of the void character of the agreement – a measure that would grant the parties the chance to take the necessary steps before unwarranted consequences ensued. This condition was not usually satisfied when peace treaties were set aside and Muslims were attacked (or were likely to be attacked soon) by the offending party.[43]

To summarise, *siyar* is fundamentally a chapter in the overall scheme of Sharia,[44] which incorporates elaborate rules on a host of issues of international concern. Akin to other branches of Islamic law, the legal parameters of *siyar* have also taken shape against the backdrop of numerous historical events and socio-political factors – a process that resulted in the growth of numerous jurist-made doctrines. Since modern times, the evolution of *siyar* has been going through a notable transformation in such crucial areas as the use of military force, immunities, diplomatic relations, human rights, and international treaties. As will be discussed in Chapter 4, in matters pertaining to war and peace, the provisions of *siyar* are now largely aligned with the principles of the United Nations Charter, which prohibits warfare as an instrument of national policy.

A. Islamic Jus in Bello Rules

Islamic law contains some important guidelines for the manner in which Muslims have to conduct themselves during an armed conflict. Islamic *jus in bello* norms become applicable only after a war has broken out between the conflicting parties. It would, therefore, normally have made more sense to deal with *jus ad bellum* principles first. But since this study focuses on *jus ad bellum* norms as its main subject matter, it will examine just war norms in reverse order to maintain an ongoing narrative. To begin with, Islamic ethical and practical guidelines as to the methods, means, permissible targets, and the overall limits of justified force correspond to some degree to the Catholic *jus in bello* principles, in that both are based on the pillars of 'proportionality' and 'discrimination'.[45] These principles require combatants to strike the right balance between the dictates of military necessity and humanitarian concerns, and, as such, demand belligerent parties to use

43 See generally, A. A. AbuSulayman, *Towards an Islamic Theory of International Relations: New Directions for Methodology and Thought,* 2nd Ed. (Herndon: The International Institute of Islamic Thought, 1993) 25; Khadduri, supra note 34, 5ff.

44 Khadduri defines *siyar* as 'a [mere] chapter in the Islamic *corpus juris*, binding upon all who believed in Islam as well as upon those who sought to protect their interests in accordance with Islamic justice.' Khadduri, supra note 34, 6.

45 See Yamanai, supra note 13, 74.

proportionate means to achieve a military objective, and to distinguish between military and civilian targets in order to minimise loss of civilian life or damage to civilian property.[46]

Unavoidably, civilian populations and objects have seldom enjoyed absolute immunity during the course of hostilities, for civilians and combatants may well be located in the close vicinity of the front line. Military attacks would be unlawful in such scenarios where anticipated civilian losses are expected to be disproportionate to the likely military gains. Obviously, any sound determination of what constitutes a legitimate military attack requires a case-by-case analysis, an onerous task due to the near impossibility of making a precise evaluation of human life as judged against any possible military advantage. Having referred to the Additional Protocol I to the Geneva Conventions,[47] the International Criminal Tribunal for the former Yugoslavia thus held in *Galić*[48] that the principal aim of proportionality is 'to spare civilians and civilian objects as much as possible', and that 'in determining whether an attack was proportionate it is necessary to examine whether a reasonably well-informed person in the circumstances of the actual perpetrator . . . could have expected excessive civilian casualties to result from the attack'.[49] This 'reasonable person' criterion appears to provide a significant, but imperfect, yardstick against which the competing interests of military achievement and civilian damage may be measured to some degree.

As touched upon earlier, Islamic law contains such humanitarian principles, applicable in warfare, as the necessity to exercise patience,[50] restraint,[51] compassion,[52] and justice[53] towards fellow human beings, who are considered to have

46 See M. R. Amstutz, *International Ethics: Concepts, Theories, and Cases in Global Politics* (Oxford: Rowman & Littlefield Publishers, 2005) 111.

47 Examples concerning the principle of proportionality may be found, among others, in Articles 51(5)(b), 57(2)(a)(iii), and 57(2)(b) of the Additional Protocol I to the Geneva Conventions. These provisions do not make explicit reference to 'proportionality', but rather employ the concept of 'excessive' incidental loss of civilian life or objects. Article 57(2) of the Protocol provides an extremely useful guideline on proportionality: 'in the conduct of military operations, constant care shall be taken to spare the civilian population . . . and civilian objects'; and that it must be verified 'that the objectives to be attacked . . . are military objectives . . .' and that 'all feasible precautions [are taken] in the choice of means and methods of attack with a view to avoiding . . . [or] minimizing, incidental loss of civilian life . . . [and] objects'; and that 'an attack shall be cancelled or suspended if it becomes apparent that . . . the attack may be expected to cause incidental loss of civilian life, injury to civilians, damage to civilian objects, or a combination thereof, which would be excessive in relation to the concrete and direct military advantage anticipated'. Protocol Additional to the Geneva Conventions of 12 August 1949, and relating to the Protection of Victims of International Armed Conflicts (Protocol 1), 8 June 1977 (entry into force: 7 December 1979).

48 *Prosecutor v. Stanislav Galić*, Case No. IT-98–29-T (Judgement, 5 December 2003).

49 Ibid. ¶ 58.

50 Q. 16:126–127.

51 Q. 16:128.

52 Q. 5:32.

53 Q. 16:90.

been part of the same family, descending 'from a single person'.[54] Arguably, one of the most important points about permissible war in Islam is that the whole concept is categorically placed within a moral realm that ultimately aims at ending structural and sectarian violence, and unifying the believers under an embracing, ideal Islamic polity, which promises peace, security, and justice. This ultimate objective is similarly held by other just war traditions, which also promise peace as an end to be attained through necessary violence directed against the enemy. Aristotle's ethics of warfare reflect this ancient notion that war is not an end in itself, but a means to attain peace: 'We work to have leisure, and wage war to live in peace', notes Aristotle, and 'since no one chooses to make war, or even starts a war, for the sake of making war; for if someone turned his friends into enemies to bring about battles and killings he would seem utterly murderous.'[55] Cicero echoed the same view that the only excuse for going to war was to secure peace,[56] and that no war would be justified unless it had been waged after a warning or an official demand for just satisfaction;[57] that is, wars had to be fought only when peaceful alternatives were exhausted. Following in the footsteps of Aristotle and Cicero, Christian scholars also held that war was merely an instrument to achieve peace. St Augustine, in this respect, wrote that 'it is obvious that peace is the end sought for by war; for every man seeks peace by waging war, but no man seeks war by making peace'.[58]

The sweeping argument that the purpose of every war is to attain peace is untenable, however; as numerous historical examples illustrate, countless wars have been fought with such ulterior motives as domination, exploitation, and subjugation. Even in cases of arguably genuine just wars, the problem surfaces when the aim of 'attaining peace' is simultaneously asserted by both warring parties. And worse yet, when viewed through the prism of both warring sides, a detached evaluation of such a subjectively defined purpose assumes complexity, as parties may equally stake a claim to attaining 'peace' as they define it. Nevertheless, the weakness of the argument does not detract from the moral endeavour of restricting the use of lethal violence to noble purposes, regardless of the possible abuse of the concept in practice.

When fought under the banner of religious cause, the objective of peace resonates more categorically. Having taken warfare as a necessary tool of last resort, the intention to achieve peace is an inherent feature of Islam. Whether fought to root out oppression and persecution, or to repel aggression, the object of Islamic war is to be directed towards the attainment of peace and salvation. Hence, even when in practice religious cause may be used as a smokescreen to cloak the real motivation (whether political or economic), a just war (in the eyes of God)

54 Q. 4:1.
55 Aristotle; R. Crisp (ed. & trans.), *Nicomachean Ethics* (Cambridge: Cambridge University Press, 2000) 195.
56 Cicero, supra note 17, 81.
57 Cicero, supra note 16, 63–65.
58 Augustine, supra note 30, 687–688.

would require Muslims to fight with the pious intention of ultimately achieving peace and security.

Since the end – establishing peace – is intertwined with the means of warfare,[59] Islamic humanitarian principles require lethal force to be used in a proportionate manner only against active enemy units, and not against civilians that have not been directly or indirectly involved in hostilities. The following verse provides a case in point, stressing the need to use restricted force in the achievement of military goals: 'Fight in the cause of Allah those who fight you, but do not transgress limits; for Allah loveth not transgressors.'[60] This verse permits warfare in self-defence within the bounds of military necessity and proportionality. Likewise, the following injunction permits defensive force only to the extent of answering the initial aggression, with the least possible expenditure of human life and suffering: 'And if one has retaliated to no greater extent than the injury he received, and is again set upon inordinately, God will help him: for God is One that blots out (sins) and forgives (again and again)'.[61] Further, the notion that one should not engage in violence any more than is necessary under the circumstances is firmly embedded in this verse: 'And fight them on until there is no more tumult or oppression, and there prevail justice and faith in God altogether and everywhere; but if they cease, verily God doth see all that they do'.[62] Here, fighting in the name of God, without using excessive or arbitrary force, is deemed synonymous with struggling for justice and liberty.

The duty to resist injustice and oppression has in fact been an important aspect of faith since the early period of Islam, when the Prophet and his small but burgeoning community had faced such forms of maltreatment as physical assaults, torture, threats, and humiliation, as well as socio-economic isolation.[63] Referring to the vulnerable situation of Muslims in Mecca, the Quran laid down an obligation to struggle, albeit not necessarily in a bellicose manner, in the name of upholding justice and of protecting the weak and vulnerable: 'And why should ye not fight in the cause of Allah and those who, being weak, are ill-treated (and oppressed)? Men, women, and children, whose cry is: "Our Lord! Rescue us from this town, whose people are oppressors; and raise . . . for us from Thee one will help"'.[64] The verses above generally suggest that believers

59 The notions of *jus ad bellum* and *jus in bello* are inextricably linked; for if warfare was fought in an unbridled manner, this would detrimentally affect the motive behind the war. A just war is one which is not only engaged with the right motive, but also with right means. In Ambrose's words, 'virtue does not lie in victory unless it is gained with honour'. Quoted in: Karoubi, supra note 26, 52.

60 Q. 2:190.

61 Q. 22:60.

62 Q. 8:39; *cf.* Q. 17:33.

63 For a detailed account of how the early Muslim community, particularly those with low social status and no tribal protection, was persecuted in Mecca, see I. Ishaq; A. Guillaume (trans.), *The Life of Muhammad: A Translation of Ibn Ishaq's Sirat Rasul Allah* (Oxford: Oxford University Press, 1955) 117ff.

64 Q. 4:75.

are to struggle (this may encompass belligerent and non-belligerent forms) against persecution, oppression, and other forms of injustice in a way that complies with humanitarian principles geared towards reducing unwarranted harm to life, limb, and property.

It is important to note that these just war principles did not emerge in a vacuum. Islam tacitly acknowledges the difficulty of achieving complete harmony in interpersonal and inter-State relations, which are accompanied by volatile swings of concord and tension or peace and violence. Given that neither perpetual peace nor constant conflict captures the real nature of human relations, Islam realistically seeks to achieve peace both by means of amicable and warlike measures – the latter being dependent on the exhaustion of peaceful methods of resolving the dispute involved. Islam calls upon Muslims to comport themselves with restraint and scrupulousness to mitigate the brutality of conflict when war becomes unavoidable.

Limitations on the manner in which wars may be waged and fought largely transpired in response to specific circumstances and needs. Indeed, such principles requiring measures and moderation in the employment of lethal force were revealed to address the pressing challenges faced by the Prophet and his followers. For instance, the necessity of exercising restraint in avenging injuries was laid down following the defeat at Uhud (625), wherein Muhammad in his anger vowed revenge as he saw the mutilated body of his uncle, Hamza: 'If God gives me power over the Quraysh', he exclaimed, 'I will mutilate seventy of their men [in the next confrontation].'[65] Yet, soon afterwards, the Prophet received a revelation that unequivocally prohibited disproportionate violence in the delivery of punishment, and recommended forbearance and patience towards the enemy:[66] 'And if ye do catch them out, catch them out no worse than they catch you out: but if ye show patience, that is indeed the best (course) for those who are patient.'[67] It follows that a Muslim soldier who fights in the name of God (*mujahid*) is ordained to suppress such destructive impulses as fury and revenge, and must remember the just cause for which he fights.

Some significant *jus in bello* norms sprang from the 'non-revealed' sources; they were mostly formulated by the Prophet himself or by his legitimate successors (caliphs) in a bid to minimise the untoward consequences of warfare. Tradition has it that Muhammad had repeatedly stressed the need for justified and proportionate force by calling on his companions to avoid incurring unnecessary casualties, respect the bodies of the living and the dead (including animals), refrain from ill-treating prisoners and from employing poisoned weapons against

65 M. Ayoub, *The Qur'an and its Interpreters* (Albany: State University of New York Press, 1992) 369. Some sources indicate that the Prophet vowed to mutilate 30 enemy corpses, not 70. See T. Ramadan, *The Messenger: The Meanings of the Life of Muhammad* (London: Penguin Books, 2007) 125.

66 See Ayoub, supra note 65, 369; A. Y. Ali, *The Meaning of the Holy Qur'an*, 11th ed. (Beltsville: Amana Publications, 2008) 670.

67 Q. 16:126.

the enemy and damaging nature, and to uphold the dignity and integrity of all combatants.[68]

A kindred tradition confirming the import of right intent and just conduct in the use of lethal force had been related by Rumi, wherein Ali, the Prophet's cousin and the fourth caliph, had once engaged in combat with a Magian chief, who, in the midst of the fight, spat in Ali's face. To the astonishment of his rival, Ali dropped his sword instead of seeking to extract vengeance on him. When the chief asked why he dropped his sword, Ali had reportedly replied that he 'did not destroy life for the satisfaction of his own vengeance, but he would simply carry out God's will'. The Magian chief was said to have been so deeply affected by this reply that he embraced Islam with all his family and clan.[69]

The emergence of the principle of distinction, which requires belligerents to distinguish between combatants and civilians, has, too, its roots in a tradition wherein the Prophet, encountering a slain woman while riding on the battlefield, expressed his disapproval of the practice of killing women and children. This later prompted a distinct code of military conduct that envisaged the prohibition of killing non-combatants (including in particular such vulnerable groups as women, children, the old, and the frail), provided that they did not partake in hostilities. The principle also came to shield civilian property and the environment (e.g. trees, orchards, and wells) from wanton destruction during an armed conflict.[70] It is so recorded that before the commencement of hostilities the Prophet would brief his soldiers on their responsibilities, instructing them thus:

> Do not handcuff or tie up the prisoners. Do not mutilate. Do not kill the wounded. Do not pursue one retreating or one who throws down his weapon. Do not use treacherous means with the enemy. Do not kill the old, the young or the women. Do not cut down trees, unless you are forced to do so. Do not deploy poison in the lands. Do not cut off water supply.[71] No house should be entered without permission and the people have safety. If any of the Muslims, whether high ranking or otherwise, give temporary refuge to any

68 See B. Lewis; B. E. Churchill, *Islam: The Religion and the People* (Indianapolis: Wharton School Publishing, 2008) 151; Zawati, supra note 9, 109.

69 M. J. M. Rumi; E. H. Whinfield (trans.), *The Masnavi-i Ma'navi of Rumi* (Charleston: The Forgotten Books, 2008) 49–50.

70 Y. H. Aboul-Enein; S. Zuhur, *Islamic Rulings on Warfare* (Carlisle Barracks: Strategic Studies Institute, 2004) 21; Haleem, supra note 32, 131; *cf.* L. C. Green, 'Cicero and Clausewitz or Quincy Wright: The Interplay of Law and War' (1999) 9 *Journal of Legal Studies* 59, 69.

71 Khadduri, citing Shaybani, wrote that Muslims were permitted to practise such warlike acts as cutting or poisoning water supplies or using poisoned arrows. See M. Khadduri, *War and Peace in the Law of Islam* (Baltimore: Johns Hopkins Press, 1955) 106. Nevertheless, this interpretation flies in the face of Muhammad's above-quoted injunction that explicitly forbids Muslims from 'cutting off water supplies' and 'deploying poison in the lands', or generally of his command not to kill the enemy in a treacherous fashion.

> of the infidels to hear the message of God then let him do so. If he follows you then he is your brother in religion; but if he refuses, secure his safety and seek help from God.[72]

These principles accentuate that not only are the lives and limbs of non-combatants considered sacred, but that the unnecessary killing of those *hors de combat*, as well as the wanton destruction of the environment and of enemy's property, are forbidden, for Islamic laws of war strictly enjoin Muslim combatants not to destroy for the sake of vengeance, hatred, or excessive wrath. Respect for the environment, in this context, features strongly within the corpus of Islamic humanitarian law. During his ministry, only once had the Prophet caused damage to the environment as a war strategy. This materialised when Muslims besieged the fort of the Jewish Banu Nadir tribe. In an effort to convince the enemy to surrender after a relatively lengthy siege, Muhammad had ordered the felling of palm trees, which were one of Madina's most valuable assets and the main source of Banu Nadir's sustenance. The message was clear: if the Nadir tribe kept up resistance, then the human and economic ramifications could reach undesirable levels. The episode was so exceptional that the Quran later made express reference to it: 'Whether ye cut down the tender palm trees, or ye left them standing on their roots, it was by leave of Allah, and in order that He might cover with shame the rebellious transgressors.'[73] The Prophet never repeated such irregularity, but admonished his adherents to pay due respect to nature even in wartime.[74]

In the course of Islamic history, such aberrations had undoubtedly taken place in the fog of warfare; nevertheless, as certain historical examples evince, transgressors of humanitarian and ethical principles were not infrequently chastised (notably during the early period of Islam), largely with intent to set an example for proper future conduct. Sahih Muslim records an incident where a singing girl was apprehended after a conquest, and thereafter subjected to amputation of her hand on account of chanting satirical poems about the then caliph, Abu Bakr. Having heard this distressing news, Abu Bakr is reported to have rebuked the decision-maker, stressing that mutilation was a 'grave offence' that had to be avoided even in manifest cases of 'polytheism' or 'infidelity'. 'Never mutilate', he pronounced, for 'God purified Islam and the Muslims from rashness and excessive wrath', and that the Prophet 'never permitted' the mutilation of his enemies.[75]

Following in the footsteps of the Prophet, the early 'rightly guided' caliphs had similarly emphasised the imperative character of humanitarian norms exhorting Muslim combatants to distinguish between military and civilian targets, and to

72 I. M. Shirazi, *War, Peace and Non-Violence: An Islamic Perspective* (London: Fountain Books, 2001) 109.

73 Q. 59:5.

74 T. Ramadan, *In the Footsteps of the Prophet: Lessons from the Life of Muhammad* (Oxford: Oxford University Press, 2007) 131–132.

75 Sahih Muslim, Bk. 19:4294.

protect the environment from undue harm during hostilities. For instance, the first caliph, Abu Bakr, spelt out a number of principles requiring respect for civilian life and property, as well as for the environment. He instructed the Muslim warriors marching on Syria as follows:

> Stop, O people, that I may give you ten rules for your guidance in the battle-field. Do not commit treachery or deviate from the right path. You must not mutilate dead bodies. Neither kill a child, nor a woman, nor an aged man. Bring no harm to the trees, nor burn them with fire, especially those which are fruitful. Slay not any of the enemy's flock, save for your food. You are likely to pass by people who have devoted their lives to monastic services; leave them alone.[76]

The profanity of inflicting unwarranted injury or mutilation on the enemy had also been stressed by the second caliph, Umar ibn al-Khattab, who would correspondingly command Muslim soldiers to spare non-combatants, in particular the women, elderly, and children, at every stage of warfare – whether at the outset of the conflict or in the heat of victory.[77] It is to be emphasised here that Islam recognises the doctrine of 'collateral damage',[78] whereby lethal damage to civilian life and property may be justified when such is unavoidable during warfare. The doctrine also applies to unintended killings of Muslims who were in the wrong place at the wrong time (particularly when they were mixed with the civilian population of the opponent), in which case their death 'would be regarded as killing by mistake'.[79] The doctrine naturally ensues from the idea of military necessity, which may excuse, but not justify, untoward behaviour against unarmed, innocuous people in pursuit of a just cause.[80] Yet, as stressed above, necessity

76 Sahih Muslim, Bk. 19:4292.

77 H. M. Zawati, '*Jus in Bello:* Civilians' Fundamental Rights under Islamic and Public International Law' in: Bassiouni, supra note 33, 167, 174; Bennoune, supra note 13, 626.

78 Today, the classical jurist Vitoria's formulation of collateral damage is frequently invoked to legitimate the deliberate or accidental harm done to civilians in the course of an armed conflict. While this concept is open to abuse, it by no means suggests that armed forces have free rein in the name of military necessity. For Vitoria's formulation of the doctrine, see F. D. Vitoria; J. P. Doyle (trans.), *Reflection on Homicide & Commentary on Summa Theologiae Iia-Iiae Q. 64 (Thomas Aquinas)* (Milwaukee: Marquette University Press, 1997) 191. Unsurprisingly, therefore, under Article 8(iv) of the Rome Statute of the International Criminal Court, intentional and disproportionate exertion of collateral damage constitutes a war crime.

79 Khadduri, supra note 71, 106–107.

80 Here Aquinas' double-effect doctrine may be recalled, according to which an act might lead to a good and bad result, yet in order for its moral permissibility, the preferred act must be good, the ensuing bad result must not be desired, and the intended good must be proportionate to the bad outcome. See T. Aquinas; R. W. Dyson (ed. & trans.), *Political Writings* (Cambridge: Cambridge University Press, 2002) 191, 263–264; also see Kelsay, supra note 30, 123ff; Elshtain, supra note 30, 5–6; Bennoune, supra note 13, 623.

never provides a licence to employ indiscriminate or disproportionate violence, even when the cause has been legitimate. Rather, it demands that lethal force be used as a final measure when peaceful alternatives have failed to thwart the threat posed or to execute a legitimate religious cause – with the least possible military damage.

Ali, the fourth caliph and the Prophet's cousin and son-in-law, thus analogously insisted that humanitarian principles be scrupulously observed. During his struggle against the Umayyads, and in particular at the Battle of Siffin (657), the first Muslim Civil War, Ali urged his soldiers to distinguish between enemy combatants and innocent civilians. To be more precise, in advance of the battle of the Camel (656),[81] Ali had reportedly commanded his followers thus:

> When you defeat them, do not kill their wounded, do not behead the prisoners, do not pursue those who return and retreat, do not enslave their women, do not mutilate their dead, do not uncover what is to remain covered, do not approach their property except what you find in their camp of weapons, beasts, male or female slaves: all the rest is to be inherited by their heirs according to the writ of God.[82]

Along with the twin pillars of proportionality and distinction, Ali's emphasis on treating captives of war humanely was in large part modelled on the example of the Prophet, who had adjured his followers to respect the rights of prisoners: 'The captives are your brothers and your companions . . . They are at your mercy, so treat them well, as though you were treating yourselves, and provide them with food, clothes and housing. Do not require them to work beyond their strengths, but help them to accomplish their tasks.'[83] When the enemy is brought under control through capture or capitulation, Muslims are hence obligated to uphold the dignity of prisoners and avoid abusing them.[84]

The fate of prisoners and the options available to Muslim captors had nonetheless proved to be a thorny question, which subjected the meaning of the relevant Quranic provisions to disparate readings. The position in the Quran in fact appears unambiguous in 47:4, which instructs Muslims to either exchange

81 This significant battle took place between the forces of Ali and those of the Prophet's widow Aisha and two of her prominent companions Zubair and Talha. The conflict, which was caused by a challenge to Ali's ascendancy to the caliphate, ended with Ali's victory. While Zubair and Talha were killed, Aisha's life was spared, yet she was compelled to spend the rest of her days at her home in Medina. For further details, see N. J. DeLong-Bas, *Wahhabi Islam: From Revival and Reform to Global Jihad* (New York: I.B. Tauris, 2004) 88ff; J. E. Lindsay, *Daily Life in the Medieval Islamic World* (Westport: Greenwood Press, 2005) 68.

82 Hamidullah, supra note 42, 363–364; Zawati, supra note 9, 31–32.

83 Quoted in: M. K. Ereksoussi, 'Le Coran et les Conventions Humanitaries' (1960) 503 *Revue Internationale de la Croix-Rouge* 641, 650.

84 According to the Quran, prisoners of war must be fed and looked after: '[F]eed for the love of Allah, the indigent, the orphan, and the captive.' Q. 76:8.

enemy prisoners for their Muslim counterparts, or to release them in exchange for ransom, or simply to free them as an act of favour. In practice, if prisoners were not exchanged with Muslim captives or not freed for ransom, they were divided up among the soldiers who had captured them,[85] albeit their release without ransom was recommended. This notwithstanding, the Quran contains a seemingly ambivalent passage in 8:67, which reads 'it is not fitting for a Prophet that he should have prisoners of war until he hath thoroughly subdued the land'. To some medieval jurists, this verse permitted a military commander to opt for the execution of prisoners when Muslim interests so required.[86] Muslims, according to this viewpoint, held the options of exchange, ransom, enslavement, execution, or release concerning prisoners. But most contemporary scholars, including Mawdudi, Hamidullah, and al-Zuhayli, maintain that medieval jurists had misread the above verse, which in effect does not provide a licence for killing prisoners, as execution is unconscionable in Islam. They thus aver that captives may in principle only be exchanged, ransomed, or freed, and not be put to death arbitrarily – drawing on the tradition of Muhammad who, during his ministry, only rarely ordered the execution of prisoners as an extreme measure.[87] While doctrinal controversy over this matter may persist, the Islamic principles on the rights of prisoners, like some other humanitarian norms, are now largely governed in keeping with the modern articulations of humanitarian and human rights law.

In subsequent years, mainly in the aftermath of the rule of the rightly guided caliphs, some humanitarian principles had not necessarily been applied faithfully or consistently, partly due to political circumstances, which at times tempered the application of some Islamic ideals, and partly due to the natural tendency of combatants to respond to an opponent's warlike conduct with disproportionate violence. While it would therefore be implausible to assume that Muslim combatants (even in the early period) had invariably adhered to the basic precepts of Islamic humanitarian law, the application of such rules was occasionally ensured through punitive or disciplinary measures taken against those who had not remained within the reasonable limits of warfare.[88] Arguably, however, it was essentially the notions

85 A. A. Mawdudi, *Human Rights in Islam* (Leicester: The Islamic Foundation, 2002) 20.

86 See Y. Friedmann, *Tolerance and Coercion in Islam: Interfaith Relations in the Muslim Tradition* (New York: Cambridge University Press, 2003) 117ff. This verse is known to have been revealed in relation to the captives of the Battle of Badr, where the Prophet had decided on the release of most prisoners for ransom (only two out of some 70 prisoners were executed), upon which the divine command disapproving of such conduct is considered to have come down. For a discussion on the Prophet's stance, see S. Kayadibi, *Istihsan: The Doctrine of Juristic Preference in Islamic Law* (Selangor: Islamic Book Trust, 2010) 76.

87 See S. H. Hashmi, 'Saving and Taking Life in War' in: J. E. Brockopp (ed.) *Islamic Ethics of Life: Abortion, War, and Euthanasia* (Columbia: The University of South Carolina Press, 2003) 144ff; S. Khatab; G. D. Bouma, *Democracy in Islam* (New York: Routledge, 2007) 183ff.

88 For recorded examples showing the Prophet or his caliphs taking serious measures against those found responsible for engaging in pre-Islamic methods of warfare, see

of faith and/or fear of the ultimate punishment of God to be visited on the evildoer that effectively prevented many early believers from violating, to varying degrees, the basic principles of Islamic humanitarian law. As Khadduri rightly emphasises, Islamic just war principles, being part and parcel of the Sharia, apply irrespective of practical concerns such as reciprocity. The adherents of Islam are thus required to impose restrictions on their warlike conduct because such is *commanded* by God.[89] Eaton also addresses this point when he writes that Muslims generally did not fill the rivers with blood, or enrich the fields with the corpses of the vanquished during Islam's height in the seventh and eighth centuries when the young religion spread across the known world with astonishing rapidity:

> As warriors the Arabs might have been no better than others of their kind who had ravaged and slaughtered across the peopled lands but, unlike these others, they were on a leash. There were no massacres, no rapes, no cities burned. These men feared God to a degree scarcely imaginable in our time and were in awe of His all-seeing presence . . . [T]here was no place in which they could hide from this presence, and while vast distances beckoned them ever onwards they trod softly on the earth, as they had been *commanded* to do.[90]

Putting it otherwise, Muslims were obligated to abide by religio-ethical laws of warfare unilaterally, irrespective of the enemy's conduct, for such an obligation was not owed to human beings, but to God alone. Theoretically, this means that Islamic just war norms bind Muslims at all times and in all circumstances, even when the opponent descends into barbarism by disregarding all the restrictions imposed by religious or man-made laws.[91] Such a reading accords with the spirit of a tradition ascribed to Abu Bakr, who instructed his soldiers thus: 'Remember that you are always in the presence of God, on the verge of death, in the assurance

Ramadan, supra note 65, 179; Yamanai, supra note 13, 74; Bennoune, supra note 13, 623–624.

89 Khadduri, supra note 34, 5.

90 G. Eaton, *Islam and the Destiny of Man* (Albany: State University of New York Press, 1985) 17 (emphasis added); also see S. S. Ali; J. Rehman, 'The Concept of *Jihad* in Islamic International Law' (2005) 10 *Journal of Conflict & Security Law* 321, 332.

91 Al-Shafi'i also highlighted the notion that Muslims are to act regardless of reciprocity in every act they perform and irrespective of their whereabouts: 'Whatever is accepted by the Muslims and receives their consensus as being permissible in the Land of Islam is not forbidden in the land of unbelievers, and whatever is forbidden in the land of Islam is also forbidden in the land of unbelievers. He who commits a forbidden act will receive the punishment prescribed by *Allah* for his offence.' M. I. I. al-Shafi'i, *Kitab al-Umm*, 7 Vols. (Cairo: al-Hay'a al-Miriyya al 'Amma lil-Kitab, 1987) 7:322; cited in: Zawati, supra note 77, 175.

of judgement, and the hope of paradise.'[92] The idea of the divine settlement of accounts for good and bad conduct in the body surely compelled Muslims to comport themselves in conformity with humanitarian principles of Islam. As alluded to above, whilst such an ideal normative framework could not have been observed at all times, Muslim military magnanimity shown by warriors of Salah al-Din (Saladin) toward their non-reciprocating crusading rivals constitutes an illustrative case in point (and an ideal paradigm) concerning such unilateralism in the conduct of warfare.[93]

Islamic *jus in bello* norms accord with, and complement, Islamic *jus ad bellum* principles, which, in brief, proscribe wars waged for satisfying such ulterior motives as the desire to obtain power over others, or to acquire undeserved wealth and influence. Legitimate Islamic wars are chiefly those fought in the cause of God; and for hallowed purposes like resisting oppression or tyranny, securing peace and justice, or spreading the word of God. However, as seen above, the right to war in Islam is qualified by the strict demand to achieve military aims with minimum damage to life, limb, property, and the environment. Hence, there exists a symbiotic relationship between the manner in which an Islamic war is induced and the manner in which it is conducted, as the end and means of Islamic warfare are interlocked and ultimately directed towards the achievement of God's will on earth.

B. Islamic Jus ad Bellum Rules

As seen above, during the course of Muhammad's prophetic career, both the Quran and the Sunnah carved out norms to regulate Islamic warlike conduct, drawing a pattern of behaviour before, during, and after armed hostilities. In addition to humanitarian norms, Sharia contains rules on *jus ad bellum,* according to which wars must not only be fought in accordance with religious

92 Quoted in: G. Bush, *The Life of Mohammed: Founder of the Religion of Islam, and of the Empire of the Saracens* (London: J. & J. Harper, 1883) 199.

93 When Saladin recaptured Jerusalem in 1187, his troops had not unjustifiably killed or mistreated its inhabitants (for whose protection he arranged patrols instead). He released rich prisoners in exchange for ransom, and released the poor ones for nothing. Saladin's adherence to humanitarian notions was radically different from his Christian opponents (to whom the Church had given remission of all sins in advance for their would-be offences) who had, at times, committed unspeakable crimes including the massacre of the entire population of Jerusalem in 1099. Raymond d'Agiles, an eye-witness to the massacre, wrote, 'so much blood flowed in the ancient temple of Solomon, where 10,000 Muslims had taken refuge, that bodies were floating in it, drifting this way and that in the court, together with hacked-off hands and arms.' See J. S. Pictek, *Development and Principles of International Humanitarian Law* (Lancaster: Kluwer Academic Publishers, 1985) 17; C. Hillenbrand, *The Crusades: Islamic Perspectives* (New York: Routledge, 2000) 22ff, 316ff; *cf.* A. Maalouf, *Les Croisades vues par les Arabes* (Paris: J.C. Lattès, 1986).

values, but also be engaged in with the right motive: not for the spoils of war,[94] nor for exploitation or personal glory, but for the cause and in the name of God.[95] At the same time, the purpose of each war must be the promotion of Islamic values and the achievement of peace, justice, and order.[96] Again, as stressed earlier, akin to the Christian just war tradition, the notions of just cause (defence against aggression or fighting in the name of God), right intent or motive (in pursuit of Islamic ideals), competent and rightful authority (the Prophet and his successors), reasonable chance of success,[97] and the objective of securing peace and justice in tandem with the teachings of Islam[98] constitute the backbone of Islamic *jus ad bellum* rules.[99]

Having derived their inspiration from the firm belief that God has communicated His unadulterated and final message to humankind through Islam, Muslims considered that the ultimate victory impended, for truth would eventually triumph over falsehood and right over wrong. Bound together with such faith, Muslims whittled away fault lines of their sectarian divisions in an effort to spread the word of God. Islam thus declared all forms of secular wars *(harb)* evil, and said they were to be avoided at all costs. To this end, the Prophet worked towards ending inter-tribal wars, which were prevalent among pagan Arabs. He unified the fragmented clans in the cause of Islam, and introduced the concept of jihad as the sole legitimate form of military force under the banner of religion.[100] In order to prevent wanton violence, wars were to be carried out with right

94 Although Islamic tradition accepts booty as a legitimate reward, it forbids Muslims to be motivated by it. See Lewis, supra note 68, 151.

95 According to a *hadith,* when '[a] man came to the Prophet and asked: "A man fights for war booty; another fights for fame and a third fights for showing off; which of them fights in Allah's Cause?" The Prophet said: "He who fights that Allah's Word, Islam, should be superior, fights in Allah's Cause."' Hadith Reported by al-Bukhari, *Hadith of Bukhari* (Hadith 4:65).

96 Khadduri, supra note 34, 10.

97 This element is considered to be based on the following Quranic verse: 'And spend of your substance in the cause of God, and make not your own hands contribute to (your) destruction; but do good; for God loveth those who do good.' Q. 2:195. This verse is also interpreted to forbid self-sacrificing warlike acts, suicide, or suicide attacks, which particularly in recent times came to be used as a weapon to conduct asymmetrical wars. See Ali, supra note 66, 78; A. V. Engeland-Nourai, 'The Challenge of Fragmentation of International Humanitarian Law' in: Bassiouni, supra note 33, 139, 160.

98 While the Quran advises Muslims to be ready for war (when necessary), it also notes that '. . . if the enemy inclines towards peace, do thou (also) incline towards peace and trust in God: for He is One that heareth and knoweth (all things)'. Q. 8:60–61.

99 J. Kelsay, *Islam and War: A Study in Comparative Ethics* (Louisville: John Knox Press, 1993) 36; S. Mahmoudi, 'The Islamic Perception of the Use of Force in the Contemporary World' (2005) 7 *Journal of the History of International Law* 55, 59.

100 See G. F. Nafziger; M. W. Walton, *Islam at War: A History* (Westport: Praeger Publishers, 2003) 207–208; Mohammad, supra note 1, 384.

intentions under the leadership of a competent imam[101] who would assume responsibility in ensuring that hostilities were conducted within the limits of just war principles.

While the Islamic tradition is heavily concerned with restraining the use of lethal force, and it thus discusses a myriad of war-related questions in extensive legal and theological texts, it remains a challenging task to identify a clear canon of Muslim attitude towards legitimate warfare. Certainly, the problem of identifying explicit principles on, or unequivocal interpretation of, vexatious questions is not particular to Islam, but is shared by almost any religious and ethical system based on sacred texts attributed to divine revelation. Such somewhat esoteric texts may support theses and moral positions that seem to offer conflicting alternatives.[102] Within the context of the Quran, the matter assumes a more complicated character due to the poetic style and complex structure of the text, in which later verses appear to be at variance with earlier ones. It would hence be incorrect to presume that Islamic sources provide a catalogue of clear-cut standards governing the doctrine of jihad.[103]

The issue with the doctrine of jihad resides in the key question of whether armed force is justified only in defence against oppression or aggression, or whether it further encompasses expansionist wars against non-Muslims. The Quranic text appears to have an ambivalent attitude: whilst some passages clearly condemn aggression and the oppression of the weak, declaring that believers should fight only in self-defence, other passages seem to provide unequivocal justification for fighting in pursuit of subduing unbelievers. As will be discussed below, a good number of verses may be relied upon in support of these two positions.[104]

Since Islamic sources are not always linear in format, or unambiguous in their message on the nature of warfare, Muslim thinkers are unsurprisingly divided upon the legal and factual implications of jihad: while some scholars vehemently stress that there is 'no compulsion in Islam',[105] that the very purpose of Islamic warfare is to deter aggression or oppression against believers, and that Islam, at its core, conveys a universal message of peace, tolerance, reconciliation, and unity of

101 Ibn Khaldun, one of the most influential Muslim intellectuals of the medieval world, argued that the institution of imamate requires such qualities as knowledge, competence and probity so that public order and administration of justice could be maintained, and that religious wars against the enemy could be led with rigour and care. I. Khaldun; F. Rosenthal (trans.), *The Muqaddimah: An Introduction to History* (Princeton: Princeton University Press, 2005) 158.

102 See Bar, supra note 2, 4; Kelsay, supra note 99, 43.

103 See G. Kepel, *Jihad: The Trail of Political Islam* (London: I.B. Tauris, 2009) 23–43; D. W. Simon, 'US Foreign Policy and the World of Islam' (1995) 3 *Willamette Bulletin of International Law & Policy* 69, 70; R. L. Euben, 'Killing (for) Politics: *Jihad,* Martyrdom, and Political Action' (2002) 30 *Political Theory* 4, 12.

104 See, for instance, Q. 2:190; Q. 9:13; *cf.* Q. 9:5; Q. 9:29.

105 Q. 2:256.

humankind,[106] others rely upon a rather rigid reading, which envisages a universal struggle to eradicate the forces of immorality or unbelief, a global Muslim rule, conversions, and the re-establishment of the caliphate through military force if necessary.[107] It follows that any conclusion as to whether the Islamic just war tradition condones offensive wars carried out in the name of faith appears to be left to the interpretation of the analyst.[108] Contemporary discussions of military jihad discourse (which will be explored in detail in the following chapter) thus unsurprisingly often lean on selective portions of primary sources, and of the historical manifestations of Islamic State practice. This method expectedly leads to sweeping generalisations about the theory and practice of Islam, mainly in order to further a particular political posture at the practical level.

The possibility of deriving mutually exclusive interpretations from the same sources relate to the absence of a hard-and-fast Muslim response to the question of warfare, a phenomenon that requires an exploration of the meaning and roots of the doctrine of jihad, whose conceptual contours have largely taken shape against the background of complex challenges that beleaguered Muslims over time. Any serious attempt to assess the implications of military jihad must accordingly trace the concept to its origins in a bid to contextualise the debate and reframe its current manifestations.

1. The Concept of Jihad

In the Western world, the term jihad has generally been translated as 'holy war', yet this loose designation could be misleading as it reduces the concept to simple belligerency. Jihad literally means 'striving' or 'struggling', and in its narrow sense it may refer to military force.[109] Despite widespread reference to this concept, military force is treated under various headings in Islam: while the Quran makes occasional reference to 'war' (*harb*), it makes frequent reference to 'fighting' (*qital*), and even more frequent reference to the notions of 'struggle' or 'striving' (jihad and other derivations).[110] Significantly, in inter-Muslim wars, the term jihad was

106 See I. S. M. Al-Qazwini, 'Just War: An Islamic Perspective' (2004) 9 *Nexus* 79, 83; N. A. Shah, *Self-Defence in Islamic and International Law: Assessing Al-Qaeda and the Invasion of Iraq* (New York: Palgrave Macmillan, 2008) 17ff.

107 See S. Jackson, 'Jihad and the Modern World' in: Donohue, supra note 11, 408; Z. Baran, 'Fighting the War of Ideas' (2005) 84 *Foreign Affairs* 6, 68–73.

108 F. M. Donner, 'The Sources of Islamic Conceptions of War' in: Kelsay, supra note 5, 47. As Firestone notes, because the Quran's message on warfare is spread out throughout the text, 'it is difficult to know whether a verse is supposed to be read in relation to the verses among which it is currently situated or whether it should be read independently'. R. Firestone, *Jihad: The Origin of Holy War in Islam* (New York: Oxford University Press, 1999) 47.

109 Khadduri, supra note 71, 55–56; S. K. Mirza, 'An Exegesis on *Jihad* in Islam' in: K. E. Shienbaum; J. Hasan (eds.), *Beyond Jihad: Critical Voices from Inside Islam* (Bethesda: Academica Press, 2006) 77.

110 Donner, supra note 108, 46.

seldom invoked to describe the nature of the conflict. The label jihad was generally invoked to describe wars waged by Muslims against their non-Muslim enemies.[111]

As will be explored below, military jihad involves armed engagement with the adversary. However, jihad technically requires a *casus belli*, which may include the motivation to repel oppression and unjust aggression, or to spread God's message and Islam's sphere of influence. Since warfare is considered to be a weapon of last resort, peaceful measures must first be exhausted before any form of military measure can be taken. Peaceable measures may encompass inviting the adversary to embrace Islam under fair circumstances, or entering into an agreement that has reconciliation as its objective. It will later be seen that the consequences of military engagement with polytheists and non-Muslim monotheists differ; suffice to say here that the latter may choose to keep their faith in return for the payment of a poll tax (*jizyah*), which in turn would provide them with protection and exemption from military service.[112] But, to reiterate the point made earlier, in each case of military jihad, the interrelated humanitarian elements of necessity and proportionality must be observed in order to moderate the irretrievable consequences of deadly force.

Jihad's military facet is manifest when the Quran exhorts believers to 'fight those who believe not in Allah nor the Last Day, nor hold that forbidden which hath been forbidden by Allah and His Messenger, nor acknowledge the Religion of Truth, from among the People of the Book, until they pay the *jizyah*. . .'[113] It is accepted that this revelation, received in relation to the raid on Tabuk (630),[114] was the first command to call for military engagement with those who had received Holy Scriptures before Muhammad's time.[115] Here the role of jihad was to mobilise the believers to fight their pagan and monotheist challengers – although

111 See D. Cook, *Understanding Jihad* (London: University of California Press, 2005) 2–3.

112 In this sense, the poll tax was basically a relationship between disarmed non-Muslim populations and Muslims who, by force of arms, assumed the former's defence in return for regular payment. See further, B. Ye'or, *Islam and Dhimitude: Where Civilisations Collide* (Ontario: Associated University Press, 2002) 69ff; A. G. Bostom, 'Jihad Conquests and the Imposition of Dhimmitude: A Survey' in: A. G. Bostom (ed.), *The Legacy of Jihad: Islamic Holy War and the Fate of Non-Muslims* (New York: Prometheus Books, 2008) 29–37.

113 Q. 9:29. It must be noted that the poll tax was to be levied on the People of the Book in line with the principle of justice. Shaybani pointed out that women, children, the poor, and the sick (including those suffering from chronic diseases or disabilities) were normally exempt from this tax, whereas priests, monks, and abbots had to pay it if they owned property. See Khadduri, supra note 34, 276.

114 This military campaign was mounted against the Byzantine Syria, when Muslims subdued the Hijaz region in an apparent attempt to expand the sphere of Islam (albeit the exact motive behind this expedition remains somewhat obscure). It is recorded that since the expedition was undertaken at an unfavourable time of the year, when harsh climatic conditions threatened men, animals, and crops, the Prophet faced considerable opposition levelled against the campaign. See R. A. Gabriel, *Muhammad: Islam's First Great General* (Norman: University of Oklahoma, 2007) 191–192.

115 See Firestone, supra note 108, 64, 82.

the latter, as stressed above, could choose to keep their beliefs.[116] Jihad's association with belligerency seems more explicit in the associated revelation below, where some Muslims were reproved for refusing to engage the enemy in Tabuk:

> 'O ye who believe, what is the matter with you, that when ye are asked to go forth [march onward] in the Cause of Allah, ye cling heavy to the earth? Do ye prefer the life of this world to the Hereafter? . . . Unless you go forth, He will punish you with a grievous penalty as others . . . Go ye forth (whether equipped) lightly or heavily, and strive and struggle, with your goods and your persons, in the Cause of Allah . . .'[117]

This and analogous injunctions generally call upon Muslims to proceed against the enemy valiantly[118] with such aims as supressing immorality, conveying God's word, warding off aggression or oppression, or fortifying Islamic influence. No doubt, such bellicose verses have hitherto been invoked by political authorities to mobilise Muslims to fight not only religiously motivated wars, but also wars of political or economic character.[119]

Having this warlike facet of jihad in mind, it is now imperative to stress that jihad in its broader sense may also refer to non-violent methods of struggle in the cause of God, whether through deed, speech, wealth, or devotion: 'and strive in His cause as ye ought to strive (with sincerity and under discipline)', says the Quran, expressing this wider sense.[120] Hence, lethal force represents but one dimension of jihad, for the concept implies not merely sheer force, but also

116 As will be made clear in the following pages, the unbeliever is conspicuously distinguished from the Scriptuaries (who yield to the authority and accept the protection of the Muslim polity in exchange for the poll tax). In Lewis' language, 'the unsubjugated unbeliever is by definition an enemy', against whom 'the jihad par excellence is waged'. B. Lewis, *The Political Language of Islam* (Chicago: The University of Chicago Press, 1991) 77; also see C. Huart, 'Le Droit de La Guerre' (1907) 2 *Revue du Monde Musulman* 331, 331. As will be touched upon in the following chapter, the system of levying *jizya* upon non-Muslims continued mainly until the nineteenth century, when it broke down under the influence of the European intellectual movement which promoted such ideas as freedom, equality, and non-discrimination. For more on *jizya*, see Lewis, supra note 68, 188–199; M. K. Nawaz, 'The Concept of Human Rights in Islamic Law' (1965) 11 *Howard Law Journal* 325, 327; A. A. An-Na'im, 'Islamic Law, International Relations, and Human Rights: Challenge and Response' (1987) 20 *Cornell International Law Journal* 317, 330.

117 Q. 9:38–41.

118 The opposition to the Tabuk expedition was so strong that it gave rise to further revelations, including the verses Q. 9:42–46, where those who avoided partaking in the war were accused of being hypocrites, and hence were threatened with divine punishment.

119 For a general account, see A. G. Bostom (ed.), *The Legacy of Jihad: Islamic Holy War and the Fate of Non-Muslims* (New York: Prometheus Books, 2008); H. Kennedy, *The Armies of the Caliphs: Military and Society in the Early Islamic State* (New York: Routledge, 2001).

120 Q. 22:78.

debate and persuasion through dialogue and other peaceable methods.[121] Majid Khadduri, in his seminal work *War and Peace in the Law of Islam*, defines the concept of jihad thus:

> The term jihad . . . means 'exerted'. Its juridical-theological meaning is exertion of one's power in Allah's path, that is, the spread of the belief in Allah and in making His word supreme over this world . . . The jihad, *in the broad sense of exertion, does not necessarily mean war or fight, since exertion in Allah's path may be achieved by peaceful means as well as violent means.* The jihad may be regarded as a form of religious propaganda that can be carried on by persuasion or by sword.[122]

The notion of 'exerting one's power for God', therefore, opens up doors for various alternatives as to what may constitute jihad. Since jihad incorporates both militant and non-militant elements, Muslim scholars usually distinguish between four distinct ways to perform it: (1) jihad by the sword, i.e. fighting in God's cause against oppressors, aggressors, or unbelievers; (2) jihad by the heart, i.e. purification of oneself of inner and outer sins; (3) jihad by the tongue, i.e. peaceful propagation of Islamic teachings; and (4) jihad by the hands, i.e. fighting against evil through pious acts.[123]

Jihad thus not merely refers to external struggle against the enemies of Islam, but also to internal struggle against evil temptations within (*nafs*), with a view to becoming a better Muslim. The duty of jihad may accordingly be undertaken both internally and externally. While external jihad is directed against hostile forces, the target of the inner jihad is the individual himself, who is to strive against evil proclivities and keep vigilant over forces that may corrupt one's willpower – by suppressing base inclinations, the individual is expected to reach higher levels of spirituality.[124] It is worth noting that not until recent times has inner jihad

121 See J. Rehman, 'Islam, "War on Terror" and the Future of Muslim Minorities in the United Kingdom: Dilemmas of Multiculturalism in the Aftermath of the London Bombings' (2007) 29 *Human Rights Quarterly* 831, 839.

122 Khadduri, supra note 71, 55–56 (emphasis added).

123 Some scholars use other categories of jihad, such as jihad against the self, against non-believers or the hypocrites, or against the agents of immorality and corruption. The concept is further subcategorised according to the means by which it may be performed: jihad of the heart, jihad of the tongue, jihad by means of wealth, and jihad by person. Most of these forms involve peaceful struggle undertaken for a good cause. See further, M. H. Kamali, 'Jihad and the Interpretation of the Qur'an: Contextualising Islamic Tradition' in: Bassiouni, supra note 33, 39–48; M. Parvin; M. Sommer, 'Dar al-Islam: The Evolution of Muslim Territoriality and its Implications for Conflict Resolution in the Middle East' (1980) 11 *International Journal of Middle East Studies* 1, 4ff; J. F. Whalen, 'In Search of *Jihad*: Toward a Policy of Constructive Islamic Engagement' (1998) 5 *Brown Journal of World Affairs* 279, 282.

124 See generally, J. Renard, 'Al-Jihad Al-Akbar: Notes on a Theme in Islamic Spirituality' (1988) 78 *The Muslim World* 225.

received sufficient attention from the Sunni and Shiite traditions, both of which focused instead on the belligerent aspect of the concept.[125]

It is in large part to the credit of the Sufi tradition that the importance of purifying the self, overcoming the wickedness within, and protecting the frontiers of one's soul have been emphasised. To Sufis, perpetual self-examination, resistance against evil, persistent refinement of inner thoughts, as well as the attempt to achieve harmony with God and His creations have been the most important and demanding constituents of jihad.[126] This notion is epitomised in the following saying, attributed to an influential Muslim thinker, Sufyan Ibn Uyaynah (d. 814): 'jihad in the way of God consists of ten parts, of which only one is fighting against the enemy while other nine are fighting against the self'.[127] The idea of self-purification to achieve tolerance, peace, and justice for humanity, therefore, constitutes the backbone of Sufi thinking on jihad, which rejects wars waged for land, resources, glory, and punishment.[128]

The position that lays emphasis on the peaceful and tolerant aspects of jihad has sparked controversy over the question as to whether there exists a hierarchy between the external and spiritual forms of jihad. According to the Sufis, peaceful jihad is more demanding than its warlike counterpart, on the basis that, unlike the external foe, the inner adversary may not be directly confronted and defeated. This debate finds its genesis in an oft-cited *hadith* of disputed reliability,[129] in which the Prophet, upon his return from the battle of Tabuk (630), is reported to have told his companions: 'We return from the lesser jihad to the greater jihad [*al-jihad al-akbar*].'[130] A parallel tradition, which similarly brings the notion of spiritual growth to the fore, defines the *mujahid* as one 'who wages a struggle against himself'.[131] These *hadiths* bear signal importance as they unmistakably give ground to the above position that spiritual accomplishments are not merely more

125 While some scholars consider the external form of jihad to have entered the picture much earlier than that of the internal jihad, contemporary Muslim opinion generally rejects that the spiritual aspect of jihad had been originally derivate or subordinate in nature. See M. Bonner, *Jihad in Islamic History: Doctrines and Practice* (Princeton: Princeton University Press, 2006) 13–14.

126 See M. Koylu, *Islam and its Quest for Peace: Jihad, Justice and Education* (Washington: The Council for Research in Values and Philosophy, 2003) 54.

127 Ibid. 55.

128 Refusing rectification or punishment as valid grounds for justified war, the Sufi philosophy holds that 'God does not kill His children because they have evil qualities'. See M. R. B. Muhaiyadeen, *Islam and World Peace: Explanations of a SUFI* (Philadelphia: The Fellowship Press, 2004) 49.

129 Some commentators, including Hasan al-Banna (the founder of the Muslim Brotherhood), challenged the authenticity of this *hadith* by expressing doubts as to the reliability of the chain of transmission for this report. See N. Lahoud, 'The Pitfalls of Jihad as an Individual Duty (*Fard 'Ayn*)' in: Bassiouni, supra note 33, 87–91.

130 See Z. Sardar, *The Future of Muslim Civilisation* (London: Croom Helm, 1979) 193; J. L. Esposito, *Unholy War: Terror in the Name of Islam* (New York: Oxford University Press, 2003) 28.

131 See Kamali, supra note 123, 44.

demanding, but more consequential, than the battles fought against the external enemy.

Challenging the notion that unwarlike jihad is the greater form of striving in the cause of God, some espouse that 'paradise lies in the shadow of the sword'[132] – a saying also attributed to the Prophet. This stance, as will be explored later in greater detail, is bolstered by such verses that extol the virtues of those who fight for God: 'Not equal are those believers who sit (at home) and receive no hurt, and those who strive and fight in the cause of Allah . . . Allah hath granted a grade higher to those who strive and fight with their persons and goods than to who sit (at home). . .'[133] Those who highlight the military sense of jihad thus essentially maintain that the self-sacrificing duty of taking up arms against the enemy for purposes like repelling oppression and propagating Islam has been the most remarkable manifestation of jihad. If the Muslim warrior is martyred, he would be cleared of his sins to ascend to 'the highest chambers in heaven'.[134] Such line of thinking appears to have dominated the Sunni intellectual scene since classical times. Lewis, in this connection, maintains that 'the overwhelming majority of classical theologians, jurists, and traditionists . . . understood the obligation of jihad in a military sense, and have examined and expounded it accordingly'.[135] As discussed in the following chapter, it was mainly due to the efforts of modernisers and reformists of the nineteenth and twentieth centuries (who were to a large degree influenced by the aforementioned posture) that the moral and spiritual sense of jihad came to receive its share of attention.

It must nevertheless be noted that the debate as to whether the doctrine of jihad is essentially warlike or spiritual in nature arguably misses the point that these two facets of jihad may overlap, for without peace, stability, and public order (which must at times be secured or maintained through force), spiritual and moral growth may not be readily achievable, and without moral maturity wars may not be fought humanely. More precisely, warfare may prove to be a necessary evil to procure public peace, independence, and security that may in turn be vital ingredients for spiritual growth, which, in a cyclical pattern, may feed into the process of humanely and responsibly initiated and fought wars.

By the same token, any question of priority on the exercise of belligerent or peaceful jihad must be considered after ascertaining the broader socio-political context. It follows that while the above tradition may be so interpreted that the Prophet had attached more weight to spiritual struggle than to actual

132 This saying is attributed to the Prophet. See al-Bukhari 56:22:1. The Hadith of Bukhari is available at: http://sunnah.com/bukhari/56.

133 Q. 4:95.

134 Lahoud, supra note 129, 88. Kennedy shows that the reason behind the great successes of Muslim armies of conquest lie partially in their military and numerical superiority, but notably in their mobility, faith, and morale. See Kennedy, supra note 119, 6ff.

135 Lewis, supra note 116, 72.

warfare,[136] the context that prompted such utterance appears to be one of a post-war scenario in which Muslims had already overcome a serious military threat. If such were the case, some qualifications would be essential before drawing definitive conclusions on the question of hierarchy. A contextual approach demands an analysis of broader circumstances; for instance, in aggressive cases of Muslim belligerency, and perhaps in less exigent cases of self-defensive wars, where believers are not individually bound to partake in war efforts (this theme will be considered below), non-militant types of jihad may be exercised without notable difficulty. Yet in cases of overwhelming aggression directed against Muslims – where every qualified Muslim might be obliged to fight – prolonged periods of detached, spiritual jihad may not readily be undertaken in view of the urgent need for communal survival that triumphs over other competing needs – at least transitorily.[137]

In fact, the above-quoted bellicose verses[138] decidedly rebuke, and promise punishment to, those who wilfully shunned the military campaign of Tabuk – a phenomenon which confirmed that, in pressing conditions, believers had to strive in God's cause even at the expense of bodily death. Unsurprisingly, the Quran gives martyrs the pride of place by bestowing upon them an honourable place and eternal bliss in heaven: 'Think not of those who are slain in Allah's way as dead. Nay, they live, finding their sustenance in the presence of their Lord.'[139] While Muslim jurists recognise some other categories of martyrdom – based on traditions – attained through such ways as death in childbirth or in pursuit of noble purposes,[140] dying in justified warfare has conventionally been at the heart of the martyrdom discourse.[141] This fact should, of course, not downplay the importance of believers' spiritual battle against their debilitating tendencies;[142] but it should be clear that when there exists a fatal threat to be concerned about, Muslims may first and foremost direct their resources to secure the survival or preservation of the Islamic polity.[143]

136 As noted above, as in all religious and mundane activities, in matters of war and peace, the Prophet's practices constitute the ideal pattern of practical and spiritual perfection, and as such his model remains exemplary for Muslims.

137 This argument, however, must not be so read as to justify the advocacy of refraining critical self-examination or spiritual jihad – even in circumstances when this is possible – whenever public peace and security are at stake.

138 Q. 9:38–41.

139 Q. 3:169; also see Q. 3:170–171; Q. 3:140.

140 See further, D. Cook, *Martyrdom in Islam* (Cambridge: Cambridge University Press, 2007) 33–34.

141 J. Mitchell, *Martyrdom: A Very Short Introduction* (Oxford: Oxford University Press, 2012) 61ff.

142 According to some, the status of martyrdom must above all be accorded to those who have overcome their evil qualities. Bonner notes that such spiritualisation of the martyrdom discourse had not been a late phenomenon, as 'martyrdom in Islam had been close to ascetic practice and belief from quite early on.' See Bonner, supra note 125, 79.

143 In the final analysis, however, the interconnectedness of non-military and military forms of jihad must arguably occupy a central point in any discussion on war in Islam,

This point brings us to the issue of whether the duty of military jihad must be undertaken in an individual or collective fashion. As alluded to above, the nature of the obligation to partake in warlike jihad depends on military exigencies. In cases of martial emergencies that gravely threaten the land of Islam, defensive jihad becomes an individual duty (*fard al-ayn*). The doctrine of individual jihad – as formulated and understood by such classical jurists as al-Shafi'i (d. 820) – thus assumes pertinence when the existence of the Islamic polity is jeopardised by external forces.[144] The obligation to join in such defensive warfare is principally expected to be shouldered by Muslim males of fighting age and fitness, dwelling in areas subjected to military threat. Yet in life-or-death scenarios, all Muslims – whether young or old, men or women, free man or slave, rich or poor – might be required to fight;[145] because, unlike any other type of military conduct, defensive jihad carries so much importance that people's physical, financial, or family circumstances are of no consequence for the purpose of defending Islam.[146]

So far as the expansion of Islam, repelling inconsequential enemy encroachments, or prevention of potential but non-material threats are concerned, the duty of jihad may acquire a collective character. The doctrine of collective jihad, which was developed by the Iraqi jurists of the Abbasid period, thus imposes a communal obligation that may be deemed satisfied when a sufficient number of Muslims' war efforts are secured. To clarify this further, the doctrine envisages that some Muslims could execute military jihad on behalf of others, since the obligation to fight does not fall on each individual in such cases as offensive incursions into enemy territory, or negligible exterior threats posed against the Muslim rule.[147]

for spiritual elevation informs the quality and pureness of each warlike conduct; i.e. one may not legitimately initiate a just war and conduct it humanely unless one continually seeks to get the better of unvirtuous elements in one's constitution – this holds true even in the heat of battle, when a believer must ideally exercise restraint and display elevated conduct lest religious wars degenerate into barbarism.

144 However, later commentaries also postulate that the duty to fight is of collective character, unless a military emergency demands that all able-bodied male Muslims bear arms. See Bonner, supra note 125, 107; Firestone, supra note 108, 60.

145 Khadduri, supra note 71, 60.

146 In defensive jihad, certain rules could be further relaxed; e.g. a Muslim rulers theoretically does not have to announce the duty to engage in individual jihad, nor officially conscript Muslims when circumstances so warrant. Likewise, dependent groups are not obliged to seek their custodians' permission to join the cause. See further, Jackson, supra note 107, 17.

147 See Bonner, supra note 125, 14; M. Syed; B. College, 'Jihad in Classical Islamic Legal and Moral Thought' in: J. Neusner *et al* (eds.), *Just War in Religion and Politics* (Lanham: University Press of America, 2013) 145ff.

Significantly, some present-day radical movements consider the collective duty of jihad to have disappeared altogether, only to be replaced by the duty of individual jihad.[148] This interpretation apparently has to do with the perception that the land of Islam is under constant politico-military threat emanating from 'Western imperialism' and its corrupt local allies.[149] The meta-narrative of Muslims being under persistent siege from all quarters by imperialism, nonetheless, does not capture the normative position in Islam concerning the duty of individual military jihad, which may become due only when there exists an actual or imminent martial threat – and not only an economic, political, or ideological one – that brooks no alternative but to strike back to ward off the threat involved. In today's context, the oft-invoked rhetoric of blaming imperial powers for all ills of the Muslim world – even when it contains some elements of truth – is not conducive to resolving some of the crises faced by Muslim societies. Furthermore, as Chapter 4 will make clearer, aggression is no longer an accepted method of resolving international disputes; hence, any legitimate State response to a military threat must be considered within the framework of the UN Charter. The doctrine of individual jihad, like other legal artefacts, was formulated in a particular epoch to meet the prevailing socio-political conditions of its milieu; and, as such, it must not be read as a dogmatic formulation governing Islamic warfare regardless of changing circumstances. It must further be remembered that, today, Muslims may readily resort to unwarlike aspects of jihad, like dialogue, diplomacy, lobbying, and agreements, to resolve issues of contention and conflict, before directly turning to drastic lethal measures.

Viewed in this light, and to summarise, it may be observed that the doctrine of jihad has a dual character, coloured by both military and peaceful elements. Be that as it may, and despite modern endeavours to promote peaceful aspects of jihad, it is primarily the military facet thereof that generally attracts most headlines and stirs heated controversy in the non-Muslim world. Such military sense generally arouses feelings of distress and misgiving in the West, for jihad is often associated with the use of wanton violence in the name, or under the pretext, of religion. There is certainly a reason behind such apprehensions concerning the just war tradition in Islam, which encompasses two main interpretations. According

148 J. T. Johnson, *Ethics and the Use of Force: Just War in Historical Perspective* (Surrey: Ashgate Publishing, 2011) 71.

149 The founder of the Muslim Brotherhood, Hasan al-Banna, for instance, noted that 'today the Muslims . . . are compelled to humble themselves before non-Muslims, and are ruled by unbelievers. Their lands have been trampled over, and their honour besmirched. Their adversaries are in charge of their affairs; . . . hence it has become an individual obligation, which there is no evading, on every Muslim to prepare his equipment, to make up his mind to engage in jihad, and to get ready for it until the opportunity is ripe. . .' H. al-Banna; C. Wendell (trans.), *Five Tracts of Hasan al-Banna (1906–1946): A Selection from the Majmuat rasail al-Imam al-shahid Hasan al-Banna* (Berkeley: University of California Press, 1978) 150; also see M. A. Dayem; F. Ayub 'In the Path of Allah: Evolving Interpretations of Jihad and its Modern Challenges' (2009) 7 *UCLA Journal of Islamic and Near Eastern Law* 67.

to the first interpretation, the creation of a universal dominion under an all-embracing Islamic polity – within which unbelief, immorality, oppression, and injustice are eradicated[150] – is incumbent on Muslims through jihad in all its forms. This position – which will receive greater attention in the following chapter – then roughly seeks to establish a socio-political order—ideally a universal one—wherein God's law reigns supreme. Jihad, in its peaceful manifestations, is merely a means for the realisation of such state of affairs.[151] The second intellectual stance, however, puts more stress on the peaceful dimensions of jihad with a view to dissociating Islam from sectarian violence, terrorist atrocities, and wars of aggression, and to promoting the view that Islam stands for peace, tolerance, and justice for everyone. Having rejected all forms of religious aggression, some pacifist jurists went so far as to reducing the concept of jihad exclusively to spiritual struggle, arguing that jihad only 'represents the exertion of spiritual warfare waged by the faithful against the lower, or evil, soul'.[152]

In order to clear such conceptual haze surrounding the Islamic *jus ad bellum,* and hence set the stage for the next chapter, it is now imperative to trace the genesis of Islam in general, and the broader socio-political context wherein militant jihad gradually evolved in particular. Such contextual approach will be seen to deliver us from the constraints of sharply discordant normative stances advanced by radical and reformist streams of Islam. The rest of this book will attempt to prove that the Islamic just war tradition has been dynamically shaped, not merely through the primary and secondary sources of Islam, but through varying Islamic State practice – all of which have neither emerged in a vacuum, nor followed a linear line of development.

150 This idea partly finds its reflection in the Quran: 'And fight them on until there is no more tumult or oppression, and there prevail justice and faith in Allah.' Q. 2:193. Yet this seemingly categorical command is qualified in the second paragraph of the verse: 'But if they cease, let there be no hostility except to those who practise oppression'. This indicates that if the opponent ceases to oppress Muslims, then hostilities must be brought to an end. But this does not mean resistance cannot be undertaken once again, if conditions warrant it, for the Quran clearly commands resistance, through peaceful or belligerent means, in the face of persecution.

151 Khadduri, supra note 71, 51. Contemporary radical groups, such as al-Qaeda, advocate the universality of Islam. In its 'letter to the American People', bin Laden, for instance, wrote that Islam is the religion of unity and 'the seal of all the previous religions. . . . It is the religion of Unification of God, sincerity, the best manners, righteousness, mercy, honour, purity, and piety. . . . It is the religion of enjoining the good and forbidding the evil with the hand, tongue and heart. It is the religion of jihad in the way of Allah so that Allah's word and religion reign supreme.' See O. bin Laden, 'Letter to America' 24 November 2002. Available at: http://www.guardian.co.uk/world/2002/nov/24/theobserver.

152 Cook, supra note 111, 2.

2. *The Contextual Formation of Jihad*

Islam emerged in seventh-century Arabia, where warfare was in essence regarded as a matter-of-fact, i.e. a relatively ordinary feature of existence. The employment and threat of armed force as well as cyclical blood feuds had been the most prevalent methods of resolving disputes,[153] and of managing relations among political entities in the region, which included various Arab tribes and the powerful Sasanian and Byzantine empires. The Prophet Muhammad initially resided, and received his early revelations, in the city of Mecca, which was beset by tribal raids, cycles of vengeance and incessant blood feud.[154] Some Quranic verses portray such a ubiquitous state of war in Arabia: 'Do they not then see that We have made a sanctuary secure, and that men are being snatched away from all around them?'[155] An analogous verse depicts the precarious situation of Muhammad's early community in Mecca: 'Call to mind when ye were a small (band), despised through the land, and afraid that men might despoil and kidnap you.'[156] It was this sort of endemic belligerency that induced pre-Islamic Arabs to introduce a period of 'forbidden months' (*al-Ashhur al-hurum*) that corresponded to the eleventh, twelfth, first, and seventh months of the lunar calendar, during which hostilities had been categorically outlawed. The 'forbidden months' served an economic purpose, too, since this peaceful period not only allowed trade caravans to freely move into the neighbouring regions and engage in commerce, but enabled potential pilgrims to safely carry out their pilgrimage in Mecca – which formed one of the most lucrative assets of the city.[157]

At this time, however, Arabia was subjected to rivalry among fragmented Arab tribes, and to the competition and interventions of its powerful neighbours, largely because it was located at the centre of one of the most gainful international trade

153 In pre-Islamic Arabia, occasional recourse would also be made to peaceful dispute settlement mechanisms, including arbitration (*al-tahkim*), which gained popularity during the Islamic period. Arabs turned to arbitrators – whose main merits comprised fairness and wisdom – for numerous disputes over such matters as inheritance, water rights, and blood revenge. As Islam gained predominance, some of the customary arbitration procedures were incorporated, with necessary changes, within the corpus of Islamic law. See further, Zawati, supra note 9, 70ff; A. S. Moussalli, 'An Islamic Model for Political Conflict Resolution: *Tahkim* (Arbitration)' in: P. Salem (ed.) *Conflict Resolution in the Arab World: Selected Essays* (Beirut: American University of Beirut Press, 1997) 44ff.

154 Some scholars maintain that Islam would probably not have survived if military jihad had not been employed in defending and spreading the faith 'at a time when violent force was the law'. See A. A. An-Na'im, *Toward and Islamic Reformation: Civil Liberties, Human Rights, and International Law* (Syracuse: Syracuse University Press, 1996) 142, 158.

155 Q. 29:67.

156 Q. 8:26.

157 See Jackson, supra note 107, 12; M. A. Bamyeh, *The Social Origins of Islam: Mind, Economy, Discourse* (Minneapolis: University of Minnesota Press, 1999) 40.

routes.[158] In the home town of the Prophet, religious and economic lives were essentially entwined. While Mecca benefited from some measure of trade, the city's main economic resource relied upon the control of the Kaaba, and associated pilgrimage rites, which attracted a considerable number of pilgrims from almost the whole of Hijaz. This religio-economic system was essentially controlled by the Quraysh tribe, which dominated the political, economic, and cultural landscape of the city.[159]

It should be stressed that the socio-political setting in which the Prophet Muhammad lived, and to which he was opposed, was marked by corruption and immorality – a period known as *jahiliyyah* ('age of ignorance'). The salient features of *jahiliyyah* included polytheism, idolatry, ignorance, sensual decadence, female infanticide, and incessant bloodshed.[160] It was against such a backdrop that Muhammad's reformist message defied the economic, political, and religious status quo. Muhammad radically challenged the establishment, called for social justice and equality for the vulnerable and needy, and denounced polytheism, immorality, and idolatry. He summoned people to abandon the iniquities and dissoluteness of the pagan mode of existence in favour of an Islamic life. Muhammad's preaching had accordingly negated some of the most entrenched customs and norms of Arabia – depicting them as signs of moral decay.

Having identified himself with the disadvantaged and having concern for the ills of society, Muhammad advanced such ideas and ethical principles that progressively but inexorably questioned the prevailing paradigms of his period – a phenomenon that was to place Muhammad at loggerheads with the ruling elite.[161] He indeed opposed such deep-rooted values as the sacredness of blood revenge, the undisputed primacy of familial and tribal affiliations, and the unconditional protection granted to members of the kindred group. Muhammad's message envisaged an identity based on piousness and religious brethren, not on blood or tribal liaisons. Furthermore, the Prophet's new faith encouraged forgiveness rather than cyclical revenge for the harm suffered.[162] It proscribed morally illicit conduct, debauchery, alcohol consumption, female infanticide, and iniquity in all forms. When such novelties were accompanied by the

158 Esposito, supra note 130, 29.

159 See R. Aslan, *No god but God: The Origins, Evolution and Future of Islam* (London: Arrow Books, 2005) 27–31.

160 G. R. Hawting, *The Idea of Idolatry and the Emergence of Islam: From Polemic to History* (Cambridge: Cambridge University Press, 1999) 1–2.

161 See Esposito, supra note 130, 30; M. Rodinson, *Muhammad: Prophet of Islam* (New York: Pantheon Books, 1980) 82.

162 Islam neither envisages complete passivism in the face of injury, nor a never-ending blood feud; rather, a middle path is advised for Muslims to seek justice on a scale proportionate to the wrong suffered; this notwithstanding, forgiveness is advised. The Quran is explicit on this: 'The recompense for an injury is an equal thereto (in degree): but if a person forgives and makes reconciliation, his reward is due from Allah: for (Allah) loveth not those who do wrong.' Q. 42:40.

denunciation of pagan gods of Mecca as mere idols devoid of any meaning and power (whose followers would be consigned to hell), and by the introduction of new religious ceremonies, rites, prayers, and abstinences for the Lord, a stronger resistance naturally grew against Islam, which called for radical changes in the day-to-day lives of pagan Arabs.[163]

Nevertheless, as alluded to above, the alienation of the pagan population at large and of the ruling elite in particular was also connected with the prospect of losing Mecca's mystical centrality – an asset that yielded notable revenue from pilgrimage.[164] Faced with the challenges mounted by the new faith, the notables of Mecca first tried to dissuade the Prophet from preaching his message and deprecating ancient customs and traditions.[165] When these attempts had failed, they sought to discredit him by such claims that he was a mere oracle (*kahin*) or simply a possessed poet.[166] Yet, as Muhammad increased his sphere of influence and proved relentless in his pursuit of spreading the teachings of Islam, he came to be perceived as a force to be reckoned with – a development that triggered severe pressure upon the burgeoning Muslim community[167] in an effort to preserve the political, economic, and cultural state of affairs. Rejecting any compromise, including the suggestion to so modify Islam as to encompass pagan gods as intercessors with Allah, Muhammad and early Muslims became subject to embittered persecution, with those who lacked any clan protection bearing the brunt of ill-treatment, insults, torture, and socio-economic isolation.[168]

163 For detailed analysis, see I. Goldziher; S. M. Stern (ed.); C. R. Barber; S. M. Stern (trans.) *Muslim Studies* (London: Aldine Transaction, 2008) 18–27, 39–42.

164 Although the degree to which trade played role in the financial life of Mecca remains a matter for controversy, Watt notes that Mecca was more than a mere trading centre, but was essentially a financial centre where economic activities of considerable complexity were carried out. 'The Qur'an', Watt writes, 'appeared not in the atmosphere of the desert, but in that of high finance.' W. M. Watt, *Muhammad at Mecca* (Oxford: Oxford University Press, 1953) 3; *cf.* P. Crone, *Meccan Trade and the Rise of Islam* (Piscataway: Gorgias Press, 2004); Aslan, supra note 159, 24–26; Rodinson, supra note 161, 108.

165 See further, F. Rahman, *Major Themes of the Qur'an* (Chicago: Chicago University Press, 2009) 157ff.

166 The detractors of Muhammad's mission, according to the Quran, asked: 'What! Shall we give up our gods for the sake of a poet possessed?' Q. 37:36.

167 The first Muslim converts comprised members of Muhammad's household and the very close circle of his relatives. Significantly, most of the early disciples are known to be in need and search of spiritual guidance, some of whom belonged to powerful Meccan families. R. H. Salmi *et al, Islam And Conflict Resolution: Theories And Practices* (Lanham: University Press of America, 1998) 23.

168 M. M. Pickthall, *The Glorious Qur'an: The Arabic Text with a Translation in English* (New York: TTQ, Inc., 2001) v–vii.

3. The Meccan and Medinan Approach to Resistance and Warfare

While the primary sources of Islam have never commanded Muslims to turn the other cheek,[169] during the Meccan period (610–622) lethal force was not permitted to avert aggression, persecution, or oppression, or to secure Muslims' right to freely exercise their faith. Over the course of Islam's formative years, which corresponded to the first 12 years of Muhammad's ministry in Mecca, the Quran continually stressed the notions of patience, persistence, and perseverance in the face of adverse opposition from the chiefs of the Meccan society whose vested interests – both political and religious – were threatened by Muhammad's unprecedented preaching. The Quran reaffirmed the future success of God's cause, and exhorted patience in the presence of unwavering disbelief: 'Seek (Allah's) help with patient perseverance and prayer. . .'[170] because 'Allah will defend thee [Muslims] from men (who mean mischief).'[171] Muhammad had therefore preferred peaceful alternatives to secure and consolidate the well-being of the Muslim community, and to spread the message of Islam.[172] Even though assiduousness in proclaiming the word of God did not convince a large number of Meccan pagans to mend their ways and to take heed of the divine message; God's revelations reminded the Prophet that his mere duty was to 'make (the message) reach them', for it was for God to 'call them [pagans] to account'.[173] Rather than belligerency, peaceable means, such as preaching and dialogue, were thus advised for the Prophet, who was assured of God's protection despite severe opposition to his mission: 'Now await in patience the command of thy Lord: for verily thou art in Our eyes.'[174] Even in the most trying moments, the Quran adjured the Prophet not be anxious,[175] but to be determinate in 'expounding openly' what he was commanded – irrespective of the bitter antagonism and hopelessness of the situation.[176]

169 Islam clearly differs from early Christianity on the question of pacifism. For early Christians, participation in warfare had to be avoided, because military service was deemed contrary to the peaceful spirit of the Gospel which condemned killing, and commanded non-resistance to the evildoer. See Lewis, supra note 68, 2; Bachrach, supra note 19, 24.

170 Q. 2:45.

171 Q. 5:67.

172 As Hashmi points out, Muhammad regarded warfare as a necessary evil of last resort. S. H. Hashmi, 'Interpreting the Islamic Ethics of War and Peace' in: T. Nardin (ed.), *The Ethics of War and Peace: Religious and Secular Perspectives* (Princeton: Princeton University Press, 1996) 146–152.

173 Q. 13:40.

174 Q. 52:48.

175 The Quran urged the Prophet not to grieve over a pagan's rejection of God's message: 'Thou wouldst only, perchance, fret thyself to death, following after them, in grief, if they believe not in this Message.' Q. 18:6.

176 Q. 15:94.

Parallel verses during this period hence largely commanded believers to be forbearing and forgiving: 'overlook (any human faults) with gracious forgiveness';[177] 'turn away from them [the oppressors]' peacefully;[178] and 'repel (evil) with what is better'.[179] Since God's commands in the Meccan period required Muhammad to handle wrongs and threats of aggression with peaceful methods, he avoided direct confrontations with the enemy and employed dialogue and negotiations with his opponents. At times, he engaged in trade relations and other sorts of confidence-building alliances with non-Muslims; and when necessary he even sought protection from those who plainly rejected Islam.[180] Apart from moral imperatives, the Meccan emphasis on non-violent methods of striving was also to do with the physical vulnerability of the believers, who regularly faced threats against their lives by opponents that vastly outnumbered and overpowered the Muslims. Indeed, because the Prophet lacked many supporters and followers – hence was bereft of such political and military might as to counter his recalcitrant foes – the propagation of the faith as well as the defence of the young Muslim community had to be done in a non-aggressive fashion.[181] The conciliatory tone of the Meccan verses thus makes better sense when read in light of the broader context, wherein believers were clearly overpowered by those who were intent on preserving the hitherto prevailing system by any means necessary. Considering such unpropitious circumstances, Muslim converts were understandably commanded to use merely peaceful methods to propagate their beliefs, to counter their stronger pagan enemies, and to engage with the 'People of the Book' (Jews, Christians, Sabaeans and Zoroastrians).[182] Nevertheless, as expounded below, non-violent methods of dealing with practical challenges, or of facing the enemy, were not confined to the embryonic phase of Islam, but were also utilised at later stages, where lethal force began to figure in Islamic dispute settlement mechanisms as an exceptional measure.[183]

177 Q. 15:85.
178 Q. 43:89.
179 Q. 41:34.
180 For example, while in Mecca, Muhammad was granted protection by his uncle (Abu Talib) who never pronounced the profession of Islamic faith. See Ramadan, supra note 65, 68.
181 See Mohammad, supra note 1, 385; Mirza, supra note 109, 78.
182 Among others, the injunctions to non-violence in Q. 2:109; Q. 2:256; Q. 22:78; Q. 25:52; Q. 109:1–6 belong to this period. During the formation of Islam, the main groups that were alluded to in the Quran were Christians, Jews, polytheists, animists, Zoroastrians, Yazidis, and the Hunafa (Hunafas were considered to have belonged to the monotheistic tradition and were thus respected by Muslims). See P. Sarris, *Empires of Faith: The Fall of Rome to the Rise of Islam, 500–700* (Oxford: Oxford University Press, 2011) 264.
183 As shown in the following chapter, in subsequent years Muhammad would conclude agreements with some neighbouring Jewish and pagan tribes, and even with the pagan clan of the Quraysh, which proved to be the most effective opponent of believers during the early phase of Islam. See further, T. Ramadan, *Western Muslims and the Future of Islam* (Oxford: Oxford University Press, 2004) 92.

Islam's first engagement with deadly force entered into the picture in the Medinan period, which witnessed the first Islamic polity founded by emigrant Muslims. The emigration (*hijrah*) resulted from the aforementioned unwavering Meccan opposition, which grew more threatening against the burgeoning Muslim community that saw its survival in moving to Yathrib in 622,[184] a year that marked the beginning of the Islamic calendar. Yathrib was an oasis town, about 250 miles to the north of Mecca, of which Muhammad was invited by a few Medinan converts to become the *de facto* ruler, and neutral arbiter between, feuding tribes that were engulfed in intractable internal conflicts. Muhammad was expected to deliver this conflict-torn society from its long-standing troubles and establish peace and order therein[185] – a challenge he undertook with the support of his followers. Soon after their settlement in Yathrib, Muhammad and his companions began to sow the seeds of a peaceful socio-political order based on Islamic principles. Except for the Jewish clans,[186] the general population of the town – which was henceforth to be known as Medina[187] – recognised Muhammad's politico-religious leadership.

The establishment of a theologico-political unit in Medina marked a radical transition from a position of weakness to strength for Muslims, who had never been so unified and bound together in their beliefs and fresh aspirations. The number and capabilities of Muslims grew drastically with the joining of Medinan converts (*ansars*, i.e. helpers) who embraced, protected, and supported the emigrants (*muhajiruns*). The emergent Muslim body politic aspired to create a consolidated socio-religious order under Muhammad's spiritual and political guidance, which, first and foremost, required Muslims not to shed blood among each other, for feuding was simply divisive and pernicious. Islam ushered in a new stage of society formation in seventh-century Arabia, one that did not lean upon familial, tribal, racial, linguistic, and cultural affiliations, but on piety and faith.[188] More precisely, adherents to this new faith (*ummah*) were no longer to be identified by profane alignments, but by Islamic principles that provided a novel blueprint as to how a meaningful, pious, and righteous life should be led.

A social organisation largely based on religious considerations, rather than temporal ideologies or associations, was the first of its kind in the history of the

184 For a detailed treatment of the *hijrah* phenomenon, see Ramadan, supra note 74, 81ff.

185 W. M. Watt, *Muhammad: Prophet and Statesman* (Oxford: Oxford University Press, 1961) 89.

186 In Medina there existed three major Jewish clans at the time; these were the Banu Qaynuqa, Banu al-Nadir, and Banu Qurayza. See S. Carimokam, *Muhammad and the People of the Book* (Bloomington: Xlibris, 2010) 304.

187 Al-Madinah (Medina) literally meant 'the city' which was also called Madinah ar-Rasul (the city of the Prophet) or al-Madinah al Munawwarah (the enlightened city). See Ramadan, supra note 74, 82; J. L. Esposito, *The Oxford History of Islam* (Oxford: Oxford University Press, 1999) 8.

188 See J. L. Esposito, *Islam: The Straight Path* (Oxford: Oxford University Press, 1994) 8–9; Watt, supra note 185, 94ff.

Arabs.[189] In his capacity as God's messenger, Muhammad's charismatic leadership, which extended to religious, judicial, and political realms, ultimately aimed at creating a united front for Muslims – an objective memorably reiterated in Muhammad's farewell sermon delivered in 632,[190] and unambiguously stated in the Quran: 'and hold fast, all together . . . and be not divided among yourselves; and remember with gratitude Allah's favour on you; for ye were enemies and He joined your hearts in love, so that by His Grace, ye became brethren. . .'[191] In an attempt to consolidate the political power in the new centre and to create a seamless Muslim unity, the Prophet regulated relations between the emigrants and local believers, gradually settled disputes between warring tribes, and entered into treaties with the Jewish clans of the area. Clearly, the first and foremost priority was given to ending conflicts among Arabs and between Arabs and Jews.[192]

To these ends, peaceful means were employed to create a legal basis for the regulation of clear rights and duties of various communities. One of the remarkable documents in this regard was the *sahifa* – generally referred to as the Constitution of Medina or the Medina Declaration – the terms of which were accepted by the local and emigrant Arabs and by the Jews of Medina. The fundamental object of the document was to build cooperation between the residents of Medina, and consequently to form a working heterogeneous polity.[193] Whilst the *sahifa* might be viewed as the first treaty between Muslims and non-Muslims, it may also be seen as the first constitution of the Islamic city-State in Medina,[194] which governed relations between the Muslim and Jewish tribes of Medina, recognised such basic rights as the right to life and freedom of religion for each community, and confirmed Muhammad's leadership and his status as the neutral arbitrator (*hakam*) of present and potential conflicts between Muslim and non-Muslim communities of Medina.[195] The document was both practical

189 See P. K. Hitti, *The Arabs: A Short History* (Washington: Regnery Publishing, 1996) 39–40.

190 'Learn', the Prophet remarked, 'that every Muslim is a brother to every Muslim and that the Muslims constitute one brotherhood. Nothing shall be legitimate to a Muslim which belongs to a fellow Muslim unless it was given freely and willingly. Do not, therefore, do injustice to yourselves.' Muhammad, 'The Prophet Muhammad's Farewell Sermon' (632). Available at: http://www.iium.edu.my/deed/articles/the-lastsermon.html.

191 Q. 3:103.

192 See generally, W. M. Watt, *Muhammad at Medina* (Oxford: Oxford University Press, 1956).

193 It is worth noting that while the Prophet did not modify some of the ancient customs, he did prohibit such un-Islamic practices as infanticide for all, and wine drinking for Muslims. Moussalli, supra note 153, 47ff.

194 Note that the exact legal character of the document remains contentious; see generally M. Gil, *Jews in Islamic Countries in the Middle Ages* (Leiden: Brill, 2004) 21ff.

195 The Prophet, both before and after his ministry, was known for his honesty and wisdom as an arbitrator. In Medina, Muhammad's role as the final arbitrator of all disputes had become prominent through the Constitution of Medina. While the prophet at times relied on customary law and tribal practices, he mainly applied

and political in nature, for it sought to jettison old bonds based merely upon tribal connections, to replace the old judicial system with one that was more attuned to the community's new multi-religious character, to regulate such tangible issues as the common defence of Medina in cases of warfare,[196] and to encompass agreements of cooperation and non-aggression between the Muslims and the Jews as well as the pagan clans of Yathrib.[197]

As will be touched upon later, the polity established in Medina was to inspire almost all Islamic revivalist or reformist movements of modern times, which strive for reviving the values of Muhammad's close-knit early politico-religious community with a view to liberating and prospering Muslim societies. While what constituted such quintessential values has remained somewhat moot, Muslims, by and large, have considered the Medinan model as representing the ideal paradigm of Islamic society and political system.[198]

As stated above, it was in Medina – wherein Muslim political thought and practice had come of age – that the early necessity of non-violent resistance against aggression and oppression had ceased to be the unavoidable fate of Muslims. Having secured a position to defend themselves, Muslims were finally permitted to take lethal action against their enemies that caused them to suffer exile.[199] Indeed, a verse revealed in Medina unequivocally authorised Muslims to invoke warlike measures, when necessary, to repel aggression: 'to those against whom war is made, permission is given (to fight), because they are wronged'.[200] This verse is generally considered to have been revealed soon after the emigration, being the first verse allowing defensive force.[201]

Such novel latitude of action conferred upon Muslims marked a dramatic sea-change in Muhammad's prophetic career, as he no longer had to demand that his followers remain passive against unprovoked aggression or persecution.

the Islamic law to Muslims, and the Old and/or New Testament to Jews and Christians as a method of arbitration in their legal, social, and religious disputes. The Quran explicitly required Muhammad to judge the Scriptuaries in line with their religious norms, probably to prevent the Prophet from delivering arbitrary judgements, but judgements based on God's revelations for each religious community: 'so judge between them by what Allah hath revealed, and follow not their vain desires . . . to each among you have We prescribed a law and an open way. . . .' See Q. 5:48–49; W. B. Hallaq, *A History of Islamic Legal Theories: An Introduction to Sunni usul al-fiqh* (Cambridge: Cambridge University Press, 1997) 4–5; I. M. Lapidus, *A History of Islamic Societies* 2nd ed., (Cambridge: Cambridge University Press, 2002) 23; Zawati, supra note 9, 56.

196 Gil, supra note 194, 21.

197 Aslan, supra note 159, 55.

198 Esposito, supra note 130, 31; Aslan, supra note 159, 52.

199 See generally, A. L. Silverman, 'Just War, *Jihad*, and Terrorism: A Comparison of Western and Islamic Norms for the Use of Political Violence' (2002) 44 *Journal of Church & State* 1, 73–78.

200 Q. 22:39.

201 See J. L. Esposito, *The Oxford Encyclopaedia of the Modern Islamic World*, Vol. II (Oxford: Oxford University Press, 1995) 370.

Muslims could henceforth resort to forceful defensive measures against aggressors. In the Medina period (622–632), it was thus made clear that as long as there was oppression, torture, or murder of people because of their beliefs, the religion permitted the employment of the sword to stop such practices.[202] And the Quran assured believers that if they were to be slain in religious cause they would be granted 'forgiveness and mercy'[203] as well as an eternal life with great rewards.[204] Nonetheless, as stressed earlier, the right to defensive war had never been unqualified, because before the sword could be unsheathed, peaceful means of dispute resolution had to be exhausted, and when the sword was unsheathed it had to be used in accord with humanitarian principles.[205]

The divine authorisation for the use of the sword and exhortation to strive against the enemy accentuated the acute necessity for, and the incipient capability of, Muslims to counter external threats by all possible means. During this period, such practical warlike pronouncements were envisaged by the Quran as the exemption from military service (for those who were weak in body and with no economic means to financially contribute to war efforts),[206] taking up arms in self-defence during the sacred months or places,[207] the fate of the enemy prisoners of war,[208] provision of asylum or safe conduct to non-Muslims,[209] and truce or peace with the enemy.[210]

Some of these warlike norms will later be explored in more detail; suffice it to remind the reader here that in the early Medina period, whilst self-defensive war is permitted to repel aggression or redress grave injustice, any recourse to lethal force is limited by the twin concepts of necessity and proportionality. Indeed, some important verses of this period unequivocally demand Muslims to fight when strictly necessary to face up to aggression or obscene injustice within the rigid bounds of proportionality.[211] Putting it otherwise, Islam's concern at this early Medinan stage is mainly confined to repelling armed intrusions or persecution within the confines of humanitarian norms. In fact, none of the warlike verses

202 J. Said, 'Law, Religion and the Prophetic Method of Social Change' (2001) 15 *Journal of Law and Religion* 83, 140; Mohammad, supra note 1, 387.

203 Q. 3:157–158.

204 The Quran read, 'those who . . . strive with might and main in God's cause, with their goods and their people, have the highest rank in the sight of God. They are the people who will achieve salvation'. Q. 9:20; also see Q. 3:169–172; *cf.* Q. 22:40.

205 The requirement to exhaust peaceful alternatives first before taking recourse to fighting may also be found in the way one must seek redress for the evils one encounters. The Prophet is reported to have said that 'whoever among you sees an evil action, let him change it with his hand (by taking action); if he cannot, then with his tongue [by speaking out]; if he cannot, then with his heart [by hating it and feeling that it is wrong], and that is the weakest of faith'. Narrated by Muslim, 49.

206 Q. 9:91; Q. 48:17.

207 Q. 2:217; Q. 2:191.

208 Q. 47:4.

209 Q. 9:6.

210 Q. 8:61.

211 Q. 2:190; Q. 2:191; Q. 2:192; Q. 2:193; Q. 2:194.

cited above suggest the sense of total elimination of the enemy or forceful conversion thereof.

Warfare at this period thus seems to have been considered a measure of final resort to secure the existence of the Muslim community caught in the midst of implacable opposition. In other words, the underlying idea was neither pacifism by necessity, nor the pursuit of justice and/or survival through disproportionate violence; rather, it was a quest for freedom from fear and for the right to religious freedom by proportionate violence, which had to be turned to when peaceful means fell short of success. Islamic laws of warfare at this stage accordingly emphasised the desirability of resolving disputes peaceably whenever this was feasible. Furthermore, while the Quran stipulated that 'the recompense for an injury is an injury equal thereto',[212] it in effect encouraged reconciliation and forgiveness; for Islamic just war principles, as a rule, called for redress, not blind vengeance.[213]

Bearing in mind these humanitarian restrictions, the need to survive, prosper, and exercise religious freedoms in a secure environment eventually brought Muslims into confrontation with those who forced them into exile. The first large-scale engagement with Meccan forces took place in 624 at the battle of Badr, which resulted in Islam's first decisive victory. Through the inspiring leadership of the Prophet, a mere three hundred Muslims defeated a well-equipped Meccan force of about one thousand soldiers.[214] This astonishing triumph was generally regarded as divine approval of the new religion. Emboldened by such a victory, believers were to invoke military jihad when necessary as an instrument for self-defence and religio-political expansion. It must be added that the extraordinary victory of Badr reinforced Muhammad's secular power, as he was no longer predominantly considered to be God's Messenger, but also a political leader and military commander of the fledging Muslim polity. The war correspondingly marked a distinct stage in Islamic history; after Badr, Islam assumed a more political character, one that fused with the State itself as opposed to merely being a State religion.[215]

Notably, at Badr and in many wars to follow, Muslims fought with extraordinary valour, which was often accompanied by a firm conviction that the Islamic cause was justified. Death probably did not frighten the believers greatly, since Muslim soldiers believed in the eventual success of their cause and considered military martyrdom to be a gate to heaven. Confirming this point, according to a well-known tradition, narrated by Bukhari, 'paradise [lay] . . . under the shades of swords'.[216] The Quran also supported the idea by heralding the immorality

212 Q. 42:40.
213 Q. 42:40 reads that 'if a person forgives and makes reconciliation, his reward is due from Allah'.
214 Watt, supra note 185, 119ff.
215 Hitti, supra note 189, 116–117.
216 *Hadith of Bukhari,* Vol. IV, Hadith 4:73.

of those slain on the battlefield in the path of God.[217] The martyrdom discourse assured that Muslims would effectively attain victory, come what may. As may be expected, such conviction made Muslims brave in action and determined in mind, even in the face of potential defeat. The Battle of Uhud (625) was a case in point, where the Prophet suffered his sole defeat at the hands of Meccan forces, who were intent on avenging their crushing defeat at Badr. In this battle, while the Muslim army was outnumbered almost four times by rival forces, it could have attained victory against their numerically superior rivals had Muslim archers followed orders and not abandoned a strategic position, from whence the rear of the Muslim army was to be guarded. Agitated by the ephemeral Muslim victory, when the archers rushed forward in an untimely manner to get their would-be share of booty, the Meccan cavalrymen struck the Muslim rear with such strength that it brought about the collapse of the Muslim defence. The defeat proved to be dramatic in that Muhammad was severely wounded, and many Muslims, including the Prophet's uncle (Hamza), were slain.[218]

Muslims, however, were to draw notable lessons from this misfortune, the foremost of which was that such impure motives as greed for material goods would often lead to failure. Hence, patience, moral strength, and purification of the soul were advised. The Quran said: 'Lose not heart, nor fall into despair: for you must gain mastery if ye are true in faith.'[219] The defeat was accordingly put within the context of God testing the mettle and piousness of the Muslims: 'What ye suffered', the Quran declared, 'on the day the two armies met, was with the leave of Allah, in order that He might test the believers.'[220] And Muslims were promised victory and success if they avoided greed and stood disciplined in their cause: 'How many of the Prophets fought (in Allah's way), and with them (fought) large bands of godly men? But they never lost heart if they met with disaster in Allah's way, nor did they weaken (in will) nor give in. And Allah loves those who are firm and steadfast.'[221] To be sure, these lessons and precepts were largely drawn on in subsequent battles of early Islamic history, most of which resulted in military success via the fervent spirit and discipline of Muslim armies. Merely two years after Muhammad's demise, not merely insurrections of the apostates were quelled,[222] but well-equipped and highly organised armies

217 Q. 3:170.

218 See generally, Nafziger, supra note 100, 8–9; S. Akhtar, *Islam as Political Religion: The Future of an Imperial Faith* (New York: Routledge, 2011) 116–118; Gabriel, supra note 114, 119ff.

219 Q. 3:139.

220 Q. 3:166.

221 Q. 3:146.

222 Because Islamic unification was initially linked to Muhammad's leadership, almost immediately after the Prophet's death the Muslim community was beset by divisions, among which the most important split was to emerge between the Sunnis and Shiites on the issue of legitimate leadership. Further, as Muhammad's charismatic leadership played a cohesive role for Muslims, in the wake of his demise some tribes returned to their pre-Islamic beliefs, while some others refused to pay tax to, or to be ruled by, the

of the Byzantine and Persian empires were defeated by the Muslims. Likewise, during the course of the seventh and eighth centuries, Muslims conquered vast territories including Jerusalem, Damascus, Antioch, Aleppo, and, further in the north, marched into the borders of the Byzantine Empire, and into the heartlands of the Sassanid Empire, and then up to the Caspian. It is to be briefly noted that the pale of Islam would later encompass Basra and Isfahan, whence it expanded into central Asia, reaching to Afghanistan and large portions of the Indian subcontinent. Having brought the North African coast under control, Muslim armies also crossed the Strait of Gibraltar, spreading Muslim power into southern Europe, the Iberian Peninsula, wherein Islamic dominion lasted more than seven centuries until the fall of Grenada in 1492. [223]

Revisiting the above theme of distinct Medinan attitude towards warfare, it should be noted that as the strength of the Islamic polity grew further and the opposition of the pagans continued, Islam progressively acquired a more assertive character. Lethal force was henceforth unambiguously permitted to ward off aggression and to vindicate religious rights against persecuting pagans. As An-Na'im posits, the Medinan verses and the related Sunna referring to warfare must be considered within their historical context in which the survival and cohesion of the vulnerable Muslim community had to be secured against the unrelenting violent opposition.[224] Nevertheless, having started with the concern to secure the well-being of the burgeoning Muslim community, the doctrine of military jihad came to include the goal of expanding the Muslim sphere of influence. As discussed in the next chapter, it is these two distinguishable positions on the doctrine of military jihad – one laying stress on defensive measures, the other exhorting Muslims to fight when necessary – that led commentators to disagree on the precise contours of Islamic warfare. It is to be briefly noted here that the Muslim struggle against the pagans increasingly exceeded the bounds of self-defensive force to include the aim of invading the enemy's homes to stop their 'ungodly mischief',[225] and of preventing their anticipated attacks.[226] This notwithstanding,

new leadership. Rising to the challenge, the first caliph, Abu Bakr (d. 634), largely spent his reign fighting the so-called 'wars of apostasy' (*ridda*) to forge the Muslim reunion. And under the skilful military leadership of Khalid ibn-al-Walid, the secessionist tribes were eventually reduced to submission. See N. N. Ayubi, *Over-Stating the Arab State: Politics and Society in the Middle East* (New York: I.B. Tauris, 2008) 55ff; I. M. Zeitlin, *The Historical Muhammad* (London: Polity, 2008) 162ff.

223 See further, M. J. Akbar, *The Shade of Swords: Jihad and the Conflict between Islam and Christianity* (London: Routledge, 2002) 2ff; *cf.* C. E. Bosworth, 'The Formation of the Early Islamic Polity and Society: General Characteristics' in: M. A. Al-Bakhit; S. M. Cissoko, *History of Humanity: From the Seventh Century to the Sixteenth Century* Vol. IV (New York: Routledge, 2000) 271ff.

224 An-Na'im, supra note 154, 144.

225 See M. Abo-Kazleh, 'Rethinking International Relations Theory in Islam: Toward a More Adequate Approach' (2006) 5 *Turkish Journal of International Relations* 4, 41–44.

226 Haleem, supra note 32, 113.

as a matter of custom, before directly engaging in hostilities with the pagans, the Prophet would first send an official letter to the polytheistic tribes inviting them to embrace Islam.[227] Tradition has it that Muhammad sent letters of invitation to such personalities as Heraclius, the ruler of the Byzantine Empire; Chosroes, the Persian king;[228] Negus, the ruler of Abyssinia; and Muqawqis, the ruler of Egypt.[229] Military jihad was launched against those who did not acknowledge Islam as their faith.[230]

Viewed in this light, it may be seen that the growing community of Muslims, by degrees, moved away from the attitude of peaceful compromise perforce with the opponents and detractors of their faith. What is more, having experienced untoward events with the pagans and Scriptuaries of Medina (e.g. collaboration with the enemy),[231] the Quran advised caution against non-Muslims by demanding

227 Drawing on an analogy between the ancient Roman and Islamic customs of warfare, Khadduri notes that '[l]ike the *jus fetiale* of ancient Rome, which required that a set of rules must be followed so that war would be lawful, the jihad was regarded as lawful only if it were proceeded by an invitation to adopt Islam. If the enemy refused (or if they were People of the Book and refused to pay the poll tax), fighting would become lawful for the Muslims'. Khadduri, supra note 34, 95.

228 Muslim tradition contrasts the deference shown by Heraclius with the arrogance displayed by the Persian ruler toward the invitation to embrace Islam. Heraclius is praised for his deeply respectful behaviour in handling the matter, and for his assumed acceptance of Muhammad as the awaited messenger of God, which (albeit his eventual refusal to submit to the new faith) was read to have been an important gesture that legitimized Muhammad's divine call. See *Hadith of Bukhari*, Vol. I, Hadith 1:6; N. M. E. Cheikh, *Byzantium Viewed by the Arabs* (Cambridge, MA: Harvard University Press, 2004) 39–47.

229 Some scholars challenged the authenticity of the letters believed to have been sent by the Prophet on the ground that the letters contained some anachronistic items. For further details see, R. B. Serjeant, 'Early Arabic Prose' in: A. F. L. Beeston *et al* (eds.), *Arabic Literature to the End of the Umayyad Period* (Cambridge: Cambridge University Press, 1983) 141ff.

230 Mirza, supra note 109, 77. The duty of waging war against the pagans was, among others, stipulated in the following verses: Q. 9:36; Q. 47:4; Q. 9:5.

231 Muhammad, for instance, cancelled a peace treaty concluded with the Jewish clan of Qurayzah on the basis that the latter had entered into secret agreements with the enemies of Muslims, and at one point they were about to attack Muslim forces from the rear during the siege of Medina laid by the Meccan confederacy in 627. As soon as the Meccan threat was over, the Prophet decided to settle scores with the Qurayzah largely because he wanted to secure his power base and set an example for current and potential enemies. He instituted a siege against the Qurayzah, which lasted for 25 days and resulted in the surrender of the latter. In consonance with the prevalent custom of the era and with the consent of the Qurayzah, an arbiter was appointed to decide upon the fate of the Qurayzah. The decision had drastic consequences in that it was decreed that all men of Qurayzah were to be executed for treachery and their women and children to be sold as slaves. See Watt, supra note 185, 171–173; Aslan, supra note 159, 90ff. After the elimination of the Qurayzah no notable Jewish presence was left in Medina; but, as Watt observes, insofar as, the Jews avoided open or covert hostility towards Muslims, 'Muhammad allowed them to live in Medina unmolested.' Ibid. 174–175.

Muslims not to take unbelievers for allies,[232] nor to consider the Jews and Christians as their *awliya* (supporters or guides).[233] Such a cautionary attitude was largely due to the spatial and temporal necessity for Muslims to keep vigilant against possible threats emerging from the competing groups or faiths of the time. This did not imply that the Quran denied the significance of the monotheistic religions preceding Islam, or the relatively privileged status of the Scriptuaries.[234] Nor did the Quran deem the Scriptuaries a monolithic entity: 'Not all of them are alike', the Quran declared, 'of the People of the Book are a portion that stand (for the right); they rehearse the signs of Allah all night long, and they prostrate themselves in adoration.'[235] A parallel verse similarly read: 'And there are, certainly, among the People of the Book, those who believe in Allah, in the revelation to you, and in the revelation to them . . .: They will not sell the signs of Allah for a miserable gain! For them is a reward with their Lord. . .'[236] Finally, the Quran encapsulated the principles of tolerance and equality for all nations: 'O mankind! We created you from a single (pair) of a male and a female, and made you into nations and tribes, that ye may know each other (not that ye may despise each other). . .'[237]

Taken together, it is evident that the sword verses of Medina must be subjected to judicious interpretation, one that takes into account the overall ethical framework of Islam and the broader socio-political context within which some of the consequential warlike precepts had taken shape. Admittedly, however, as the Meccan and Medinan periods represent different approaches to military jihad, the question of whether Islamic warfare may exceed the confines of self-defensive aggression to further incorporate the vindication of rights and the pursuit of Islamic supremacy through military force still stands unanswered satisfactorily.

As will be seen in the following chapter, there are mainly two schools of thought, both of which employ an exegetical method of appealing to a select set of injunctions found in the Quran and the tradition with a view to bolstering a specific

232 The Quran reads: 'O ye who believe! Take not for allies unbelievers rather than believers: do ye wish to offer Allah an open proof against yourselves?' Q. 4:144.

233 The wording of the Quran is: 'O ye who believe! Take not the Jews and the Christians for your allies and protectors; they are but allies and protectors to each other. And he amongst you that turns to them (for protection) is of them. . . .' Q. 5:51.

234 According to the Quran: 'And . . . We sent Jesus. . ., confirming the Law that had come before him: We sent him the Gospel: therein was guidance and light, and confirmation of the Law that had come before him: a guidance and an admonition to those who fear Allah.' Q. 5:46.

235 Ibn Ishaq notes that this verse came in reference to those People of the Book who eventually embraced Islam. See Ishaq, supra note 63, 262. However, this claim does explain the language of the Quran that clearly refers to 'the People of the Book', who, had they converted to Islam, would no longer have been considered as such, but simply as 'Muslims'.

236 Q. 3:199. For a similar Quranic message, see Q. 2:62.

237 Q. 49:13.

approach to warfare, and thereby to undercutting any countervailing stance. Clearly, a selective collection and narrow interpretation of authoritative sources, with the main goal of promoting a dogmatic, one-sided view of military jihad, may not be said to contribute to revealing the contextual realities of the Islamic just war tradition – which, as the pages that follow will show in detail, has never followed a linear historical evolution and practical application.

3 Shades of Jihad: Moderate and Radical Interpretations

Introduction

As the previous chapter demonstrated, there has hitherto been no commanding interpretation of the doctrine of jihad. The selective reading of, and reference to, authoritative sources has similarly contributed little to the emergence of a coherent narrative on the defining features of Islamic just war. Rather, the prevalent insistence on laying the foundations for a monolithic theory of militant jihad often led Muslim scholars to avoid relative (non-absolute) positions, contingent on such contextual considerations as the socio-political and cultural characteristics of diverse, ever-fluid Muslim societies. Muslim scholars who draw an antithetical distinction between defensive and offensive forms of jihad generally rely upon 'cherry-picked' verses, traditions, facts, or doctrines to advance their viewpoint – often at the expense of a more subtle, refined representation of Islamic use of force discourse. Although students of Islamic just war tradition stand for a broader spectrum of political stances, ranging from traditionalist to radical, from revivalist to liberal, from progressive to reformist, and from critical to moderate (or perhaps an amalgamation of some of these) modes of thinking, it is, as stressed earlier, possible to identify two main streams of thought on the justifiability and legitimacy of invoking military jihad, namely the moderate and radical schools. This chapter will first provide a critical, general overview of some of the pivotal ideas advanced by these schools of thought; it will then proceed with the presentation of a more nuanced picture of the military jihad doctrine.

I. The Moderate School of Thought

The first of these schools (which, for lack of a better term, may be called the 'moderate school') vehemently posits that military force in the cause of God is approved by the Quran and prophetic tradition only for self-defensive purposes. Muslims are accordingly empowered to wage warfare merely against those who fight or take up arms against them. It follows that Muslims may not initiate hostilities or launch aggressive campaigns to aggrandise their power and wealth. Sheikh al-Zuhili, in this context, categorically writes that 'warfare is only for defence, to prevent injustice and fend off aggression'.[1] Defensive lethal force, however, is by no means unlimited for the proponents of this view; it must not only accord with the dictates of humanitarian concerns and principles discussed earlier, but it must also be discontinued when the opposing party desists, or oppression comes to a halt.[2]

Proponents of the moderate school principally seek to prove that at the core of Islam lies the notion of peace that forms the very essence of Islamic just war. Being part of this mode of thinking, Sufi scholars, for example, hold that God is the source of peace,[3] a state that neither springs from the absence of warfare, nor from the defeat of the enemy. Sufis view military jihad as an anomalous condition on the ground that Islamic faith prioritises permanent personal and public peace, and not religio-political domination through brute force. To experience such peace, believers are said to undergo a process of continuous spiritual cleansing (inner jihad), and learn to coexist and collaborate with people of diverse ethnic, racial or religious backgrounds.[4] This accords with the view that Islam is a religion of respect and toleration, the chief proof of which is rooted in the plain message of the Quran: 'Let there be no compulsion in religion: truth stands out clear from error: whoever rejects evil and believes in Allah hath grasped the most trustworthy handhold that never breaks.'[5] For moderate or modernist Muslims, this verse is one of the mighty pillars of Islam, and is a scriptural confirmation that Islam constitutes a religion of broad-mindedness and toleration. The verse is hence argued to rebut the broad assertion that Islam has been a religion of the sword that spread through forced conversions.[6] In other words, since the non-compulsion principle is stressed to represent one of the cardinal tenets of Islam, the sweeping assumption that jihad merely connotes aggressive warfare or irrational violence is untenable.

1 S. al-Zuhili, 'Islam and International Law' (2005) 87 *International Review of the Red Cross* 269, 273. Al-Zuhili goes as far as to say that in early Islamic wars 'with Arabs, Persians or Romans, Muslims resorted to combat only in defence of their existence, to repel aggression, to empower themselves in order to raise the banner of freedom among all nations on an equal footing, to declare the absolute truth, namely servitude and submission to God alone, without any influence from an oppressive [and unjust] ruler. . .' Ibid. 271.

2 See generally, H. Zawati, *Is Jihad a Just War: War, Peace, and Human Rights under Islamic and Public International Law* (New York: The Edwin Mellen Press, 2001); N. Mohammad, 'The Doctrine of *Jihad*: An Introduction' (1985) 3 *Journal of Law and Religion* 381; J. Rehman, *Islamic State Practices, International Law and the Threat from Terrorism: A Critique of the 'Clash of Civilisations' in the New World Order* (Oxford: Hart Publishing, 2005); H. A. Haleem *et al* (eds.), *The Crescent and the Cross* (London: Macmillan Press, 1998).

3 See Q. 59:23.

4 See A. A. Engineer, *Islam in Contemporary World* (New Delhi: New Dawn Press Group, 2007) 142.

5 Q. 2:256.

6 See M. Cook, *The Koran: A Very Short Introduction* (New York: Oxford University Press, 2000) 35ff; A. Y. Ali, *The Meaning of the Holy Qur'an*, 11th ed. (Beltsville: Amana Publications, 2008) 106.

If forced conversions and suppression of non-conformist views or belief systems do not sit comfortably with the general tenor of Islam, then the imperial conquests of Islamic polities over the course of history must be considered as predominantly motivated by political and economic considerations. As is well known, Islamic States came to dominate a wide array of foreign lands, not through defensive wars, but largely through wars fought to establish Islam's political, economic, cultural, or religious ascendancy.[7] Yet this phenomenon may well be explained away by moderates as the 'mundane practice' of rulers who claimed to have acted in furtherance of the religious cause. Indeed, the essential narrative of those stressing the peaceful facet of Islam is based on the postulate that military jihad may principally be invoked as an exceptional tool to thwart aggressive or oppressive assaults mounted against Muslims. Warlike measures must consequently not go beyond the objective of defending the pale of Islam wherein justice and equity should prevail for all people.[8] The spread of Islam's message through forceful means, within this understanding, is to be viewed as a practical upshot rather than the normative state of Islam. In fact, the 'non-compulsion' norm may readily be supported by a parallel verse that reads: 'If it had been the Lord's will, they would all have believed. All who are on earth, wilt thou then compel mankind, against their will, to believe?'[9] This verse conspicuously rejects conversions imposed upon non-Muslims by means of military force, as forced belief may not stem from the exercise of free will through which, Islam holds, humankind would eventually be held to judgement.

The moderate narrative of jihad thus appears to accentuate the spiritual aspect of the doctrine – reducing its warlike component to the exceptional, necessary, and proportionate use of force undertaken to fend off unjustified harm and injustice. The salient purpose of martial jihad is thus argued to be the interception of aggression or challenging persecution through temperate armed action geared towards maintaining or reconstructing the peace. To stress the notion that Islam has been a religion of peace, rather than that of the sword, moderate scholars, including An-Naim, Rehman, Zawati, and Shah,[10] have in effect laid stress on pacific verses and corresponding prophetic traditions

7 It is to be reiterated that only within the first two decades following the Prophet's death, Arab armies conquered vast areas including Syria, Jerusalem, Persia, Iraq, and Egypt. In the first century of Islam, Muslims made astounding conquests towards the heart of Byzantium to the north, India and present-day Afghanistan to the east, and North Africa and Spain to the west. Where Muslim rule had been established, poll and land taxes were levied on non-Muslim subjects (of tolerated monotheist religions) that did not embrace Islam. See further D. E. Arzt, 'The Treatment of Religious Dissidents under Classical and Contemporary Islamic Law' in: J. Witte; J. D. Vyver (eds.), *Religious Human Rights in Global Perspective: Religious Perspectives*, Vol. I (The Hague: Kluwer Law International, 1996) 412.

8 See Zawati, supra note 2, 4; Rehman, supra note 2, 70.

9 Q. 10:99.

10 A. A. An-Na'im, *Islam and the Secular State: Negotiating the Future of Shari'a* (Cambridge, MA: Harvard University Press, 2008); Rehman, supra note 2; Zawati, supra note 2; N. A.

rather than on classical secondary sources produced during the heyday of Islamic civilisation.[11]

Naturally, moderates denounce wanton violence or acts of terrorism committed in the name of Islam by such extremist groups as al-Qaeda, Boko Haram, or al-Shabab, maintaining that wars of aggression in general, and terrorism in particular, are diametrically opposed to the very essence of the Quran, which plainly proclaims: 'If anyone slew a person – unless it be for murder or for spreading mischief in the land – it would be as if he slew the whole people: and if anyone saved a life, it would be as if he saved the life of the whole people.'[12] Cognate arguments are also advanced to denounce suicide bombings, which often claim many innocent lives and damage civilian property.

In fact, sanctity of life is correctly noted to occupy a central position in Islam; the Quran commands Muslims to 'take not life, which Allah hath made sacred, except by way of justice and law'.[13] Underscoring the inviolability of human life, Kamali writes that 'since life is a God-given gift, and not the creation of its bearer, no one has the right to destroy it. This is why suicide is forbidden in Islam without any exception whatsoever.'[14] Kamali's point may be buttressed by the following *hadith* reported by Bukhari: 'Whoever commits suicide . . . will be punished.'[15] The prophet was recorded to have added that: 'A man was inflicted with wounds and he committed suicide, and so Allah said: "My slave has caused death on himself hurriedly, so I forbid Paradise for him."'[16]

Clearly, such arguments are not without merit. It is thus difficult to disagree with the moderates on this issue, since terrorist atrocities do flagrantly violate the above-mentioned Islamic principles of proportionality, necessity, and distinction by randomly maiming and killing defenceless civilians, or by deliberately arousing fear of harm with intent to publicise a certain cause and force authorities to address issues of concern. Being victimised abominably, targets of terrorism are simply instrumentalised for a purportedly sacred objective. As elaborated upon earlier, even when there exist compelling reasons to employ armed force against allegedly corrupt national or international regimes, Islam imposes strict humanitarian restraints in the conduct of hostilities, such as the prohibition of

Shah, *Self-Defence in Islamic and International Law: Assessing Al-Qaeda and the Invasion of Iraq* (New York: Palgrave Macmillan, 2008).

11 Guellali points out that the advocates of such views 'do not [generally] refer to the classical doctrines of *jihad* and prefer instead to cite the authoritative primary sources, [the] Quran and Sunna'. A. Guellali, 'Understanding the Discourses on Jihad in Islam' in: M. C. Bassiouni; A. Guellali (eds.), *Jihad and its Challenges to International and Domestic Law* (The Hague: Hague Academic Press, 2010) 59, 75.

12 Q. 5:32; Y. El-Ayouty, 'International Terrorism under the Law' (1999) 5 *ILSA Journal of International and & Comparative Law* 485, 490.

13 Q. 6:151.

14 M. H. Kamali, 'Jihad and the Interpretation of the Quran: Contextualising Islamic Tradition' in: Bassiouni, supra note 11, 39, 51.

15 *Hadith* Reported by al-Bukhari, *Hadith of Bukhari,* Vol. II, Hadith 2:445.

16 Ibid.

indiscriminate and disproportionate use of violence against civilian life, limb, and property. A Muslim soldier is neither allowed to combat inhumanely, nor is he entitled to take his own life[17] or the lives of those who are not directly responsible for the conditions he seeks to alter; this is so, even when recourse to indiscriminate violence might produce marked political gains.[18] It must be borne in mind that Islam does not even permit the destruction of the environment, let alone the use of murderous violence directed at defenceless civilians with an objective to gain an edge over the enemy. Since acts of terror, whether committed in reaction to oppression or in a bid to defend Muslims, often harm individuals who have no direct bearing on what has been opposed, they may readily qualify as murder – a violation of the right to life, which ranks as the most significant right in Islam. The Quran not only equates the killing of an innocent person to killing all humankind,[19] but it manifestly prohibits taking life, except in cases of self-defence or when done in accordance with due process of Islamic law.[20] The sanctity of life had likewise been accentuated by the Prophet who denounced murder as a heinous crime, which he put on a par with polytheism. A tradition ascribed to Muhammad reads thus: 'The greatest sins are to associate something with God and to kill human beings.'[21] Another relevant tradition condemns suicide in unequivocal terms: 'One who throws himself off a mountain cliff and kills himself, he will be doing the same to himself perpetually in Hell . . . And one

17 The Quran states not to 'kill (or destroy) yourselves; for verily Allah hath been to you most merciful'. Q. 4:29. Yet it must be noted that the legitimacy of suicide attacks, particularly within the context of Palestinian suicide missions against Israel, has been subject to heated controversy. While most scholars maintain that suicide operations cannot be part of jihad, since this would be at odds with Sharia principles, some radical religious authorities in Sunni Islam, including Sheik Yussuf Al-Qaradhawi of the Muslim Brotherhood, Abd Al-Aziz Al-Rantisi of Hamas and Muhammad Sayyed Tantawi of Al-Azhar, generally consider these attacks legitimate so long as they are undertaken for the benefit of the Islamic community, and the intention behind them is to harm the enemy rather than civilians. For more on this debate, see The Middle East Media Research Institute, 'Debating the Religious, Political and Moral Legitimacy of Suicide Bombings Part I: The Debate over Religious Legitimacy'. Available at: http://www.memri.org/report/en/0/0/0/0/0/0/451.htm#_edn8; Guellali, supra note 11, 83–85.

18 As Khadduri points out, Muslim jurists concur that 'non-combatants who did not take part in fighting, such as women, children, monks and hermits, the aged, blind, and insane', are to be excluded from molestation unless they have actively aided the enemy during hostilities. Khadduri cites an example, originally recorded by Ibn Hisham, wherein the Prophet condones an old man's killing due to his provision of intelligence to enemy forces during the Battle of Hunayn. See M. Khadduri, *War and Peace in the Law of Islam* (Baltimore: Johns Hopkins Press, 1955) 103–104.

19 Q. 5:32.

20 The Quran states that 'take not life, which Allah hath made sacred, except by way of justice and law' (Q. 6:151).

21 Cited in: M. I. Ashraf, *Islamic Philosophy of War and Peace* (Bloomington: iUniverse, 2008) 110; A. A. Mawdudi, *Human Rights in Islam* (Leicester: The Islamic Foundation, 2002) 17.

who kills himself with a weapon, he will be piercing his body with it perpetually in Hell.'[22]

Viewed from this perspective, Islam may be argued to disallow unwarranted killing regardless of one's racial, religious, national, social, sexual, or tribal background; the injunction against unjustified deprivation of life thus applies to all human beings.[23] What is more, in spite of crude attempts to construct inextricable affinities between Islam (as a religious and cultural practice) and terrorism (a concept that remains legally undefined), the majority of Muslims carrying out terroristic atrocities mainly pursue political (and not predominantly religious) objectives.[24] Indeed, any serious attempt at surveying the root causes of terrorism committed by Muslims is likely to establish that Islamic militancy largely stems from specific grievances, as opposed to general hatred felt towards the Western lifestyle, and that Muslim resentment has not been about 'what the West is, but what the West does'.[25] By the same token, there are often unsatisfactory political and economic policies, at national and international levels, which provoke recourse to violence purportedly under the banner of jihad.[26] While there is no gainsaying that politico-economic and religious causes may intertwine, there is no Islamic norm authorising or condoning indiscriminate killing on religious grounds.

22 Khatib al-Tabrizi, *Mishkat al-Masabih,* Vol. II, *Hadith* No. 3451, cited in: M. H. Kamali, *Shari'ah Law: An Introduction* (Oxford: Oneworld Publications, 2008) 284.

23 See Mawdudi, supra note 21, 17.

24 Since the second half of the last century, religiously motivated terroristic violence is established to have been less common than its political counterpart. For instance, political violence employed by such organised groups as the Tamil Tigers in Sri Lanka, the IRA in Northern Ireland and ETA in Spain had been more frequent than religious violence committed by radical religious groups. See M. C. Bassiouni, 'Evolving Approaches to Jihad: From Self-Defence to Revolutionary and Regime-Change Political Violence' (2008) 8 *Chicago Journal of International Law* 119, 122. In fact, modern terrorism, as emerged in the late 1960s and 1970s, largely resulted from ethnonationalist tensions. Religiously motivated terrorism, however, essentially gained momentum in the early 1980s, particularly when the architects of the Iranian revolution endeavoured to export their revolution across the region. For an analysis, see J. M. Koh, *Suppressing Terrorist Financing and Money* (New York: Springer, 2006) 3ff.

25 M. S. Berger, 'Jihad and Counter-Jihad: Western European Legal Responses to Islamic Militancy' in: Bassiouni, supra note 11, 229, 232.

26 Studies indicate that economic and political underdevelopment is one of the chief determinants in driving (particularly young) people to violence and terrorism. This argument must be qualified, though, for in some cases radicals may well come from wealthy, well-educated backgrounds – as in the case of Bin Laden. Be that as it may, most such privileged individuals similarly take issue with the general state of economic and political conditions, and at times consider violence as one legitimate means to challenge the national and/or international status quo. See generally, T. Bjørgo (ed.), *Root Causes of Terrorism: Myths, Reality and Ways Forward* (New York: Routledge, 2005); A. V. Engeland-Nourai, 'The Challenge of Fragmentation of International Humanitarian Law' in: Bassiouni, supra note 11, 162ff; A. Pedahzu (ed.), *Root Causes of Suicide Terrorism: The Globalization of Martyrdom* (New York: Routledge, 2006).

Nevertheless, some militant Muslim non-State actors draw on warmongering rhetoric to stir random and disproportionate violence in furtherance of a particular ideology. Due to the superiority of States in conventional military forces and technology, these groups often avoid direct military confrontation, invoking instead such asymmetric means of violence as terrorism to target States. Such groups are often motivated by politico-economic deprivation, various forms of injustice and exclusion, feelings of alienation, powerlessness, and indignation felt towards national authorities and hegemonic powers.[27] Radical armed networks are thus chiefly reinforced by the failures of national and international bodies in providing such values as democratic governance, political participation, accountability and transparency, non-discrimination, socio-economic development, and equality between individuals and nations.[28]

Consequently, as the moderate school of thought rightly emphasises, caution must be exercised against sweeping attempts at sacralising terrorist atrocities purportedly committed in the name of religion.[29] Any attempt at eliminating the root causes of terrorism in the cloak of religion must above all consider adopting concrete measures to advance human rights and democratic values, and to address economic and social inequities at domestic and international levels. It is also imperative that dominant Western nations, in particular the US, must cease pursuing their economic interests to the detriment of vital values and principles to which they often pay lip service, i.e. democracy, transparency, human rights, equality, self-determination, and security. Some of the most atrocious terrorist offences are committed in response to such insincerity on democratic governance, economic development, political independence, and human rights in Muslim societies.[30] Western nations need not only to follow consistent and fair policies in

27 Usama bin Laden, for instance, often stressed the need for Muslims to expel the United States from the lands of Islam, because he found the United States responsible for plundering the riches of Muslim lands, 'dictating to its rulers, humiliating its people, terrorizing its neighbours, and turning its bases in the [Arab] Peninsula into a spearhead through which to fight the neighbouring Muslim peoples'. U. bin Laden, *Jihad against Jews and Crusaders: World Islamic Front Statement* (23 February 1998). Available at: http://www.fas.org/irp/world/para/docs/980223-fatwa.htm.

28 For an analysis of how socio-economic development, democracy, and literacy relate to terrorist violence, see generally Bjørgo, supra note 26.

29 As Esposito poignantly notes, 'many Christians and Jews regard their traditions as committed to peace and social justice but are quick to believe that other traditions and peoples (such as Islam and Muslims) are more militant. Our wars are defensive and not offensive, "just wars" against aggressors. "Their" wars follow a tradition of holy war.' J. L. Esposito, *The Islamic Threat: Myth or Reality*? 3rd ed. (New York: Oxford University Press, 1992) 279.

30 Ramadan rightly points out that 'for years, the United States and Europe invested heavily in protecting their own economic interests, stability, and security in the Arab world. [Hence], if an equation that contained no unknowns (profit, stability, security) could be insured by dictatorships (like those in Tunisia and Egypt) or by kings who swore by strict, conservative Islam (as in Saudi Arabia), then such regimes were considered de facto reliable allies.' Ramadan concludes that such a hypocritical and self-interested

volatile States like Palestine, Iraq, and Afghanistan, but to desist from supporting authoritarian and corrupt regimes in the Arab world.[31] In fact, following 9/11, the then US president, George W. Bush, acknowledged the need for fairer Western policies in the Middle East that do not put economic interests above the rights and freedoms of people in the region:

> Sixty years of Western nations excusing and accommodating the lack of freedom in the Middle East did nothing to make us safe, because in the long run, stability cannot be purchased at the expense of liberty. As long as the Middle East remains a place where freedom does not flourish, it will remain a place of stagnation, resentment and violence ready for export. And with the spread of weapons that can bring catastrophic harm to our country and to our friends, it would be reckless to accept the *status quo*.[32]

Although the speech did not admit any direct responsibility of the Western powers in creating or sponsoring authoritarian rulers in the region, it nevertheless stressed the need to promote democratic values including the rule of law, human rights, and political accountability to alleviate the plight of Muslim societies. Certainly, sincere national and international efforts to enhance such values are likely to lessen reactionary violence anchored in religious rhetoric.[33] To summarise the above, contemporary manifestations of military jihad may not be duly understood without reference to modern politico-economic context, wherein inequality between individuals and nations is largely generated as a result of callous power politics. This, in turn, contributes in great measure to the escalation of sectarian violence committed by a growing number of embittered Muslims.[34] The solution

approach was demonstrated through the 'uneven response to the Arab uprisings by the US and European governments'. T. Ramadan, *Islam and the Arab Awakening* (Oxford: Oxford University Press, 2012) 54.

31 For a discussion of this point, M. Jansen, 'Terrorism is a Response to Western Hypocrisy' in: P. A. Winters (ed.), *Islam: Opposing Viewpoints* (San Diego: Greenhaven Press, Inc., 1995) 168.

32 G. W. Bush, 'Remarks on the 20th Anniversary of the National Endowment for Democracy' 6 November 2003, National Archives and Records Administration, *Public Papers of the Presidents of the United States: George W. Bush* (Washington: Government Printing Office, 2003) 1473–1474.

33 Also, as emphasised by the former UN Secretary General, any fight against terrorism must be conducted in compliance with the fundamental principles of human rights. Hence, 'while States must take measures to protect their citizens against terror, they must also recognise that security cannot be achieved at the expense of human rights. On the contrary, stronger protection of and respect for human rights, democracy and social justice are integral to the promotion of security.' Report of the Secretary-General on the work of the Organisation, A/57/1, 2002, para. 148. For parallel messages delivered by the UN Security Council, see UN Doc. S/RES/1456 (2003), para. 6; UN Doc. S/RES/1624 (2005), para. 4.

34 As Kelsay notes, 'almost all important discussions of jihad [conducted both by Sunni and Shiite scholars] over the last 150 years have stressed that it is a war in defense of

to the problem of violence committed in the name of jihad does not lie in undertaking equally irresponsible counter-violence, or blaming the religion itself, but in eradicating, or at least enfeebling, the breeding grounds for religious sectarianism.[35]

Revisiting the notion of whether Islam essentially aims at establishing personal and public peace – since it encompasses such humane principles as 'non-compulsion' in religion, peaceful tolerance, broad-mindedness, and patience and forbearance in the face of hardship, oppression or aggression – it may be said that modernists have felt compelled to offer a rationale for some of the belligerent (sword) verses that ostensibly sanction wars of conversion against polytheists. The so-called 'sword' verses, including Q. 9:5,[36] Q. 2:191,[37] Q. 9:123,[38] Q. 8:65[39] and Q.47:4,[40] do not indeed appear to readily square with the principles of non-compulsion and tolerance. As will be discussed in more detail below, it is largely on

Islamic values'. J. Kelsay, *Islam and War: A Study in Comparative Ethics* (Louisville: John Knox Press, 1993) 48. Cook also supports this point, noting that 'one of the factors binding globalist radical Muslims together is the shared belief that the entire world is united in a concerted effort to destroy Islam'. D. Cook, *Understanding Jihad* (London: University of California Press, 2005) 136.

35 As the UN Policy Working Group on Terrorism indicated, 'the protection and promotion of human rights under the rule of law is essential in the prevention of terrorism.' For 'terrorism often thrives in environments in which human rights are violated'; and 'terrorists may [readily] exploit human rights violations to gain support for their cause'. In light of such observations, the report's overall focus was consequently laid upon the significance of promoting respect for human rights at domestic and international levels for effective anti-terrorism strategies. See Report of the Policy Working Group on the United Nations and Terrorism A/57/273-S/2002/875, para. 26.

36 Q. 9:5 reads: 'But when the forbidden months are past, then fight and slay the pagans wherever ye find them, and lie in wait for them, and seize them, beleaguer them, and lie in wait for them in every stratagem (of war); but it they repent, and establish regular prayers and practice regular charity, then open the way for them: for Allah is oft-forgiving, most merciful.' It is to be noted that the so-called 'forbidden months' refer to a four-month period during which tribes were prohibited from warring among themselves. This period was important so that pilgrimage and trade could take place in a secure environment.

37 Q. 2:191 commands: 'And slay them wherever ye catch them, and turn them out from where they have Turned you out; for tumult and oppression are worse than slaughter; but fight them not at the Sacred Mosque, unless they (first) fight you there; but if they fight you, slay them. Such is the reward of those who suppress faith.'

38 Q. 9:123 reads: 'O ye who believe! Fight the unbelievers who gird you about, and let them find firmness in you: and know that Allah is with those who fear Him.'

39 This verse says: 'O Messenger! Rouse the Believers to the fight. If there are twenty amongst you, patient and persevering, they will vanquish two hundred: if a hundred, they will vanquish a thousand of the Unbelievers: for these are a people without understanding.' Q. 8:65.

40 According to Q. 47:4: 'Therefore, when ye meet the unbelievers (in fight), smite at their necks; at length, when ye have thoroughly subdued them, bind a bond firmly (on them): thereafter (is the time for) either generosity or ransom: until the war lays down its burdens. . .'

account of such injunctions that some jurists submit that the sword verses had cancelled all other earlier verses that called for tolerance, patience, compassion, and peace. In response, the moderates generally maintain that these warlike verses had never authorised lethal force against polytheists as a whole; rather, the Quran merely referred to those who openly assaulted or oppressed the Muslim community.[41] It is accordingly unjustified for Muslims to wage unprovoked wars against passive unbelievers, for there have to be legitimate grounds for Islamic warfare – like warding off aggression or preventing injustice or persecution. To borrow Sachedina's language, moderates thus argue that 'it is not unbelievers, as such, who are the object of force, but unbelievers who demonstrate their hostility to Islam by, for example, persecution of the Muslims'.[42]

In an effort to place the warlike verses in their historical context, moderates have further asserted that the application of these verses had been chiefly limited to pagan Arab tribes, who were implacably opposed to – or already at war with – the nascent Muslim community in Medina. The object of military jihad was therefore the suppression of hostile powers that actively sought to overpower the early Muslim community.[43] Under this reading of the Quran, the sword verses do not grant an unqualified right to kill the 'infidels'. In fact, moderates could further support their interpretation by referring to a Chapter 9 verse of the Quran, which enjoins Muslims from forming a league with 'pagans except those with whom . . . [Muslims] made a treaty'.[44] Arguably, if unqualified warfare against the pagans had indeed been the general order of the day, the said verse would never have been revealed – a point that will be revisited later.

To recapitulate the key teachings of the moderate school, it may be said that the works of this tradition largely focus on the spiritual and social aspects of the doctrine of jihad. Emphasising the principle of non-aggression, moderates generally maintain that only in cases of self-defence may Muslims resort to lethal force as a measure of last resort – subject to the rigorous humanitarian principles of necessity and proportionality. In terms of objective and coverage, the works of the moderate school essentially challenge the oversimplified claim that Islam has intimately been bound up with indiscriminate violence. While this school advances weighty arguments to shore up the point that Islamic laws of warfare have been compatible with contemporary humanitarian principles, what is in the main absent from the works of moderates is a critical analysis of the doctrinal and practical diversity within the Muslim tradition of just war. In the following pages,

41 See J. L. Esposito, *Unholy War: Terror in the Name of Islam* (New York: Oxford University Press, 2003) 68.

42 A. A. Sachedina, 'The Development of *Jihad* in Islamic Revelation and History' in: J. T. Johnson; J. Kelsay (eds.), *Cross, Crescent, and Sword* (London: Greenwood Press, 1990) 35, 43.

43 See S. H. Hashmi, 'War and Peace' in: S. H. Hashmi (ed.), *Islamic Political Ethics: Civil Society, Pluralism, and Conflict* (Princeton: Princeton University Press, 2002) 206–207.

44 Q. 9:7.

a critical portrayal of the opposing doctrinal position concerning the meaning and implications of jihad will be presented.

II. The Radical School of Thought

Classical works on jihad had paid scant attention to the spiritual dimension of the concept; what dominated scholarly debates, particularly until the 'closure of the gates of *ijtihad*', had mainly been the issue of legitimate force under various circumstances.[45] Nonetheless, because many modern Muslim commentators seek to distance Islam from any associations with sectarian violence, terrorism, or aggressive warfare, they, as highlighted above, often focus on the spiritual and other unwarlike facets of jihad. Denouncing both distorted militant rhetoric and acts of wanton violence, imbued with politico-religious motives, modern-minded jurists have attempted to revive Islam as a paradigm to promote peace, justice, and humanitarian values. To this end, some prominent Muslim jurists have gone so far as to argue that jihad is 'entirely peaceable and represents the exertion of spiritual warfare waged by the faithful against the lower, or evil, soul'.[46]

At the other end of the spectrum, however, have been those who reject a rigid dichotomy between offensive and defensive forms of jihad. It should be noted at the outset that these commentators, similar to the moderates, are generally unwilling to emphasise the diversity within the Islamic just war discourse; rather they, in large measure, selectively quote from the primary and secondary sources of Islamic law, and generally provide a one-sided reading thereof with intent to mobilise masses to fight against corruption, oppression, and imperial exploitation in the land of Islam.

This relatively radical streak of Islam customarily considers military jihad both as a right and a duty to defend and propagate the message of Islam. Although this line of thinking – which is not characterised by a monolithic dispensation – acknowledges peaceful facets of jihad, it essentially underscores the mandatory duty of protecting and promoting Islam by all means necessary. This, in effect, implies that the doctrine of jihad may assume a defensive or offensive posture, depending upon the dictates of a particular situation. As will be seen soon, the recurring theme in the works of radicals is that the early model of Islam may be reinstituted if Muslims display courage, piety, and determination to overwhelm the enemies of Islam. More precisely, the ultimate aim of replacing politically, economically, and morally impoverished Muslim societies with ideal socio-political orders (as experienced under the leadership or Muhammad and his immediate successors) underscores the rhetoric of radical thinkers and groups. Linked with this objective is the ambition to revive the institution of the caliphate in its uncorrupted form. The idea of reforming the caliphate to its pristine form is

45 See generally, R. Peters, *Jihad in Classical and Modern Islam* (Princeton: Markus Wiener Publishers, 1996) 79; Khadduri, supra note 18.

46 See Cook, supra note 34, 2.

based on the premise that originally the institution had a divinely guided mission of even-handedly applying the laws of God and developing or maintaining a just society. The sultanates or kingdoms, however, are argued to have subsequently moved away from this mission by engaging in untoward practices – including arbitrariness in making and applying the law, unfair taxation and public policies, and creating decadence in cultural and moral affairs.[47] The radical or revivalist reading of the doctrine of jihad hence incorporates an aspiration to restore the original, ideal Islamic polity headed by a caliph.

In contrast to moderates, radical commentators insist that jihad must, above all, be understood within its primary context of military striving. Accordingly, the principal roles of jihad are to fight, by all necessary means, against aggression, oppression, and injustice, and to promulgate Islam's universal message.[48] In modern times, such thinking has gained prominence due, in large part, to the colonial and postcolonial policies in the Muslim world. The calls for all modalities of jihad by Sayyid Ahmad of India, the Mahdist movement of Sudan, the Sanusiyya order of North Africa and the Wahhabiyya of Saudi Arabia constitute examples of universal appeals to struggle to break free of imperial incursions.[49] The stress laid on the need to employ all means necessary to deliver Islam from colonial and postcolonial shackles, and to reinstate the pristine Islam of early Muslims, was particularly pronounced in views advocated by Hasan al-Banna, founder of the Muslim Brotherhood.[50] Banna declared that members of the Brotherhood formed an army of liberation, or rather the troops of God, charged with the sacred duty of reviving the Islamic morality proper. While he accepted that jihad was part of *ijtihad*, which thus also comprised peaceful methods of exertion, he scorned those who reduced the role of jihad to peaceful methods alone. To Banna, military struggle (*qital*) captured the very essence of jihad, a duty that had to be shouldered by every Muslim individually in the same manner as other obligatory acts of

47 J. R. Willis, 'Jihad Fi Sabil Allah—its Doctrinal Basis in Islam and Some Aspects of its Evolution in Nineteenth-Century West Africa' (1967) 3 *Journal of African History* 395, 395–396.

48 S. K. Mirza, 'An Exegesis on *Jihad* in Islam' in: K. E. Shienbaum; J. Hasan (eds.), *Beyond Jihad: Critical Voices from Inside Islam* (Bethesda: Academica Press, 2006) 74, 85–86.

49 D. Brown, 'Martyrdom in Sunni Revivalist Thought' in: M. Cormack (ed.), *Sacrificing the Self: Perspectives on Martyrdom and Religion* (Oxford: Oxford University Press, 2001) 107, 109–110. See generally, A. Schimmel, *Islam in the Indian Subcontinent* (Leiden: Brill, 1980) 182ff; K. Searcy, *The Formation of the Sudanese Mahdist State—Ceremony and Symbols of Authority: 1882–1898* (Leiden: Brill, 2011); A. A. Ahmida, *The Making of Modern Libya: State Formation, Colonization, and Resistance* (Albany: State University of New York Press, 2009) 86ff.

50 The Muslim Brotherhood is one of the first highly organised politico-religious groups that has grown into a considerable network, covering also the diaspora in Europe. It is to be noted that Hamas is the Palestinian branch of the Muslim Brotherhood. Being distinguished by its relatively belligerent agenda, Hamas envisages a rather urgent duty of jihad against the enemies of Islam. See M. Levitt; D. Ross, *Hamas: Politics, Charity, and Terrorism in the Service of Jihad* (Virginia: Yale University Press, 2006) 30–32.

worship like the testimony of faith, praying, almsgiving, fasting, and pilgrimage. Abstention from military struggle, from this angle, constituted a major sin, as the victory of the Islamic cause was inextricably intertwined with the uninterrupted and dedicated effort of jihad.[51]

Arguments of this sort, as we shall see, have later figured prominently in the works of other radical thinkers. Mawdudi, a well-known representative of this intellectual tradition, posited that unity among Muslims is not based upon the mundane ties of race, history, geography, language, mutual interests, economics, or culture, but upon Islam and the commitment of believers to follow the path of God.[52] Mawdudi denies the possibility of any positive change in Muslim societies, unless the evil agents of the *jahiliyyah* (i.e. the pre-Islamic ignorance, immorality, and barbarism of Arabia) are removed from their positions of power, whereby they propagate sacrilegious values and practices.[53] Jihad, the argument runs, must accordingly be launched to wipe out all un-Islamic systems, and to re-establish pious polities instead,[54] because Muslims are not to accept the bondage of unrighteous regimes, rather they are obliged to invoke jihad as a revolutionary tool to transform the *status quo*, and propel humanity towards greater peace, liberty, and moral achievement. Hence, reminiscent of the Marxist rhetoric, Mawdudi regards Islam as a *revolutionary* force to free humankind of tyranny and immorality:

> Islam is a revolutionary ideology which seeks to alter the social order of the entire world and rebuild it in conformity with its own tenets and ideals. 'Muslims' is the title of that 'International Revolutionary Party' organized by Islam to carry out its revolutionary programme. '*Jihad*' refers to that revolutionary struggle and utmost exertion which the Islamic Nation/Party brings into play in order to achieve this objective . . .[55]

Syed Qutb, whose views continue to inspire such militant groups as the Taliban and al-Qaeda, represents a more radical conception of Islam.[56] Strongly influenced by Mawdudi and the influential thirteenth-century thinker Ibn Taymiyya, Qutb avers that the modern world has been plagued by pre-Islamic ignorance

51 R. P. Mitchell, *The Society of the Muslim Brothers* (Oxford: Oxford University Press, 1969) 207–208; Brown, supra note 49, 111.

52 C. J. Adams, 'Mawdudi and the Islamic State' in: J. L. Esposito (ed.), *Voices of Resurgent Islam* (New York: Oxford University Press, 1983) 103.

53 Ibid. 102.

54 Translation from Mawdudi Al-*Jihad* fi'l-Islam, cited in: S. V. R. Nasr, *Mawdudi and the Making of Islamic Revivalism* (New York: Oxford University Press, 1996) 83.

55 A. A. Mawdudi, 1997b. '*Jihad* fi Sabilillah' 3–9; cited in: D. Zeidan, *The Resurgence of Religion: A Comparative Study of Selected Themes in Christian and Islamic Fundamentalist Discourses* (Boston: Brill, 2003) 237. It must be noted that over the years the radical position of Mawdudi softened. In 1939, he declared that the military form of jihad should be a weapon of last resort to achieve victory for Islam. See Nasr, supra note 54, 74.

56 Esposito, supra note 29, 143.

(*jahiliyyah*), which is 'based on rebellion against God's sovereignty on earth'.[57] The establishment of God's sovereignty on earth through the abolishment of man's dominion (i.e. 'taking away of sovereignty from the usurper to revert it to God'), and the enforcement of the Sharia instead of man-made laws may not be readily achieved by peaceful means alone. This is because those who usurp the supremacy of God, according to Qutb, would not give up their domination solely through preaching; if this had been possible, the task of establishing God's law on earth would have been easy for the prophets of all times.[58] Hence, in order to free humankind from servitude to anyone other than God and secure God's supremacy over all nations, both preaching and military jihad must be employed.[59] Islam is not a 'defensive movement', claims Qutb; on the contrary, it has always been 'a movement to wipe out tyranny and to introduce true freedom to mankind'. He thus scorns those scholars who are apologetic and defensive while discussing the implications of jihad.[60] Qutb's intellectual reaction does indeed stand in stark contradiction to that of 'apologetic scholars' who, in an effort to rebuff the mainstream Western conception of Islam's purportedly aggressive nature, generally adopt a defensive posture to meet the criticisms or calumnies directed against Islam. Qutb's stance radically denounces the legacy of imperialism – with all its residual institutions or practices – and the 'condescending' Western attitude towards the Orient in general, and Islam in particular. Qutb was one of the staunchest voices to defy the moderate Muslim position of solely stressing the non-belligerent features of the Islamic just war tradition; he argued that any divinely ordained system had in fact 'a God-given right to step forward and take control of the political authority so that it may establish the Divine system on earth'.[61] To him, therefore, the doctrine of jihad could legitimately go beyond the contours of peaceful propagation of the faith to encompass the sword as an instrument of fighting worldly corruption and liberating humankind.

Of course, the debate over whether military jihad could merely be defensive or whether it could assume an offensive role is an old one. Classical scholars, too, had differed on the subject: for example, while al-Thawri and Abu Hanifah posited that fighting against non-believers was restricted to wars of self-defence alone, al-Sarakhsi argued that Quranic injunctions on military jihad had been revealed in stages, the last of which commanded Muslims to exalt Islam over other faiths or

57 S. Qutb, *Milestones* (SIME E-Publishing, 2005) 5; *cf.* I. M. Abu-Rabi, *Intellectual Origins of Islamic Resurgence in the Modern Arab World* (Albany: State University of New York Press, 1996) 195.

58 Qutb, supra note 57, 52; *cf.* Y. Y. Haddad, 'Sayyid Qutb: Ideologue of Islamic Revival' in: Esposito, supra note 52, 84–87.

59 Qutb, supra note 57, 52–53.

60 Qutb disparagingly viewed apologetic scholars as spiritually and mentally defeated 'by the wily attacks of the Orientalists, who distort the concept of Islamic *Jihad*'. Ibid. 55; Abu-Rabi, supra note 57, 193–194.

61 Qutb, supra note 57, 68–69; D. Bukay, *From Muhammad to bin Laden: Religious and Ideological Sources of the Homicide Bombers Phenomenon* (New Brunswick: Transaction Publishers, 2008) 223–224.

ideologies and subdue the pagans. Similar to al-Sarakhsi, al-Shafi'i opined that jihad became a military obligation to be undertaken by every single capable man, save when there were sufficient forces to ensure that polytheists turned to Islam and the scriptuaries paid the poll tax to the Muslim State.[62]

As alluded to earlier, the modern version of this radical streak survived, notably in discussions over the liberation of the Muslim world from the shackles of imperialism, and over the prospective reform of domestic and international public orders according to the basic tenets of Islam. Being inspired by thinkers like Mawdudi and Qutb, radical groups often stress that Muslims may resort to belligerent jihad to wipe out all forms of injustice, oppression and immorality.[63] It was such thinking that underpinned the decision to assassinate the Egyptian president Anwar Sadat in 1981, who led Egypt to sign a peace treaty with Israel – a political move which proved to be fatal for Sadat – who was considered by radicals to have abused his power. In fact, whilst the treaty was blessed by leading scholars of the al-Azhar university, the group behind the assassination denounced the validity thereof due to its ostensible treachery to the Islamic cause in general and to the Palestinian cause in particular – calling for an internal insurgency to institute a truly Islamic government as an initial step towards fighting Zionism as well as foreign intervention.[64]

Remarkably, while classical debates on just war and its limits related almost entirely to engagements with external enemies, modern radical groups draw on classical texts with intent to legitimate both external and internal struggles. This latter form of strife is directed against national authorities that are believed to have usurped the political power. The killing of President Anwar al-Sadat of Egypt, for instance, could be construed within this framework, for Sadat was deemed an apostate on account of his setting aside the Sharia norms by abandoning the Islamic cause. And since apostasy was deemed a grave offence punishable by death, the basic Muslim duty of doing the right and preventing the wrong required, according to them, the enforcement of such a penalty. Similar arguments were employed to overthrow the Shah of Iran, and are being invoked against other Muslim governments that are thought not to follow such radical groups' interpretation of what Islam entails.[65]

It is worth noting that the modern reassertion of Islam's role as a socio-political force to challenge Western imperialism, along with its moral, legal, and political

62 A. A. AbuSulayman, *Towards an Islamic Theory of International Relations: New Directions for Methodology and Thought,* 2nd ed. (Herndon: The International Institute of Islamic Thought, 1993) 9–10.

63 D. R. Springer *et al, Islamic Radicalism and Global Jihad* (Washington DC: Georgetown University Press, 2009) 32–34.

64 See S. Lacroix, 'Ayman al-Zawahiri, Veteran of Jihad' in: G. Kepel; J. P. Milelli (eds.); P. Ghazaleh (trans.) *Al Qaeda in its Own Words* (Cambridge, MA: Harvard University Press, 2008) 150–154; also see E. Rogan, *The Arabs: A History* (London: Penguin, 2010) 486–497.

65 See B. Lewis, *The Political Language of Islam* (Chicago: University of Chicago Press, 1988) 90.

legacies, to overthrow autocratic governments; and to instigate social change in Muslim societies in accord with the eternal teachings of Islam, largely relates with the frustration felt by Islamist movements towards incompetent Muslim authorities that failed to deliver what they promised. While radical movements' calls for military jihad did not generally elicit widespread response, Muslim grassroots certainly shared the frustration felt for biased Western policies in the Middle East, the plight of Palestinians, and corrupt authoritarianism across Muslim States.[66] Hence, radical movements did not find it particularly difficult to recruit supporters challenging the legitimacy of corrupt Muslim States, which were blamed for their failure to challenge the material and cultural imperialism imposed by the West. These criticisms proved to be valid since, following the colonial period, most Muslim States came to be ruled by unprincipled and inefficient leaders who remained politically and economically subservient to former colonial, or new imperialist, powers, while keeping large parts of their populations politically repressed, uneducated, and in poverty.

When such Muslim polities failed to institute fair and effective institutions to address socio-economic and political inequalities within the society, people on the ground grew disillusioned. This in turn strengthened reactionary movements' appeals for bellicose jihad in a bid to construct fairer Muslim societies that reject Western political artefacts and embrace Sharia principles instead.[67] Common themes in Islamic revivalism included the rejection of Western hegemony, restoration of Islam's original spirit and morality, and expansion of Islam's influence to society and politics. Muslim Brotherhood's well-known slogan, 'Islam is the answer' (*al-Islam huwa al-hal*), epitomised such aspiration to create a fresh socio-political order, both at domestic and international levels, built on the pillars of Islam.

Significantly, those who stress the obligatory nature of jihad to build fairer societies commonly refer to Islam's universal mission, which aims to convert polytheists, and to bring the scriptuaries under the pale of Islam wherein they may practise their original faiths in return for their fiscal and political tributes. The universalist outlook has certainly not been a novel notion; and radicals often justify their position by echoing a saying attributed to the Prophet, which reads: 'I have been ordered to fight with the people till they say, "none has the right to be worshipped but Allah". . .'[68] In fact, according to Karsh, the ambition to universalise Islam was behind many early Muslim conquests, since the Prophet not merely aimed to thwart external aggression, but strived 'for a new universal order

66 One of the decisive turning points in marking the political and military weakness of Muslims was the defeat of Arab States at the hands of Israel during the Six-Day War of 1967, which radically shattered the faith and confidence of Arabs. The defeat triggered self-criticism and questions about what went wrong. This eventually led to calls for religio-cultural reform, which, it was thought, necessitated greater self-reliance and reclamation of Islam's glorious past. See J. L. Esposito, *Islam and Politics* 4th ed. (Syracuse: Syracuse University Press, 1998) 160–161.

67 See M. C. Bassiouni, 'Introduction' in: Bassiouni, supra note 11, 2.

68 *Hadith* Reported by al-Bukhari, *Hadith of Bukhari,* Vol. IV, Hadith 4:196.

in which the whole of humanity would embrace Islam or live under its domination'.[69] Karsh supports his argument by adding that Muhammad had devised the concept of jihad initially to entice his followers to fight for worldly reasons like raiding Meccan caravans, but then he transformed this ancient practice into a holy duty to spread the dominion of Islam. Muhammad, according to this analysis, 'developed and amplified this concept with the expansion of his political ambitions until it became a rallying call for world domination', whereby all believers could practise the Islamic faith 'in all territories [they] conquered'.[70]

It should be noted that the above thesis does not fit neatly into the overall Islamic philosophy, which placed itself within the framework of Abrahamic religions, acknowledging monotheistic faiths as the previous mediums of God's truth.[71] Correspondingly, it will be remembered that one of Muhammad's declared missions was to remind humankind of God's 'original' message. Had Muhammad's principal objective been the extension of his political influence, he arguably could have materialised this without having to suffer, along with his followers, hardship, mockery, or socio-economic isolation in Mecca, wherein he had already been offered significant political power and influence in exchange for his cooperation with the Meccan elite. But when Muhammad was asked to cease his preaching in return for power and prestige, he had reportedly replied that he would not forsake his mission even if his enemies or detractors 'put the sun in . . . [his] right hand and the moon in . . . [his] left'.[72] His refusal to cooperate with the polytheists eventually led to increasing levels of adversity against the nascent community of believers who were finally compelled to leave their homes. Muhammad's farewell address may also be adduced to highlight his commitment to the fraternity of humankind, where, in unmistakably plain words, he declared: 'All mankind is from Adam and Eve, an Arab has no superiority over a non-Arab, nor does a non-Arab have any superiority over an Arab; also a white has no superiority over black, nor does a black have any superiority over white *except by piety and good action.*'[73]

Undoubtedly, Muhammad had deemed the community of believers a seamless unity (*ummah*) that jointly strove for God's cause and bore unique qualities distinguishing them from the subscribers to other belief systems. This was only natural considering his mission as God's final messenger. Besides, the fact that his religious role was interlaced with his roles as the political and military leader of his community does not necessarily suggest that his mission was overwhelmingly political,

69 E. Karsh, *Islamic Imperialism: A History* (London: Yale University Press, 2007) 4.

70 Ibid. 5.

71 'The same religion has He established for you [the Arabs] as that which He enjoined on Noah . . . on Abraham, Moses, and Jesus . . .' the Qur'an says. Q. 42:13.

72 See A. A. Azzam, *The Life of the Prophet Muhammad* (Riyadh: International Islamic Publishing House, 1987) 16ff; A. Wessels, *A Modern Arabic Biography of Muhammad* (Leiden: Brill, 1972) 63ff.

73 The Prophet Muhammad, 'The Prophet Muhammad's Farewell Sermon' (632). Available at: http://isites.harvard.edu/fs/docs/icb.topic747373.files/The%20Prophet%20Muhammads%20Farewell%20Sermon.pdf (emphasis added).

nor does it suggest that it was not moral or religious. To reason otherwise would require the analyst to take the entire pre-Medinan period of Islam out of account in an effort to force the facts to fit the theory. In consequence, the reductionist argument that the main motivation of jihad has simply been to further Islam's imperialistic ambitions falls short of capturing the much richer tapestry of Islamic tradition on warfare.

The above argument is not to suggest that Islam lacked the goal of universality; on the contrary, Islam, from its inception, regarded humanity as the children of Adam and Eve, led astray and to be brought back to the right path.[74] Indeed, Islam has always claimed universality, calling for the union of all believers regardless of their distinctions based on race, wealth, class, ethnicity, and language. Muhammad's appeal to embrace God's original design was thus not directed to the Arabs alone, but to the whole world. While some verses and other primary sources bear relevance to certain characteristics of seventh-century Arabia and its intractable problems, which beleaguered the Muslims, references to such notions as justice, fairness, equality of nations, and the supremacy of the pious act (as a measure of divine judgement) shore up Islam's universal appeal. Expressed differently, the ideal of Islam has been the unification of all humans under a single law and authority. Consequently, different from Judaism, whose monotheistic perspective – despite its universalist streak[75] – is tilted towards a particular ethnic group, Islam makes its appeal to all humankind.[76] Viewed through this prism, the reduction of the role of jihad simply to an instrument of power and imperial expansion oversimplifies the concept – a restricted approach that does not take richer dimensions of jihad into account.

74 Furthermore, Muslims consider Islam as a complete and perfect system, covering almost all aspects of human life. Hence, Islam is believed to occupy the centre stage of history with its timeless, universal, and all-embracing message. See further, A. Tayob 'The Shifting Politics of Identity' in: M. K. Masud, M. A. Salvatore; M. V. Bruinessen, *Islam and Modernity: Key Issues and Debates* (Edinburgh: Edinburgh University Press, 2009) 270ff; *cf.* J. Berkey, *The Formation of Islam: Religion and Society in the Near East 600–1800* (Cambridge: Cambridge University Press, 2003) 7.

75 Some commentators, in this context, argue that the moral and ethical lessons of Judaism have not been peculiar to Jews alone, but to the entire human family, even when 'Jewish particularity' is one of the defining qualities of Judaism. For a fuller account, see S. D. Breslauer, *Toward a Jewish (M)orality: Speaking of a Postmodern Jewish Ethics* (Westport: Greenwood Press, 1998) 27ff.

76 Such an aspiration likewise underpins the structure of Christianity, which considers humanity as part of a single race – namely the human race – which has to dismantle all artificial barriers that separate them. Judaism, in this respect, differs from Christianity and Islam in that Jews in Torah are deemed the chosen people of God: "You are a people holy to the Lord your God. The Lord your God has chosen you out of all the peoples on the face of the earth to be his people, his treasured possession." Deuteronomy (7:6). Given such a special relationship between God and Israelis, there is no claim to fraternity of nations in Judaism. See further, T. Frymer-Kensky 'Biblical Voices on Chosenness' in: R. Jospe *et al* (eds.), *Covenant and Chosenness in Judaism and Mormonism* (Cranbury: Fairleigh Dickinson University Press, 2001) 23, 23ff.

Regrettably, militant groups generally take a similarly restricted approach to what the doctrine of jihad entails. The hermeneutic method they generally adopt is based upon a select portion of sources, casting aside competing verses, traditions, and scholarly views that might dictate alternative conclusions. Informed by their varying political agendas, their reading of Islamic warfare is largely characterised by a literal, rigid exegesis of Islamic sources, rather than a contextual and purposive appraisal thereof. Such a hermeneutic approach thus generally construes relevant norms in their narrow senses, and in isolation from qualifying considerations and the context that gave rise to their formulation and use. Naturally, this strategy often results in overlooking the broader rationale and concrete implications of pertinent verses, traditions, and scholarly opinions.

The rhetoric of warlike jihad is certainly not merely utilised by militant organisations. Radical rulers, such as Khomeini, Hussein, or Gaddafi, might likewise assert that military jihad could be pivotal in ensuring the political liberation of Muslims and spreading the word of God.[77] Following the Islamic revolution of 1979, Khomeini, for instance, pursued a policy of 'exporting' the revolution through jihad with intent to undermine the political, economic, and cultural hegemony of the Western world. Continuous struggle against oppression and the expansion of (Shiite) Islamic influence constituted the cardinal tenets of the Iranian constitution – drafted by Khomeini and his close associates – and of Iranian foreign policy. The preamble of the constitution clearly reflected such pan-Islamism: '[the Iranian army]. . .will be responsible not only for guarding and preserving the frontiers of the country, but also for fulfilling the ideological mission of jihad in God's way; that is, extending the sovereignty of God's law throughout the world'.[78] Nevertheless, despite this seemingly radical posture, Khomeini occasionally denounced aggression to expand Islam's frontiers or to export the principles of Iranian revolution, probably in a bid to avoid contradicting the norms of international law. In such statements, he professed that Islamic values had to be exported peacefully: 'When we say we want to export our revolution we mean we want to export this spirituality which dominates Iran . . . We have no intention to attack anyone with swords or other arms.'[79] Here, the notion of jihad was declared to include exclusively peaceful means.

It is worth briefly noting here that there exists little difference between the radical exegeses of jihad in the Sunni and Shiite traditions. Indeed, notwithstanding some doctrinal divergences, Sunnis and Shiites have a comparable conception of warlike jihad, in that both recognise jihad as a religious duty incumbent upon Muslims (whether individually or collectively) to resist oppression, ward off

77 See I. Detter, *The Law of War* (Cambridge: University of Cambridge, 2000) 157.

78 See H. E. Chehabi; H. I. Mneimneh, 'Five Centuries of Lebanese-Iranian Encounters' in: H. E. Chehabi (ed.) *Distant Relations: Iran and Lebanon in the last 500 Years* (Oxford: The Centre for Lebanese Studies, 2006) 32; also see M. A. M. Khan, *Jihad for Jerusalem: Identity and Strategy in International Relations* (Westport: Praeger, 2004) 154ff.

79 Cited in: S. Hunter, *The Future of Islam and the West: Clash of Civilizations or Peaceful Coexistence?* (Westport: Praeger, 1998) 133.

aggression, intercept a palpable threat, or expand the pale of Islam. The main difference lies in the concept of 'legitimate authority' that can declare jihad. For Sunnis, it is the caliph or ruler (with the backing of religious scholars); for the Shiites, it is the legitimate successor to Muhammad, or rather, the divinely appointed ruler (Imam). Most Shiite jurists delineate defensive and aggressive forms of military jihad in respect of legitimate authority.[80] To Shiites, an aggressive or expansionist form of jihad requires the presence of the Imam – and not an ordinary Muslim leader – who is deemed (by Twelve Shiites) to have gone into occultation at the close of the ninth century.[81] Shiites believe that only with the re-emergence of the occult Imam may the ultimate triumph of good over evil transpire, and may religious purity be restored.[82] The emphasis on the currently 'occult' ruler to declare offensive jihad is to ensure that lethal force against the enemies of Islam is strictly undertaken for the cause of God. In cases of self-defensive jihad, on the other hand, an ordinary (legitimate) Shiite ruler may authorise armed force. It is in congruence with such reasoning that Khomeini (and the Lebanese Hezbollah) advocated the export of the Iranian Revolution through the sole form of warlike jihad permitted in the classical Shiite tradition, i.e. the defensive military jihad.[83]

Before examining some other radical theories of jihad, it should be stressed that when radical groups and/or political leaders aim to shore up their ideological agendas, rather than attempting to get to the bottom of things, they often interpret sources on jihad in such a manner as to take advantage of the outward discrepancies on legitimate force outlined above.[84] It is accordingly incumbent on contemporary scholars to engage more rigorously with the theme of Islamic just war, for such efforts may promote constructive debates on the subject involved. As will be discussed in the next chapter, since the Islamic tradition on just war carries the potential to comply with the modern demands of international law, scholars should hammer out a more progressive framework – informed by a holistic and contextual exegesis of Islamic sources, which should then be read in conjunction with the fundamental norms of international law – in order that regressive interpretations cannot block the development of the inherently dynamic Islamic law.

80 J. P. Piscatori, *Islam in a World of Nation-States* (Cambridge: Cambridge University Press, 1986) 116.

81 For more on the doctrine of occult Imam, see I. M. Lapidus, 'Sultanates and Gunpowder Empires: The Middle East' in: J. L. Esposito, *The Oxford History of Islam* (Oxford: Oxford University Press, 1999) 347, 366ff; W. O. Beeman, 'Iran's Islamic Republic' in: J. L. Esposito; E. El-Din Shahin (eds.), *The Oxford Handbook of Islam and Politics* (Oxford: Oxford University Press, 2013) 399ff.

82 See further Sachedina, supra note 42, 41ff.

83 Esposito, supra note 41, 38–39.

84 To be sure, the rhetoric of jihad may also be invoked to advance a peaceful or noble cause. A case in point is the former Tunisian President Habib Bourguiba's appeal to eradicate the phenomenon of under-development under the banner of jihad. See Bassiouni, supra note 67, 2.

A. Warlike Jihad and the Doctrine of Abrogation

While the 'unapologetic' views presented above provide the major reference points for radical movements, some proponents of militant jihad (to be used as a drastic measure to effect change) have grounded their arguments on other doctrines. Among the apologists of warlike jihad, there are in particular those who maintain that peaceful verses of the early Islamic period had been abrogated by the sword verses revealed later in Medina – wherein the first Muslim polity progressively became a force with which the enemies of Islam had to reckon. Initially, the Muslim exegetical tradition invoked the method of abrogation (*naskh*) to explicate and contextualise the seemingly conflicting passages of the Quran by linking the disputed verses with traditions midwifed by specific historical incidents.[85] This method follows the traditional Muslim outlook, which holds that divine revelations had been imparted in response to disparate and inconstant predicaments faced by the Prophet and his followers. God is thus believed to have guided the Muslims through His varying revelations in testing and uncertain times. And in cases of apparent contradiction, it is accordingly suggested that the earlier verses should be considered to have been revealed to answer the contingency of the moment, whereas subsequent revelations are to be read as normative and binding.[86]

The theory of abrogation (or annulment) also finds its roots in the Quran, which states that 'none of Our revelations do we abrogate or cause to be forgotten, but We substitute something better or similar: knowest thou not that Allah hath power over all things?'[87] This verse may be construed to mean that an injunction could be replaced by another if the exigencies of the time so warranted. Nonetheless, the verse does not unequivocally suggest that subsequent verses axiomatically supersede the earlier ones – although it leaves room for such a conclusion. It is of course also arguable that the verse refers to earlier holy revelations sent to the Jews or Christians, which were subsequently superseded by the Quran's novel (or pristine) messages.[88] But there are also suggestions that this verse came in response to challenges mounted by non-Muslims about the consistency of the text of the Quran, with claims that there existed stark contradictions between some early and later revelations.[89] The following verse, which apparently responds to such a critique, attests that God might permit progressive revelation when necessary: 'When we substitute one revelation for

85 See O. Leaman (ed.), *The Qur'an: An Encyclopaedia* (New York: Routledge, 2006) 5.

86 See R. Firestone, *Jihad: The Origin of Holy War in Islam* (New York: Oxford University Press, 1999) 49–50

87 Q. 2:106.

88 Ali, supra note 6, 46.

89 Carimokam notes that Muhammad had been compelled to counter the arguments of the Jews in particular, who sought to raise doubts as to the authenticity and coherence of some Quranic verses. S. Carimokam, *Muhammad and the People of the Book* (Bloomington: Xlibris Corporation, 2010) 257.

another – and Allah knows best what He reveals (in stages) – they say, "thou art but a forger": but most of them understand not.'[90]

Having recognised the notion of progressive divine guidance, proponents of the warlike jihad draw attention to Chapter 9 of the Quran, which incorporates some of the most prominent 'sword' verses revealed in circa 631, a year before the demise of the Prophet, when he was at the height of his power.[91] As Chapter 9 authorised aggression against polytheists, unless they embraced Islam or lawfully concluded a peace treaty with Muslims[92] – and against the monotheists, until they paid the poll tax[93] – these commentators maintain that Chapter 9 of the Quran abrogated previous revelations that generally enjoined Muslims to be tolerant towards non-Muslims, accommodate other monotheistic traditions, display forgiveness, and employ peaceful methods to resolve disputes.[94] It is consequently posited that these belligerent Medinan verses took precedence over the earlier peaceful verses.[95] It follows from this hypothesis that Q. 2:256[96] (which states 'let there be no compulsion in religion'[97]) had been abrogated by Q. 9:73,[98] with regard to polytheists, and by Q. 9:29, with respect to the 'People of the Book'.[99] Put differently, although the 'no compulsion' principle was held to have categorically

90 Q. 16:101.

91 Some non-Muslim commentators argue that Chapter 9 might also contain verses belonging to different periods, because the verses were claimed not to be listed in chronological order. See further L. Fatoohi, *Abrogation in the Quran and Islamic Law: A Critical Study of the Concept of 'Naskh' and its Impact* (New York: Routledge, 2013) 119ff.

92 See Q. 9:7.

93 See Q. 9:29.

94 See generally, D. Bukay, 'Peace of Jihad? Abrogation in Islam' (2007) 14 *Middle East Quarterly* 3–11; Fatoohi, supra note 91, 8ff.

95 M. Abo-Kazleh, 'Rethinking International Relations Theory in Islam: Toward a More Adequate Approach' (2006) 5 *Turkish Journal of International Relations* 41, 43.

96 This verse is generally believed to have been revealed at the onset of Muhammad's prophetic career in Medina – where the fortification of the new religio-political unit was prioritised. The Prophet at this stage is known to seek the support and co-operation of the Jews and Christians of Medina. Muslim expeditions against the pagan enemies of Islam had started only when Muslims grew more confident to confront them. As will be remembered from the previous chapter, it was at this stage that the Quran granted Muslims the right to fight. See Q. 22:39–40; Q. 2:244; also see I. Ishaq; A. Guillaume (trans.), *The Life of Muhammad: A Translation of Ibn Ishaq's Sirat Rasul Allah* (Oxford: Oxford University Press, 1965) 247–270; W. M. Watt, *Muhammad at Medina* (Oxford: Oxford University Press, 1956) 2–4.

97 'Let there be no compulsion in religion: Truth stands out clear from Error: whoever rejects evil and believes in God hath grasped the most trustworthy hand-hold that never breaks. And God heareth and knoweth all things.' Q. 2:256.

98 'O Prophet! Strive hard against the unbelievers and the hypocrites, and be firm against them. Their abode is hell – an evil refuge indeed.' Q. 9:73.

99 'Fight those who believe not in Allah nor the last day, nor hold that forbidden which hath been forbidden by Allah and His Messenger, nor acknowledge the religion of truth, even if they are of the People of the Book, until they pay the *jizya* (poll tax) with willing submission, and feel themselves subdued.' Q. 9:29.

prohibited various forms of religious coercion following the revelation of later verses, its ruling, it was argued, was not fully enforced. Some jurists went so far as to contend that subsequent warlike verses abrogated some 114 verses – spread into 54 chapters – that had hitherto regulated peaceful relations with non-Muslims.[100]

The advocates of the abrogation theory also suggest that the prominent sword verse of Q. 9:5[101] epitomised a sea change in the progressive scheme of divine guidance, since it came down in the wake of the violation of the Hudaybiyyah Agreement by the Meccan forces. The verse in question called upon Muslims to fight the pagans until the latter repented, established regular prayers, and corrected their immoral ways.[102] Supporting the thesis of such a sea change in strategy, Friedmann contends that the deeds of the Prophet largely followed the lead of the sword verses, which required Muslims of the late prophetic phase to use coercive measures when dealing with their non-Muslim foes. Friedmann adds that the Prophet had, in effect, given the Arab pagans the choice of the sword or conversion; the Prophet, the argument runs, would not have acted this way had he felt obliged to follow the principle of 'no compulsion'.[103]

Plausible though the above arguments may appear, it must be borne in mind that the Quran does not clearly annul its earlier verses, nor for that matter does it specifically substitute one verse for another. There lacks, therefore, explicit norms clarifying the set of verses being replaced by subsequent verses. More importantly, divine injunctions of the early period, some of which are claimed to have been annulled, were not merely germane to matters of war and peace, but to the overall normative and ethical framework of Islam, which is informed by such consequential notions as peace, justice, equity, tolerance, patience, respect, fairness, and solidarity. And it is such a framework that has hitherto guided the manner in which Muslims conducted their interpersonal, national, and international relations. Hence, the unqualified proposition that subsequent verses have perforce abrogated the previous ones is highly questionable.

Furthermore, the fact that both peaceful and belligerent verses form part and parcel of the 'timeless' text of the Quran also reinforces the counter-proposition that all verses, regardless of their chronological order, retain their relevance. Viewed in this light, non-belligerent verses may be said to remain valid and applicable in contemporary times which, among others, is characterised by its

100 For a fuller account of such arguments, see M. A. S. Faraj, 'The Neglected Duty' in: R. L. Euben; M. Q. Zaman (eds.), *Princeton Readings in Islamic Thought: Texts and Contexts from al-Banna to bin Laden* (Princeton: Princeton, 2009) 327, 338–339.

101 See supra note 36.

102 But because the pagans of Mecca submitted to the Muslims before actual warfare broke out, Mecca was conquered without serious bloodshed, and thus the verse was not acted upon on this occasion. See Kamali, supra note 14, 46; J. E. Brockopp, 'Introduction' in: J. E. Brockopp (ed.), *The Cambridge Companion to Muhammad* (New York: Cambridge University Press, 2010) 10ff.

103 See Y. Friedmann, *Tolerance and Coercion in Islam: Interfaith Relations in the Muslim Tradition* (New York: Cambridge University Press, 2003) 102.

prohibition on unilateral aggression as an instrument of resolving differences among nations. As the following chapter will make clear, the monopoly on the use of legitimate aggression is exclusively reserved for central international organs that are charged with the responsibility of maintaining or restoring international peace and security.[104] It follows that the early verses concerning peaceable or self-defensive forms of jihad may, and should, continue to bind Muslims of the contemporary age.

In support of the argument that the Quran cannot be robbed of its peaceful verses arbitrarily – with a consequence of its ethical framework being largely impaired – it may be adduced that God may not be conceived as having revealed contradicting principles in respect of the same matter; rather, He may more plausibly be perceived as having guided the community of Muslims through practical challenges of versatile nature. The seemingly conflicting norms should thus retain their validity and field of applicability, for they may be acted upon whenever circumstances provide the grounds for adaptable responses. As considered earlier, Muslims coped with the challenges thrown their way generally commensurate with the degree of power they possessed at various stages of Muhammad's ministry – a fact that informed the non-linear Islamic approach to war, at a time when varying strategies (whether peaceful or otherwise) had to be invoked to secure one's very existence and fundamental freedoms.[105]

Indeed, when the Quran had been taking form, Muslims – who were still relatively small in number and weak in strength – had been compelled to take up arms against their foes to ensure their survival and liberty and to practise as well as to promulgate their creed.[106] As history does not repeat itself in exact cycles, and as only a single type of response to the exigencies of circumstances cannot always yield desired outcomes, Muslims of all times should be given the opportunity to adopt flexible approaches by drawing on the alternative teachings of the Quran, rather than solely on those that appear to advocate warlike measures against the

104 It is for this reason that the right to self-defence is merely an interim measure, which does not affect the general authority and responsibility of the Security Council. See O. Bakircioglu, *Self-Defence in International and Criminal Law: The Doctrine of Imminence* (London: Routledge, 2011) 194ff.

105 One of the prominent reasons why the sword verses are said to have abrogated the peaceful verses is that the pre-Islamic concept of warfare envisaged perpetual conflict between warring tribes unless these had concluded a truce or peace agreement. The Muslim community was born within such socio-political setting, wherein political and military might could ensure one's survival as well as command recognition. Whilst Islam dramatically transformed the divisive violence of the pre-Islamic era by uniting most of the erstwhile warring tribes through the cement of its religious principles, it may not be said to have obliterated all pre-Islamic conceptions of war and peace – at least in practice. For a fuller account, see R. Firestone, *An Introduction to Islam for Jews* (Philadelphia: Jewish Publication Society, 2008) 13–16.

106 As alluded to above, the doctrine of abrogation appears to be a product of its turbulent age, which required Muslims to be constantly ready for battle against the actual or potential enemy. See AbuSulayman, supra note 62, 84.

adversary. It must further be noted that the modern state of international affairs neither threatens Muslims' existence, nor does it prevent them from relying on peaceful means of religious practice and propagation. Islamic laws of war and peace, in other words, operate in a distinct socio-political framework, wherein international disputes are meant to be resolved peacefully and amicably. Contemporary Muslims, therefore, need to use the rich reserve of Islamic norms in order not only to conform to the demands of this age, but also to consolidate the hard-won system of collective security in international affairs.

The major weakness of the abrogation doctrine is that it gives pride of place to warlike verses and traditions – often by taking them out of context – to the detriment of Islam's overall ethical system, which is built on such fundamental concepts as peace, justice, compassion, tolerance, forgiveness, and patience. Taken together, one may conclude that the abrogation theory stands on shaky ground due to its avoidance of purposive and holistic hermeneutics – which is characterised by its appraisal of primary sources dialectically and in conjunction with parallel sources, and by reference to spatial and temporal assessments.[107] The radical school has also fallen back on certain military doctrines of Muslim States that were mainly formulated during the imperial phase of Islam. In order to gain a better appreciation of warlike jihad, as understood by the 'radicals', one such doctrine – whose intellectual foundations were rooted in medieval State practice – must now be examined.

B. Dar al-Islam and Dar al-Harb

Notwithstanding the conceptual haze as to the precise implications of military jihad, it should now be clear that primary sources on warfare appear to take warlike jihad as a legitimate means of dealing with the adversary, particularly in cases where Muslims are attacked. It is also evident that during the period of great Muslim conquests, military struggle against non-Muslims had been the dominant form of jihad – mainly undertaken as a collective duty – albeit peaceful propagation methods were also relied upon to expand and consolidate the frontiers of Islam.[108]

At the height of far-reaching Islamic conquests, Muslim jurists developed a military doctrine that categorically divided the world into two broad domains: the House of Islam (*dar al-Islam*) and the House of War (*dar al-harb*). According to this doctrine, the House of Islam included countries wherein Islamic legal order and faith prevailed, whereas in the rest of the world, named as the House of War, Islamic principles had no validity. Although such territorial distinction lacked

107 As will be remembered, this study has attributed a similar weakness to the moderate school.

108 See generally, H. Kennedy, *The Armies of the Caliphs: Military and Society in the Early Islamic State* (New York: Routledge, 2001); A. K. Bennison, *The Great Caliphs: The Golden Age of the Abbasid Empire* (London: I.B. Tauris, 2011).

a scriptural backing, it carried the authority of such influential commentators as Abu Hanifa and Abu Yusuf, who held that because there existed a continual state of war between the Islamic and non-Islamic spheres, the House of Islam was justified in going to war against the House of War, if the latter refused to embrace Islam or to pay a poll tax (in cases of scriptuaries).[109] Such bifurcation of the world evidently served the political ambitions of those rulers who aimed to spread Muslim rule or justify wars of various kinds on religious grounds, as the doctrine placed heavy emphasis on the warlike features of jihad.[110]

A legitimate Muslim authority, by this doctrine, was thence justified in waging offensive warfare to bring the domain of unbelief under the sway of Islamic order. Again, military jihad aimed at the subordination of the House of War was deemed the religious duty of the caliph, whose task to proselytise Islam would only cease when the entire world accepted Islam.[111] Theoretically, therefore, Muslims were to struggle against the unbelief until there prevailed an all-embracing, universal Muslim polity. This quest seemed attainable at the time, for Islam was confidently considered the panacea for all the problems of this world, by which humanity could achieve salvation both in this world and in the hereafter.[112] At the centre of this militant understanding, then, lay the hypothesis that only within the universal House of Islam could everlasting peace, security, and justice prevail for all – an objective that must be realised, if necessary, at the cost of warfare.[113]

It appears plausible to suggest that such a broad-brush, bipolar categorisation of the world reflected the then common tendency of major religious traditions to view their alternatives as monolithic constructs. Some have traced back such

109 See M. Khadduri, *The Islamic Law of Nations: Shaybani's Siyar* (Baltimore: Johns Hopkins Press, 1966) 52–54; A. Ali, *The Spirit of Islam: A History of the Evolution and Ideals of Islam with a Life of the Prophet* (London: Christophers, 1922) 214–215; H. Kennedy, *The Great Arab Conquests: How the Spread of Islam Changed the World We Live In* (London: Phoenix, 2008).

110 Schacht points out that the imperial legislation of the Umayyad dynasty furnished the main structure of what later became the Islamic laws of war. This suggests that only in later stages of Islamic history did jurists seek to root the tradition of warlike jihad within the soil of primary sources. Whilst this point remains controversial, there is clear evidence that later Umayyad caliphs had promoted offensive jihad, which called for subduing all opponents – be them non-Muslims or Muslim rebels. See J. Schacht, *An Introduction to Islamic Law* (Oxford: Clarendon Press, 1964) 23–24; M. Bonner, *Jihad in Islamic History: Doctrines and Practice* (Princeton: Princeton University Press, 2006) 122–123.

111 F. M. Donner, 'The Sources of Islamic Conceptions of War' in: J. Kelsay; J. T. Johnson (eds.), *Just War and Jihad: Historical and Theoretical Perspectives on War and Peace in Western and Islamic Traditions* (New York: Greenwood Press, 1991) 31, 47–51; Khadduri, supra note 109, 10.

112 The ethos that all nations would eventually be brought under a peaceful religious order is advanced by Judaism as well: "They shall beat their swords into ploughshares, and their spears into pruning-hooks: nation shall not lift up sword against nation, neither shall they learn war anymore." Isaiah 2:4.

113 Kelsay, supra note 34, 34.

categorical division of the world to one of the traditions attributed to the Prophet in which he had reportedly said 'unbelief is one nation'.[114] But the accuracy and content of this saying is so dubious as to lend itself to the inexorable conclusion that the non-Muslim world must be coerced into accepting Islam or paying a fiscal tribute. As noted earlier, neither the Quran nor the Sunna draws such a sharp distinction (with military implications) between the world of Islam and the 'heathendom'.[115] This jurist-made doctrine hence appears to mirror the realities of the prevailing circumstances of its time, whereby nations could be sweepingly categorised through religious status – as other grounds of distinction were of less import – which, accompanied by political and economic reasons, may then pave the way for hostilities.

Notably, this doctrine stood in sharp contrast to the early teachings of Islam (which encouraged the establishment of a more inclusive system) by attempting to foster a unique Muslim identity, chiefly defined against the non-Muslim 'other', with the potential to perpetuate belligerency. Nevertheless, as the historical record of Islamic State practice evinces, the doctrine had never been fully implemented. Indeed, the long-standing Muslim practice of concluding treaties of peace, friendship, and commerce with non-Muslim entities suggests that the doctrine was not taken to mean unceasing belligerency to reduce the non-Muslim rule to submission.[116] Likewise, even when jihad is accepted to be the sole means of achieving the vision of this militant doctrine, it will be remembered that jihad does not always mean war, because Islam's objective might well be achieved through peaceable forms of jihad.

It is hence unsurprising that even during the era of great conquests, Muslim rulers and jurists had recognised the legitimacy of peaceful mechanisms to govern international affairs.[117] This was possible due to the flexibility of Islamic international law (*siyar*), which, unlike many areas of Sharia, was largely developed through judicial speculations in the light of concrete historical circumstances. While such juridical speculations had to be in tandem with the basic tenets of Islam, this does not change the fact that *siyar* had largely been man-made, and as such it is, on the whole, not immutable and timeless. In other words, while *siyar's* main principles had been derived from the body of primary and subsidiary sources, its structure has hitherto been shaped by shifting realities on the ground.[118] Badr is thus right in noting that 'the Islamic law of nations is not part of the dogma of Islam, but is the product of a continuing process of juridical speculation by

114 See B. Lewis, *Politics and War in Islam* (Princeton: Princeton University Press, 1975) 174–175.

115 See Haleem, supra note 2, 71.

116 A. A. An-Na'im, *Toward and Islamic Reformation: Civil Liberties, Human Rights, and International Law* (Syracuse: Syracuse University Press, 1996) 150.

117 See M. Khadduri, 'Islam and the Modern Law of Nations' (1956) 50 *American Journal of International Law* 2, 359ff.

118 F. A. Hassan, 'The Sources of Islamic Law' (1982) 76 *American Society of International Law Proceedings* 65, 68.

authoritative jurists over the ages'.[119] And this being the case, any credible attempt to understand Islam's approach to international relations should give due consideration to the pertinent historical phenomena and Muslim statesmen's and jurists' reactions to them.

III. Siyar and the Complexity of Islamic International Relations

As summarised above, whilst *siyar* stood on the pillars of primary sources, its main corpus borrowed significantly from the secondary sources, including the practices of exemplary Muslim rulers or officials, court decisions, arbitral awards, validly concluded treaties, pacts and other binding agreements, customs and usage, official instructions for army personnel, ambassadors and other public officials, and regulations governing the conduct of foreigners.[120] Other governing principles of *siyar* were obtained from the general norms and practices of interstate relations, as well as from the experiences with the non-Muslim world. Evidently, the opinions, writings, and judgements of eminent jurists and judges further contributed to the development of the discipline. Juridical writings were not produced for academic reasons alone, but also for practical reasons. It was by no means an infrequent practice for Muslim rulers to solicit the guidance of leading jurists on the vexing legal questions of the day.

Judicial opinions and rulings on a point of Islamic law (*fatwa*) either formed precedents, serving as commanding points of reference for later cases, or they constituted an alternative interpretation for an established principle.[121] To be sure, judicial opinions formed in respect of specific legal questions not only bridged detached scholarship and practical matters, but also helped innovative thinking to mitigate the challenges of an ever-changing world. Particularly in the domain of Islamic international relations, jurists felt less restrained by dogmatic bounds, and hence formulated fresh standards to enrich the existing jurisprudence over matters of public interest.[122]

The fact that subsidiary sources, in particular scholarly opinions and practices of well-respected statesmen, laid the foundations of *siyar* refutes the suggestion that the Muslim framework for international relations constitutes the final expression of the divine will, which as such is unalterable and timeless. By contrast, *siyar* has

119 G. M. Badr, 'A Survey of Islamic International Law' (1982) 12 *American Society of International Law* 56, 56.

120 See S. S. Ali, 'The Twain Doth Meet! A Preliminary Exploration of the Theory and Practice of *As-Siyar* and International Law in the Contemporary World' in: J. Rehman; S. C. Breau (eds.), *Religion, Human Rights and International Law* (Leiden: Martinus Nijhoff Publishers, 2007) 86, 91. M. Hamidullah, *Muslim Conduct of State,* 5th Ed. (Lahore: Ashraf Press, 1968).

121 Khadduri, supra note 109, 8–9.

122 See W. B. Hallaq, 'From *Fatwas* to *Furu*: Growth and Change in Islamic Substantive Law' (1994) 1 *Islamic Law and Society* 29, 34.

been subject to various modifications in harmony with historical changes in the nature of political Islam. Badr identifies three principal stages in the progress of Islamic international law: the age of expansion, interaction, and coexistence. Hence, he concludes, 'any attempt at describing the Islamic regulation of international relations must not lose sight of this historical framework'.[123] Studies on Islamic international law should indeed take into account this living aspect of the discipline.

It follows from this analysis, and as will be fully explored in the next chapter, that the medieval theory of perpetual belligerency against the non-Muslim world may no longer be reasonably supported in the modern context of international relations. But what is more striking is that the hypothetical bifurcation of the world into Muslim and non-Muslim domains may be said to have never stood on solid ground due in large part to the political schisms in the so-called House of Islam. In fact, the disintegration of the once-unified Muslim polity started as early as the demise of the Prophet, and in particular of his immediate successors.[124] However, the most catastrophic division within the Muslim community transpired following the killing of Muhammad's grandson (Husayn ibn Ali) and some 70 members of his family in the desert of Karbala by the Umayyad family, which sought to preserve its political power at the expense of massacring members of the Prophet's family.[125]

This notorious incident markedly deepened the Sunni–Shiite disagreement on questions of qualified leadership and legitimate authority, and it eventually paved the way for the takeover of political power by the Abbasid dynasty.[126]

123 Badr further makes the general point that 'the corpus of Islamic law as it developed over the ages is manmade in the sense that it resulted from the efforts of the jurists of the various schools of law. If civil law can be described as a legislator's law as to its source and common law as a judge's law, then Islamic law is a jurist's law. There is very little that is rigid and immutable in Islamic law.' Badr, supra note 119, 56.

124 Soon after Muhammad's death, a number of Muslim tribes attempted to break away from the *umma* on the ground that they recognised nobody's authority except the Prophet's; yet they were forcibly brought back under the sway of the Muslim polity by the immediate successors to the Islamic leadership, i.e. by Abu Bakr (632–634) and Umar (634–44). The military campaigns waged against the rebellious tribes are known as the 'wars of apostasy' (*ridda*), which were completed by circa 634. The impact of these campaigns was so significant that it eventually brought almost all Arabs within the embrace of Islam, which, in turn, enabled the forces of Islam to turn their attention to the Roman and Persian Empires. See further P. Sarris, *Empires of Faith: The Fall of Rome to the Rise of Islam, 500–700* (Oxford: Oxford University Press, 2011) 263–272.

125 In time, the massacre at Karbala had attained a mythical quality in Shiite tradition. For Shiites, the event marked a dramatic pattern of suffering and martyrdom. The day on which the Karbala incident took place (10 Muharram) is commemorated annually by the Shiites as their greatest religious festival, which is marked by passion plays and flagellants' processions with a view to highlighting the frustration and regret the event still inspires. See G. R. Hawting, *The First Dynasty of Islam: The Umayyad Claiphate AD 661–750*, 2nd ed. (London: Routledge, 1996) 49–50.

126 For a discussion, see M. Khadduri, *The Islamic Conception of Justice* (Baltimore: The Johns Hopkins Press, 1984) 23ff.

It is worth noting that when the Abbasids wrested political leadership from the Umayyads in 750, the borders of the Islamic Empire had already reached global dimensions – absorbing such vast areas as the entire Persian Empire, significant portions of the Roman Empire on the east and south shores of the Mediterranean Sea, North Africa, and significant parts of the Spanish peninsula.[127]

However, dynastic struggles within this vast empire were to result in further divisions. The first serious crack within the unity of the Islamic Empire was the establishment of the Umayyad dynasty in Spain in 756, defying the Abbasid rule.[128] The founding of the Fatimid caliphate in Tunisia in 909 marked another dramatic political fragmentation in medieval Islam. Belonging to the Shiite branch of Islam, Fatimids claimed to hold the sole legitimate religious authority over all Muslims, and as they acquired more power they mounted a grave challenge to the Sunni Abbasid caliphs. The Fatimid period, marked by notable politico-religious tolerance and economic prosperity, was eventually brought to an end in 1171 by Saladin, who later established his own (Sunni) dynasty to rule Egypt and much of the Levant for almost a century.[129]

During the coexistent reigns of the Fatimids, Spanish Umayyads, and Abbasids, there were three caliphs who concurrently staked a claim over religious authority. While the fall of the caliphate of Cordova in 1031 and the collapse of the Fatimid dynasty in 1171 appeared to have once again restored the unity of the caliphate, by then it became clear that the caliphs were no longer capable of exerting effective control over central bodies.[130] Stated otherwise, as early as the eleventh century, imperial and religious authority ceased to be synonymous in the world of Islam. Particularly following the emergence of the Seljuq dynasty in the eleventh century, political sovereignty came to distinguish itself from the caliphate by assuming responsibility for public order, security, and the daily administration of the polity, leaving most religious matters to the caliph. Henceforth, a gradual but distinct separation of powers surfaced between the monarchical and religious

127 In their revolt against the Umayyads, Abbasids had frequently made an appeal to defend the purity of Islam, which, they said, was marred by the aristocratic pride and tribal exclusiveness of the Umayyads. Abbasids particularly animated the religious feelings of those converts who were denied equal opportunities promised to all Muslims. The Abbasids further benefited from the widespread sympathy felt for the massacred descendants of Ali by obtaining the support of certain Shiite factions—even though they later harvested most benefits for themselves. See H. M. Gwatkin, *The Cambridge Medieval History*, Vol. IV, Part I, (New York: Macmillan, 1966) 699–700.

128 Yet, like its Eastern counterpart, the Spanish Muslim rule was unsettled by internal conflicts and ensuing political fragmentations. See further B. Lewis, 'Politics and War' in: J. Schacht; C. E. Bosworth (eds.), *The Legacy of Islam* (London: Oxford University Press, 1974) 165; I. M. Lapidus, *A History of Islamic Societies,* 2nd ed. (Cambridge: Cambridge University Press, 2002) 311–313; Y. H. Aboul-Enein; S. Zuhur, *Islamic Rulings on Warfare* (Carlisle Barracks: Strategic Studies Institute, 2004) 3.

129 See F. Daftary, *A Short History of the Ismailis* (Edinburgh: Edinburgh University Press, 1998) 63–66, 112; see generally, Karsh, supra note 69.

130 See Lewis, supra note 128, 168; J. M. Abun-Nasr, *A History of the Maghrib in the Islamic Period* (Cambridge: Cambridge University Press, 1987) 72ff.

bodies – even when political force was expected to be exercised in conformity with the fundamental laws of God.[131]

A culmination in the decline of caliphal power was reached with the Mongol destruction of the Abbasid dynasty in Baghdad in 1258, after which only an attenuated form of the office survived in Cairo. When the Ottoman Turks conquered Egypt in 1517, they seized the title of the caliphate, adding it to other qualifying sovereign titles they had been using.[132] The caliphate thus continued to hold little value until the eighteenth century, at which time the Ottomans sought to revive its political value after their defeat in the Russo-Turkish war of 1768–1774. In the ensuing peace treaty of 1774, the title of the caliphate was indeed forcefully re-claimed to emphasise the religious and political unity of the Muslim world under the Turkish Ottoman leadership.[133] But this was a rather belated attempt, for it had long become evident that real political power rested with the possessors of military might – with religious institutions principally being employed to reinforce the authority of sovereign powers.

As the above account makes clear, the assumed unity of the 'House of Islam', militantly pitted against the 'House of War', has long become a legal fiction, rather than a reality. In today's context, the doctrine of constant hostility between the world of Islam and the world of war becomes even more problematic, given the rich variety within the Islamic tradition, which is embraced by a large number of divergent nation-States, and of adherents who have branched out across the globe. In short, the above-discussed continuous war theory is untenable due to its inability to capture the richer matrix of the Islamic just war tradition. Islamic law may not be confined to inflexible man-made formulae that are the product of their age, and not of the eternal principles of Islam. To hold otherwise would mean holding the present and future generations of Muslims hostage to temporally and geographically conditioned doctrines that are not responsive to changing circumstances. Besides, as the section below further illustrates, the world of Islam had in practice a far more complex relationship with the world of non-Muslims.

A. Islam and the Tradition of Concluding Treaties

As the discussion above suggests, because Islamic tradition has hitherto manifested itself on multifaceted political, ethnical, and cultural fronts, it has become increasingly difficult to construct all-embracing, or generally agreed upon, doctrines for

131 See Lewis, supra note 128, 169–172.

132 The Ottomans assumed such titles as *sultan*, *padisah*, *khan*, and *ghazi* to reflect their political and military status. The number of these titles augmented as the power of the Sultans grew. See H. Inalcik, *Osmanlilar: Futuhat, Imparatorluk, Avrupa ile Iliskiler* (Istanbul: Timas Yayinlari, 2010) 115ff.

133 R. Schulze, *A Modern History of the Islamic World* (London: I.B. Tauris, 2000) 16; D. Pipes, *Slave Soldiers and Islam: The Genesis of a Military System* (London: Yale University Press, 1981) 67.

Muslims of divergent backgrounds.[134] The disjointed structure of political Islam had undeniably also affected the contours of Islamic just war, as the interpretation and application of relevant primary sources significantly varied from one Muslim country to another, from one epoch to another.

But one thing was clear: Muslim States had never adopted an unceasing warlike attitude against the external world; by contrast, even during the height of Muslim expansion, Islamic international law incorporated institutional devices to relax the dichotomy of Muslim and non-Muslim nations. It will, in this context, be remembered that non-Muslim monotheists (*dhimmis*) were afforded the right to peacefully reside within the borders of the Islamic polity by keeping their beliefs in return for certain political and fiscal concessions.[135] With regard to the non-Muslim residents – even when they belonged to the 'House of War' (*harbis*) – they could be provided with a pledge of security (*aman*) during their sojourns within the borders of Islam. More precisely, *amans* gave such non-Muslims the right to work within Muslim frontiers for a maximum period of one year without granting the status of the People of the Book (*dhimmi*). After the one-year period, the protégé was in principle presented with two choices: to accept the status of the *dhimmi* or to revert back to his erstwhile status, i.e. *harbi*.[136] The provision of such temporary security did not involve a complex procedure; while a free Muslim adult could accord *aman* to a few people, a Muslim ruler could grant it to a larger entity. No doubt, this cooperative measure, coupled with other peaceful initiatives touched upon below, not merely contributed to high levels of commercial, cultural, and diplomatic exchanges between the purportedly 'mutually exclusive' worlds of Islam and other traditions, but also to the emergence of resident communities of non-Muslim traders, artisans, and workers within the domain of Islam.[137]

Such institutions palpably eased the way for peaceful contact with the outside world – a process that was complemented by a growing awareness that incessant belligerency to spread the sphere of Islam could not furnish a basis for a meaningful engagement with the rest of the world. Other peaceful agreements

134 See further, A. Ezzati, *The Spread of Islam: The Contributing Factors,* 4th ed. (London: Islamic College for Advanced Studies, 2002) 192ff; Lewis, supra note 128, 165–166, 173ff. As shown later, some Muslim States even allied with non-Muslim States against their co-religionists for politico-economic reasons. See Hashmi, supra note 43, 206–207.

135 Some commentators maintain that the main rationale for allowing *dhimmis* to practise their faiths was more related to their peaceful invitation to Islam than to fiscal considerations. See further, N. P. Aghnides, 'Classification of Persons' in: A. G. Bostom (ed.), *The Legacy of Jihad: Islamic Holy War and the Fate of Non-Muslims* (New York: Prometheus Books, 2008) 303.

136 See O. R. Constable, *Trade and Traders in Muslim Spain: The Commercial Realignment of the Iberian Peninsula, 900–1500* (Cambridge: Cambridge University Press, 1994) 64; Aghnides, supra note 135, 303; R. Israeli, *Islam in China: Religion, Ethnicity, Culture, and Politics* (Lanham: Lexington Books, 2002) 21.

137 See further, Lewis, supra note 128, 177; Khadduri, supra note 109, 158–160.

had accordingly been reached in an effort to further rapprochement with non-Muslim communities. Muslims, among others, turned to such concepts as the *hudna* (truce or armistice), *sulh* (peace or truce), *mithaq* (pact), and *ahd* (covenant) to achieve some form of amicable coexistence with external entities.[138] All these relations were constructed through *aqds* (contracts), which were considered valid when the terms therein conformed to the core principles of Islam.[139]

Viewed from this angle, the understanding that Islam should constantly battle the non-Muslim world – a state that should purportedly be broken only with occasional truces – does not dovetail with the overall practice and theory of Islam. The Quran, even in its relatively late Medinan phase, called upon Muslims to build friendly relations with other entities: 'Allah forbids you not, with regard to those who fight you not for (your) faith, nor drive you out of your homes, from dealing kindly and justly with them', read one of the verses.[140] A parallel verse confirmed this: 'Allah only forbids you, with regard to those who fight you for (your) faith, and drive you out . . . and support (others) in driving you out, from turning to them (for friendship and protection).'[141] As the verses suggest, Islam generally allows Muslims to deal kindly with non-Muslims, unless the latter have shown evidence of ill will, or have oppressed Muslims for their faith.

According to the orthodox view, however, peace treaties are temporally limited with the utmost duration of a 10-year period. This temporal limit was based on the precedent of the Hudaybiyyah Treaty (discussed below), signed by the Prophet and the Meccan leadership in 628.[142] A proper assessment of whether a peace treaty may remain valid for a longer time firstly requires a general consideration of Islam's position on treaties with non-Muslims. The Quran, to start with, acknowledges the legitimacy of peace treaties, and demands that Muslims keep their pledges so long as the other party remains loyal thereto.[143] The Prophetic Sunna also demonstrates that Muslims entered into confederal arrangements with non-Muslim Arab and Jewish clans. Of particular importance was the Covenant of Medina, which aimed to build a confederation in Medina whereby old internecine feuds between and among the Jews and Arabs could come to an end on the basis of the new religious superstructure that was to weld them into an alliance against unbelievers.[144] The covenant therefore sought to reconcile all the rival elements of Medina and to create a unified community distinct from other tribes. It further permitted the Jews to freely practise their religion and enjoy

138 See AbuSulayman, supra note 62, 24ff; Zawati, supra note 2, 61ff.
139 L. A. Bsoul, 'Historical Evolution of Islamic Law of Nations/Siyar: Between Memory and Desire' (2008) 17 *Domes* 48, 49ff.
140 Q. 60:8.
141 Q. 60:9.
142 See AbuSulayman, supra note 62, 25.
143 See Q. 9:7–13.
144 See Hamidullah, supra note 120, 199ff; I. M. Lapidus, *Islamic Societies to the Nineteenth Century: A Global History* (Cambridge: Cambridge University Press, 2012) 42ff.

equal status with the believers, provided that they supported Muslims in war and did not collaborate with the enemy.[145]

It is worth noting here that the agreement concluded with the Jewish tribes of Medina was not to last long by reason of growing alienation and mistrust felt by Muslims toward the Jews. As Armstrong notes, the Jews grew to resent Muhammad's ascendancy and became intent on deposing him whenever convenient.[146] Further, they generally derided Muhammad's claim to prophethood, as they believed the era of prophecy was over, and hence sought to weaken the religious and intellectual bases of Islam. Most importantly, the Medinan Jews were later suspected of being allied – at various stages, to varying degrees – with the polytheist enemies of the Muslims.[147] One of the Jewish tribes (Banu al-Nadir) was even thought to have plotted to assassinate Muhammad,[148] and another (Banu Qurayza) was believed to have collaborated with Meccan pagans during the Battle of the Trench in 627, which endangered the existence of the nascent Muslim community.[149] Consequently, the confederacy agreement with the Jewish tribes of Medina was ended, for Muslims held the former responsible for breaching their oaths.[150]

145 According to the agreement, the Jews were to 'contribute to the cost of battle' whenever the believers fought, and to avoid helping Muslims' enemies in the event of a war. Khadduri, supra note 18, 208.

146 K. Armstrong, *Islam: A Short History* (London: Phoenix, 2001) 15.

147 Ibid. 15–16; Watt, supra note 96, 200–204; *cf.* F. E. Peters, *Muhammad and the Origins of Islam* (Albany: Sunny Press, 1994) 218ff.

148 According to the tradition, when Muhammad tried to settle a dispute, he sought Banu al-Nadir's assistance in accordance with the agreement Muslims reached with the Jews. But during the negotiations held with the chiefs of the Nadir, Muhammad intuited that they were plotting to assassinate him. More precisely, during the talks, the Nadir tribe was recorded to have acted strangely. When Muhammad had reportedly sensed a mischief, he left the place discreetly and was visited by Gabriel who revealed to him that the Nadir was to assassinate him. The incident resulted in the expulsion of the Nadir tribe. For more on this incident, see T. Ramadan, *In the Footsteps of the Prophet: Lessons from the Life of Muhammad* (Oxford: Oxford University Press, 2007) 131; Ishaq, supra note 96, 265ff. Some Western commentators argued that although the suspected assassination was a real possibility in that some men of Nadir could indeed have planned to kill Muhammad, this did not change the fact that the ensuing expulsion of the tribe not merely secured additional living space in the city, but also fortified the political position of Muslims by neutralising a potential enemy, and hence by humbling potential rivals in Medina and elsewhere. See further J. Lassner, *Jews, Christians, and the Abode of Islam: Modern Scholarship, Medieval Realities* (Chicago: The University of Chicago Press, 2012) 146–147; M. V. McDonald, 'Translator's Foreword' in: W. M. Watt (annotator); M. V. McDonald (trans.), *The History of al-Tabari: The Foundation of the Community,* Vol. VII (Albany: State of New York Press, 1987) xxxvi.

149 Ishaq, supra note 96, 461.

150 The end of confederacy meant exile for the Banu Qaynuqa and the Banu Nadir, whereas it meant execution for the male population of the Banu Qurayzah. Ibn Ishaq reports that after the Battle of the Trench 'the apostle besieged them [the Banu Qurayzah] for 25 nights until they were sore pressed and God cast terror into their hearts'. It appears that the Jews had hoped to be banished on the same terms as the

Returning to the theme of duration, while early treaties signed between the Prophet and non-Muslims contained no temporal limitation, the Treaty of Hudaybiyyah had a specific 10-year upper limit. Signed in 628, in the aftermath of the Battle of the Trench, this treaty sought to establish a temporary peace with the formidable Meccan enemies of Islam. Broadly speaking, the treaty stipulated a 10-year truce between the parties, accompanied by clauses granting the Muslims the right to make pilgrimage to the holy Kaaba the following year in exchange for the Muslims' pledge to return Qurayshi converts to Mecca.[151] Although the treaty initially appeared to have unfairly favoured the pagans, it ultimately yielded far-reaching results for the Muslim camp. Of particular importance was the long-awaited lull in the hitherto relentless fighting between the signatories; this enabled the Muslims to channel their resources into the solidification of their fledgling power base. Further, Mecca's formal acknowledgement of the Muslim polity as a legitimate force allowed Muslims to enter into a host of agreements with neighbouring tribes, which began to recognise the growing prestige of the young Muslim city-State.[152] This 10-year truce would not last long however; for when the treaty had been violated by an assault of a confederate of the Meccans (the Banu Bakr) against a Muslim ally (the Banu Khudaah), the Prophet cancelled the agreement,[153] ordering his soldiers to march over Mecca, which was captured in 630 almost without bloodshed.[154]

As may readily be observed, the treaty appears to have eventually favoured the Muslim side, which had the chance to consolidate its political power during the lull in hostilities. Likewise, the time limit seems to have served no other purpose than to end the violence for a while, enabling parties to focus on their long-term objectives. It must be stressed here that the Quran does not envisage any specific

Qaynuqa and Nadir tribes. However, when they surrendered unconditionally, Muhammad suggested that their fate was to be determined by an arbiter, Sa'd bin Mu'adh, who had been one of the confederates of the Qurayza. The Jews submitted to the suggestion, but the appointed arbiter decreed that all male members of the tribe would be put to the sword, their property would be divided, and their women and children would be taken as captives. See Ishaq, supra note 96, 463–464; *cf.* M. A. Khan, *Islamic Jihad: A Legacy of Forced Conversion, Imperialism, and Slavery* (New York: iUniverse, 2009) 44ff.

151 The condition of returning Meccan converts initially excited significant opposition within the Muslim camp on account of its non-reciprocal character. It simply meant that when someone left Medina for Mecca, he would be able to remain there, yet if someone escaped from Mecca to join the Muslim cause, the Prophet was obligated to return him back to Mecca. See T. Ramadan, *Western Muslims and the Future of Islam* (New York: Oxford University Press, 2004) 92ff.

152 See M. W. Khan, *The Prophet of Peace: Teachings of the Prophet Muhammad* (New York: Penguin, 2009) 120.

153 A. Unal, *The Quran with Annotated Interpretation in Modern English* (Izmir: Sistem Matbaacilik, 2006) 1129.

154 The seizure of Mecca enabled Muslims to consolidate their political power in the region of Hijaz and to pay greater attention to regions outside Arabia, wherein great Arab–Muslim conquests were to take place to spread Islam. See Carimokam, supra note 89, 415–416; Unal, supra note 153, 1039ff.

time frame within which treaties may remain valid. It nevertheless openly recognises the legitimacy of treaties concluded with non-Muslims by urging Muslims to keep their pledges so long as other parties do the same.[155] The Quran's emphasis, putting it otherwise, is not laid upon the duration of agreements, but upon the sanctity of treaty undertakings. This is borne out by the unequivocal language of the Quran: 'Fulfil the Covenant of Allah when ye have entered into it, and break not your oaths after ye have confirmed them.'[156] The same point is reinforced by the sayings of the Prophet who similarly exhorted Muslims to observe their treaty commitments.[157] The Islamic State practice also evinces that Muslim rulers of various epochs had concluded numerous agreements of varying durations with non-Muslims in the light of the above enjoinments that commanded loyalty to one's word.

Regardless of the question whether the historical Muslim practice of observing treaty obligations fared better than that of non-Muslims, the long tradition of finding mediums to peacefully interact with the non-Islamic world suggests that the juristic postulation of incessant war, with brief spells of peace, between the opposing religious groups did not match up too well to reality.[158] Notwithstanding the view that the maximum term for a peace treaty could not exceed a period of 10 years, peace pacts were not necessarily framed within such time limits.[159] In fact, authoritative scholars, such as Abu Hanifa (d. 767), Malik Ibn Anas (d. 795), and Ibn Hanbal (d. 855), had never rejected the possibility of concluding indefinite agreements with non-Muslims when such was in the best interest of Muslims.[160] More precisely, these classical jurists rejected the unavoidability of constant wars in view of the notion that peace agreements (like other contracts) could be stretched out whenever peace, rather than protracted wars, better served Muslim interests. Be this as it may, the lack of a scholarly agreement about the extent and duration of peace agreements evidenced the controversial character of the matter.[161] Yet, given that the pacts Muhammad concluded with monotheist and/or pagan signatories had generally been based upon the notions of political expediency and public good, there exists no compelling reason why Islamic States should be bound by a strict time limit without good reason. Indeed, since the nature of the specific practice of Hudaybiyyah was marked by historical circumstances, one may speculate that had the political conditions of the time dictated otherwise, the

155 See Q. 9:7–13.
156 Q. 16:91.
157 See Y. al-Qaradawi, 'Islam and Democracy' in: Euben, supra note 100, 230, 245.
158 In Johnson's words, 'a tension thus existed between juristic theory and the actual practice'. J. T. Johnson, *The Holy War Idea in Western and Islamic Traditions* (University Park: The Pennsylvania State University Press, 2002) 144.
159 Badr, supra note 119, 56.
160 M. R. Zaman, 'Islamic Perspectives on Territorial Boundaries and Autonomy' in: S.H. Hashmi (ed.), *Islamic Political Ethics: Civil Society, Pluralism, and Conflict* (Princeton: Princeton University Press, 2002) 79, 93–94.
161 See A. AbuSulayman, 'Al-Dhimmah and Related Concepts in Historical Perspective' (1988) 9 *Institute of Muslim Minority Affairs* 8, 21.

Prophet could have agreed on a different time frame, or perhaps envisaged no temporal limit at all.

It is further to be borne in mind that the Islamic State practice generally defied the confines of academic speculations by demonstrating that agreements could last as long as they were possible and effective. One of the most notable and enduring instruments that contravened the idea of constant militancy as a feature of Muslim engagement with the external world was the treaty of 1535, concluded between the Ottoman Sultan and the French King. Although the treaty was initially limited to the duration of the lives of the Sultan and the King, it remained in force for centuries.[162] This treaty, also known as the 1535 Capitulations, was originally concluded as a result of the Ottoman–French alliance against the Habsburgs; but it later served such other purposes as advancing commercial, cultural, and political ties between the parties. Having recognised formal equality between the signatories, it envisaged reciprocal rights for the subjects of contracting powers by relaxing commercial restrictions and granting travel warrants. The treaty further incorporated certain judicial, diplomatic, and administrative privileges of signal import.[163] The French consuls, for instance, were provided with the right to exercise jurisdiction over all civil and criminal cases concerning French citizens residing within the Ottoman Empire. This was certainly a significant concession and it constituted a diminution of territorial jurisdiction.[164] A further illustration of how the purportedly inflexible boundaries between Muslims and non-Muslims could be relaxed came with a stipulation concerning the payment of the poll tax. The agreement provided that French subjects who resided within the Empire for less than 10 years were no longer required to pay the poll tax – and were still able to freely practise their religion.[165]

162 The treaty of 1740, containing 85 articles, renewed the Ottoman grants of 1535. Containing an explicit enumeration of extra-territorial privileges, it is mainly upon this treaty that other subsequent capitulation treaties with Christendom were modelled. See L. E. Thayer, 'The Capitulations of the Ottoman Empire and the Question of their Abrogation as its Affects the United States' (1923) 17 *American Journal of International Law* 207, 211.

163 See generally, J. Allain, 'Acculturation through the Middle Ages: The Islamic Law of Nations and its Place in the History of International Law' in: A. Orakhelashvili (ed.), *Research Handbook on the Theory and History of International Law* (Northampton, MA: Edward Elgar Publishing, 2011) 394, 406ff.

164 However, disputes (taking place within the Ottoman frontiers) between the French and Ottoman subjects were to be submitted to Ottoman juridical bodies – with the proviso that certain safeguards were to be put in place for the protection of French subjects. See further, H. J. Liebesny, 'The Development of Western Judicial Privileges' in: M. Khadduri; H. J. Liebesny (eds.), *Law in the Middle East,* Vol. I (Washington DC: Middle East Institute, 1955) 316–317.

165 The remainder of the treaty generally dealt with issues of forced labour, maritime matters, and the reciprocal freeing of slaves and prisoners of war. See further, Z. Arikan, 'Cumhuriyet Ideolojisi ve 1536 Kapitulasyonlari' in: N. Abaci (ed.), *VIII. Uluslararasi Turkiye'nin Sosyal ve Ekonomik Tarihi Kongresi* (Morrisville: Lulu Press, 2006) 154ff.

Closely modelled on the treaty of 1535, such capitulations were subsequently extended to other European States. For instance, when Queen Elizabeth I of England championed the cause of European resistance against Philip II of Spain, the Ottoman sultan warmly responded to her overtures and granted capitulations to the English monarchy in 1580 as a gesture of goodwill.[166] The Ottomans similarly supported the Dutch Calvinists' struggle against Catholic Spain, and accorded capitulations to the Dutch Republic in 1612, which in turn led to an expansion of trade between European and Mediterranean ports.[167]

While capitulations might be thought of as a notable success for the European powers of the day, the Islamic Empire's initial concessions were not a result of weakness, because at the height of their power Ottomans did not in fact require similar privileges in return. The actual purpose of the Ottoman sultans was rather to create division within the Christian frontier, which had until then acted in unison against the Islamic world.[168] In subsequent centuries, however, such capitulary agreements, which were also entered into between other Muslim nations and major European powers, went far beyond what had originally been intended. The agreements came to include an almost absolute exemption from local taxation, and a large measure of exemption from the applicability of local laws to the subjects of beneficiary States, whose consular organs began to exercise more power in juridical matters. Capitulary agreements eventually marked a turning point for Muslim States, which no longer occupied a superior or parallel position vis-à-vis their non-Muslim counterparts – a fact that set the scene for further fiscal, juridical, and administrative concessions to the detriment of the sovereignty of Muslim States.[169]

Such increasingly humiliating capitulations to the non-Muslim world would cause serious resentment for the future (nationalist) movements of the Ottoman, Persian, and Arab worlds,[170] which challenged the privileged status of foreign powers that began to act as 'States within States'.[171] It is worth noting that

166 See P. Bannerman, *Islam in Perspective: A Guide to Islamic Society, Politics and Law* (London: Routledge, 1988) 92; 154ff; Liebesny, supra note 164, 317, 330.

167 As Inalcik notes, the Ottoman support for the national monarchies and Protestants of Europe essentially aimed at breaking the Habsburg hegemony. But by opening the markets of the Levant to its European allies, the Ottomans also extended their support to the mercantile development of its European confederates. H. Inalcik, 'The Heyday and Decline of the Ottoman Empire' in: P. M. Holt *et al*, *The Cambridge History of Islam* (Cambridge: Cambridge University Press, 1970) 330; also see I. H. Kadi, *Ottoman and Dutch Merchants in the Eighteenth Century: Competition and Cooperation in Ankara, Izmir and Amsterdam* (Leiden: Brill, 2012) 60ff.

168 See Arikan, supra note 165, 154.

169 For an account of how capitulatory agreements signified a proof of diminished sovereignty in Iran, see G. G. R. Hambly, 'The Pahlavi Autocracy: Riza Shah, 1921–1941' in: P. Avery *et al* (eds.), *The Cambridge History of Iran*, Vol. VII (Cambridge: Cambridge University Press, 1991) 239ff.

170 B. Lewis; B. E. Churchill, *Islam: The Religion and the People* (Indianapolis: Wharton School Publishing, 2008) 185.

171 Thayer, supra note 162, 207.

capitulatory regimes for the Ottomans remained valid for almost four centuries; they were finally abolished with the Treaty of Lausanne in 1923, a year that also saw the annulment of such agreements for Iraq. Capitulations were similarly brought to an end in Syria and Palestine by the Mandatory Powers in 1928; the same year also marked the termination of capitulations for Iran. In Egypt, on the other hand, capitulatory privileges lasted until 1937.[172]

These agreements, notwithstanding their eventual adverse effects on Muslim interests, have patently demonstrated that the practice of temporary truces or alliances with members of the non-Muslim communities could last decidedly longer than 10 years. Indeed, capitulations and assorted international conventions were renewed time and again, and remained valid for centuries – as long as half a millennium in some cases – for reasons of expediency.[173]

As the aforementioned Islamic State practice demonstrates, what actually determined the length of treaties was not abstract doctrinal formulae, but rather socio-political considerations. This fact dovetails with Islam's general approach to engaging with other nations of various creeds, which takes its cue from practical interpretations of Islamic law rather than from inflexible dogmas. As discussed in detail earlier, since Islam's inception, Muslim scholars and leaders employed diverse forms of hermeneutics to render Islamic rules responsive to the dynamism of social forces. Likewise, supplementary legislative initiatives were undertaken to devise answers to problems for which primary sources contained no explicit provisions. In time, the human law-making agency hence midwifed a notable corpus of Islamic rules with a view to keeping the State and society running in an ever-changing world.[174]

Viewed in the light of above considerations, one may readily observe that although the basics of *siyar* were rooted in the primary sources of Islam, its superstructure is built by Muslim jurists and statesmen who sought to meet the demands of the time.[175] Since the basic canons of secondary legislative and legal interpretation practices are largely conditioned by the prevailing ideas and conditions of each epoch, it is no surprise that the first comprehensive treatises on the doctrine of warlike jihad – penned by great jurists like A. Hanifa (d. 767), A. al-Rahman al Awza'i (d. 774), and M. al-Shaybani (d. 804) – were composed at

172 Lewis, supra note 170, 185.
173 See Thayer, supra note 162, 211.
174 In practice, however, such man-made legal formulations were not presented as legislation proper, for Sharia technically admitted no *primary* legislative power exercised by humans. Secondary legislation was thus classified under various headings such as customs, regulations, or interpretations. On the role of human agency in Islamic law-making, see generally V. J. Cornell, 'Fruit of the Tree of Knowledge: The Relationship between Faith and Practice in Islam' in: Esposito, supra note 81, 63, 72ff.
175 Certainly, apart from relatively more flexible areas of Islamic law – such as *siyar* – Islamic law distinguished itself from secular codifications by its quest for rules of transcendental and universal nature, applicable at all times under the divine authority of God. For an analysis of this point, see Hassan, supra note 118, 65.

a time when Muslim rulers exhibited greater interest towards the external world. Notably, therefore, the period in which the main legal framework of military jihad was hammered out coincided with the era of great Muslim conquests, which aroused public interest in material and potential adversaries, conquered peoples, and new neighbours.[176] What is more, when Islamic laws of war and peace were fleshed out – through such methods as independent reasoning, judicial speculation, and analogical deduction – a great measure of pragmatism and flexibility had been exercised whenever basic religious principles so permitted. Muslims were, for instance, deemed permitted to enter into long-term alliances, truces, and peace agreements with their non-Muslim counterparts if necessary – a position that could be justified by reference to Quranic injunctions.[177] Such flexibility asserted itself in debates on whether Muslims were bound to fight incessant wars to achieve Islam's universal ideals, or whether religious efforts to spread Islam should primarily incorporate peaceable methods of dialogue, diplomacy, and conventions of various kinds.

As Lewis highlights, in the process of law-making, the discretionary powers of leaders and the critical thinking of learned scholars (particularly when exercised collectively) had played critical roles.[178] It must be repeated that such mundane legal efforts had by no means replaced or contravened the entrenched principles of Islamic law; rather, they elaborated or updated the extant norms, or introduced novel or alternative thinking in keeping with the spirit of primary sources. Consequently, apart from the key aspects of family law, which are considered intrinsic to the essence of Islam, many fresh principles were introduced to enrich Sharia.[179]

Such adoption or crystallisation of flexible norms transpired particularly in the field of politics. Muslim rulers, under the doctrine of *siyasa shariyya*,[180] put in place a myriad of administrative, legislative, or juridical measures to supplement those of Islamic law. The legitimacy of these measures was naturally contingent upon the question whether they served any public good without violating the fundamental tenets of Islam.[181] In essence, the concept of *siyasa shariyya* was invoked to correlate the dictates of religion with those of governance and administration with a view to assuring that all public acts were performed for the

176 See further J. L. Esposito, *The Oxford Encyclopaedia of the Modern Islamic World*, Vol. II (Oxford: Oxford University Press, 2001) 370; Khadduri, supra note 109, 23–26.

177 See, among others, Q. 9:7; Q. 9:8; Q. 9:10.

178 B. Lewis, *The Middle East: 2000 Years of History from the Rise of Christianity to the Present Day* (London: Phoenix Press, 2000) 224.

179 In his detailed empirical study, Coulson shows how some ancient principles and practices were recognised along with Islamic laws, and how new supplementary mechanisms were introduced by reason of political expediency. See further, N. J. Coulson, *A History of Islamic Law* (Edinburgh: Edinburgh University Press, 1964) 147.

180 This term roughly means governance according to the divine law.

181 F. E. Vogel, *Islamic Law and the Legal System of Saudi: Studies of Saudi Arabia* (Leiden: Brill, 2000) 173ff; Coulson, supra note 179, 147.

common good (*al-maslaha al 'amma*), the attainment of which often demanded additional norms or mechanisms supplementing those of Sharia.[182]

Taken together, it appears plain that such additional politico-legal tools provided Islam with dynamism and suppleness to remain relevant in changing circumstances. As will be discussed below, such flexibility asserted itself not merely in the field of just war, but in other areas relevant to the governance of State and society, as well as to the delivery of justice. A brief survey of such openness, pragmatism, and flexibility in Islam will equip the reader with the insight that rigid and abstract doctrines (e.g. the doctrines of constant belligerency and limited peace) are to be approached with utmost care, because Islam has largely followed a non-linear development within which inhered not only traditional and modern notions, but also religious and secular elements – all of which fused into the objective of being responsive to the demands of sacred as well as profane spheres of life.

B. Dictates of the Realpolitik: Religion and Secularism

In Islamic legal thought, there often existed a degree of dichotomy between certain areas of doctrine and practice. This forms part of the above-discussed endeavour to run society by means of dynamic norms and institutions that are not directly found in classical texts or established practices. The introduction of secular courts (*mazalim*) constitutes an excellent case in point. The foundations of these courts were laid down during the reign of Abbasides in an attempt to provide alternative forums for the provision of justice.[183] *Mazalim* courts were initially authorised by the caliph to exercise jurisdiction chiefly over administrative practices and regulations, as well as over issues of taxation and criminal justice. While the jurisdictional relationship between Sharia and *mazalim* courts was not always straightforward, it was clear that the former often decided on disputes concerning matters of private law, family law, inheritance, civil transactions, injuries, and public or familial endowments (*waqfs*),[184] whereas the latter customarily decided on matters of public policy, seeking to ensure that administrative practices were largely in conformity with public welfare.[185]

These secular *mazalim* courts similarly made an appearance during the reign of the Seljuq Empire, where they existed alongside Sharia courts to provide an

182 See D. Bramsen, 'Divine Law and Human Understanding: The Idea of Sharia in Saudi Arabia' in: J. S. Nielsen; L. Christoffersen (eds.), *Shari'a as Discourse: Legal Traditions and the Encounter with Europe* (Farnham: Ashgate Publishing, 2010) 157, 158ff.

183 See P. S. Ali, *Human Rights in Islam* (New Delhi: Adam Publishers, 1995) 81.

184 Coulson, supra note 179, 132.

185 These secular courts at times exercised jurisdiction on criminal offences over which Sharia envisaged heavy punishments (*hadd*). When authorities, for reasons of public policy, chose to impose less severe punishments for *hadd* crimes, they could authorise the *mazalim* courts. See M. Shapiro, *Courts: A Comparative and Political Analysis* (London: The University of Chicago Press, 1981) 207.

alternative medium for the sultan to hear his subjects' complaints. Apart from dealing with matters of public policy, these courts also functioned as expedient tools for the sultans to assert their authority by engaging with their people and, where necessary, dispensing justice in their personal capacities. Akin to the Abbasid experience, these courts differed from their religious counterparts by their capacity to exert a significant degree of flexibility in their application of substantive and procedural law.[186]

Such non-religious courts performed analogous functions in some other Muslim States (such as Mamluk Egypt), where they eventually came to exercise broad jurisdiction over a wide range of disputes.[187] One of the most significant advantages of these courts was that, since they operated within a secular legal framework, judges could decide cases on considerations of fairness and equity without being bound by a stringent body of law. Tyan, in this context, points out that *mazalim* courts flourished in large measure due to 'the inability of the ordinary judiciary to guarantee equal justice to all people'.[188] A kindred reason for establishing such alternative courts was the demand to surmount some rigid religious standards of procedure and evidence – such as the refusal to admit written[189] or circumstantial evidence, or the need for presenting two witnesses of the highest moral character in certain cases – which occasionally rendered the proceedings so formalistic that there was no possibility of deciding a case 'on the balance of probabilities'.[190]

Since such substantive or procedural complications in legal proceedings were recurrent, there also emerged a trend to use pre-Islamic local codes based on tradition or custom. A prominent example of this was seen in the Ottoman Empire,

186 See further, A. Black, *The History of Islamic Political Thought: From the Prophet to the Present* (New York: Routledge, 2001) 95ff.

187 The jurisdictional powers of *mazalim* courts became so broad that some scholars went as far as to write that: 'It is hardly necessary to point out that only in limited fields did the provisions of the Sharia apply. What criminal, fiscal and commercial provisions there existed were largely ignored. Sharia lawyers had themselves contributed to this state of affairs, for when at an early stage its provisions were being left behind by practical developments they had accepted stratagems . . . which avoided the intent of the law.' See J. S. Nielsen, *Secular Justice in an Islamic State: Mazalim under the Bahri Mamluks, 662/1264–789/1387* (Istanbul, 1985), as cited in: H. Gerber, *State, Society, and Law in Islam: Ottoman Law in Comparative Perspective* (Albany: State University of New York Press, 1994) 61.

188 E. Tyan, 'Judicial Organization: The General Characteristics of the Judicial Function' in: Khadduri, supra note 164, 263.

189 The issue of whether verbal or oral evidence was to be privileged over written evidence had been moot. While some Sunni jurists, particularly the Hanafis, argued that oral testimony was a more powerful form of evidence, other jurists opposed this view by stressing that, since the Prophet had not made a general ruling on the relative value of oral or written evidence, regard had to be had to the nature of the evidence in each case. For an analysis, see A. A. Ahmad, *Islam, Modernity, Violence and Everyday Life* (New York: Palgrave, 2009) 54ff.

190 See Coulson, supra note 179, 125.

where, on account of the sophistication of the State machinery that sprawled across vast territories, secular laws were employed to respond to the varying demands of a highly populous empire. The legitimacy of these laws was based on customs and the sultan's position as the supreme ruler.[191] Cognisant of fundamental religious precepts and practices, Ottomans drew on some local customs and practices. In the Hungarian provinces, for instance, tax-paying subjects of the empire (*reaya*) were required to pay one gold coin to the Sultan, which was the same amount paid to the Hungarian Kings before the Ottoman acquisition of the land in 1541. Ottomans likewise preserved some of the local customs and practices of the Akkoyunlu Turkoman confederation, which ruled Eastern Anatolia before the Ottoman control of the region.[192]

After the conquest of Constantinople in 1453, such unwritten non-religious norms, also known as the customary law (*orfi hukuk*), were collected, systematised, and codified into what is called the *Kanun-i Osmani*. The sultan's promulgation of secular codes, covering such broad areas as criminal, civil, administrative, and fiscal law, was an extraordinary development in Islamic history, which witnessed a harmonious fusion and application of secular and religious laws.[193] It appears clear that the dualistic nature of the Ottoman legal system, which incorporated laws stemming from both sacred and non-religious sources, not only enabled the sultan to devise novel responses to unprecedented socio-political conditions, but also to answer the needs of the Empire's non-Muslim populations residing in culturally diverse milieus, with their distinct local customs and pre-Islamic laws.

A culmination in the codification of secular laws was reached during the reform era of the nineteenth century (the *Tanzimat* period), at a time when it was clear that the Ottoman Empire ceased to keep pace with the scientific, industrial, and political progress of the West. The poignant realisation that the biggest Islamic Empire was on a steady decline led the Ottoman rulers to progressively adopt Western institutions and technology, as well as novel secular legal principles and mechanisms to keep up with the spirit of the age.[194] As far as the legitimation of legal reforms was concerned, the Ottoman pundits posited that eternal religious principles had to be accompanied with secular norms to govern the increasingly complex relations of modernity.[195] The justification of the legal reformation did

191 Gerber, supra note 187, 61–65.

192 G. Agoston; B. Masters, *Encyclopaedia of the Ottoman Empire* (New York: Infobase Publishing, 2009) 306–307; also see M. A. Unal, *XVI. Yuzyilda Harput Sancagi* (Ankara: Turk Tarih Kurumu, 1989) 118ff.

193 Agoston, supra note 192, 307; J. W. Sedlar, *East Central Europe in the Middle Ages, 1000–1500: A History of East Central Europe*, Vol. III (Seattle: The University of Washington Press, 1994) 332–333; Black, supra note 186, 212ff; H. Isamoglu-Inan, *State and Peasant in the Ottoman Empire: Agrarian Power Relations and Regional Economic Development in Ottoman Anatolia during the Sixteenth Century* (Leiden: Brill, 1994) 24ff.

194 See S. S. Onar, 'The Majalla' in: Khadduri, supra note 164, 293.

195 Thayer, supra note 162, 212.

not prove to be very difficult, since the traditional laws of the Empire had long fallen far short of meeting the needs of the latest financial, commercial, and banking practices. The existing laws were also inadequate or antiquated in the fields of admiralty, civil, criminal, and enforcement law.[196]

Efforts to reform and secularise the Ottoman legal system bore fruit particularly with the adoption of the Gulhane Charter of 1839, which sought to limit arbitrary exercises of executive powers and afford basic rights and equality to all subjects of the sultan.[197] In 1856, another imperial decree (*Hatt-i Humayun*) confirmed the sultan's pledge to provide equality and justice for all subjects of the Empire, irrespective of their religious, racial, and ethnic affiliations.[198] During this era of swift transformation, the Empire expanded its egalitarian assurances by increasingly recruiting non-Muslims into public offices, and by promulgating the policy of non-discrimination in taxation and education. In defiance of age-old practices, non-Muslims were also invited to perform military service for the State, but were offered exemption on payment of a substitution fee (*bedel*), which in effect replaced the fiscal obligation of the *jizya* payments levied on non-Muslims.[199] Furthermore, by moving far beyond the traditional confines, the secular reforms of the nineteenth century ushered in such radical developments as the formation of mixed secular tribunals to adjudicate commercial disputes between Ottomans and non-Ottomans, the abolishment of the capital punishment for apostasy from Islam, and the prohibition of the official and private use of derogatory epithets (e.g. *gavur*, i.e. infidel) against any class or religious category.[200]

It should be pointed out that there had been a variety of impediments to implementing the reforms. In an empire where the legal system was essentially founded

196 The introduction of Western codes occasionally produced profound confusion, as the application of both traditional Ottoman and foreign-sourced laws offered irreconcilable solutions to a legal issue. In an effort to resolve such difficulties, a novel civil code (*Mecelle*) was eventually adopted. See Onar, supra note 194, 293–296; see generally D. Quataert, *The Ottoman Empire, 1700–1922* (Cambridge: Cambridge University Press, 2000).

197 The reformation process was evidently laden with political objectives, too. Among the most urgent political goals of the Charter were the resolve to counter the rising tide of separatist nationalism simmering across the Empire, and to respond to the increasing pressure of European powers' interventionist policies over the rights of Christian minorities in the crumbling Empire. But the element of 'European pressure' should not be overestimated; for, while these reforms aimed to gain European favour and avert foreign intervention, they were largely the consequence of a genuine belief that the most effective way to save the empire from ruin was to introduce radical 'European-style' reforms. See E. J. Zurcher, *Turkey: A Modern History* (New York: I.B. Tauris, 2004) 56.

198 See Quataert, supra note 196, 66ff.

199 See C. V. Findley, *The Turks in World History* (Oxford: Oxford University Press, 2004) 160; see generally, C. V. Findley, *Turkey, Islam, Nationalism, and Modernity: A History: 1789–2007* (New Haven: Yale University Press, 2010).

200 S. Zubaida, *Law and Power in the Islamic World* (London: I.B. Tauris, 2005) 129ff; Zurcher, supra note 197, 61ff.

on religious precepts, it was one thing to accommodate religious differences, but quite another to provide practical equality between Muslims and non-Muslims.[201] Putting it another way, the Ottoman recognition of equality was not an easy compromise, for it marked a sharp turn towards Western secularism – a process that was to reach maturity by the second quarter of the following century. Nevertheless, despite some serious discordance between traditional doctrines and the new privileges accorded to non-Muslim Ottoman subjects on the basis of full civic equality, modernising reforms in this period were in full swing. In addition to the fundamental rights of life, dignity, property, due process, and non-discrimination, reformist pressures led to the adoption of the 1876 Constitution, which notably envisaged religious freedoms, and security against arbitrary intrusions on personal liberties, as well as the freedom of the press.[202]

As touched upon above, the implications of these far-reaching reforms were assuredly drastic for the Ottoman Empire, as they practically defied the hierarchical structure of the polity wherein non-Muslims had hitherto been tolerated, but not deemed equal with Muslims. The acquiescence to Western standards of equality[203] did not thus root out the official reluctance to fully implement the reforms that were largely considered to have flown in the face of entrenched values and conventions.[204] It would take the collapse of the Ottoman Empire at the end of the Great War to see a further break from religious laws.

The founders of the modern Turkish Republic, which sprang from the ruins of the old Empire, set out to turn Turkey's direction toward the West. Indeed, the establishment of the Turkish Grand National Assembly in 1920 had set in motion scores of decisive measures that marked Turkey's drastic transformation from an Islamic Empire into a nation State.[205] Among the most decisive policies of the new Republic was secularism,[206] which aimed at dismantling the political authority of

201 It was hence no wonder that many Muslims initially expressed their concerns about such far-reaching legal reforms, claiming that the new regulations breached some of the basic tenets of Islam. See generally, A. Palmer, *The Decline and Fall of the Ottoman Empire* (New York: M. Evans, 1994).

202 See Esposito, supra note 176, 143–144; Piscatori, supra note 80, 52–53.

203 It is worth noting that the Ottoman Empire was admitted as a member of the European State system following the Crimean War (1853–1856) by the Treaty of Paris, which mainly pursued the policy of upholding the post-Napoleonic balance of power by thwarting Russian encroachments upon Ottoman sovereignty. See S. D. Krasner, *Sovereignty: Organised Hypocrisy* (Princeton: Princeton University Press, 1999) 158ff; S. Akgonul, *The Minority Concept in the Turkish Context: Practices and Perceptions in Turkey, Greece and France* (Leiden: Brill, 2013) 73ff.

204 See M. Schulz, 'The Guarantees of Humanity: The Concert of Europe and the Origins of the Russo-Ottoman War of 1877' in: B. Simms; D. J. B. Trim (eds.), *Humanitarian Intervention: A History* (Cambridge: Cambridge University Press, 2011) 184, 186–187.

205 See B. Lewis, *The Emergence of Modern Turkey* (London: Oxford University Press, 1961) 327.

206 The founders of the Republic subsequently summarised their political programme with six key principles: republicanism, nationalism, populism, revolutionism,

Islam and rooting the concept of sovereignty in the popular will of the nation. To this effect, not merely were the time-honoured institutions of the sultanate and the caliphate abrogated, but also the dominion of religion over the political and legal machinery was largely brought to an end by a series of reforms, which included the abolition of religious schools, Sharia courts, the office of the *Shaykh-ul-Islam*, Ministry of Sharia and Religious Foundations, as well as the use of religious titles and garments in public spaces.[207]

The new regime's primary objective was to effect a thorough rupture with the Ottoman legacy, an ambitious goal requiring a spate of major legal reforms. For instance, in 1926 a new secular civil code replaced its former counterpart (*Mecelle*), which generally drew on Sharia principles.[208] Having originated from the Swiss Civil Code, the novel Turkish Civil Code eradicated polygamy, granted equal rights to men and women in many family matters, and regulated such issues as the upbringing and custody of children, marriage, and divorce as well as inheritance in accordance with secular and modern principles.[209] The Western influence on the legal system grew following the enactment of the 1926 Law of Obligations (of Swiss origin), the 1926 Turkish Commercial Law (of predominantly German origin), and the 1927 Turkish Code of Civil Procedure (again of Swiss origin).[210] In the realm of public law, a similar trend was followed; the 1926 Turkish Penal Code, for instance, originated from the Italian Criminal law of 1889, and the main corpus of the Turkish Administrative Law was of French origin. Expressing his surprise at the revolutionary nature of such legal changes, the eminent Swiss professor of international law, Sauser-Hall, noted that 'such a radical and rapid change is unknown to history'.[211]

Certainly, the practice of adopting secular codes to replace the religious ones was not peculiar to Turkey. In fact, the Turkish initiative of re-casting and secularising the legal system by modelling it on European legal codes inspired almost all Middle Eastern countries.[212] The experience of Persia, in this context, resembles that of Turkey in many respects. Having similarly succumbed to the growing pressures of the Western world, the Persians came to make capitulary concessions to Christian powers. A case in point was the humiliating 1828 Treaty of Turkmenchay, which compelled Persia to grant significant territorial and legal

secularism, and statism. See P. Dumont, 'The Origins of Kemalist Ideology' in: J. M. Landau (ed.), *Ataturk and the Modernization of Turkey* (Leiden: Brill, 1984) 26.

207 M. Kocak, 'Islam and National Law in Turkey' in: J. M. Otto (ed.), *Sharia Incorporated: A Comparative Overview of the Legal Systems of Twelve Muslim Countries in Past and Present* (Leiden: Leiden University Press, 2010) 231, 240–242.

208 Zubaida notes that *Mecelle* was written in keeping with a French methodology, yet its initial axioms were taken from the Sharia. The '"form" is European', he notes, but 'the "content" Muslim'. Zubaida, supra note 200, 133.

209 Kocak, supra note 207, 243.

210 See generally, S. Guran, 'Administrative Law' in: T. Ansay; D. Wallace (eds.), *Introduction to Turkish Law* (The Hague: Kluwer Law International, 2005) 53ff.

211 Cited in: A. Guriz, 'Sources of Turkish Law' in: Ansay, supra note 210, 1, 9.

212 Coulson, supra note 179, 152.

concessions to Russia. Apart from inflicting vast land losses on Persia, Russia wrested such extra-territorial privileges as consular jurisdiction for its subjects and preferential tariffs for its commercial activities.[213] Perhaps more dramatic than this treaty was the Treaty of Tehran, signed between Britain and Persia in 1814, where the Shah, among others, pledged to provide Britain with military aid in the event of a British–Afghan conflict.[214] This simply meant that Persia had committed itself to taking up arms against a Muslim State, along with a non-Muslim State, when necessary – a political manoeuvre that clearly defied basic Islamic ideals and precepts.

Following the ordeal of the Great War, Persia – renamed Iran in 1935 – ventured into an unprecedented modernisation programme. Following in the footsteps of the Kemalist revolution in Turkey, the Shah of Iran, Reza Khan, set out to secularise the society in a top-down fashion. Illustrative examples of this process included the inception of secular education for boys and girls alike, the banning of the veil, the requirement for mullahs to shave and wear the kepi instead of the customary turban, as well as the proscription of the accustomed celebrations held in honour of the martyred Imam Husayn.[215] Although such authoritarian reformism might have contributed to Iran's rapid modernisation along Western lines, the process had marked a traumatic break from some of the entrenched cultural and religious values;[216] for secularism and its accompanying institutions were in large part introduced in disregard of the general will of the people, respect for which generally constitutes an essential element of any successful social-engineering project. The Iranian reformers' top-down measures of modernisation are known to have ultimately paved the way for a reactionary Islamic Revolution in 1979.

Similar reform efforts also took place in other Islamic States, Egypt being a case in point. In a bid to reshape the society along European lines, Egyptian reformers, since the time of the radical moderniser Muhammad Ali (r. 1805–1848), embarked upon a wide-ranging transformation of the society in political, financial, administrative, educational, and military spheres. As this process required significant legal reorientation, Western codes – particularly of French origin – were adopted to restrict the applicability of the Sharia mainly to cases concerning the personal status of Muslims.[217] Such comprehensive political and legal reforms

213 See S. Hunter, *Iran's Foreign Policy in the Post-Soviet Era: Resisting the New International Order* (California: ABC-CLIO, 2010) 181ff; F. Rajaee, 'Conclusion: Why "Alone"' in: T. Juneau; S. Razavi (eds.) *Iranian Foreign Policy since 2001* (New York: Routledge, 2013) 208, 215.

214 R. Greaves, 'Iranian Relations with Great Britain and British India, 1798–1921' in: Avery, supra note 169, 374, 387ff.

215 For an assessment, see K. Armstrong, *A History of God* (London: Vintage, 1993) 424ff.

216 See J. Tolan *et al, Europe and the Islamic World: A History* (Princeton: Princeton University Press, 2013) 376–377.

217 See J. Marlowe, *A History of Modern Egypt and Anglo-Egyptian Relations: 1800–1953* (New York: Praeger, 1954) 135; F. R. Hunter, *Egypt under the Khedives 1805–1879: From*

to keep up with changing realities were also undertaken by Tunisia, which, as early as 1857, guaranteed civic equality for all before the law and in taxation, and promised security to everyone irrespective of religious and racial standing.[218]

To be sure, the introduction of secular laws into Muslim legal systems gained significant momentum with the European colonisation of large parts of the Muslim world. Radical secular legal reforms may be observed to have occurred particularly after the Great War, a period when Western codes were sometimes copied verbatim.[219] Yet, even in the post-colonial period, Muslim States did not generally revert to Islamic public law concepts. It was merely in the area of family and personal status law – which relates to such questions as marriage, divorce, child custody, and inheritance – that the majority of Muslim States (with the notable exception of Turkey) have continued to observe Sharia principles.[220] Even in stricter regimes, secular codes in large part remained in force. For instance, in the post-Khomeini Iran, Iranian authorities applied Islamic penal measures restrictively to such acts as murder, adultery, and theft (albeit criminal sanctions were selectively applied due to political considerations). More significantly, by dint of the 1989 amendments to the Constitution, sanctioned by Khomeini himself before his demise, the Iranian executive was empowered to set aside certain Sharia principles if such was deemed necessary 'in the interests of the Islamic community'.[221]

In light of the above observations, it should be evident that the application of the Sharia has never been uniform across the Muslim world; rather, it was contingent on the socio-political character of each society, and on the dictates of *realpolitik*. Not surprisingly, therefore, the ambit of the Sharia at times grew extensively, and at other times its scope narrowed, depending on the broader circumstances. The same finding holds valid for the way in which Islamic international law in general, and the laws of war in particular have been interpreted and applied. As discussed above, when it was deemed expedient or necessary, assorted agreements of peace were concluded with non-Muslim entities for short or long durations.

Flexibility, innovation and adaptability have thus been key qualities underpinning Islamic international law. At the practical level, the historical record of Islamic

Household Government to Modern (Cairo: The American University in Cairo Press, 1984) 21–22.

218 Esposito, supra note 176, 143.

219 See W. G. Clarence-Smith, *Islam and the Abolition of Slavery* (Oxford: Oxford University Press, 2006) 98–99.

220 But it must be noted that the reformist-minded scholars in the post-colonial period have altered some of the key concepts of the customary family and personal law to keep up with modern circumstances. One of the most prominent manifestations of this process was the progressive ascent of the rights of women in family and inheritance matters. For an analysis, see E. Moosa, 'Colonialism and Islamic Law' in: Masud, supra note 74, 158, 168ff.

221 See S. Zubaida, 'Is Iran an Islamic State?' in: J. Beinin; J. Stork (eds.), *Political Islam: Essays from Middle East Report* (London: I.B. Tauris, 1997) 119.

State practice attests to the fact that Muslim States have constantly been in touch with the changing realities of the world. Indeed, the conduct of most exemplary rulers suggests that theoretical formulations of certain epochs – most of which were moot even in their own times – have not petrified the general contours of Muslim engagement with the outside world, particularly when such formulations dictated incessant religious aggression against non-Muslims. It is on this account to be stressed that neither socio-politically contingent doctrines of pre-modern ages, nor decontextualised formulations on warlike measures should mould the framework of Islamic laws of war and peace.

IV. Going Beyond Partisan Positions

As established above, the scope of jihad reaches beyond the use of lethal force by also encompassing peaceful methods of religious striving. Furthermore, the implications of warlike jihad against the pagans have been shown to have more dramatic consequences relative to the 'People of the Book'. This meant that no forceful conversion to Islam was imposed on scriptuaries, who in return were to avoid proselytising their beliefs, to participate in shouldering the financial burdens of the Islamic polity by paying a poll tax,[222] and to contribute in various ways to the commonweal.[223] The payment of the poll tax, until modern times, largely allowed the non-Muslim monotheists of conquered lands to abide by their religious convictions in a relatively protected environment, where they did not have to perform military service.[224]

222 See R. C. Martin, 'The Religious Foundations of War, Peace and Statecraft in Islam' in: Kelsay, supra note 111, 91, 98; B. Lewis, *The Arabs in History* (London: Hutchinson's University Library, 1950) 93–94.

223 As stated earlier, the system of levying *jizya* upon non-Muslims was abolished in many Muslim States – a development set in motion with the Tanzimat reformation of the Ottoman Empire, which sought to erase the customary lines of demarcation drawn between the Muslim and non-Muslim subjects of the Empire. See Findley, supra note 199, 160; also see K. Hidemitsu, 'Mobility of Non-Muslims in Mid-Nineteenth-Century Aleppo' in: K. Hidemitsu (ed.), *The Influence of Human Mobility in Muslim Societies* (New York: Routledge, 2009) 117, 135. In modern Muslim nation-States, the rationale for imposing *jizya* may be said to have become invalid, because all citizens, who are no longer defined via religious affiliations, generally bear equal rights and responsibilities, which include the duty to perform military service.

224 It is highlighted that the poll tax had also a symbolic meaning of 'submission and desistance from harmful acts'. See R. Peters (ed. and trans.), *Jihad in Medieval and Modern Islam* (Leiden: Brill, 1977) 51; M. Shaltut, 'The Koran and Fighting' in: Peters, supra note 45, 79; also see Q. 9:29. Ali similarly explains that 'the jizyah was . . . partly symbolic and partly a commutation for military service, but as the amount was insignificant and the exemptions numerous, its symbolic character predominated.' Ali, supra note 6, 445.

It was further highlighted that while military conquests were among the chief means of promulgating Islam,[225] Muslim armies customarily set off on campaigns against non-Muslim monotheists only when the Muslim invitation to embrace the Islamic faith or to pay the poll tax was rejected by the latter. The focal concern of the conquerors was not to impose Islam by means of arms on those who held monotheistic beliefs and revered the holy scriptures that were recognised by the Muslims, as the Quran explicitly forbids forceful conversions by not only envisaging the 'no compulsion' principle,[226] but also by recognising the merits of monotheists who sincerely believe in God and perform pious acts.[227] Hence, those with revered scriptures were always given the freedom to accept Islam or to retain their faiths by accepting the status of 'protected people' (*dhimmi*) with accompanying fiscal measures.[228]

Admittedly, the 'People of the Book' were not on equal footing with Muslim subjects, yet they were generally accorded a degree of liberty and tolerance with no comparable parallel within Christian Europe of the Middle Ages.[229] The Ottoman Empire's *millet* system constitutes an illustrative paradigm of the distinct Muslim attitude toward recognised religious communities (known as *millets*), which were given a reasonable level of cultural and religious autonomy. The *millet* system

225 As discussed above, the Sharia sanctioned lethal force not merely in cases of self-defence, but also as an instrument of spreading the sphere of Islam – albeit this could be done in peaceful ways, too.

226 See Q. 2:256.

227 While this is not the place to discuss the moot point whether the Quran acknowledges the possibility for a scriptuary to be rewarded in the hereafter, it is worth noting that some verses appear to support the idea that a believer (whether a Muslim, Jew, Christian, or Sabian) may be rewarded in the afterlife provided that he truly believes in God and acts righteously. See Q. 2:111; Q. 2:112; Q. 2:62; Q. 5:48; 49:13. Some other verses, on the other hand, seem to defy such interpretation. Generally see Q. 3:85; Q. 3:19. Scholars are divided on this thorny question; for more on this debate, see F. Rahman, *Major Themes of the Qur'an*, 2nd ed. (London: the University of the Chicago Press, 2009) 166ff; I. A. Omar (ed.), A *Muslim View of Christianity: Essays on Dialogue by Mahmoud Ayoub* (New Delhi: Logos Presss, 2010) 199ff; M. Koylu, *Islam and its Quest for Peace: Jihad, Justice and Education* (Washington: The Council for Research in Values and Philosophy, 2003) 66ff.

228 Shaybani wrote that when a Muslim army besieged a city of non-Muslim residents, the latter would likewise be asked to embrace Islam first. If the residents accepted the offer, they would be entitled to the same rights as Muslims; but when they refused, they would be demanded to pay the *jizya* in order for the hostilities to cease. See Khadduri, supra note 109, 159.

229 While it would be erroneous to measure medieval Islamic practices against the yardstick of contemporary human rights principles, it is fair to note that the Muslim record of treating monotheistic minorities had been significantly better than its Christian counterpart. This fact has been emphasised by Lewis: 'There is nothing in Islamic history to compare with the massacres and expulsions, the inquisitions and persecutions that Christians habitually inflicted on non-Christians and still more on each other. In the lands of Islam, persecution was the exception; in Christendom, sadly, it was often the norm.' B. W. Lewis, *The Multiple Identities of the Middle East* (New York: Schocken Books, 2001) 129.

was chiefly founded upon legal pluralism that entitled denominational groups to follow their own laws, particularly in matters germane to family law, personal status, and succession. Moreover, this unique system did not merely empower each group to practise religious rites, but also to enforce its own laws, establish its communal organisations, and to regulate its education and social life – on condition that such measures did not contravene the basic tenets of Islamic law.[230] Although the decisive military and political power rested with Muslims in this system, non-Muslims had substantial impact on the management of economic life and, in part, on the political process.[231]

The *millet* system, which expired under the secular Republic of Turkey, was certainly not born in a vacuum; Islamic law, since its inception, has recognised the special position of the scriptuaries.[232] As alluded to above, Muslims were urged to respect the lives, customs, rituals, and traditions of the protected groups, whose places of worship were not to be interfered with, even in times of war.[233] The Quran explicitly enjoins Muslims from disputing with the 'People of the Book' – unless there exist compelling reasons for so doing – but exhorts them to 'say "we believe in the Revelation which has come down to us and in that which came down to you; our God and your God is One; and it is to Him we bow (in Islam)"'.[234] This verse underscores the Islamic belief that since all believers worship the same God, differences between them should primarily be settled peacefully, before lethal measures could be resorted to, and that all monotheists are to be respected. As pointed out earlier, the principal reason why the scriptuaries could have been the legitimate objects of military or supplemental fiscal measures relates to the Muslim belief that while they shared the monotheistic understanding of the Deity, they subsequently failed to acknowledge God's final effort, conveyed through His last Prophet, to reconstruct the original, but long-forgotten or distorted, message preached by earlier prophets.[235]

230 B. Masters, *Christians and Jews in the Ottoman Arab World: The Roots of Sectarianism* (Cambridge: Cambridge University Press, 2001) 61ff; I. Yilmaz, *Muslim Laws, Politics and Society in Modern Nation States: Dynamic Legal Pluralisms in England, Turkey and Pakistan* (Aldershot: Ashgate Publishing, 2005) 99.

231 B. Lewis, *What Went Wrong: Western Impact and Middle Eastern Response* (London: Phoenix, 2002) 37–38. Historically, protected peoples had restricted participation in public affairs and authority over Muslims, yet the actual terms of the *dhimmi* status, as Naim points out, varied over time and place depending on a variety of factors. See An-Na'im, supra note 10, 130.

232 See generally, A. A. An-Na'im, 'Religious Freedom in Egypt under the Shadow of the Islamic *Dhimma* System' in: L. Swidler (ed.), *Religious Liberty and Human Rights in Nations and in Religions* (Philadelphia: Ecumenical Press, 1986) 50ff.

233 See H. M. Zawati, '*Jus in Bello:* Civilians' Fundamental Rights under Islamic and Public International Law' in: Bassiouni, supra note 11, 167, 180.

234 Q. 29:46.

235 Q. 33:40; Q. 2:127–130.

The situation was somewhat different for the pagans, however. Indeed, 'for those who were not monotheists and possessed no recognised scriptures,' in Lewis' language, 'the alternatives were harsher';[236] for, as pointed out earlier, one of the main objectives of jihad was to proselytise unbelievers either through violent or non-violent means.[237] Undoubtedly, the common Muslim practice was first to invite pagans to accept Islam;[238] it was only on their resistance that the pagans were fought.[239] According to Khadduri, polytheists had the limited choice of either embracing Islam or facing the sword, since, unlike the monotheists, they could not choose to pay the poll tax. This, he argued, was on account of several sword verses that enjoined Muslims to 'fight and slay the pagans wherever [they were found]',[240] to 'fight the unbelievers [firmly]',[241] and to 'smite at their [pagans'] necks' when they were met in fight.[242] Khadduri supports his argument by citing one of the *hadiths* ascribed to Muhammad,[243] who is reported to have said: 'I have been commanded to fight against people [polytheists] till they testify that there is no god but Allah, that Muhammad is the Messenger of Allah.'[244] Khadduri's reasoning shows parallels with that of Shafi, who had also asserted that the option of paying the poll tax was restricted to the scriptuaries. In this view, pagans had thus to be fought until they eventually accepted Islam on pain of death.[245] However, the Muslim position on polytheists appears to have a more complex character than that proposed by Khadduri and Shafi. In fact, both of these scholars failed to cite an important *hadith*, narrated by Muslim, where the Prophet is reported to have allowed polytheists to pay the *jizyah* as one of the options presented to them:

> When you [Muslims] meet your enemies who are polytheists, invite them to three courses of action. If they respond to any one of these, you also accept it and withhold yourself from doing them any harm. Invite them to (accept) Islam; if they respond to you, accept it from them and desist from fighting against them. . . . If they refuse to accept Islam, demand from them the *jizya*. If they agree to pay, accept it from them and hold off your hands. If they refuse to pay the tax, seek Allah's help and fight them.[246]

236 B. Lewis, *The Middle East* (London: Weidenfeld & Nicolson, 1995) 57; also see Khadduri, supra note 18, 80.
237 See M. Khadduri, 'International Law' in: Khadduri, supra note 164, 349, 355.
238 There was no pre-determined period of reflection and consideration; this depended upon the context.
239 See G. F. Nafziger; M. W. Walton, *Islam at War: A History* (Westport: Praeger Publishers, 2003) 217.
240 Q. 9:5.
241 Q. 9:123.
242 Q. 47:4.
243 Khadduri, supra note 18, 75.
244 Sahih Muslim, Bk. 1:33.
245 Haleem, supra note 2, 76–77.
246 Sahih Muslim, Bk. 19:4294

Apart from this tradition, which plainly recognises the possibility of tolerating pagans in return for the poll tax, there are numerous verses in the Quran that evince agreements of peace signed between the Muslim and pagan forces. The following verse, for example, commands loyalty to the terms of the treaty concluded with the pagans: 'How can there be a league . . . with the pagans, except those with whom ye made a treaty . . . as long as these stand true to you, stand ye true to them.'[247] The following verse, however, laments that Arab pagans broke their oaths when they had the edge over the Muslims: 'How (can there be such a league), seeing that if they get an advantage over you, they respect not in you the ties either of kinship or of covenant.'[248] Again, the following verse expresses regret over the 'treacherous' pagans who denounced their covenants: 'In a believer they respect not the ties either of kinship or of covenant. It is they who have transgressed all bounds.'[249] The presence of these verses suggests that the proposed option of Islam or deadly force for the pagans does not match historical evidence.[250] While there is no gainsaying that once the Islamic polity had asserted its dominance over the Arabian Peninsula, it became almost impossible to come upon an openly polytheist tribe in the region, but this had been a socio-political consequence, not a doctrinal necessity of Islam.

The early Islamic position towards polytheists may be further qualified by a practical point of distinction drawn between various categories of polytheists, who were not deemed a monolithic entity. In fact, the Hanafi and Maliki schools had propounded that Arab and non-Arab pagans needed to be treated differently, in that the latter could be subject to a more lenient regime. These schools further maintained that the *jizyah* could only be levied on pagans of non-Arab descent.[251] Friedmann argues that the harsher policy adopted by the embryonic Muslim polity against Arab pagans might be explained by the fact that since the Quran had been revealed in Arabic, its divine nature was expected to be clearer to Arabs more than to other groups. 'Being the Prophet's kith and kin', Friedmann adds, 'they [Arabs] had the obligation to support him and respond to his call. Their rejection of Muhammad's message . . . [was thus] deemed more reprehensible than . . . [a comparable] behaviour of other unbelievers.'[252] One may also maintain that because the pagan Arabs had posed a rather immediate threat to the very existence of Islam, the Prophet and his immediate successors might have felt that sterner

247 Q. 9:7.
248 Q. 9:8.
249 Q. 9:10.
250 Significantly, some pagan tribes, including the Banu Hamzah and Banu Kinana, had remained true to their treaties concluded with the early Muslim community. See Ali, supra note 6, 439.
251 However, this view was not shared by the Shafi'i and Hanbali schools, which posited that the *jizyah* was only acceptable from the People of the Book and the Magians. An alternative position, generally attributed to Malik, defended the extreme position that *jizyah* was acceptable from all non-believers. AbuSulayman, supra note 62, 11.
252 Friedmann, supra note 103, 80.

measures had to be taken against them – particularly when peace treaties had failed to provide lasting security in the volatile region of Arabia. Islam's categorical renunciation of idolatry and its utter break with Arab polytheism may likewise account for the uncompromising posture of the Muslim leaders toward Arab idolaters in the region, wherein Muslims were in urgent need of securing a stronghold.

Bearing the above considerations and qualifications in mind, it should be reiterated that the Islamic just war tradition has never assumed an entirely pacifistic stance; and hence legitimate means of jihad, in all its forms, have been recognised and encouraged by Muslim sources and rulers alike with a view to establishing the universality of Islam. Stressing the relatively assertive character of Islam, the great Muslim philosopher and historian Ibn Khaldun (d. 1406) pointed out that major monotheistic systems other than Islam do not impose a religious obligation of war 'save only for purposes of defence'.[253] Khaldun distinguished this aspect of Islam thus:

> In the Muslim community, the holy war is a religious duty, because of the universalism of the Muslim mission and (the obligation to) convert everybody to Islam either by persuasion or by force. Therefore, caliphate and royal authority are united in Islam, so that the person in charge can devote the available strength to both of them at the same time.[254]

While Khaldun's ensuing postulate that 'other religious groups did not have a universal mission'[255] to forcefully spread their spheres of influence practically proved untrue – considering the historical record of international politics – there is certainly merit in arguing that Islam and the idea of pious struggle (conducted peacefully or otherwise) are inextricably interlaced with Islam's mission to extend God's word to all nations.[256] Be that as it may, the characteristics of struggling to attain Islam's objectives were shown not to have been straightforward; for the contours of striving in God's path (jihad) had become subject to various changes in keeping with the exigencies of times and circumstances. Hence, when the conditions so dictated, the sword was employed to defend Muslims;

253 I. Khaldun; F. Rosenthal (trans.), *The Muqaddimah: An Introduction to History* (Princeton: Princeton University Press, 2005) 183.

254 Ibid. It is to be noted that Khaldun distinguished between four types of war: (1) tribal wars, which occurred between neighbouring tribes or families; (2) raids or 'wars caused by hostility', which were undertaken by 'savage nations' with a view to depriving people of their possessions; (3) religious wars; and (4) dynastic wars against seceders or rebels. To Khaldun, only the latter two types of war were holy and just. Ibid. 224.

255 Ibid. 183.

256 Lewis, in this connection, writes that 'Muhammad. . . was not only a prophet and a teacher, like the founders of other religions; he was also the head of a polity and of a community, a ruler and a soldier. Hence his struggle involved a state and its armed forces.' B. Lewis, 'The Roots of Muslim Rage' (1990) 266 *The Atlantic Monthly* 47, 49.

likewise, when it was expedient or beneficial, military expeditions were carried out and/or peace treaties were concluded to advance the interests of Islam. Given the complex history and non-linear evolution of the doctrine of jihad, it is thus not possible to construct a monolithic metanarrative of an entirely defensive or aggressive jihad; rather, as previous chapters have shown, the tapestry of the doctrine is much richer than suggested by the moderate and radical schools. Having established the multifaceted nature of the use of force discourse in Islam, the next chapter will turn to the main question of whether the Islamic just war tradition may accord with the contemporary precepts of international law, which are essentially geared towards promoting and maintaining international peace and security.

4 Jihad in the United Nations Era

Introduction

The above account made it clear that a line of demarcation between defensive and offensive jihad has thus far not been drawn. What remains uncontroversial, however, is that during the Prophet's lifetime, the notion of jihad acquired various tenors in harmony with the historical predicaments faced by the early Muslim community. Jihad, accordingly, moved from being pacifistic to defensive in character, and thereafter to a somewhat bellicose form in order to eliminate idolatry and immoral practices, and to expand the sphere of Islam. Historically, therefore, the doctrine of military jihad has been invoked to legitimate both defensive wars and offensive wars of religious, economic, or political character.

Such doctrinal and practical imprecision concerning the legal boundaries of jihad had reached an unparalleled level particularly since the late nineteenth and early twentieth centuries, when the Ottoman Empire, the final great Islamic dynasty, began to disintegrate into smaller States, which by and large later fell under the yoke of Western colonialism in the wake of the Great War.[1] This development not only further augmented the fragmentation of the Islamic world, but also led Islamist movements to turn to jihad's transformative mission in political and socio-cultural domains in a bid to stir up anti-colonialism. In the aftermath of colonial independence of Islamic nations – politically organised into nation-States – Islamist movements similarly invoked the rhetoric of jihad to mobilise the masses to fight against various forms of exploitation, efforts at top-down secularisation, or against the political, economic, and cultural subordination of the Islamic world.[2] Jihad even formed a vital reference point during the Arab uprisings to affect transition from authoritarianism to democracy in the so-called

1 See M. C. Bassiouni, 'Evolving Approaches to Jihad: From Self-Defence to Revolutionary and Regime-Change Political Violence' (2008) 8 *Chicago Journal of International Law* 119, 120.

2 See generally, J. Beinin; J. Stork, 'On the Modernity, Historical Specificity, and International Context of Political Islam' in: J. Beinin; J. Stork (eds.), *Political Islam: Essays from Middle East Report* (London: I.B. Tauis, 1997) 3.

'Arab Spring' States[3] – wherein, nevertheless, the initial aspiration to solidify such values as human rights, the rule of law, good governance, transparency, and justice somewhat withered away. But the point to be drawn here is that the doctrine of jihad continues to hold diverse meanings for contemporary Muslim actors who, like their forefathers, have proved adaptable to change, and have thus been able to use the concept of jihad with intent to achieve (*inter alia*) fundamental rights and freedoms based on justice and the rule of law. This has only been possible through a dynamic reading of relevant Islamic principles.

I. Dynamism of Islamic Approach to International Relations

Since the Islamic approach to legitimate warfare has been construed from various perspectives in conformity with the dictates of changing socio-political circumstances, this book has argued that a one-sided or rigid understanding of jihad – without due regard to the overall spirit and genealogical framework of Islamic thought – is unlikely to yield constructive results. As the earlier chapters highlighted, there is much evidence to suggest that Muslim jurists have long articulated juridical concepts in order to adjust classical precepts and doctrines to new socio-political realities. Accordingly, as Kelsay puts it, 'it must never be said that the Sharia is closed; . . . [t]o take such a position is to deny the freedom of God. It is to render God static, whereas the voice speaking in the Quran, and to which the Prophet's Sunna bears witness, is very much dynamic and living.'[4]

It will be remembered that Muslim jurists, particularly during the classical age of Islamic thought (roughly from the seventh to the thirteenth centuries), had often sought to respond to the shifting demands of international relations.[5] A paradigm case in point was the theoretical division of the world between the House of Islam and the House of War at the height of Islamic expansion. But this strict categorisation was subsequently mitigated, or at times totally ignored, by the conclusion of numerous agreements with non-Muslims – at a time when Muslim rulers and jurists recognised the near impossibility of establishing Islam as the sole

3 See generally, T. Ramadan, *Islam and the Arab Awakening* (Oxford: Oxford University Press, 2012) 95–102, 194–201; J. R. Bradley, *After the Arab Spring: How Islamists Hijacked The Middle East Revolts* (New York: Palgrave Macmillan, 2012).

4 J. Kelsay, *Arguing the Just War in Islam* (Cambridge, MA: Harvard University Press, 2007) 177.

5 Muslim jurists have always tried to generate practical solutions to keep Islam relevant to society. In so doing, they occasionally suspended the application of some legal injunctions. For instance, as attested by John of Damascus (d. 749), flogging had occasionally replaced the penalty of amputating thieves' hands. Another illustrative example was the practice of restricting legal proof to witness evidence to the exclusion of written documents, which was at odds with the explicit verse of the Quran which dictates that transactions involving future obligations are to be put in writing (Q: 2:282). See further J. Schacht, *An Introduction of Islamic Law* (Oxford: Oxford University Press, 1982) 18–19.

belief system across the globe.[6] Muslims had accordingly concluded treaties of short and long durations with their material or potential rivals on numerous occasions, for Muslim rulers had to adjust their goals and practices to the realities of power politics where Muslim forces could not always prove to be compelling enough to dictate their will forcibly. The implication of such a juridical bifurcation of the world was not a state of unceasing hostility between the two 'Houses'; instead, it was the 'non-recognition' of the non-Muslim enemy,[7] with whom Muslims could still suspend hostilities and engage in peaceful relations.

The regular reliance of Muslims on agreements as instruments of foreign policy further induced some jurists, particularly those of the Shafi'i school, to coin another controversial category, namely *dar al-sulh* (House of Peace) or *Dar al-Ahd* (House of Covenant), which referred to non-Muslim nations with whom Muslims had armistice, diplomatic ties, or peace agreements.[8] Al-Shafi'i, one of the pioneers of this thinking, opined that Muslims could suspend hostilities with other nations when the dictates of *realpolitik* or the welfare of the Muslim community so required.[9] But because the concept of *dar al-sulh* did not necessarily entail a state of permanent peace, the lethal contest between the House of Islam and House of War theoretically persisted; Muslims, on that account, had to maintain constant vigilance against the latter. It must be stressed that other jurists, notably those of the Hanefi school, did not subscribe to this further conceptual division of the world on account of the understanding that the inhabitants of a territory with whom Muslims concluded peace agreements had to be considered part of the Abode of Islam – and, being such, they were thought to possess the right to be protected by the Muslim polity.[10]

Notwithstanding its controversial status, the third categorical division – *dar al-sulh* – gained currency with the stark realisation that neither Muslims nor

6 It is worth noting that the palpable decline of Islamic politico-military power vis-à-vis the non-Muslim world began on the whole from the seventeenth century onwards. See generally, A. E. Mayer, 'War and Peace in the Islamic Tradition and International Law' in: J. Kelsay; J. T. Johnson (eds.), *Just War and Jihad: Historical and Theoretical Perspectives on War and Peace in Western and Islamic Traditions* (New York: Greenwood Press, 1991) 195, 196.

7 The non-recognition of the enemy referred to the incapacity of non-Muslims to possess equal legal status under Islamic law, on the ground that non-Muslims failed to embrace the true faith. Yet such non-recognition did not suggest the impossibility of constructing peaceful relations between these theoretically conflicting parties. See generally, M. Khadduri, 'International Law' in: M. Khadduri; H. J. Lienbesny (eds.), *Law in the Middle East*, Vol. I (Washington DC: Middle East Institute, 1955) 349, 359ff.

8 A. Al-Dawoody, *The Islamic Law of War: Justifications and Regulations* (New York: Palgrave, 2011) 91–92.

9 See M. Abo-Kazleh, 'Rethinking International Relations Theory in Islam: Toward a More Adequate Approach' (2006) 5 *Turkish Journal of International Relations* 4, 46.

10 See M. Khadduri, *The Islamic Law of Nations: Shaybani's Siyar* (Baltimore: The Johns Hopkins Press, 1966) 14; S. H. Hashmi, 'Islamic Ethics in International Society' in: S. H. Hashmi (ed.), *Islamic Political Ethics: Civil Society, Pluralism, and Conflict* (Princeton: Princeton University Press, 2002) 148, 160.

other nations (particularly Christians) could establish ultimate mastery over one another any time soon through lethal force. The cognisance of this phenomenon, which became prominent after the disintegration of Muslim political unity, markedly contributed to the mitigation of the rigid bifurcation of the world by the acceptance of treaty relations with non-hostile nations.[11] The formulation of this doctrine openly reflected the reality that Muslims could not be in a state of permanent warfare against the rest the world, against which they found themselves – to varying degrees – declining in adeptness and military capacity. The new non-Muslim actors at times possessed far stronger political and military might than those confronted during the early years of Islam. When confronted by politically organised Christians – who had also been trying to universalise their politico-religious sway – Muslims found an enemy much more organised than the dispersed Jewish or polytheistic tribes of the seventh century. As illustrated above, after its adoption as the official religion of the Roman Empire, Christianity acquired a formidable political force with a capacity to contend for supremacy, paired with a conviction in its divine mission to proselytise the unconverted.[12] Additionally, the Islamic polity over time progressively broke into diverse and rival dominions that competed for control and religious legitimacy. The most ravaging form of such disunity transpired along the lines of Shia and Sunni Islam, which in turn later subdivided into a variety of factions.[13]

In light of these considerations, the attitude adopted during Islam's ascent to world power, which called for the acquisition of non-Muslim lands within the embrace of Islam through jihad in all forms, took on a more compromising tone.

11 See L. B. Ware, 'A Radical Islamist Concept of Conflict' in: S. C. Pelletiere (ed.), *Terrorism: National Security Policy and the Home Front* (US Army War College: Diane Publishing, 1995) 31–32; I. Bantekas, 'Religion as a Source of International Law' in: J. Rehman; S. C. Breau (eds.), *Religion, Human Rights and International Law: A Critical Examination of Islamic State Practices* (Leiden: Martinus Nijhoff Publishers, 2007) 115, 120.

12 See M. Parvin; M. Sommer, 'Dar-al-Islam: The Evolution of Muslim Territoriality and its Implications for Conflict Resolution in the Middle East' (1980) 11 *International Journal of Middle East Studies* 1, 21. As stressed earlier, the idea that all nations are to be eventually converted and be brought under a single world order – in an environment free of warfare and bitter divisions – is also advanced by Judaism. Illustrative of this point is Isaiah 2:4: 'They shall beat their swords into ploughshares, and their spears into pruning-hooks: nation shall not lift up sword against nation, neither shall they learn war anymore.'

13 In contemporary Muslim world, the difference between Shiite and Sunni Islam continues to play a decisive role in determining the nature of governmental policies at home and abroad. This religious disunity also prevents Muslim States from forming a unified religio-political voice. Olivier Roy, in this context, stresses that 'the great ethnic, religious, and national divisions of the Muslim world are turning out to be stronger than all the calls to Islamic solidarity'. See O. Roy; C. Volk (trans.), *The Failure of Political Islam* (Cambridge, MA: Harvard University Press, 1994) 124. Hence, while Islamic identity has the relative power to mobilise popular support, it does not provide a very solid basis for a global Muslim unity.

The widening gap between the legal theory and political realities had hence driven the Muslim rulers to increasingly adopt policies of mutual tolerance, as long as such were feasible. An important corollary of this process was the practical rejection of the early-mentioned idea that only temporally limited agreements were permissible with non-Muslim entities.[14] Indeed, when the doctrine of permanent hostilities was considered practically unsustainable, pragmatic Muslim rulers did not wish to bind themselves within an iron-clad 10-year upper limit, modelled on the Hudaybiyyah Agreement.[15] The Hudaybiyyah example, as argued earlier, was to all intents and purposes a tailor-made response to a particular occasion,[16] and was therefore not designed to tie Muslims to a pre-ordained 10-year threshold irrespective of the individual circumstances of each case. Although the treaty undoubtedly constituted a prophetic tradition, it would be far-fetched to conclude that it was Muhammad's real objective to set a blanket temporal precedent for future treaties to which Muslims would accede.

As the above-discussed Islamic State practice amply demonstrates, it was in effect political considerations that informed the content and duration of peace treaties with non-Muslim powers.[17] Illustrative of this point is the Peace of Zsitvatorok of 1606, signed between the Ottoman Empire and the Habsburg Monarchy for a term of 20 years. Marking the first check on Ottoman expansion into the Habsburg territory, the treaty nominally recognised the equal sovereignty of Habsburg emperors, and stabilised relations between the signatories for

14 Hanafi and Shafi'i schools generally supported the view that a treaty concluded with the enemy could not exceed a period of 10 years. But some other jurists, including al-Hajjawi, advised that an imam could conclude a treaty for more than 10 years when this was expedient, or when the Muslims were not in a position to resume the war with the adversary. See M. Khadduri, *War and Peace in the Law of Islam* (Baltimore: Johns Hopkins Press, 1955) 219–220.

15 It will be remembered that the Hudaybiyyah Agreement, among others, envisaged that all hostilities between the Muslims and the Quraysh would cease for 10 years, that Muslims would renounce their right to pilgrimage in Mecca until the following year, and that Muslims would return any member of the Quraysh who adopted Islam without permission from his or her guardian or from the clan chief. The Meccans, on the other hand, were given the assurance that their caravans to Syria and Damascus would not be assaulted by the Muslim forces. See M. Ruthven, *Islam in the World*, 3rd ed. (Oxford: Oxford University Press, 2006) 57; S. Gunbey, *Veda Haccinda Islam Ummetine Hz. Peygamber (S.A.V.)' in Vasiyeti* (Istanbul: Zinde Ofset Matbaacilik, 2010) 10–12.

16 The treaty, as pointed out earlier, allowed the Muslims to be formally recognised as a legitimate polity in the region and to consolidate their power in the absence of the Meccan threat. As such, it created such favourable conditions that within a span of merely two years, Mecca was brought within the fold of Islam almost without bloodshed, which accelerated the expansion of Islam to all of Arabia, and thenceforth to other parts of the world. Referring to the treaty, the Quran noted that 'verily We have granted thee a manifest victory'. Q. 48:1.

17 Significantly, treaties signed with the 'protected people' (*dhimmis*) were perpetual in character; for the parties of such treaties were considered to be on unequal footing, with Muslims providing constitutional guarantees to protected communities. See further, Khadduri, supra note 14, 219–220.

a considerable period.[18] Significantly, the Zsitvatorok Treaty was not particularly affected by dogmatic temporal considerations, and it was thus regularly renewed (e.g. in 1642 the treaty was extended for another 20 years).[19] The Treaty of Karlowitz of 1699, which heralded the termination of Ottoman expansion in Europe, had also envisaged a relatively long period of 25 years. Likewise, the Treaty of Passarowitz of 1718, which compelled the Ottomans to cede sizeable territory in Eastern Europe, was to last for 24 years. The Treaty of Belgrade of 1739 is another illustrative case, agreed for the duration of 27 years. In 1747, a new Ottoman–Habsburg treaty was concluded, which anomalously sought to lay the basis for perpetual peace and friendship between the parties,[20] marking a break with the tradition of concluding temporally limited peace agreements. Later, through the Paris Peace Treaty of 1856, which ended the Crimean War, the Ottoman Empire was admitted into the Concert of Europe, thereby becoming part of European public international relations and law. Guaranteeing the territorial integrity of the Ottoman Empire by rendering any violation thereof a matter for general concern, Article 7 of the Treaty read that 'the Sublime Porte [is] admitted to participate in the advantages of the public law and system (Concert) of Europe'.[21] While short-lived, a Muslim State was for the first time, through the Concert, deemed part of Europe, a development that further undercut the perception that Muslim and Christian nations could never establish long-term confederacies.

The admission of the Ottomans within the European legal order laid the groundwork for further alliances in the years to follow. Muslim States would soon thereafter begin to contribute to the nascent norms of international law. For instance, the Ottoman Empire became part of the First Geneva Convention in 1865, and Persia followed suit in 1874. The Ottomans and Persians were also present at the Hague Peace Conferences of 1899 and 1907, wherein their insistent attempts resulted in the confirmation of the principle of religious non-discrimination as one of the basic tenets of international humanitarian law (IHL).[22] The steady accession of Muslim polities to international organisations

18 See generally, H. Rudolph, 'The Ottoman Empire and the Institutionalization of European Diplomacy, 1500–1700' in: M. L. Frick; A. T. Muller (eds.), *Islam and International Law: Engaging Self-Centrism from a Plurality of Perspectives* (Leiden: Brill, 2013) 161, 169.

19 See K. H. Ziegler, 'The Peace Treaties of the Ottoman Empire with European Christian Powers' in: R. Lesaffer (ed.), *Peace Treaties and International Law in European History: From the Late Middle Ages to World War One* (Cambridge: Cambridge University Press, 2004) 345–351.

20 J. Tolan *et al*, *Europe and the Islamic World: A History* (Princeton: Princeton University Press, 2012) 213; Foreign Office, *Treaties between Turkey and Foreign Powers: 1535–1855* (London: Harrison and Sons, 1855) 679ff.

21 S. Halperin, *War and Social Change in Modern Europe: The Great Transformation Revisited* (Cambridge: Cambridge University Press, 2004) 297ff; C. Badem, *The Ottoman Crimean War (1853–1856)* (Leiden: Brill, 2010) 287ff.

22 See S. H. Hashmi, 'Jihad and the Geneva Conventions: The Impact of International Law on Islamic Theory' in: S. H. Hashmi (ed.), *Just Wars, Holy Wars, and Jihads: Christian,*

and treaties would, over the years, accelerate the universalisation and secularisation of international law, which had previously been considered as 'an artefact of the law of nations of the *res publica christiana,* embedded in the notion of a shared, pan-European Christian culture'.[23]

This notwithstanding, it was in large degree after the decolonisation period that Muslim States, acting in tandem with the so-called 'Third World', sought to modify the prevailing standards of international law by challenging, among other things, racism, apartheid, foreign occupation, and the use of aggression against liberation movements fighting colonialism or alien domination.[24] By the same token, since the dawn of the UN, Islamic States have contributed to the drafting of such significant human rights instruments as the International Bill of Rights, the UN Convention on the Rights of the Child (CRC), and the Convention on the Elimination of All Forms of Discrimination against Women (CEDAW).

It must be stressed that although all Muslim States ratified such key international instruments, in the main they entered certain reservations therein. The nature of such reservations largely depended on the degree to which Islam exercised influence on the interpretation of legal rights and obligations in society. The application of treaty obligations proved particularly thorny concerning the law of personal status; as most Muslim jurisdictions strictly preserve Islamic laws of personal status, wherein some key individual and familial matters – including conjugal rights and divorce, custody and guardianship of children, inheritance and succession – are generally governed by religious standards.[25] This area of Islamic law has a broad field of applicability on account of its significance for Muslim identity. Naturally, reservations based on the stipulations of Islamic laws reflect the tension between the rights and obligations set out in international treaties and Sharia principles.[26] A representative example is the reservations placed by most

Jewish, and Muslim Encounters and Exchanges (Oxford: Oxford University Press, 2012) 325, 329.

23 J. Cockayne, 'Islam and International Humanitarian Law: From a Clash to a Conversation between Civilisations' (2002) 84 *International Review of the Red Cross* 597, 600.

24 J. Rehman, *Islamic State Practices, International Law and the Threat from Terrorism: A Critique of the 'Clash of Civilisations' in the New World Order* (Oxford: Hart Publishing, 2005) 103; A. Cassese, *International Law in a Divided World* (Oxford: Clarendon Press, 1994) 138–140.

25 S. S. Ali, 'The Twain Doth Meet! A Preliminary Exploration of the Theory and Practice of *As-Siyar* and International Law in the Contemporary World' in: J. Rehman; S. C. Breau (eds.), *Religion, Human Rights and International Law* (Leiden: Martinus Nijhoff Publishers, 2007) 81, 93–94; see generally, J. J. Nasir, *Islamic Laws of Personal Status* (London: Kluwer Academic Publishers, 1986).

26 Among Muslim States, Turkey stands as a prime example of relative legal modernisation, even within the field of personal status laws. Despite its political, cultural, and religious sensitivities, Turkey has not yet entered reservations to international treaties on religious grounds. Nevertheless, it is worth noting that even Turkey had initially entered reservations (which were later withdrawn in 1999) on various aspects of Articles 15 and 16 of CEDAW. But Turkey justified its limitations with the relevant provisions of the Turkish Civil Code, not with Islamic principles. See E. Brems, *Human Rights:*

Islamic States on Article 16 of CEDAW, which aims to eliminate 'discrimination against women in all matters relating to marriage and family relations [. . .] on a basis of equality of men and women'. Such reserving States justified their limitations imposed on this article by reference to their Sharia obligations. But it must be stressed that not all reservations entered into human rights treaties are Islamic in nature, nor is there a uniform or consistent Islamic approach thereto.[27] Islamic States, in other words, display a non-uniform approach to making reservations – which are made in large part due to particular political, cultural and religious reasons.[28]

In contrast to personal status laws, Islamic States have not assumed a comparably protective stance vis-à-vis multinational treaties prohibiting aggressive force and terrorism, as well as treaties seeking to promote and facilitate international cooperation, dialogue, and friendship. Undoubtedly, accession to international organisations or agreements alone does not guarantee compliance with relevant rules geared towards preserving or restoring international peace and security. But the same holds true for each and every other State. It is therefore incumbent on the international community to ensure that hegemonic or aggressive conduct is controlled and discouraged by collective security measures – a theme to which the following pages will turn.

II. Modern International Law and State Aggression

It was alluded to above that modern international law, as it emerged in the wake of the horrors of World War II, is no longer a wholly Euro-centric construct – the erstwhile expression of which indeed bore the hallmarks of the post-Westphalian world order. This observation is borne out by the above-discussed phenomenon that Muslim States (with other non-European nations) have been increasingly exerting influence over the development and enforcement of international law.[29] Starting from the nineteenth century in particular, Muslim polities had already

Universality and Diversity (The Hague: Kluwer Law International, 2001) 268ff; also see N. Abiad, *Sharia, Muslim States and International Human Rights Obligations: A Comparative Study* (London: BIICL, 2008) 97ff.

27 Whilst the validity of religion-based reservations had seldom been an object of dispute at the UN level, in the context of CEDAW a heated controversy arose on the validity of such reservations – with some members of the Muslim camp in effect claiming that the discourse of universal human rights is tied to cultural imperialism. The debate, however, did not bring forth any resolution specifically addressing the question of whether religion-based reservations could be considered contrary to the overall object and purpose of CEDAW. See S. Jeleff (ed.), *The Gender Perspective* (Strasbourg: Council of Europe Publishing, 1995) 132; D. P. Forsythe (ed.), *Encyclopaedia of Human Rights,* Vol. I (Oxford University Press, Oxford, 2009) 237.

28 Such reasons include issues relating to marriage, abortion, religious freedoms, criminal punishments, rights of women and children, and some other key personal and familial matters. For an analysis, see Abiad, supra note 26, 85–92.

29 See further, Bantekas, supra note 11, 115, 115ff.

conceded that they had to keep pace with the demands of the modern nation-State model, which is marked by receding emphasis on religious, cultural, and linguistic particularisms, and progress toward the formation of highly centralised, secular, and national socio-political constructs.[30] In the aftermath of World War II and classical colonialism, the active participation of Muslim States in the political and administrative structures of international law have particularly increased.

Today, all Islamic States, with their diverse socio-political and economic backgrounds, have become parties to international agreements of various types. Significantly, they form a large portion of the UN, which in its Charter lays down the fundamental tenets of modern international law. The most salient goal of international law is to maintain and restore global peace and security, which, according to the Charter, may be secured through the promotion of amicable relations and cooperation among States, as well as the establishment of 'conditions under which justice and respect for the obligations arising from treaties and other sources of international law can be maintained'.[31] The Charter, unsurprisingly, places heavy emphasis on peace as its principal objective, expressing a determination 'to save succeeding generations from the scourge of war'.[32] Having built itself upon the pillars of international solidarity and amicable solution of international disputes, the Charter further envisages the adoption of collective security measures with a view to containing material or potential breaches of international peace and security. Chapter VII of the Charter grants specific powers to the Security Council to achieve this objective in conformity with the principles of justice and equality of nations.[33]

In an effort to prevent unwarranted conflicts, the Charter stipulates in no uncertain terms that 'armed force shall not be used, save in the common interest'[34] and in the exercise of the right to self-defence pursuant to Article 51 of the Charter. With its absolute prohibition on the use of unilateral aggression, the UN is clearly distinguished from its predecessor, the League of Nations, which attempted to restrict recourse to war in the settlement of international disputes, rather than outlawing it completely.[35] Members of the UN, upon witnessing the unprecedented devastation of World War II, renounced their sovereign prerogative to use or

30 The Ottoman and Egyptian experiences during the nineteenth and twentieth centuries constitute good examples of how some of the then Muslim polities were heavily influenced by the political and administrative structures of their European counterparts. See further N. S. Al-Ali, *Secularism, Gender and the State in the Middle East: The Egyptian Women's Movement* (Cambridge: Cambridge University Press, 2000) 42ff.

31 Charter of the United Nations, 24 October 1945, Preamble.

32 Ibid.

33 Ibid; see Articles 39–49.

34 Ibid, Preamble.

35 See, in particular, Articles 10, 12 and 16 of the Covenant of the League of Nations (adopted in December, 1924). For an analysis, see I. Brownlie, *International Law and the Use of Force by States* (Oxford: Clarendon Press, 1963) 62–66; A. C. Arend; R. J. Beck, *International Law and the Use of Force* (London: Routledge, 1993) 19–21.

threaten to use armed force as a means of settling disputes.[36] Today, Article 2(4) of the Charter, which prohibits 'the threat or use of force against the territorial integrity or political independence of any state, or in any other manner inconsistent with the purpose of the United Nations', is considered to be a peremptory norm of international law.[37] Absent Security Council authorisation for coercive enforcement measures, self-defence remains the only ground for legitimate armed force (*casus belli*) against unlawful aggression.[38]

The modern laws of war accordingly not only abolished the sovereign right to wage wars as a means of achieving foreign policy objectives,[39] but also reduced the conventional just war reasons (including the recovery of property, securing redress for wrongdoings or avenging injuries) to self-defence.[40] Certainly, there have been attempts to broaden the scope of exceptions to the general prohibition on the use of unilateral force under the Charter. Some States, for instance, attempted to legitimate unilateral aggression on such grounds as the protection of nationals, humanitarian intervention, or fighting terrorism.[41] Nonetheless, such

36 See M. A. Weightman, 'Self-Defense in International Law' (1951) 37 *Virginia Law Review* 1095, 1102–1108; D. Kennedy, *Of War and Law* (Oxford: Princeton University Press, 2006) 75–76; C. Hsiung, *Anarchy & Order: The Interplay of Politics and Law in International Relations* (London: Lynne Rienner Publishers, 1997) 51.

37 In *Nicaragua v United States of America*, the International Court of Justice (ICJ) described Article 2(4) as a peremptory norm of international law from which Members could not derogate. See *Case Concerning the Military and Paramilitary Activities in and Against Nicaragua (Nicaragua v United States of America)* Judgment of 27 June 1986, ICJ 14, ¶ 190; also see M. N. Shaw, *International Law*, 6th ed. (Cambridge: Cambridge University Press, 2008) 1123.

38 But self-defensive measures, according to Article 51 of the Charter, may persist only until the Security Council has taken measures to maintain or restore international peace and security. See generally Y. Dinstein, *War, Aggression and Self-Defence*, 4th ed. (Cambridge: Cambridge University Press, 2005) 85ff; L. Henkin, *How Nations Behave*, 2nd ed. (New York: Columbia University Press, 1979) 204ff; C. Gray, *International Law and the Use of Force*, 3rd ed. (Oxford: Oxford University Press, 2008) 144–166.

39 For more on the positivist legal position, which accorded the 'sovereign' an unlimited right to make war, see K. Nabulsi, *Traditions of War: Occupation, Resistance, and the Law* (Oxford: Oxford University Press, 2005) 241; S. C. Neff, 'A Short History of International Law' in: M. D. Evans, *International Law,* 2nd ed. (New York: Oxford University Press, 2006) 29–38; A. Anghie, 'Finding the Peripheries: Sovereignty and Colonialism in Nineteenth-Century International Law' (1999) 40 *Harvard International Law Journal* 1.

40 While some commentators maintain that humanitarian intervention, an unauthorised coercive action undertaken on professed humanitarian grounds, may be a legitimate cause for the use of force, compatible with Article 2(4) of the UN Charter, this reading of the UN Charter is controversial. See Dinstein, supra note 38, 90; *cf.* E. Schroeder, 'Kosovo Crisis: Humanitarian Imperative versus International Law' (2004) 28 *Fletcher Forum of World Affairs* 181; J. Mertus, 'Reconsidering the Legality of Humanitarian Intervention: Lessons from Kosovo' (2000) 41 *William and Mary Law Review* 1751.

41 See N. Krisch, 'More Equal than the Rest? Hierarchy, Equality and US Predominance in International Law' in: M. Byers; G. Nolte (eds.), *United States Hegemony and the Foundations of International Law* (Cambridge: Cambridge University Press, 2003) 150.

expansive reading of the Charter has not elicited much international or academic support for fear of abuse. As it currently stands, therefore, only in cases of self-defence may States turn to unilateral force, as a means of last resort, to fend off actual or imminent aggression.[42] As alluded to above, States may also adopt collective coercive measures, with the Security Council's blessing, in order to prevent or remove threats to international peace and order.[43]

Since the prohibition against aggressive war constitutes today's secular *jus ad bellum* norm and the cornerstone of modern international law, the religious and moral justness of a given conflict bears no relevance in determining whether the use or threat of armed force by one State against another complies with the UN Charter. The contemporary regulation of warfare thus takes no account of religious, ideological, or political justifications professed by States in their efforts to justify force. As Kunz observes, under the UN collective security system, the concept of *bellum justum* is replaced by that of *bellum legale*;[44] this is because moral and religious considerations of justice, in view of their 'subjective' texture, no longer feature in the relatively 'objective' assessment of the *legality* of wars. While moral and religious principles may certainly interface with contemporary norms of international law, only the latter may be invoked to ascertain whether a given war is defensive or aggressive in character.

A radical shift such as this in just war thinking is intricately related to the destructive military capacities of States that have reached unparalleled proportions. Hence, the drafters of the UN Charter – who rejected warfare as an instrument of national policy[45] – were not driven by naïve idealism; rather, they prudently presumed that a possible third world war would endanger the survival of the human race.[46] Certainly, the sea change in just war tradition has also been related to the secularisation process of international law, which mainly started

42 For a detailed treatment of the legality of preventive or anticipatory self-defence, see my previous work, *Self-Defence in International and Criminal Law: The Doctrine of Imminence* (London: Routledge, 2011).

43 See generally, ibid.148ff; Dinstein, supra note 38, 90; *cf.* Schroeder, supra note 40, 181.

44 J. L. Kunz, 'Bellum Justum and Bellum Legale' (1951) 45 *American Journal of International Law* 528, 532.

45 Before the UN Charter, the Kellogg–Briand Pact of 1928 renounced warfare as an instrument of *national* policy. While the Pact was silent on the theme of self-defence, the Contracting Parties had an understanding that the 'inherent' right of self-defence had been unimpaired by the Pact. Indeed, the reference to the term 'inherent' was generally interpreted to suggest that self-defence was a natural right, one that was beyond the domain of positive international law. However, the Pact was criticised for not openly addressing the issue of self-defence, for not being clear about whether war could be waged as a means of *international* policy, for not having universal applicability, and for not regulating the category of forcible measures short of war. See Weightman, supra note 36, 1108ff; Dinstein, supra note 38, 84–85.

46 As some scholars rightly pointed out, 'the history of twentieth-century international law' may be read 'as an attempt to reduce recourse to the use of force in international relations'. See J. Brunnée; S. J. Toope, 'Slouching Towards New "Just" Wars: The Hegemon after September 11th' (2004) 18 *International Relations* 405, 406.

in the early modern period, particularly with the writings of Vitoria (d. 1546), Suarez (d. 1617), Gentili (d. 1608), and Grotius (d. 1645). Having witnessed some horrendous wars of religious intolerance, these scholars, first and foremost, made recourse to natural law and human reason to underpin the foundations of the law of nations, rather than merely appealing to religion as the sole moral authority.[47]

The secularisation of international law has reached complete maturity with the formation of the UN, which prohibited States from falling back on religious concepts to justify their wars – notwithstanding that some basic humanitarian notions like distinction, proportionality, and necessity are genealogically rooted in the soil of moral and religious traditions.[48] Undoubtedly, both in religious and legal scenarios of self-defence, States may claim the right to decide whether they are justified to invoke force and what is necessary for their own self-defence. But if States were to be the sole judges to subjectively appraise the nature of attacks or threats ostensibly directed against them, there would emerge a grave risk of abuse in the exercise of such discretion.[49] In religious justifications, the said risk has been conspicuous, as the warring parties almost always concurrently claim the justness of their causes. In legal cases, the danger of conferring exclusive legal competence to a State in determining what is necessary for its own security is no less serious. Writing as early as in 1933, Lauterpacht thus pointed out that self-defence claims had to be subjected to close scrutiny. To reason otherwise, the argument went, would run counter to the spirit of the law, because the idea that claims of self-defence are not amenable to evaluation by law 'is self-contradictory, inasmuch as it purports to be based on legal right, and as, at the same time, it dissociates itself from regulation and evaluation by the law'.[50] The Nuremberg Tribunal confirmed

47 Grotius, for instance, held that the law of nations derived its power 'from the will of nations', and not from morality, universal reason, or religion. H. Grotius, A. C. Campbell (trans.) *The Rights of War and Peace* (London: M. Walter Dunne Publisher, 1901), bk. I/I/XIV/I. See generally, M. Evans, 'Moral Theory and the Idea of a Just War' in: M. Evans (ed.), *Just War Theory: A Reappraisal* (Edinburgh: Edinburgh University Press, 2005) 1; F. D. Vitoria; E. Nys (ed.), J. P. Bate (trans.), *De Indis Et De Ivre Belli Reflectiones* (New York: Oceana Publications, 1963); C. F. Murphy, 'The Grotian Vision of World Order' (1982) 76 *American Journal of International Law* 477.

48 For a discussion on how religions have influenced international law, see Bantekas, supra note 11, 116ff.

49 The purported necessity for the exercise of such discretion to decide upon measures to preserve one's existence was given formal expression by the US during the negotiation of the Kellogg–Briand Pact. 'Every nation alone', declared the US representative, 'is competent to decide whether circumstances require recourse to war in self-defence.' See Q. Wright, 'The Meaning of the Pact of Paris' (1933) 27 *American Journal of International Law* 39, 43. However, the US qualified its argument by adding that 'if it [the State claiming to be acting in self-defence] has a good case, the world will applaud and not condemn its action'. Such qualification suggested that the international community could reject an alleged claim of self-defence. See P. B. Potter, 'As Determined by the United States' (1946) 40 *American Journal of International Law* 792, 794.

50 H. Lauterpacht, *The Function of Law in the International Community* (Oxford: Oxford University Press, 2011; first published in 1933) 188; O. Schachter, 'Self-Defence and the Rule of Law' (1989) 83 *American Journal of International Law* 259, 261.

this line of reasoning when it rejected the German contention that it was ultimately for each State to decide whether it entertained the right to self-defence under particular conditions. The Tribunal rightly held that 'whether action taken under the claim of self-defence was in fact aggressive or defensive must ultimately be subject to investigation or adjudication if international law is ever to be enforced'.[51] The International Court of Justice (ICJ) upheld this position in the case of *Oil Platforms*.[52] Having referred to its ruling in *Nicaragua*,[53] the Court unequivocally remarked that a decision involving the use of armed force to defend a State's national security was 'not purely a question for the subjective judgement of the party'; such a far-reaching decision must be 'assessed by the Court'.[54]

It follows that a State resorting to the legal right of self-defence bears the burden of proof as to the absolute necessity of its action in order for the international community to make an objective judgement of the justifiability of its claim.[55] Such a State must demonstrate beyond reasonable doubt that all peaceful efforts had failed – including the exhaustion of diplomatic and economic avenues[56] – and that there had been no alternative other than taking military action. Above all, the presence of an actual or imminent attack must be substantiated by hard evidence, which must reveal that the defending State has actually been attacked or imminently threatened, and that the harm involved was serious enough to warrant defensive force. Since self-defence is an act of emergency, it must also be temporally and materially confined to the narrow purpose of warding off an actual or imminently impending unlawful attack. Relatedly, any measure of self-defence must forthwith be reported to the Council, whose authority to maintain or restore international peace remains unaffected.[57] Self-defensive force may indeed persist only until the Council has effectively contained the situation. Furthermore, the defending State must at some stage provide evidence as to how it has honoured the rules of proportionality and necessity in its use of lethal force.[58]

51 *Judgement of the International Military Tribunal for the Trial of German Major War Criminals*, Nuremburg 30th September and 1st October 1946, Cmd. 6964, HMSO, Lond. 1946, 30; also see H. Waldock, *The Law of Nations: An Introduction to the International Law of Peace* (New York: Oxford University Press, 1963) 407–408.

52 *Oil Platforms (Islamic Republic of Iran v United States of America)* (Judgement, 2003), ICJ Reports 161.

53 *Nicaragua v United States of America*, supra note 37.

54 *Oil Platforms*, supra note 52, ¶ 43; *cf. Nicaragua v United States of America*, supra note 37, ¶ 282.

55 See *Oil Platforms*, supra note 52, ¶ 51; also see D. Raab, 'Armed Attack after the *Oil Platforms* Case' (2004) 17 *Leiden Journal of International Law* 719, 723.

56 See D. Kaye, 'Adjudicating Self-Defense: Discretion, Perception, and the Resort to Force in International Law' (2005) 44 *Columbia Journal of Transnational Law* 134, 161.

57 See generally, Brierly, supra note 51, 416.

58 Whilst customary principles of necessity and proportionality are not clearly spelt out in the UN Charter, as the ICJ held in *Nicaragua*, they play an important role in the correct interpretation of the self-defence doctrine. See *Nicaragua v United States of America*, supra note 37, ¶ 176.

In view of all this, the legal regulation of modern warfare provides structure and a measure of accountability to just war thinking. States may therefore no longer offer their mere assertions as unassailable religious justifications for their war efforts. Instead, every unilateral action in the name of self-defence must legally be justified to the satisfaction of the international community. In summary, the divorce of the modern laws of war from religion-based just war thinking allowed all members of the UN – irrespective of their religious, cultural, and political affiliations – to come together under the umbrella of a relatively neutral legal order designed to prevent unlawful aggression as a means of settling differences.

Being part and parcel of such a secularised international legal system, Muslim States now attempt to justify their employment of military force by reference to the UN Charter, rather than to the doctrine of military jihad. Whilst some Muslim States occasionally turn to the rhetoric of jihad to rally popular support at home, internationally they seek to legitimate their warlike conduct by legal means.[59] Like other States, Muslim States by and large categorise their wars under the rubric of self-defence – nevertheless, such a characterisation must stand up to legal scrutiny in order to be deemed valid.[60]

III. War and Martyrdom in the World of Nation-States

The above has shown that Islamic States are disinclined to resort to the concept of jihad in their bids to legitimate their wars at the international level. While there is nothing to prevent Muslim States from invoking defensive military jihad in conjunction with the legal right to self-defence, no Muslim government has hitherto brought claims of jihad before the UN to justify its warlike conduct.[61] Muslim

59 Recent examples of drawing upon religious warlike concepts as a spur to fight other nations include Afghan Muslims' waging of jihad against the Russian occupation of Afghanistan in 1979; Iran's call for military jihad against Iraq in 1980; the Taliban's appeal for jihad against the US before the Afghanistan War in 2001; and Iraq's declaration of jihad against the US before the 2003 US occupation of Iraq. See G. Kepel, *Jihad: The Trail of Political Islam* (London: I.B. Tauris, 2004) 205ff; S. Mahmoudi, 'The Islamic Perception of the Use of Force in the Contemporary World' (2005) 7 *Journal of the History of International Law* 55, 68ff; J. Rex, 'Islam in the United Kingdom' in: S. T. Hunter (ed.), *Islam, Europe's Second Religion: The New Social, Cultural, and Political Landscape* (Westport, CT: Praeger, 2002) 70ff.

60 It will be remembered that *defensive* military jihad similarly constitutes the least problematic form of religious war, which received its divine approval in the early Medinan era when fighting was permitted in self-defence within the bounds of necessity and proportionality. See Q. 22:39; Q. 2:190.

61 An instance where reliance on military jihad coincided with the invocation of the legal right to international self-defence transpired in the Iran–Iraq War, in which parties sought to mobilise their populations for hostilities by reference to jihad at the domestic level, while at the same time they sought to justify their use of force under the right of self-defence before the UN. See K. T. Szabó, 'Self-Defense Arguments in Jihad and Western International Law' in: M. C. Bassiouni; A. Guellali (eds.), *Jihad and its*

States' official avoidance of drawing on militant religious concepts before international organs, however, does not mean that Muslim groups as a whole ceased to perceive matters of war and peace from a theological perspective. As discussed extensively in the previous chapter, fundamentalist non-State actors, who come from varying ethnic, linguistic, and denominational backgrounds, continue to exhort believers to undertake warlike jihad against the perceived moral, political, and economic corruption of the ruling elite both at home and abroad. Notwithstanding the considerable difficulty of drawing a clear line of demarcation between the fundamentalist, revivalist, or reformist Islamist groups,[62] these radical movements, it will be recalled, may be said to have engaged in an effort to cleanse Islam of 'heretical' practices and to revert it to its pure form – as it is believed to have existed during the time of Muhammad and the rightly guided caliphs. Stressing the indivisibility of religion and political order, radicals generally undertake a non-contextual exegesis of primary sources, calling for jihad to overthrow oppressive regimes and to revive the original values and principles of Islam.[63]

Radical movements vehemently disapprove of contemporary Muslim polities for following the Western nation-State model, which stands in sharp contrast to the Islamic concept of *ummah*, where emphasis is laid on religious fraternalism as the common denominator between believers of diverse ethnic, cultural, and linguistic backgrounds. Challenging the vestiges of past Muslim subjugation and holding contemporary Muslim polities responsible for not rising up against the evils of imperialism and modernity, and for being morally and politically corrupt, radicals insist that true salvation lies in the rejection of non-Islamic ideologies (such as nationalism) and socio-political institutions, and in the restoration of a purified Muslim theocracy predicated on fundamental religious tenets.[64]

Radicals generally utilise the discourse of martyrdom (*sahadat*) to mobilise the masses – particularly the impoverished, disadvantaged, and disenchanted young Muslims – to undertake military operations or commit terrorist atrocities, usually

Challenges to International and Domestic Law (The Hague, Hague Academic Press, 2010) 209, 225–226.

62 See generally, B. M. Edwards, *Islamic Fundamentalism since 1945,* 2nd ed. (London: Routledge, 2013).

63 As noted earlier, the above world view by no means entirely captures the complex and multifaceted nature of various fundamentalist groups. See generally, V. V. Naumkin, *Radical Islam in Central Asia: Between Pen and Rifle* (Oxford: Rowman & Littlefield Publishers, 2005) 1–7.

64 Such views found their most forceful expressions in the writings of Hasan al-Banna and Sayyid Qutb of the Muslim Brotherhood, Abu'l-A'la Mawdudi of Jama'at-i Islami, and the Shia cleric Ayatollah Khomeini, who led the Iranian Revolution of 1979. See further, S. H. Hashmi, 'Is There an Islamic Ethic of Humanitarian Intervention' in: M. A. Baderin (ed.), *International Law and Islamic Law* (Aldershot: Ashgate, 2008) 122; P. Harvey, *Hybrids of Modernity: Anthropology, the Nation State and the Universal Exhibition* (London: Routledge, 1996) 94ff; M. A. Raja, 'Muslim Modernity: Poetics, Politics, and Metaphysics' in: G. Marranci (ed.) *Muslim Societies and the Challenge of Secularization: An Interdisciplinary Approach* (London: Springer, 2010) 99, 108ff.

against randomly chosen or intentionally selected individuals – the latter category mostly embodies a particular group like politicians, journalists, or military personnel.[65] Such militant measures generally hinge upon the symbolic and communicative ramifications of violence, with the ultimate objective being to effectuate the sort of change that radical groups demand.[66] The role of the martyrdom discourse, in such a context, is to make the would-be jihadists believe that their lethal activities would result in eternal afterlife, wherein immeasurable benefits and endless bliss are promised to those who lose their lives for the religious cause. Hence, the main motivator behind the concept of military jihad is the conviction that whoever perishes on the battlefield in the path of God will become a martyr (*shahid*) and go to Paradise. Evidently, faith in the absolute righteousness of one's beliefs and the idea of martyrdom, rewarded by heavenly bliss, must provide indomitable resolve and valour to those who face adversity or death.[67]

Today, the theme of martyrdom is resorted to by Islamist groups in such volatile regions as Palestine, Chechnya, Kashmir, Afghanistan, Iraq, Syria, and Egypt with a view to motivating Muslim fighters in conflicts of predominantly asymmetric character.[68] Notwithstanding its diminishing prevalence in inter-State settings, Muslim States also make occasional reference to martyrdom to further their war

65 Internet-based forums, blogs, and chat-boards have lately been used extensively to recruit people from all backgrounds for suicide attacks. Cook and Allison note that 'these internet sites have mass appeal among Arabic-speaking youths and, in some cases, among converts in Europe and the United States (even those who know little or no Arabic [may have access to most of such sites], because many sites have translated sections)'. See D. Cook; O. Allison, *Understanding and Addressing Suicide Attacks: The Faith and Politics of Martyrdom Operations* (Westport: Greenwood Publishing Group, 2007) 105.

66 Certainly, such atrocities may, in the short term, also aim at voicing certain grievances, damaging the credibility of public authorities, or gaining concessions from governments. See generally, P. R. Neumann, *Old & New Terrorism* (Cambridge: Polity Press, 2009).

67 Modern States and intelligence services regularly express grave concern over the possibility of terrorist atrocities through suicide missions, reinforced by the idea of martyrdom. In an effort to discredit the purported nobility of religious violence perpetrated through terrorism and suicide bombings, the post-9/11 US narrative sought to depict the radical Islamist 'terrorist' as a contemptible person, whose fanatical ideology is based on hatred, intolerance, ruthlessness, and devastation, and whose indiscriminate violence leads to the decimation of countless innocent civilians. For more on this theme, see G. Kepel, *Beyond Terror and Martyrdom: The Future of the Middle East* (Cambridge, MA: Harvard University Press, 2008). But the sincerity of this narrative is undercut by many illegitimate US practices during the 'war on terror' campaign, which included widespread practices of torture (or the so-called 'enhanced interrogation techniques'), secret detentions, the denial of fair trial rights, and the arbitrary killings of many civilians – often disguised as 'collateral damage'. See further, Bakircioglu, supra note 42, 176–182.

68 As noted earlier, the Quran has explicit verses concerning martyrdom; see, in particular, Q. 4:74; Q. 9:111; Q. 61:10–12.

efforts.[69] The Iran–Iraq war constitutes a case in point, where both the Iraqi and Iranian authorities had promised the would-be martyrs the highest rank in paradise.[70] But due in large part to the overuses and misuses of martyrdom in Islamic history, contemporary invocations of the discourse no longer elicit a significant Muslim response. It therefore appears that martyrdom has, in particular since the modern period, become one of those notions whose widespread use eroded its practical import.

Perhaps the last credible attempt to mobilise Muslims on a global scale through the notions of jihad and martyrdom transpired in the run-up to the Great War, when the crumbling Ottoman Empire had desperately appealed to the global Muslim community to take up arms against the Allied Powers.[71] Whilst the call for military jihad initially generated apprehension among the Allied Powers – which were concerned about the possibility of a destabilising impact over their Muslim subjects living under their rules – the Sultan's plea for Muslim solidarity against the enemy proved rather ineffective. Indeed, the appeal to religious concepts not only failed to convince most Muslim subjects of the Empire[72] that the circumstances warranted the duty of military jihad regardless of what the sultan-caliph declared, but also failed to prevent the British-backed Arab revolt against Turkish rule.[73]

69 See J. L. Esposito, *Unholy War: Terror in the Name of Islam* (New York: Oxford University Press, 2003) 69.

70 See ibid; J. L. Esposito, *What Everyone Needs to Know about Islam*, 2nd ed. (Oxford: Oxford University Press, 2011) 152–153. In particular during the early years of Islam, the firm belief in the inevitable triumph of the Islamic cause and in the heavenly rewards envisaged for martyrs rendered Muslim warriors much more valiant in wars. See generally, D. MacEoin, 'Suicide Bombing as Worship Dimensions of Jihad' (2009) *Middle East Quarterly* 15.

71 See generally, M. Kamrava, *The Modern Middle East: A Political History since the First World War* (Berkeley: University of California Press, 2011) 40ff.

72 The proclamation of jihad in particular was directed at the Empire's Arab inhabitants, whose leaders had been making alliances with the British and, in a few instances, with the French Empires. See further, M. Aksakal, '"Holy War Made in Germany?" Ottoman Origins of the 1914 Jihad' in: H. Gulalp; G. Seufert (eds.), *Religion, Identity and Politics: Germany and Turkey in Interaction* (London: Routledge, 2013) 34, 35.

73 The successful Arab revolt against the Ottomans proved to have consequential results for the Allied Powers; it notably ensured that the British and French Empires could maintain their authority over their Muslim subjects. B. Lewis, *The Middle East: 2000 Years of History from the Rise of Christianity to the Present Day* (London: Phoenix, 2000) 340–341; M. A. Reynolds, *Shattering Empires: The Clash and Collapse of the Ottoman and Russian Empires 1908–1918* (Cambridge: Cambridge University Press, 2011) 122ff. It is argued that the Arab revolt was not merely based on nationalistic motivations, but on religious reasons, on the basis that the ruling elite of the declining Ottoman Empire (the so-called Young Turks) were not considered pious enough to rule over the Arabs. For more on this, see B. Lewis, *From Babel to Dragomans: Interpreting the Middle East* (Oxford: Oxford University Press, 2004) 164–165; J. Jankowski, 'Egypt and Early Arab Nationalism, 1908–1922' in: R. Khalidi *et al* (eds.), *The Origins of Arab Nationalism* (New York: Columbia University Press, 1991) 257–264.

A recent illustration of how the political impact of holy war and martyrdom discourse has lost its erstwhile power for most Muslims was the former Iraqi leader Saddam Hussein's failed attempt to unite Muslims in opposition to the impending US-led military action against Iraq in 2003.[74] Despite worldwide protests against the anticipated war, Muslim nations did not respond to Hussein's ostensible religious overture to galvanise Muslims into military action. The long-standing Palestinian–Israeli conflict likewise demonstrates that religious appeals to jihad or promises of heavenly rewards have not hitherto elicited direct support from Muslim States, which prefer to act according to the dictates of international law and power politics. Because contemporary Muslim State practice is informed by legal and political factors, it is primarily radical non-State actors who turn to religious claims to justify their actions and to effect change at the national or international level.

By the same token, while radical groups usually aspire to restore theocratic orders predicated upon the fundamental tenets of Islam,[75] Muslim States have long recognised the legitimacy of modern nation-States, where sovereignty is not premised upon divine authority, but upon the general will of the governed. This, of course, does not mean that all Muslim organisations are intent on discarding the machinery of the modern nation-State in favour of primitive polities based on pre-modern forms of tribal solidarity. Rather, non-extreme Islamist movements principally aim at building fair State machineries based on timeless Muslim values without rejecting such notions as popular sovereignty, citizenry participation, basic human rights, and other pertinent constructs of the current socio-political conjuncture.[76] Supporting this point, Ali's work on modern *fatwas* demonstrates that many contemporary Muftis and non-fundamentalist Muslim groups have come to accept the legitimacy of territorial nation-States, the UN and its institutions, as well as other regional mechanisms including the Organisation of Islamic Cooperation (OIC, formerly known as the Organization of the Islamic Conference).[77] Furthermore, according to Ali's work, both Muslim State practice and public opinion suggest that mechanisms of Islamic international law (*siyar*) are becoming more and more open to the 'contemporary realities of co-existence in an increasingly globalised world'.[78]

74 Bantekas, supra note 11, 125.

75 See O. Mehmet, *Islamic Identity and Development: Studies of the Islamic Periphery* (London: Routledge, 1990) 72; J. P. Piscatori, *Islam in a World of Nation-States* (Cambridge: Cambridge University Press, 1986) 22ff.

76 See generally, S. Zubaida, 'Is Iran an Islamic State?' in: Beinin, supra note 2, 103, 104ff.

77 Ali notes that 'despite the rhetoric of many Muslims that international law and the language of globalisation is an alien and oppressive construct, almost all the *fatwas* reviewed in . . . [my] study, employ contemporary language of international law and international relations'. S. S. Ali, 'Resurrecting *Siyar* through *Fatwas*? (Re)Constructing Islamic International Law in a Post (Iraq) Invasion World' in: Bassiouni, supra note 61, 107, 135.

78 Ibid. 132.

If such is the case, then the above-discussed bellicose norms and time-bound formulations are to be subjected to renewed reading in keeping with the spirit of this age, which is defined by pluralism, tolerance, broadmindedness, and peaceful solidarity of all nations.[79] Since the post-colonial era, Muslim States have not often invoked religious notions of war and peace, favouring instead the modern concepts of international law, which permit unilateral force in cases of self-defence alone. This modern approach has not been too radical a shift for Muslim States, which, by religious standards, are entitled to employ lethal force to ward off an armed attack.[80] However, as the previous pages have demonstrated, because religious claims of self-defence did not readily lend themselves to dispassionate evaluation, modern international law has provided a legal structure to assess the validity of self-defence claims from a more factual standpoint.

It should now be plain that Muslim States have recourse to international mechanisms in order to deal with security issues and resolve international disputes. By repudiating the legitimacy of national and international legal orders, radical movements, however, arrogate to themselves the right to launch military jihad to further their religio-political agendas. But given the sheer range and diversity of such fragmented movements, and considering their widespread use of indiscriminate and disproportionate violence, it is inconceivable to suggest that radical groups hold any form of legitimacy. In contrast, militant Islamists' increasing reliance upon illicit means significantly erodes sympathy felt for them.[81]

It should, in this context, be recalled that the declaration of warlike jihad presupposes the presence of a supreme leader whose legitimacy is acknowledged by the Muslim community at large, not just by marginal militant groups. The legitimate ruler (or his deputy) alone wields the ultimate power to wage and direct defensive or offensive wars – albeit such power bears particular significance in offensive campaigns – for nations are inherently justified to counter force with force in genuine cases of self-defence.[82] Evidently, the doctrine of legitimate

79 As the UN General Assembly rightly stressed, the creation of the UN system 'has been a major act towards transformation from a culture of war and violence to a culture of peace and non-violence.' A/RES/52/13, 15 January 1998.

80 Q. 2:192. Muslims are likewise allowed to pursue defensive measures until a point when 'there is no more tumult or oppression'. Q. 2:193.

81 As Selvik and Stenslie rightly stress, many secular Muslims and non-Muslim minority groups feel apprehension about the possibility of fundamentalist movements coming to power, lest they restrain religious freedoms and minority rights, and adopt restrictive measures. See K. Selvik; S. Stenslie, *Stability and Change in the Modern Middle East* (London: I.B. Tauris, 2011) 140.

82 As stressed earlier, the Shiite doctrine of legitimate authority draws a sharp line between offensive and defensive forms of jihad. According to the Shiite tradition, offensive jihads may not be fought in the absence of the just Imam (who is believed to have gone in occultation). In the absence of an infallible Imam, so the reasoning goes, there is no way of avoiding an error of judgement concerning the imperative to wage offensive wars, which may unduly endanger the lives of countless innocent people. Consequently, until the hidden Imam reappears (or appoints a deputy), the only form of jihad is held to be defensive. For a detailed treatment of this point,

authority is formulated to ensure that military jihad is undertaken strictly for the cause of God. Connected with this principle is the rule that any declaration of jihad must be made openly – and if such is made on account of an alleged breach of a treaty, the treaty in question must be proclaimed null and void before the initiation of hostilities.[83] The necessity for an open declaration of war is geared towards granting one final opportunity to the enemy who might offer an alternative to military confrontation. This requirement, in turn, is the corollary of the notion that wars are to be fought only when all peaceful means of dispute settlement are exhausted.[84]

In the contemporary world of nation-States, political and sectarian divisions among Muslims have become more pronounced; no Islamic political entity may therefore be said to represent the Muslim community as a whole.[85] The net ramification of this phenomenon is that in inter-Muslim hostilities, whether between States or between a State and a militant non-State group, none of the parties may authoritatively exercise jihad proper against the adversary. Indeed, the idea of legitimate authority often assumes a problematic nature in inter-Muslim disputes. For instance, in disputes between Morocco and Algeria, Pakistan and Bangladesh, Egypt and Saudi Arabia (in the Yemen), Libya and Chad, Syria and Lebanon, and Iran and Iraq, parties to the conflict could hardly lay an authoritative claim to justified force exercised by a 'legitimate authority'.

The same logic applies to civil wars raging in Muslim States; for absent a universal Muslim body politic, all conflicting parties could subjectively assert possession of legitimacy and just cause. Nevertheless, subjective characterisations of justifiability hardly dispel the spectre of one-sidedness. Worse still, since the earliest epochs of Muslim history, political power has been fragmented and polarised – a phenomenon that often led to concurrent pretentions to the right to rule over Muslims.[86] Viewed from this angle, the necessity for international legal mechanisms to gauge the nature and justifiability of particular international behaviour seems all the more judicious. The secular UN system of collective security (albeit imperfect) is thus vital in efforts to prevent wars waged for political, economic, or religious reasons. By placing the onus on aggressors to legitimate

see A. A. Sachedina, *The Just Ruler in Shi'ite Islam: The Comprehensive Authority of the Jurist in Imamite Jurisprudence* (Oxford: Oxford University Press, 1988) 110–111.

83 See M. H. Kamali, 'Jihad and the Interpretation of the Qur'an: Contextualising Islamic Tradition' in: Bassiouni, supra note 61, 39, 49.

84 The Quran, however, recommends that even when hostilities break out, Muslims should stop fighting when the enemy 'ceases' or 'inclines to peace'. See Q. 2:193; Q. 8:61.

85 The Quran describes humankind, in its original state, as 'one single nation', which was later splintered into various nations. Q. 2:213.

86 The institution of the caliphate was shown to have lost its consolidating value soon after the period of the first rightful caliphates. In 1924, Turkish modernists, led by Mustafa Kemal, brought to an end this symbolic institution that had long ceased to represent the political unity of Muslims as a whole. For an analysis see S. Aoun, *Aujourd'hui L'islam: Fractures, Intégrisme et Modernité* (Montréal: Médiaspaul, 2007) 18ff.

their warlike conduct, the UN system compels States to substantiate their assertions by facts rather than by religious or speculative notions.

IV. Muslim State Conduct in the UN Era

There is certainly no monolithic pattern of Muslim State conduct, as the extent to which the law and religion shape the way that national and international relations are conducted varies across the Muslim world.[87] This notwithstanding, present-day Muslim States on the whole denounce aggressive force, including sectarian violence and terror attacks, perpetrated in the name or under the pretence of religion.[88] Whilst Muslim States may not yet be at the forefront of human rights protection, they have perceptibly been going through a major political transition in an increasingly globalised world, wherein respect for human rights and peaceful resolution of international disputes are playing an ever-increasing role.

Today, almost all Islamic States adhere to the basic precepts of international law, recognising such fundamental rights and values as self-determination of peoples, national sovereignty and territorial integrity of States, and the right to life, security, and equality of individuals.[89] One of the most noteworthy declarations on human rights issued by Muslim States, the Universal Islamic Declaration of Human Rights (IDHR),[90] enshrines most political and socio-economic rights, including the right to life, the right to equality and justice, the right to fair judicial proceedings, the right to protection against abuses of power, the right to freedom from torture and inhuman and degrading treatment, the right to freedom of expression and belief, the right to education, the right to status and dignity of workers, and the right to social security. Although some of the above rights are qualified by the 'limits prescribed by the Law' (the Law denotes the Sharia),[91]

87 Hence, as Esposito puts, 'Islam represents ideals that have taken many forms through the centuries. While the life of Muhammad and the Medinan State he created remain ideal paradigms, historically there has been no single, agreed-upon model for an Islamic State. Muslim empires, sultanates, and modern States have varied [and been] conditioned by diverse historical and social contexts. . .' J. L. Esposito, *The Future of Islam* (Oxford: Oxford University Press, 2010) 139.

88 For instance, Saudi Arabia (which is known for its strict application of Sharia rules) in its report to the Security Council on counter-terrorism, expressed its 'resolute stance on rejecting terrorism in all its forms and manifestations', and its desire for 'active cooperation and participation in and contribution to international and bilateral efforts to combat terrorism and the financing thereof'. Report Submitted by the Government of the Kingdom of Saudi Arabia pursuant to para 6 of Security Council Resolution 1455 (2003), S/AC.37/2003/(1455)/42.

89 See Arab Charter on Human Rights Articles 2, 3, 4, 5, 8, 10.

90 See Universal Islamic Declaration of Human Rights (*21 Dhul Qaidah 1401*, 19 September 1981). Available at: http://www.alhewar.com/ISLAMDECL.html.

91 The vagueness of this restriction renders the document somewhat restrictive, in that some Sharia rules may come into conflict with modern rights and liberties. This difficulty may be exacerbated in view of the diversity of opinions and practice across time and space as to what constitutes an Islamic rule on a certain subject or right.

the IDHR carries considerable political and moral weight in view of its recognition of parallel rights enshrined in the 1948 Universal Declaration of Human Rights (UDHR). Among the most striking provisions of the IDHR is Article 13, which guarantees that 'every person has the right to freedom of conscience and worship in accordance with his religious beliefs'. This Article evinces that Islamic States have moved beyond the peaceful toleration of non-Muslim groups by recognising the principle of non-discrimination and respect for people of various beliefs without imposing additional fiscal burdens on the latter.[92] Fundamentally, however, the disallowance of religious discrimination (particularly in respect of the Scriptuaries) has never been an alien phenomenon to Islam. It is therefore unsurprising that in Article 10 of the IDHR rests the protection of minority rights on the 'no compulsion in religion' injunction of the Quran.[93]

A similar trend is followed in the Cairo Declaration on Human Rights in Islam (CDHRI),[94] which, penned with a religious tenor, guarantees some of the most prominent civil and political, and social and economic rights – including the prohibition of discrimination, forced religious conversions, unlawful arrests, slavery, torture and other forms of ill-treatment; the protection of life, dignity, equality, privacy, honour, and property; the assurance of the rights to education, work, medical care, clean environment, and social security.[95] Affirming the basic principles of humanitarian law, Article 3 of CDHRI further demands the principles of proportionality and distinction be respected in armed conflicts, the wounded and the sick benefit from medical treatment, and prisoners of war be provided with essential rights to food, clothing, and shelter, and the right to be returned home. Notwithstanding that the said declarations incorporate limitations on the substantive content of some rights by reference to Sharia law – which has been read or applied in divergent ways – they nevertheless constitute outstanding steps in aligning Islamic State practice with the current standards of international law, where individual rights and liberties acquire increasing significance. In 2004, the League of Arab States adopted a more muscular legal instrument, the Arab Charter on Human Rights,[96] which reaffirmed the principles of the UN

92 As touched upon earlier, Muslim States had at times imposed certain limitations on the rights and freedoms of the People of the Book. Such restrictions included the way they had to dress in public, or the conditions they had to satisfy to build or restore religious places of worship. Nevertheless, there did not exist an unvarying practice concerning the treatment of the Scriptuaries. See further, Khadduri, supra note 10, 277–278.

93 Q. 2:256. Article 10(b) of the IDHR further grants religious minorities residing in Muslim countries the right to 'have the choice to be governed in respect of their civil and personal matters by Islamic Law, or by their own laws'.

94 Cairo Declaration on Human Rights in Islam, issued by the Member States of the Organisation of the Islamic Conference, Cairo, 5 August 1990. Available at: http://www.oic-oci.org/english/article/human.htm.

95 See, in particular, Articles 1, 2, 7, 10, 13, 15, 17, 18, and 20.

96 League of Arab States, Arab Charter on Human Rights, 22 May 2004, entered into force on 15 March 2008.

Charter and the Cairo Declaration, and recognised the civil and political, and social, cultural, and economic rights envisaged in the International Bill of Human Rights.[97]

Moreover, in 1969, Muslim leaders established the OIC[98] to promote cooperation among Muslim States in political, economic, social, cultural, and scientific matters, and to achieve solidarity in foreign policy goals.[99] In its Preamble, the Charter of the OIC reaffirms Member States' commitment 'to adhere . . . to the principles of the United Nations Charter . . . and [of] international law [in general]'.[100] Correspondingly, the Charter stresses that Member States will uphold such values as democracy, good governance, human rights, and the rule of law; that they will respect the sovereignty and territorial integrity of other nations, and settle international disputes through peaceful means; that they will contribute to global peace and security in conformity with the principles of the UN Charter; and that they will work together with the international community in ensuring respect for non-interference in domestic affairs, and in combating aggression and terrorism in all forms.[101] In effect, then, the OIC Charter confirms the willingness of Muslim States to enter into relations with non-Muslim nations on the basis of equality, reciprocity, and mutual respect for territorial sovereignty.

The OIC appears to fulfil two main functions: it acts as a special instrument to enable Muslim States to engage with each other on the common ground of core religio-political precepts; and it endorses the secular rules of modern international law on matters of war and peace. The second function naturally requires the OIC members to partake in collective international efforts to arrest or suppress aggressive State conduct, even when this means forcibly opposing an illegitimate policy of a Muslim State. A case in point was the OIC's condemnation of the Iraqi invasion of Kuwait – an unlawful move that eventually led to Security

97 Ibid. See, in particular, the Preamble and Articles 2, 3, 5, 8, 9, 10, 11, 13, 14, 24, 25, 30, 31, 34, 38, and 41.

98 Among the significant events that prepared the ground for the establishment of the Islamic Conference were the crushing Arab defeat in the Six-Day War of 1967 (which reshaped the foreign policy objectives of the Arab leaders involved), and the 1969 arson attack against the al-Aqsa mosque by an Australian citizen of unsound mind. King Faisal, in reaction to such phenomena, called for an Islamic summit in Rabat, Morocco, where it was decided to construct a permanent Muslim organisation. See further, I. Warde, 'Global Politics, Islamic Finance and Islamist Politics Before and After 11 September 2001' in: C. M. Henry; R. Wilson (eds.), *The Politics of Islamic Finance* (Edinburgh: Edinburgh University Press, 2004) 37, 38ff.

99 S. S Ali, *Gender and Human Rights in Islam and International Law* (London: Kluwer Law International, 2000) 195–196; S. S. Ali; J. Rehman, 'The Concept of *Jihad* in Islamic International Law' (2005) 10 *Journal of Conflict & Security Law* 321, 343.

100 Charter of the Organisation of the Islamic Conference (1972). Available at: http://www.oic-oci.org/is11/english/Charter-en.pdf.

101 See Article 1(3), (6), (14), (18) and Article 2(3), (4), (5), (7) of the Charter of the Organisation of the Islamic Conference (1972). Available at: http://www.oic-oci.org/is11/english/Charter-en.pdf.

Council-authorised military action against Iraq.[102] While a few Muslim States did not approve the OIC's denunciation of the Iraqi aggression, the Muslim World League also deplored the Iraqi attempt to annex Kuwait, and found it justified 'in the name of Islam' to 'appeal for help . . . [to] non-Muslim armies'.[103]

Muslim States have, in addition, developed regional conventions that require Member States to criminalise and punish terrorist activities. Examples of these instruments include the Arab Convention on the Suppression of Terrorism 1998,[104] and the OIC Convention on Combating International Terrorism,[105] which, among others, reaffirms the resolve of Muslim States to adhere to procedures of relevant international instruments directed towards the elimination of international terrorism and other unlawful acts that undermine territorial integrity, political independence, and general security of other States.

At the practical level, Muslim States have frequently turned to diplomacy and other peaceful methods of international dispute settlement. Illustrative of such efforts are the conclusion of a peace treaty between Israel and Egypt;[106] the settlement of territorial questions between Qatar and Bahrain,[107] Egypt and Israel,[108] Emirates of Dubai and Sharjah,[109] Libya and Tunisia;[110] and recourse to settlement of legal disputes between Algeria, Mauretania, and Morocco,[111] Libya and the United Kingdom and the United States.[112] As these examples suggest, mechanisms of modern international law have been employed by Muslim States

102 Ever since its establishment, the OIC has been criticised, in particular by radical Muslims, for not advancing the interests of the Islamic community as a whole, and for being a mere assortment of fifty-odd Muslim States. However, despite its generally ineffective role in the Bosnian conflict and the Second Iraq War, many Muslims hoped that the OIC would evolve into a stronger political force for the Muslim community in the future. See Hashmi, supra note 10, 224.

103 Kepel, supra note 59, 210.

104 Arab Convention on the Suppression of Terrorism, signed on 22 April 1998. Available at: https://www.unodc.org/tldb/pdf/conv_arab_terrorism.en.pdf

105 Convention of the Organisation of the Islamic Conference on Combating International Terrorism (1990). Available at: http://www.oic-oci.org/english/convenion/terrorism_convention.htm

106 Peace Treaty between the State of Israel and the Arab Republic of Egypt (26 March 1979). Available at: http://www.mfa.gov.il/MFA/Peace%20Process/Guide%20to%20the%20Peace%20Process/Israel-Egypt%20Peace%20Treaty.

107 *Maritime Delimitation and Territorial Questions between Qatar and Bahrain* (*Qatar v Bahrain*) ICJ Reports 2001, 40.

108 *Boundary Dispute concerning the Taba Area* (*Egypt v Israel*) 27 ILM (1988) 1421.

109 *Boundary Dispute between Dubai and Sharjah* (*Emirate of Dubai v Emirate of Sharjah*) (Arbitral Award of 19 October 1981) ILR Vol. 91, 543ff.

110 *Continental Shelf* (*Tunisia/Libyan Arab Jamahiriya*) ICJ Rep1982, 18.

111 *Western Sahara Case*, Advisory Opinion, ICJ Rep 1975 12.

112 *Case Concerning Questions of Interpretation and Application of the 1971 Montreal Convention Arising from the Aerial Incident at Lockerbie* (*Libya v UK and Libya v United States of America*) ICJ Rep 1998, 115. For more on peaceful settlement of disputes in the Middle East, see J. Allain, *International Law in the Middle East* (Aldershot: Ashgate Publishing Limited, 2004) 229–262.

as a medium for resolving differences. However, it is fair to add that Muslim States do not merely benefit from the mechanisms of public international law; in some measure they also contribute to its functioning through such means as drafting and reviewing international agreements,[113] supporting peace-keeping missions, dispatching humanitarian aid to conflict-torn countries, partaking in collective security measures, and shaping such global policies as environmental protection and nuclear non-proliferation.[114]

Evidently, it is in the interests of Muslim States to support the framework of international law in general, and human rights law in particular,[115] which provide important rights including the right to freedom from unilateral aggression, the right to non-interference in domestic matters, equality of nations, self-determination and freedom of religion. All these rights and freedoms allow Muslims to practise their religion and preserve their way of life – the need to protect such interests, it will be recalled, originally brought forth the emergence of the doctrine of military jihad. Such fundamental rights, when practicable and applicable, could render most militant verses and traditions (save the ones concerning self-defence) non-applicable in the contemporary world.[116]

113 Ali, supra note 25, 97.

114 While the issue of nuclear disarmament, as the current Iranian nuclear crisis showcases, is a highly politically charged matter, Muslim States are generally no different from other self-interested States that wish to enhance their national securities by gaining the upper hand vis-à-vis their present or potential adversaries. For an analysis of the Middle Eastern States' attitude toward nuclear policies, see generally H. Tosaki, 'Nuclear Weapons Issues in the Middle East' in: W. L. Huntley *et al* (eds.), *Nuclear Disarmament in the Twenty-First Century* (Hiroshima: The Hiroshima Peace Institute, 2004) 184–197.

115 Challenging the intellectual stance that seeks to categorically distance Islam from the human rights discourse, some Muslim jurists have (particularly since the 1980s) vehemently attempted to prove that Islamic values and fundamental human rights have never been mutually exclusive. Such moderate Muslim defence against the aforesaid sceptic position at times goes to such lengths as to assert – and not without some strong evidence – that Islam's historical record of human rights until modern times had been far better than that of its Western counterparts, which is argued to be replete with massive human rights violations like racism, religious discrimination, slavery, genocide, and the exploitation of the non-European world. For more on this point, see E. Sahliyeh, 'Islam and Human Rights' in: D. P. Forsythe; P. C. McMahon (eds.), *Human Rights and Diversity: Area Studies Revisited* (Lincoln: University of Nebraska Press, 2003) 262ff; A. E. Mayer, *Islam and Human Rights: Tradition and Politics*, 4th ed. (Oxford: Westview Press, 2007); A. A'la Mawdudi, *Human Rights in Islam* (Leicester: The Islamic Foundation, 2002).

116 Nevertheless, as discussed earlier, many contemporary jihadist groups believe that the pressing responsibility to establish a truly Islamic order on earth requires preventing the constant decline of Islam by forcibly opposing corrupt regimes and fighting imperialism. Such a struggle, it is argued, would require weeding out all un-Islamic customs, practices, rituals, and value systems. See further, Kepel, supra note 59, 36ff.

V. The Reconciliation of Siyar with Modern International Law

The above account has made it clear that, notwithstanding the Islamic ideal to bring the entire Muslim community (and eventually the whole of humankind) under an all-encompassing polity, socio-political forces had long coerced Muslims into reconciling the universalist tendencies of Islam with dynamic practical realities. Contemporary *siyar* has correspondingly responded positively to the reality of nation-States, and to the norms of modern international law, which aim at ensuring peaceful coexistence of all nations regardless of race, creed, ideology, size, or strength. Likewise, the manner in which *siyar* is understood and applied has gone through notable changes, both structurally and ideologically. Islamic public law, in this context, draws less on rigid or obsolete dogmas to regulate domestic or foreign affairs; instead, it makes itself increasingly subject to political dynamics (*siyasa*) in a changing socio-political and economic landscape.[117]

Present-day Muslim States have accordingly forged novel norms – whether by introducing new laws or by subjecting extant principles or doctrines to purposive reinterpretation – to generate fresh approaches to the burning challenges of the day. Islamic external relations are consequently conducted in compliance with the normative order of secular international law; albeit at the domestic level regulations may in varying degrees still hinge upon Sharia norms, particularly in matters concerning personal and family law. This holds true for conservative societies too, such as Saudi Arabia, where some Sharia norms are applied internally, while international matters are chiefly carried out in accordance with secular universal standards.[118] Nevertheless, in relatively secular Muslim States, including Turkey and the Central Asian republics, both national law and international politics are largely informed by non-religious sources of authority.[119]

It would, however, be erroneous to assume that Muslim societies' amenability to politico-legal adjustment is due to pragmatic concerns alone; for in Islam inheres the policies of peaceful negotiation and dialogue as substitutes for undue armed

117 O. Arabi, *Studies in Modern Islamic Law and Jurisprudence* (The Hague: Kluwer Law International, 2001) 16–18.

118 However, Saudi Arabia does not always adhere to international standards when it comes to certain aspects of international human rights law. Indeed, despite the universalist language of human rights instruments, Saudi Arabia has long advocated the view of cultural relativism, which, for instance, provided it with the excuse to abstain from casting a vote for the UDHR – on the grounds that Article 16 of the UDHR grants equal rights to men and women in marriage, and Article 18 contains freedom of religious belief. Although Saudi Arabia acceded to such important human rights instruments as the CRC, CERD, CEDAW, and CAT, it entered reservations thereto (with the exception of CAT), declaring that the terms of such treaties would be inapplicable if they conflicted with Sharia norms. See further, C. Wilcke, 'Saudi Arabia' in: Forsythe, supra note 27, 397ff; J. Morsink, *The Universal Declaration of Human Rights: Origins, Drafting, and Intent* (Philadelphia: University of Pennsylvania Press, 1999) 24–26.

119 See Bantekas, supra note 11, 116–120.

confrontations (which are increasingly becoming more destructive in the current climate overshadowed by nuclear weaponry). This unwarlike facet of the Muslim tradition may readily dovetail with the UN collective security system, which seeks to replace internecine conflicts with amicable compromises between all nations. True, Islam does not reject aggression outright, but it considerably qualifies its employment through norms enshrined in the Quran and relevant traditions,[120] exhorting Muslims to have recourse to alternative channels of dispute resolution before resorting to lethal force against their material or potential enemies. Besides, as discussed earlier, when military jihad is deemed unavoidable, hostilities must be conducted within the strict bounds of necessity, proportionality, and discrimination with a view to reducing, among others, harm to life, which is considered sacred in Islam.[121]

Considering the capabilities of modern military technology, the need to protect life, limb, and property from undue, disproportionate, and irreparable damage becomes all the more pressing. Viewed from this angle, it is imperative that non-militant forms of jihad must be given proper consideration with intent to further the objectives of the UN Charter and foster the conditions of peaceful coexistence. While humankind has not yet devised ways to ensure lasting world peace, it is plain that currently among the most significant mechanisms to terminate wars (at least temporally) and promote amicable relations between nations are treaties of peace and cooperation – which may be signed in diverse areas ranging from commercial to diplomatic, scientific, and cultural exchanges, and from the prevention of organised crime and terrorism to treaties of extradition. While such treaties may evidently not guarantee lasting peace, they may nonetheless provide opportunities for nations to reduce recourse to conflicts, and to address the root causes of potential wars.[122]

Since moral and religious imperatives can tangibly bolster corresponding legal duties, Islamic tradition on war and peace and its approach to treaty obligations may be drawn on to uphold the notion of peaceful and amicable relations between the Members of the UN. This book has demonstrated that Sharia allows Muslim States to conclude peace treaties with other Muslim and non-Muslim nations alike, and recognises the binding nature thereof in keeping with the maxim *pacta sunt*

120 The Quran contains abundant verses about the desirability of peaceful resolution of conflicts. See, among others, Q. 49:9; Q. 49:10; Q. 8:60–61; Q. 4:90.

121 Islam considers all human beings, regardless of colour, race, or creed, to be God's creation; and being such, human life is sacred. The Quran states that it has been God's will to create nations separately: 'If Allah had so willed', the Quran says, 'He would have made you a single people, but (His plan is) to test you in what He hath given you; so strive as in a race in all virtues. . .' Q. 5:48; *cf.* Q. 10:19; Q. 11:118. See also G. C. Decasa, *The Qur'anic Concept of Umma and its Function in Philippine Muslim Society* (Rome: Editrice Pontificia Universita Gregoriana, 1999) 134–135.

122 As Dinstein correctly notes, because the life expectancy of an average peace treaty is relatively short, 'each generation must work out for itself a fresh formula for peaceful coexistence.' Dinstein, supra note 38, 36.

servanda,[123] which constitutes one of the cardinal pillars of *siyar*. Hence, if an Islamic State enters into a valid agreement of its own accord, it is obligated – both by secular and religious norms – to take all necessary measures to honour its undertakings. The classical Islamic formulation of the duty to fulfil contractual duties is as follows: 'Muslims are bound by their stipulations' ('*al-muslimun 'ala shurutihim*').[124] Although some classical jurists posited that Muslims could unilaterally renounce their treaties whenever circumstances turn to their advantage, this viewpoint had not been generally supported on grounds that such action would violate treaty pledges made by the Muslims, and that Muslims' anticipated advantages must be carefully assessed at the time of the agreement, rather than at a later point in time.[125] It must be added that such 'pragmatism' would defeat the purpose of having peace agreements in the first place. If non-Muslims suspect the candour of Muslims in making treaty promises, or distrust that Muslims would keep true to their pledges, they would probably either not willingly enter into contractual relations with Muslims, or they would renege on their vows whenever conditions are propitious. This purportedly pragmatic position is, therefore, neither plausible, nor is it supported by the Quran, which lays emphasis on the necessity of honouring pacts, even when they are concluded with polytheists:

> How can there be a league, before God and His Apostle, with the Pagans, except those with whom ye made a treaty near the sacred Mosque? As long as these stand true to you, stand ye true to them: for God doth love the righteous (Q. 9:7); But if they violate their oaths after their covenant, and taunt you for your Faith—fight ye the chiefs of Unfaith: for their oaths are nothing to them: that thus they may be restrained (Q. 9:12); [A]nd fulfil (every) engagement, for (every) engagement will be enquired into (on the Day of Reckoning) (Q. 17:34); And those who respect their trusts and covenants; [a]nd those who stand firm in their testimonies . . . such will be the honoured ones in the Gardens (of Bliss). (Q. 70: 32–35)

In parallel to such verses, the exposition of the relevant prophetic tradition in earlier chapters has shown that Muhammad had engaged in various pacts with non-Muslim tribes, and abided by the stipulations of these accords so long as other

123 The customary rule of *pacta sunt servanda* requires that parties to a treaty fulfil their duties in good faith. Being universally recognised, the norm stressing the binding force of international agreements serves as one of the basic tenets of modern international law. See M. E. Villiger, *Commentary on the 1969 Vienna Convention on the Law of Treaties* (Leiden: Bill, 2009) 366ff; M. C. Bassiouni, 'Protection of Diplomats under Islamic Law' (1980) 74 *American Journal of International Law* 609, 614.

124 J. Schacht, 'Islamic Law in Contemporary States' (1959) 8 *American Journal of Comparative Law* 133, 139; D. E. Arzt, 'The Application of International Human Rights Law in Islamic States' (1990) 12 *Human Rights Quarterly* 202, 212.

125 A. A. AbuSulayman, *Towards an Islamic Theory of International Relations: New Directions for Methodology and Thought*, 2nd ed., (Herndon: The International Institute of Islamic Thought, 1993) 25–26.

parties had not acted in grave misconduct and performed their treaty obligations in good faith.[126] The peace agreement signed between the Prophet and the Christian people of Najran constitutes an illustrative case in point, where in return for the Najrans' pledge to pay a certain sum to Muslims and not to collaborate with anti-Muslim forces, Muhammad assured that they would be secured 'their lives, property, lands, creed . . . their buildings and their churches'; that they would be free from any hardship, humiliation, or oppression; and that they would not be compelled to pay tithe, nor would they be denied justice. The agreement further guaranteed that no clergyman would be displaced from his church, nor would he be forced to abandon his pastoral occupation. Temporally, the agreement was to be valid 'so long as the people of Najran remain[ed] faithful [thereto] and act[ed] in accordance with their obligations, giving no support to oppression'.[127] This example is not singular, as Muhammad, it should be reiterated, forged numerous pacts with the neighbouring Jewish and pagan tribes without insisting that they adopt Islam – although generally requiring a payment of contributions to Muslims in return for their protection.[128]It follows from the Quran and the prophetic tradition that lawfully concluded treaties (such as the present-day UN Charter) are binding on Muslims not only for secular reasons, but also due to the fundamental premises of Islamic jurisprudence that manifestly call for fastidious observance of lawfully concluded treaties. As Hassan puts it, 'in Islam a contract or treaty is not merely a secular affair, but in fact a religious one; it is, therefore, safeguarded by divine as well as human sanctions'.[129] The Quran conspicuously condemns those who unjustifiably break their contractual oaths as being treacherous and lacking the fear of God.[130] Only in the event of material or suspected breaches of contract does the Quran permit Muslims to renounce their covenants.[131] Yet, in suspected breaches of contractual obligations, it is only fair to require that Muslims substantiate their claims with credible evidence, lest they unwarrantedly repudiate their responsibilities. For all intents and purposes, in alleged violations of contract terms, the burden to prove beyond reasonable doubt that the other side is about to abdicate its responsibilities should rest with the claimant to prevent or reduce scenarios of abuse. Whilst the Quran contains no such hard-and-fast evidentiary rule, it would be judicious to place the onus of proof on the party that suspects

126 See further, T. Ramadan, *Western Muslims and the Future of Islam* (New York: Oxford University Press, 2004) 92ff.

127 Khadduri, supra note 10, 279; I. Ishaq; A. Guillaume (trans.), *The Life of Muhammad: A Translation of Ibn Ishaq's Sirat Rasul Allah* (Oxford: Oxford University Press, 1955)14ff.

128 The prophet, as touched upon above, even signed a treaty with the polytheistic Quraysh, which had initially coerced the early Muslim community into exile in Medina. See further W. M. Watt, *Muhammad: Prophet and Statesman* (Oxford: Oxford University Press, 1961) 214–220; Ramadan, supra note 126, 92ff.

129 F. A. Hassan, 'The Sources of Islamic Law' (1982) 76 *American Society of International Law Proceedings* 65, 73.

130 Q. 8:56.

131 See Q. 8:58, which reads: 'If thou fearest treachery from any group, throw back (their covenant) on them, (so as to be) on equal terms; for Allah loveth not the treacherous.'

a violation would transpire. This would also meet the requirements of contemporary international law, which in treaties of indefinite duration[132] customarily allow parties to rescind their contractual duties for justifiable reasons and in line with termination clauses.[133]

Returning to the role of covenants within the Islamic tradition, it must be added that the post-prophetic practice followed the route of signing strategic agreements of peace with external communities. Islamic State practice, in this respect, has hitherto corroborated the textual and traditional teachings regarding the legitimacy of Muslim engagement with non-Muslims on a contractual basis, the binding force of which is confirmed by the primary sources of Islamic law.[134] From this standpoint, it appears implausible to suggest that Islam does not contain mechanisms for resolving material and potential conflicts peacefully, or that Muslims remain within a constant state of belligerency against the non-Muslim camp. Historical evidence laid out above unmistakably points to the rich repertoire of peaceful Muslim dealings with nations of various creeds.

This peaceful facet of Islam neatly corresponds with the general mechanisms and institutions of contemporary public international law that are, among others, geared towards the mission to prevent nations from using aggression in furtherance of their political, economic, or religious objectives. Whilst Muslims occasionally entertain misgivings about the fairness of 'Western-emplaced' structures and processes of international order, they nevertheless, as Falk writes, invoke the equality of nations discourse with a view to advancing 'the quest for peace and justice in the relations among the peoples of the world'.[135] What is more, in an

132 In international law, bilateral treaties generally make no reference to duration; rather, they include termination clauses that allow either party to terminate the treaty by means of written notice to be served on the other party. Likewise, multilateral treaties of unlimited duration mainly allow a party the right to withdraw when necessary. In cases of UN treaties, parties are usually allowed to withdraw by giving 12 months' prior notice in writing. It must be stressed that when parties are unsure about the duration of the treaty, they often include a clause that provides for an initial term, which may later be extended, whether explicitly or tacitly. For a detailed treatment of this matter, see A. Aust, *Handbook of International Law* (Cambridge: Cambridge University Press, 2005) 100ff.

133 Certainly, the gravity of such evidential and procedural norms is paramount in cases where an anticipated breach of a covenant carries the threat of aggression. As discussed above, even when there are reasonable grounds to believe that a State would act in breach of the UN Convention concerning the principle of non-use of armed force, the putative defender has the burden to prove the necessity of its anticipatory military action, so that the international community would evaluate the legitimacy of such a would-be military response from an objective viewpoint. See *Oil Platforms,* supra note 52, ¶ 51; also see Raab, supra note 55, 723.

134 A prophetic tradition has it that 'Muslims are bound by their obligations, except an obligation that renders the lawful unlawful, and the unlawful lawful'. See Bassiouni, supra note 123, 615.

135 R. Falk, 'False Universalism and the Geopolitics of Exclusion: The Case of Islam' in: J. Allain (ed.), *Unlocking the Middle East: The Writings of Richard Falk* (Gloucestershire: Apris Books, 2003) 50.

effort to positively influence the normative architecture of the international legal order, Muslim States increasingly utilise and seek to improve the extant tools of friendly relations and cooperation among States, in line with the basic premises of the UN Charter.

It would undoubtedly be far-fetched to maintain that the Islamic law of nations is fully congruent with its modern counterpart, not least because the former roots itself in the soil of 'divine sovereignty' – naturally assigning a special function to religious identity – as opposed to the latter, which is 'theoretically' a product of the will of nations, large and small,[136] as well as of a mixture of secular natural law and positivism.[137] Moreover, while Muslim State practice and jurists have relegated some of the belligerent and uncompromising doctrines of Islamic war and peace to a condition of desuetude or insignificance,[138] it has been demonstrated in earlier chapters that Islamic wars may, *inter alia*, be fought to root out oppression, persecution, and other forms of injustice, and to expand the Islamic sphere of influence (albeit such expansion, it will be recalled, may be realised via peaceful means, too). International law, on the other hand, confines the lawful exercise of unilateral force to the single case of self-defence. Aside from this principal exception, States must be expressly authorised by the Security Council to take military measures.[139] Another difference is the fact that Islamic just war principles cover less ground than those of detailed contemporary rules. Being formulated at an

136 It is generally accepted that the international legal system has not yet freed itself from the political, ideological, and economic interests of dominant States and social classes. In Yasuaki's words, '[t]he international system tends to reflect predominant ideas and institutions of the major powers in the system.' See O. Yasuaki, *A Transcivilizational Perspective on International Law* (The Hague: Hague Academy of International Law, 2010) 165; also see T. E. Paupp, *Redefining Human Rights in the Struggle for Peace and Development* (Cambridge: Cambridge University Press, 2014) 36ff.

137 For a discussion on how international law rose above religious considerations and progressively acquired a rather secular character, see J. O'Brien, *International Law* (London: Cavendish, 2001) 2–28.

138 As discussed in earlier chapters, Islamic legal theory, since the very beginning, allowed judges and rulers to rely on such concepts as 'equitable solution' (*istihsan*) or 'public interest' (*siyasa Sharia)* so as to deviate from the conventional means of reasoning, when necessary. The exercise of such discretion – done in the light of guiding religious principles – allowed decision-makers to find fair or politically expedient solutions in cases where the rigid application of orthodox norms or doctrines could cause iniquity or undue hardship. See generally M. H. Kamali, *Shari'ah Law: An Introduction* (Oxford: Oneworld Publications, 2011); C. A. Ford, 'Siyar-ization and its Discontents: International Law and Islam's Constitutional Crisis' (1995) 30 *Texas International Law Journal* 499.

139 Accordingly, if the UN Members believe that a given State has breached international law or posed a grave threat to international peace and security, they do not possess the right to act unilaterally to ensure adherence to the norms of international law, for this is a matter for the Security Council. See generally, *Nicaragua v United States of America*, supra note 37, ¶ 190; S. A. Alexandrov, *Self-Defence against the Use of Force in International Law* (London: Kluwer Law International, 1996) 19–27; S. C. Neff, *War and the Law of Nations: A General History* (New York: Cambridge University Press, 2005) 168–170; Dinstein, supra note 38, 90ff; Y. Dinstein, 'Comments on War' (2004) 27 *Harvard Journal of Law & Public Policy* 877, 877.

early phase of Islamic history, Islamic norms naturally provide scant guidance as to where Islam stands on such modern-day problems as economic coercion, collective security measures, organised or State-sponsored terrorism, the prosecution and punishment of grave international crimes, peacekeeping missions, and weapons of mass destruction. Likewise, the conventional layout of the Islamic law of nations does not envisage an international organisation like the UN. But the intrinsic flexibility of Sharia has readily permitted Muslim States to adapt to the modern State system, characterised by sovereign territorial States, and to significantly revise their national laws and practices, and international policies pursuant to the stipulations of the UN Charter.

Admittedly, radical Muslim groups are not prepared to acknowledge the legitimacy of public international law and its pertinent institutions. Extremist movements generally denounce the UN and other international bodies as mere pawns of imperialism, which is argued to stand for immorality, unbelief, and callous exploitation of the weak.[140] Relatedly, such fundamentalist groups as the Taliban and al-Qaeda hold that most Muslim States are mainly the agents of dominant powers, particularly the United States, the likes of which are accused of controlling or manipulating the institutions of the international legal order. Being committed to literalism in their methods of reading the authoritative sources, fundamentalists often follow their rigid, one-sided understanding of Sharia, drawing in the main on pre-modern religious dogmas and juristic interpretations.[141] This anachronistic approach unsurprisingly leads to the overall rejection of non-religious politico-legal constructs on grounds that sacred laws are commonly at variance with profane laws, and that the main edifice of both the nation-State model and international legal system has been Euro-centric, and thus essentially un-Islamic.[142]

Although the Euro-centric imprint in contemporary international law may not be denied,[143] the racist, hierarchical, and imperial underpinnings of public

140 See J. Burke, *Al-Qaeda: The True Story of Radical Islam,* 3rd ed. (London: Penguin Books, 2007) 179–198.

141 Most political Islamist movements also distrust 'conventional' Muslim scholars (*ulema*) who have ties with regimes accused of being corrupt. Hence, such movements either seek religious opinions from 'militant clergies' or form their own opinions (in keeping with the idea that any Muslim who is well-versed in Islamic teachings may rely on his own interpretations). Ibid. 184–185.

142 It must, however, be noted that non-fundamentalist Muslim groups condemn (in their declarations or *fatwas*) all forms of wanton violence. Such groups generally recognise the legitimacy of modern international law, and hence support peaceful methods of conflict resolution, calling for defensive jihad only against unjust aggression. See Ali, supra note 77, 127.

143 As Anghie observes, the initial development and universalisation of public international law had largely been the product of the imperial expansion of the Great Powers toward the end of the nineteenth century, when the conquest and colonisation of non-European peoples shaped the main parameters of international relations. By the start of the First World War, by virtue of many colonial wars, large swathes of the non-European world fell under the control of the major European Powers, which led to the assimilation of non-European peoples into a legal matrix that was

international law are progressively waning – a process that gained particular traction in the aftermath of World War II and the creation of the UN. The post-war evolution of the human rights discourse – with its emphasis on multilateralism, non-aggression in international relations, (nominal) equality of nations, and self-determination of peoples – figured prominently in the emancipation of the so-called 'Third World' from the shackles of colonial rule. Today, the growing participation of non-European and Muslim States in the workings of international law is further chipping away at the barriers to freedom and equality of all nations.

Certainly, if international law is to become more effective, it must command widespread and voluntary compliance with its imperative norms from nations regardless of the economic and political power they wield, or of their cultural and religious affiliations. While the post-World War II era altered the trend of excluding the non-European world from the sovereign equality discourse, aiming also to curb hegemonic and aggressive conduct,[144] international law has not yet acquired a fully impartial character detached from power politics.[145] The failure of international actors to bring forth a more egalitarian and encompassing framework – wherein all nations may enjoy equal treatment under comparable conditions – has in the main resulted in visible distrust on the part of radical Islamist groups, which preferred to rely on pre-modern conceptions of Islamic international relations, as viewed through their own lenses.

The drafters of the UN Charter evidently saw that absence of war did not mean real peace, or that deterrence of conflicts could not be secured by coercive measures alone. Since peace was correctly thought to be interlaced with justice and fundamental freedoms, the Preamble of the Charter draws particular attention to the importance of promoting fairness and equality for all humans and nations alike as a foundation for securing international peace and security.[146] In his

fundamentally begotten by a European mode of thinking and experience. *See* Anghie, supra note 39, 1–3; also see H. Bull, *The Anarchical Society: A Study of Order in World Politics,* 3rd ed. (London: Palgrave, 2002) 32–33.

144 It is well known that international law in earlier centuries heavily reflected crude power politics, in that warfare was a legitimate tool in international politics and that acquisition of territory through sheer aggression was perfectly acceptable – so much so that the *right of conquest* meant that the victor could confer rights or imposed obligations upon the vanquished. See further S. Korman, *The Right of Conquest: The Acquisition of Territory by Force in International Law and Practice* (Oxford: Clarendon Press, 1996) 7–8.

145 The way in which the permanent members of the Security Council were chosen is an example of power politics in international affairs. Indeed, the permanent members were not chosen for the sole reason that they had the capability to prevent a threat to the peace or to restore the international order, but mainly because they were the victors in World War II. See H. H. Lentner, 'Politics, Power and States in Globalization' in: H. Goverde *et al* (eds.), *Power in Contemporary Politics: Theories, Practices, Globalizations* (London: Sage Publications, 2000) 198ff; see generally J. B. Scott, 'The Legal Nature of International Law' (1905) 5 *Columbia Law Review* 124.

146 Articles 1(3), 13, and 55 of the Charter similarly underline the necessity of advancing fundamental rights and liberties for individuals, and of developing friendly relations and cooperation between nations. See The Charter of the United Nations, 24 October 1945.

concluding speech at the San Francisco Conference, President Truman summarised this underlying philosophy of the Charter by remarking that justice, equality, and human rights are inextricably connected to the attainment of world peace.[147] This line of thought was followed by C. Wilfred Jenks, the late director of the International Labour Organization, who noted that without equality, 'human rights and social justice, there can be no solid foundation for an enduring peace'.[148]

If the maintenance or re-establishment of international peace and security is linked with socio-economic progress and justice, fundamental rights and liberties, and equality and solidarity of nations, then, as the Declaration on Social Progress and Development makes plain, all States and international organisations should undertake the task of eliminating from social life 'such evils as inequality, exploitation, war, colonialism and racism'.[149] The international society, in a word, is to unite in its efforts to eradicate, or reduce so far as possible, social and economic injustice and all forms of discrimination in a bid to root out the scourge of war, whose prime causes lie more in the pursuit of economic and political dominance, and increasingly less in the search for religious hegemony. Among the consequential implications of this reasoning is that a sustainable world peace hinges, *inter alia*, on equitable participation of each civilisation in the cosmopolitan governance of global matters. Muslims, who constitute about 23 per cent of the world population,[150] may significantly have a hand in conducting such an intercivilisational dialogue. But, as the former ICJ judge C. G. Weeramantry highlighted, if a meaningful international dialogue is to be achieved, it is imperative that intercommunication between Islamic and other legal traditions be progressively strengthened, and efforts be made to raise awareness about Islam's overall involvement[151] in the development of international

147 'The Charter', Truman said, 'is dedicated to the achievement and observance of human rights and fundamental freedoms', and that 'unless we can attain those objectives for all men and women everywhere, without regard to race, language, or religion, we cannot have permanent peace and security in the world'. H. S. Truman, 'Verbatim Minutes of the Closing Plenary Session' (26 June 1945) in: UNIO Documents, 1: 715–16. The same wisdom permeated into the language of the UDHR, the Preamble of which provides that 'the recognition of the inherent dignity and of the equal and inalienable rights of all members of the human family', and 'the development of friendly relations between nations' constitute 'the foundation of freedom, justice and peace in the world'. See The Universal Declaration of Human Rights, adopted by the UN GA on 10 December 1948.

148 Report of the Director-General to the ILO Conference, 48th Session 1964, Part I, pp. 71–72, cited in: M. Moskowitz, *International Concern with Human Rights* (Leiden: Sijthoff International Publishing, 1974) 157.

149 GA Res. 2542 (XXIV) of 11 December 1969.

150 At the time of writing there are about 1.6 billion Muslims in the world. See P. Ferrara, *Global Religions and International Relations* (New York: Palgrave, 2014) 82.

151 One should not, of course, ignore the contribution of other civilisations to the evolution of international law; see generally A. Altman, *Tracing the Earliest Recorded Concepts of International Law: The Ancient Near East (2500–330 BCE)* (Leiden: Brill, 2012).

law.[152] This would arguably not only bring into question the sweeping assumption that public international law has its roots in Western civilisation alone,[153] but promote the universality and legitimacy of international norms and standards – with a possibility of ensuring further compliance therewith.

As the chapters above have illustrated, the doctrine of military jihad has undergone dramatic transformations over the course of Islamic history in keeping with the wider circumstances of each epoch. What is more, notwithstanding the classical Muslim theory advocating the unity of all believers bound together by ties of their common creed, Muslims have, in practice, long conceded the reality of nation-States, whose foundations were laid with the 1648 Treaty of Westphalia, which ended the Thirty Years' War (1618–1648) – a pan-European territorial and religious struggle of cataclysmic proportions.[154] Yet even before this era, Muslims are shown to have peacefully coexisted with nations of various beliefs or socio-political systems, without repudiating the theological and cultural differences involved.[155] This practical position finds its expression in the Quran, which reads that God created humankind 'from a single (pair) of a male and a female', and then divided it 'into nations and tribes' for the purpose of letting them 'know each other'.[156] In the same verse, the Quran accentuates the equality of human beings by declaring that 'the most honoured of you in the sight of God is (he who is) the

152 C. G. Weeramantry, *Islamic Jurisprudence: An International Perspective* (New York: St. Martin's Press, 1988) 166–169.

153 In the sensitive case of *US v Iran*, the ICJ, for instance, recognised that the Islamic tradition had substantially contributed to the development of international norms and conventions regarding the protection of diplomatic envoys. See *United States Diplomatic and Consular Staff in Tehran* (*US v Iran*), 1980 ICJ 3 (24 May 1980) ¶ 40. This acknowledgment, however, was in essence made in an effort to convince Iran that the ICJ was indeed a legitimate body to resolve the case involved, and that international law was indebted to Islamic law in some key areas. It is worth noting that prior to 1969, no ICJ judgement or judge had ever mentioned the contribution of the Islamic legal tradition to the development of modern international law. Starting from the *North Sea Continental Shelf* case (1969, ICJ 3), separate opinions (albeit unsystematically) sought to demonstrate that Islamic law had in fact provided contemporary international law with some substantial principles including equity, modalities of establishing statehood and territorial control through identities characterised by religion, and various techniques of legal interpretation. See *Aegean Sea Continental Shelf* (*Greece v Turkey*), 1978 ICJ 3. Also see C. B. Bombardi, 'Islamic Law in the Jurisprudence of the International Court of Justice: An Analysis' (2008) 8 *Chicago Journal of International Law* 85; E. J. Powell, 'Islamic Law States and the International Court of Justice' (2013) *Journal of Peace Research* 1.

154 See C. P. Potholm, *Winning at War: Seven Keys to Military Victory Throughout History* (Plymouth: Rowman & Littlefield Publishers, 2010) 206; G. Jusdanis, *The Necessary Nation* (Princeton: Princeton University Press, 2001) 54.

155 For interesting examples of how Muslims and members of other religions coexisted side by side, see M. Hasan, *Moderate or Militant Images of India's Muslims* (Oxford: Oxford University Press, 2009) 117ff.

156 Q. 49:13

most righteous of you'.[157] The Muslim attitude towards peaceful cohabitation with the followers of monotheistic religions has been demonstrated to be particularly encouraging. As the Quran assures, those who worship God alone and follow the Quran or other Holy Scriptures need not fear; instead, provided that they act righteously and perform their duties, they 'shall have their reward[s]'.[158]

Muslim nations' propensity for territorial plurality and peaceable conduct has been borne out by their institution of regular treaty relations with non-Muslim States – with which Islamic polities have in practice rejected to have been in an unmitigated state of hostilities on account of religious differences. As the aforementioned historical evidence demonstrates, Muslim polities – which had, since the demise of Muhammad, fallen prey to political fragmentation and internal conflicts[159] – have long ceased to pursue the juridical ideal of universalising Islam through incessant wars. They have rather adapted themselves to the dynamic circumstances of international relations. Unsurprisingly therefore, even such medieval thinkers as al-Ghazzali, Ibn Taymiyya, and Ibn Khaldun had realistically envisioned an Islamic legal order that acknowledges the phenomena of political divisions and multifarious power centres.[160] The evolution of Islamic international law and its adaptation to changing external parameters have proven particularly remarkable in this atomic age, in which aggressive international behaviour is prohibited – except in self-defence or under the authority of the Security Council.

All things considered, those fundamentalist Muslim movements that defy the basic canons of international legal order, governing the rights and obligations of all nations concerning the maintenance of global peace, tend to disregard the above-discussed complexity of Islamic theory and practice of international relations. Rather, making in large part selective references to the whole corpus of Sharia, they generally produce a single-sided, belligerent portrayal of the Islamic just war tradition.[161] However, the idea that the decline of Islamic civilisations is

157 Ibid.

158 Q. 2:62.

159 The so-called House of Islam (*dar al-Islam*) has almost never been a seamless unity; that is, Islam has never been a monolithic political and religious force. This point is underscored by Edward Said, who censured the crude and monolithic image of Islam as portrayed by Bernard Lewis in one of his controversial articles, 'The Roots of Muslim Rage'. Said argues that Lewis travesties historical truth and serious scholarship to depict 'Muslims as one terrifyingly collective person enraged at an outside world that has disturbed his almost primeval calm and unchallenged rule'. See E. Said, *Covering Islam: How the Media and the Experts Determine How We See the Rest of the World* (London: Vintage Books, 1997) xxxii.

160 See J. P. Piscatori, *Islam in a World of Nation-States* (Cambridge University Press: Cambridge, 1986) 144–145.

161 See generally, D. Bukay, *From Muhammad to Bin Laden: Religious and Ideological Sources of the Homicide Bombers Phenomenon* (New Brunswick: Transaction Publishers, 2008) 223–224; C. J. Adams, 'Mawdudi and the Islamic State' in: J. L. Esposito (ed.), *Voices of Resurgent Islam* (New York: Oxford University Press, 1983) 103ff; D. Zeidan, *The Resurgence of Religion: A Comparative Study of Selected Themes in Christian and Islamic Fundamentalist Discourses* (Boston: Brill, 2003) 237ff; S. Qutb, *Milestones* (SIME E-Publishing, 2005) 5ff.

attributable to Muslim States' adoption of Western legal, cultural and political institutions is myopic in that it fails to thoroughly diagnose the root causes of the problem. Undoubtedly, Western colonialism and imperial disrespect for the sovereignty and independence of Muslim States are important reasons for the non-conformist attitude of radical Muslims. However, the salient reasons underpinning Muslim dissatisfaction lie in corrupt domestic leadership; the gaping chasm between the haves and have-nots; dysfunctional public institutions; the unequal distribution of opportunities to gain access to education, jobs, or offices; the generally servile attitude of Muslim States towards dominant world powers; the presence of American military bases in Muslim States; and the unwillingness of global actors (whether Muslim or otherwise) to duly address the plight of the Palestinians.[162]

Certainly, the remedy to some of such socio-political ills of the modern world does not reside in blind adherence to obsolete doctrines that no longer meet new exigencies. Although radical Muslims may understandably feel disenchanted about the grossly unequal distribution of wealth, political power, and status domestically and internationally, the invocation of warlike jihad – in total disregard of basic humanitarian principles – as a means of fighting perceived injustices would not only yield counterproductive results, but also nurture the prevalent crude perception that Islam is an aggressive religion. As shown earlier, the translation of feelings of grievance into random violence against civilians would violate both secular and religious laws. The rationalisation of militant jihad to fight perceived 'injustice' or 'oppression' cannot entail renunciation of humanitarian restrictions on lethal force, because deliberate refusal to comply with Islamic just war principles would render any potentially justified aggression utterly unjustified; i.e. indiscriminate violence by means of terrorist atrocities can never be legitimated under Islamic law.

True, international law and its institutions are not perfect artefacts, not least because power politics or self-interested machinations of global actors adversely impact on the assumed neutrality thereof. Yet the growing economic, political, and cultural interdependence of nations does, more often than not, deter nations from engaging in internecine conflicts with one another.[163] In this increasingly globalised world, nations generally demand more security, order, and predictability in international relations – which, at the current stage of history, could to some

162 This by no means constitutes an exhaustive list of why radicals are disillusioned with their governments and generally dissatisfied with the international legal system. For more on this, see generally E. Rogan, *The Arabs: A History* (London: Penguin, 2010); D. Cook, *Understanding Jihad* (London: University of California Press, 2005); Burke, supra note 140; B. Lewis, *The Arabs in History* (London: Hutchinson's University Library, 1950).

163 See generally, T. J. Schoenbaum, *International Relations—The Path Not Taken: Using International Law to Promote World Peace and Security* (Cambridge: Cambridge University Press, 2006) 96ff.

degree be secured by relying upon, and supporting, the mechanisms of international law.

Suffice it to recall that the whole edifice of the UN system is built in reaction to the horrors of two World Wars, which brought about devastation on a scale larger than any that humankind has ever suffered. Given the unprecedented nature of these wars, the elimination of short-sighted imperialistic policies and the scourge of war has unsurprisingly become a major concern for the international community. It is thus no exaggeration to say that 'the history of twentieth-century international law' may primarily be read 'as an attempt to reduce recourse to the use of force in international relations'.[164] It is in this context that Muslim nations, along with other nations, have frequent recourse to dispute-settlement procedures available under international law – these include diplomacy, regular exchange of emissaries, and the conclusion of bilateral or multilateral agreements in numerous areas.

In an age where warfare threatens the survival of all life on this planet, nations are obligated – morally and legally – to settle their differences peacefully, without resort to force and within the framework of the UN Charter. Forming a sizeable portion of the international society, and being part of all major international agreements, Muslims should accordingly draw solely on peaceful forms of jihad in their endeavours to effectuate any political, economic, social, and/or individual transformation. Whilst Muslims may not fall back on militant measures to advance their ambitions, Article 51 of the UN Charter allows States to adopt self-defensive measures in response to unjustified aggressive conduct 'until the Security Council has taken measures necessary to maintain international peace and security'. Technically speaking, Muslim States are thus not precluded from invoking the rhetoric of defensive military jihad against unlawful aggression in the absence of Security Council protection – albeit Muslim States are shown to have hitherto preferred to make references to the UN Charter in their claims of self-defence.

In summary, in contemporary international relations, where States are bound by the principles of the UN Charter and are parties to numerous peace agreements, religious partitioning of the world and the idea of unceasing belligerency against a particular group of people for political, economic, or religious domination have become unacceptable. Considering the current state of military technology and the exigencies of modern-day life, it is imperative that Muslim jurists intensify their efforts to reinterpret the normative contours of *siyar* to enable the doctrine of jihad to be understood contextually, and to be fought within the confines of public international law. It is high time that Muslims drew a distinct demarcation between licit and illicit uses of force – taking a determined stand against the latter – and that the international community as a whole made concerted efforts to address the root causes of violence undertaken in pursuit of politico-religious objectives.

164 Brunnée, supra note 46, 405–406.

5 Conclusion

At the heart of this book lies the effort to depict a contextual, multifaceted vision of Islamic just war, which – in contrast to what the scaremongering popular narrative suggests – has never followed a linear line of development. Rather, in keeping with the ever-changing demands and circumstances of each epoch, the notion of striving in God's path, namely jihad, has been subject to various changes. This evolution may be traced back as far as the very inception of Islam, whose warlike precepts have taken shape against the backdrop of political, religious, and martial predicaments that betided the nascent Islamic community. Over time, Muslim pundits, rulers, and reformers have also resorted to such flexible concepts as 'public interest', 'juristic preference', 'equity', and 'fairness' with a view to generating reasonable, just, and legitimate answers to some of the burning issues of war and peace. Muslims, accordingly, at times adopted a pacifistic posture towards an enemy that was comparatively formidable in military power; at times they used the sword to defend themselves, while at other times, especially when it was opportune or expedient, they undertook offensive campaigns or concluded peace treaties of various types in order to further the interests of Islam.

From the vantage point of such conceptualisation, and given the complex and non-linear evolution of the just war doctrine in Islam, it is not possible to devise a monolithic metanarrative of an entirely defensive or aggressive jihad. Instead, within the context of divergent historical experiences, the tapestry of the Islamic just war has grown much richer than suggested by the moderate or radical schools of thought. Throughout Islamic history, jihad has thus been employed to legitimate both defensive and offensive wars to eliminate injustice, oppression, idolatry, and immorality, and to expand the sphere of Islam. What in essence characterised the nature of Islamic wars has not then been a pre-ordained, all-encompassing abstract principle, but the religious and socio-political exigencies of a given period – albeit in order for a war to qualify as 'just', it had to be fought within the ethico-legal framework of Islam.

The doctrinal and practical imprecision concerning the legal contours of jihad appears more pronounced when one considers that military force constitutes just one – and not the highest – aspect of jihad, which further contains peaceful and pious forms of striving for the religious cause. Hence, those who seek to reduce the application of jihad to merely aggressive war, or to wanton acts of violence, generally disregard the peaceful facets of jihad and adopt a dogmatic, literal interpretation thereof, detaching the concept from its wider historical context. The idea of just war in Islam may indeed not be confined to offensive measures, for not only would this dismiss a significant portion of peaceful verses and traditions from consideration, but it would also overlook the fact that Islam has constantly sought to keep up with the tenor of the times.

As this book has repeatedly stressed, Islamic laws of war did not emerge in a vacuum; they were moulded by everyday life. It is therefore not surprising that rules on the contours of jihad have not remained stable, except for the core precepts found in the primary sources of Islamic law. It should, in this connection, be recalled that the bulk of Muslim laws of nations is not found in the primary sources of Sharia, but in the secondary sources developed through juridical speculation and dynamic interpretation of Islamic principles – in particular during the classical period of Islamic civilisation, when critical (collective and individual) thinking was encouraged with the aim of preventing Sharia from becoming rigid or unresponsive to change. The categorical division of the world between the House of Islam and House of War, and the formulation of House of Peace or House of Covenant, are all illustrative examples of how the Muslim world sought to remain dynamic by devising flexible doctrines to interact with non-Muslim communities at the international level.

The historical record of Islamic State practice suggests that, rather than vainly attempting to universalise the message of Islam through forcible methods, Muslim rulers generally conceded the reality of territorial pluralism. Muslim propensity for peaceful coexistence with other nations was supported by the institution of regular treaty relations with non-Muslim nations, with whom Muslims clearly rejected to be in an unrelenting state of hostilities. The legitimacy of peace covenants with non-Muslim entities was originally envisaged by the Quran, and supported by the practice of Muhammad, who concluded many agreements both with the neighbouring Scriptuaries and pagans of his time. Over time, Muslim polities of various sizes and shapes have entered into countless treaties of both short and long durations with their material or potential rivals. The frequency of such treaty relations increased in recent centuries in parallel with the growing awareness that peaceful coexistence of nations, where possible, is preferable to the horrors of internecine conflicts.

Today, Muslim States, with their diverse composition and socio-political structures, form part of the legal infrastructure that is – albeit still imperfect – indispensable for international peace and security. With its universal and equal membership, the UN and its organisations endeavour to promote peaceful forms of political change and fruitful cooperation among sovereign States. The UN Charter, the centrepiece of the modern law of nations, categorically prohibits aggressive wars for resolving international disputes. The underlying philosophy behind the Charter is that peaceful resolution of conflicts and sustainable world peace are only possible through the promotion of multilateralism and human rights, and the creation of efficient international organisations and instruments, whereby increased international cooperation may be achieved. This strategy distinctly differs from the one advanced by the proponents of power politics, who prioritise the national interests of their States by augmenting the military and economic capabilities thereof, irrespective of whether such a course of action would promote international peace and security. The drafters of the UN Charter, having witnessed two cataclysmic global wars, exhorted all States to settle their disputes peacefully by resorting to such measures as negotiation, enquiry, mediation, conciliation, and judicial settlement.

Being parties to the UN Charter, Islamic States, just like other members, have committed themselves not to use armed force – except in self-defence or in execution of a mandate issued by the Security Council – but to resolve their disagreements by peaceful means. For Muslim States, infringement of contractual commitments has both material (e.g. enforcement measures ordered by the Council) and religious ramifications, because Muslims are bound by the terms of lawfully concluded treaties not only for secular reasons, but also due to the fundamental principles of Sharia that command adherence thereto: 'O ye who believe! Fulfil (all) obligations',[1] declares the Quran. As Yusuf Ali, in his commentary on the Quran, makes clear, all Muslims must honour their contractual obligations, whether sacred or profane. Hence, when a Muslim State concludes a treaty, it becomes incumbent on every individual living in that State to ensure that – so far as is reasonably possible – 'such obligations are faithfully discharged; . . . [because] truth and fidelity are parts of religion in all relations of life'.[2] Islamic teaching can thus be seen to require Muslims to abide by the principles of the UN Charter, which are geared towards ensuring international peace and security.

There is no doubt that Islam has in practice spread its universal message through both peaceable and belligerent methods. It may further be admitted that many battles fought during the expansionist phase of Islam were offensive in order to eradicate idolatry and communicate the word of Islam. But this book has shown that aggression constitutes only one facet of the highly qualified notion of jihad, which also comprises peaceful and spiritual types of struggling for God's cause. Depending on historical context, Muslims have made recourse to both warlike and peaceful forms of jihad. Arguably, the present-day circumstances of international relations call for a contextual understanding of the Quranic verses and the *hadith* on the doctrine of jihad. This may be done by identifying and analysing specific historical events and conditions that gave rise to textual and/or prophetic responses, and by reading the primary sources in their unity – taking into account the overall purpose of Islamic tradition on just war. While the primary sources of Islamic law are deemed immutable, it is clear that in cases of ambiguity or apparent conflict in textual or prophetic injunctions, these sources must be subjected to independent critical scrutiny (*ijtihad*) – a method that had once significantly

1 Q. 5:1.
2 A. Y. Ali, *The Meaning of the Holy Qur'an*, 11th ed. (Beltsville: Amana Publications, 2008) 242–243.

enriched Islamic law and theology, enabling Islamic concepts to remain relevant to everyday life.

Treating all Islamic just war principles as timeless and immutable, by robbing them of their contextual meanings, would be an unjust practice that would hold Muslims of all periods hostage to temporally constricted articulations of law. Islamic laws of war must be attentive to modern dilemmas. Any interpretation of Islamic just war that does not duly consider the relevant historical circumstances along with abundant verses and traditions devoted to peace and tolerance will fall short of addressing the demands of the modern world, in which wars may bring about the ultimate destruction of humanity. Today, aggressive wars are neither legitimate nor viable to solve international disputes; nor does the Muslim community – which is spread across the globe and comprises almost a quarter of the world's population – need the sword to communicate the call of Islam.[3] Jihad, in conclusion, must be conducted in accordance with the current dictates of the time; that is, not by the sword, but by the heart, hand, and tongue.

3 The Quran is replete with messages that call for the peaceful propagation of the faith; verse Q. 16:125, for instance, states that 'invite (all) to the way of thy Lord with wisdom and beautiful preaching; and argue with them in ways that are best and most gracious'.

Select Bibliography

I. Books

Abiad, N., *Sharia, Muslim States and International Human Rights Treaty Obligations: A Comparative Study* (London: BIICL, 2008).

Aboul-Enein, Y. H.; Zuhur, S., *Islamic Rulings on Warfare* (Carlisle Barracks: Strategic Studies Institute, 2004).

Abu-Rabi, I. M., *Intellectual Origins of Islamic Resurgence in the Modern Arab World* (Albany: State University of New York Press, 1996).

Abun-Nasr, J. M., *A History of the Maghrib in the Islamic Period* (Cambridge: Cambridge University Press, 1987).

AbuSulayman, A. A., *Towards an Islamic Theory of International Relations: New Directions for Methodology and Thought*, 2nd Ed. (Herndon: The International Institute of Islamic Thought, 1993).

Afsaruddin, A., *Excellence and Precedence: Medieval Islamic Discourse on Legitimate Leadership* (The Hague: Brill, 2002).

Agoston, G.; Masters, B., *Encyclopaedia of the Ottoman Empire* (New York: Infobase Publishing, 2009).

Ahmad, A. A., *Islam, Modernity, Violence and Everyday Life* (New York: Palgrave, 2009).

Ahmida, A. A., *The Making of Modern Libya: State Formation, Colonization, and Resistance* (Albany: State University of New York Press, 2009).

Akbar, M. J., *The Shade of Swords: Jihad and the Conflict between Islam and Christianity* (London: Routledge, 2002).

Akgonul, S., *The Minority Concept in the Turkish Context: Practices and Perceptions in Turkey, Greece and France* (Leiden: Brill, 2013).

Akhtar, S., *Islam as Political Religion: The Future of an Imperial Faith* (New York: Routledge, 2011).

Al-Ali, N. S., *Secularism, Gender and the State in the Middle East: The Egyptian Women's Movement* (Cambridge: Cambridge University Press, 2000).

A'la Mawdudi, A., *Human Rights in Islam* (Leicester: The Islamic Foundation, 2002).

Al-Azami, M. M., *On Schacht's Origins of Muhammadan Jurisprudence* (Oxford: Oxford Centre for Islamic Studies, 1996).

Al-Banna, H.; C. Wendell (trans.), *Five Tracts of Hasan al-Banna (1906–1946): A Selection from the Majmuat rasail al-Imam al-shahid Hasan al-Banna* (Berkeley: University of California Press, 1978).

Al-Dawoody, A., *The Islamic Law of War: Justifications and Regulations* (New York: Palgrave, 2011).

Alexandrov, S. A., *Self-Defence against the Use of Force in International Law* (London: Kluwer Law International, 1996).

Al-Faruqi, I. R.; Al-Faruqi, L. I., *The Cultural Atlas of Islam* (London: Macmillan, 1986).

Al-Khui, A. Q. M., *Prolegomena to the Qur'an* (New York: Oxford University Press, 1998).

Ali, A., *The Spirit of Islam: A History of the Evolution and Ideals of Islam with a Life of the Prophet* (London: Christophers, 1922).

Ali, A. Y., *The Meaning of the Holy Qur'an,* 11th ed. (Beltsville: Amana Publications, 2008).

Ali, P. S., *Human Rights in Islam* (New Delhi: Adam Publishers, 1995).

Ali, S. S., *Gender and Human Rights in Islam and International Law* (London: Kluwer Law International, 2000).

Allain, J., *International Law in the Middle East* (Aldershot: Ashgate Publishing Limited, 2004).

Altman, A., *Tracing the Earliest Recorded Concepts of International Law: The Ancient Near East (2500–330 BCE)* (Leiden: Brill, 2012).

Amstutz, M. R., *International Ethics: Concepts, Theories, and Cases in Global Politics* (Oxford: Rowman & Littlefield Publishers, 2005).

Anghie, A., *Imperialism, Sovereignty and the Making of International Law* (Cambridge: Cambridge University Press, 2005).

An-Na'im, A. A., *Islam and the Secular State: Negotiating the Future of Shari'a* (Cambridge, MA: Harvard University Press, 2008).

An-Na'im, A. A., *Toward and Islamic Reformation: Civil Liberties, Human Rights, and International Law* (Syracuse: Syracuse University Press, 1996).

Aoun, S., *Aujourd'hui L'islam: Fractures, Intégrisme et Modernité* (Montréal: Médiaspaul, 2007).

Aquinas, S. T.; Dyson, R. W. (ed. and trans.), *Political Writings* (Cambridge: Cambridge University Press, 2002).

Aquinas, S. T.; Heath, T. R. (trans.), *Summa Theologiae,* Vol. XXXV, (London: Blackfriars, 1972).

Arabi, O., *Studies in Modern Islamic Law and Jurisprudence* (The Hague: Kluwer Law International, 2001).

Arend, A. C.; Beck, R. J., *International Law and the Use of Force* (London: Routledge, 1993).

Aristotle; Crisp, R. (ed. and trans.), *Nicomachean Ethics* (Cambridge: Cambridge University Press, 2000).

Armstrong, K., *Islam: A Short History* (London: Phoenix, 2001).

Armstrong, K., *A History of God* (London: Vintage, 1993).

Ashraf, M. I., *Islamic Philosophy of War and Peace* (Bloomington: iUniverse, 2008).

Aslan, R., *No god but God: The Origins, Evolution and Future of Islam* (London: Arrow Books, 2005).

Augustine, St; Dods, M. (trans.), *The City of God* (New York: Modern Library, 1950).

Aust, A., *Handbook of International Law* (Cambridge: Cambridge University Press, 2005).

Ayoub, M., *The Qur'an and its Interpreters* (Albany: State University of New York Press, 1992).

Ayubi, N. N., *Over-Stating the Arab State: Politics and Society in the Middle East* (New York: I.B. Tauris, 2008).

Bachrach, D. S., *Religion and the Conduct of War* (Woodbridge: The Boydell Press, 2003).

Badem, C., *The Ottoman Crimean War (1853–1856)* (Leiden: Brill, 2010).

Badran, M., *Feminists, Islam, and Nation: Gender and the Making of Modern Egypt* (Princeton: Princeton University Press, 1995).

Bailey, S. D., *Prohibitions and Restraints in War* (Oxford: Oxford University Press, 1972).

Bakircioglu, O., *Self-Defence in International and Criminal Law: The Doctrine of Imminence* (London: Routledge, 2011).

Bamyeh, M. A., *The Social Origins of Islam: Mind, Economy, Discourse* (Minneapolis: University of Minnesota Press, 1999).
Bannerman, P., *Islam in Perspective: A Guide to Islamic Society, Politics and Law* (London: Routledge, 1988).
Bar, S., *The Fatwas of Radical Islam and the Duty to Jihad* (Oxford: Rowman & Littlefield Publishers, 2006).
Bello, I. A., *Medieval Islamic Controversy between Philosophy and Orthodoxy: Ijma and ta'wil in the Conflict between al-Ghazali and Ibn Rushd* (Leiden: Brill, 1989).
Bennison, A. K., *The Great Caliphs: The Golden Age of the Abbasid Empire* (London: I.B. Tauris, 2011).
Berkey, J. P., *The Formation of Islam: Religion and Society in the Near East, 600–1800* (Cambridge: Cambridge University Press, 2003).
Black, A., *The History of Islamic Political Thought: From the Prophet to the Present* (New York: Routledge, 2001).
Bonner, M., *Jihad in Islamic History: Doctrines and Practice* (Princeton: Princeton University Press, 2006).
Bradley, J. R., *After the Arab Spring: How Islamists Hijacked The Middle East Revolts* (New York: Palgrave Macmillan, 2012).
Brems, E., *Human Rights: Universality and Diversity* (The Hague: Kluwer Law International, 2001).
Breslauer, S. D., *Toward a Jewish (M)orality: Speaking of a Postmodern Jewish Ethics* (Westport: Greenwood Press, 1998).
Brierly, J. L., *The Law of Nations: An Introduction to the International Law of Peace,* 6th ed. (London: Oxford University Press, 1963).
Brown, L. C., *Religion and State: The Muslim Approach to Politics* (New York: Columbia University Press, 2000).
Brownlie, I., *International Law and the Use of Force by States* (Oxford: Clarendon Press, 1963).
Bukay, D., *From Muhammad to Bin Laden: Religious and Ideological Sources of the Homicide Bombers Phenomenon* (New Brunswick: Transaction Publishers, 2008).
Bull, H., *The Anarchical Society: A Study of Order in World Politics,* 3rd Ed. (London: Palgrave, 2002).
Burke, J., *Al-Qaeda: The True Story of Radical Islam,* 3rd ed. (London: Penguin Books, 2007).
Burton, J., *An Introduction to the Hadith Tradition* (Edinburgh: Edinburgh University Press, 1994).
Burton, J., *The Collection of the Quran* (Cambridge: Cambridge University Press, 1977).
Bush, G., *The Life of Mohammed: Founder of the Religion of Islam, and of the Empire of the Saracens* (London: J. & J. Harper, 1883).
Campbell, D., *Writing Security: United States Foreign Policy and the Politics of Identity* (Minnesota: University of Minnesota Press, 1998).
Carimokam, S., *Muhammad and the People of the Book* (Bloomington: Xlibris Corporation, 2010).
Cassese, A., *International Law in a Divided World* (Oxford: Clarendon Press, 1994).
Cheikh, N. M. E., *Byzantium Viewed by the Arabs* (Cambridge, MA: Harvard University Press, 2004).
Cicero, M. T.; Miller, W. (trans.), *Cicero de Officiis* (London: Heinemann, 1928).
Ciceoro, M. T.; J. Powell (ed.); Rudd, N. (trans.), *The Republic and the Laws* (Oxford: Oxford University Press, 1998).
Clarence-Smith, W. G., *Islam and the Abolition of Slavery* (Oxford: Oxford University Press, 2006).

Constable, O. R., *Trade and Traders in Muslim Spain: The Commercial Realignment of the Iberian Peninsula, 900–1500* (Cambridge: Cambridge University Press, 1994).
Cook, D., *Martyrdom in Islam* (Cambridge: Cambridge University Press, 2007).
Cook, D., *Understanding Jihad* (London: University of California Press, 2005).
Cook, M., *The Koran: A Very Short Introduction* (New York: Oxford University Press, 2000).
Cornell, V. J., *Voices of Islam: Voices of Tradition* (Westport: Praeger Publishers, 2007).
Coulson, N. J., *A History of Islamic Law* (Edinburgh: Edinburgh University Press, 1964).
Crone, P., *Meccan Trade and the Rise of Islam* (Piscataway: Gorgias Press, 2004).
Daftary, F., *A Short History of the Ismailis* (Edinburgh: Edinburgh University Press, 1998).
Davis, M., *The Politics of Philosophy: A Commentary on Aristotle's Politics* (Lanham: Rowman & Littlefield, 1996).
Decasa, G. C., *The Qur'anic Concept of Umma and its Function in Philippine Muslim Society* (Rome: Editrice Pontificia Universita Gregoriana, 1999).
DeLong-Bas, N. J., *Wahhabi Islam: From Revival and Reform to Global Jihad* (New York: I.B. Tauris, 2004).
Detter, I., *The Law of War* (Cambridge: University of Cambridge, 2000).
Dickinson, E., *The Development of Early Sunnite Hadith Criticism: The Taqdima of Ibn Abi Hatim al-Razi (240/854–327/938)* (Leiden: Brill, 2001).
Dien, M. I., *Islamic Law: From Historical Foundations to Contemporary Practice* (Edinburgh: Edinburgh University Press, 2004).
Dinstein, Y., *War, Aggression and Self-Defence*, 4th ed. (Cambridge: Cambridge University Press, 2005).
Eaton, G., *Islam and the Destiny of Man* (Albany: State University of New York Press, 1985).
Eickelman, D. F.; Piscatori, J., *Muslim Politics* (Princeton: Princeton University Press, 2004).
El-Fadl, K. A., *Rebellion & Violence in Islamic Law* (Cambridge: Cambridge University Press, 2003).
Elias, J. J., *Islam* (London: Routledge, 1999).
Engineer, A. A., *Islam in Contemporary World* (New Delhi: New Dawn Press Group, 2007).
Esposito, J. L., *The Future of Islam* (Oxford: Oxford University Press, 2010).
Esposito, J. L., *Islam and Politics*, 4th ed. (Syracuse: Syracuse University Press, 1998).
Esposito, J. L., *Islam in Transition: Muslim Perspectives*, 2nd ed. (Oxford: Oxford University Press, 2007).
Esposito, J. L., *Islam: The Straight Path* (Oxford: Oxford University Press, 1994).
Esposito, J. L., *The Islamic Threat: Myth or Reality*? 3rd ed. (New York: Oxford University Press, 1992).
Esposito, J. L., *The Oxford Dictionary of Islam* (Oxford: Oxford University Press, 2003).
Esposito, J. L., *The Oxford History of Islam* (Oxford: Oxford University Press, 1999).
Esposito, J. L., *Unholy War: Terror in the Name of Islam* (New York: Oxford University Press, 2003).
Esposito, J. L., *What Everyone Needs to Know about Islam*, 2nd ed. (Oxford: Oxford University Press, 2011).
Esposito, J. L., *Women in Muslim Family Law* (Oxford: Oxford University Press, 2001).
Ezzati, A., *The Spread of Islam: The Contributing Factors*, 4th ed. (London: Islamic College for Advanced Studies, 2002).
Fahmy, K., *All the Pasha's Men: Mehmed Ali, His Army and the Making of Modern Egypt* (Cairo: The American University in Cairo Press, 1997).
Faksh, M. A., *The Future of Islam in the Middle East: Fundamentalism in Egypt, Algeria, and Saudi Arabia* (Westport: Praeger Publishers, 1997).

Fatoohi, L., *Abrogation in the Quran and Islamic Law: A Critical Study of the Concept of 'Naskh' and its Impact* (New York: Routledge, 2013).

Ferrara, P., *Global Religions and International Relations* (New York: Palgrave, 2014).

Findley, C. V., *Turkey, Islam, Nationalism, and Modernity: A History: 1789–2007* (New Haven: Yale University Press, 2010).

Findley, C. V., *The Turks in World History* (Oxford: Oxford University Press, 2004).

Firestone, R., *An Introduction to Islam for Jews* (Philadelphia: Jewish Publication Society, 2008).

Firestone, R., *Jihad: The Origin of Holy War in Islam* (New York: Oxford University Press, 1999).

Fraade, S. D., *Legal Fictions: Studies of Law and Narrative in the Discursive Worlds of Ancient Jewish Sectarians and Sages* (Leiden: Brill, 2011).

Friedmann, Y., *Tolerance and Coercion in Islam: Interfaith Relations in the Muslim Tradition* (New York: Cambridge University Press, 2003).

Gabriel, R. A., *Muhammad: Islam's First Great General* (Norman: University of Oklahoma Press, 2007).

Gerber, H., *Islamic Law and Culture 1600–1840* (Leiden: Brill, 1999).

Gil, M., *Jews in Islamic Countries in the Middle Ages* (Leiden: Brill, 2004).

Goffart, W., *Barbarians and Romans A.D. 418–584: The Techniques of Accommodation* (Princeton: Princeton University Press, 1980).

Goldziher, I., *Introduction to Islamic Theology and Law* (Princeton: Princeton University Press, 1981).

Goldziher, I.; Stern, S. M. (ed.); Barber, C. R; Stern, S. M. (trans.), *Muslim Studies* (London: Aldine Transaction, 2008).

Gray, C., *International Law and the Use of Force*, 3rd ed. (Oxford: Oxford University Press, 2008).

Green, A. H., *The Tunisian Ulama 1873–1915: Social Structure and Response to Ideological Currents* (Leiden: Brill, 1978).

Grotius, H.; Campbell, A. C. (trans.), *The Rights of War and Peace* (London: M. Walter Dunne Publisher, 1901).

Gunbey, S., *Veda Haccinda Islam Ummetine Hz. Peygamber (S.A.V.)'in Vasiyeti* (Istanbul: Zinde Ofset Matbaacilik, 2010).

Haleem, H. A.; Ramsbotham, O.; Risaluddin, S.; Wicker, B., *The Crescent and the Cross: Muslim and Christian Approaches to War and Peace* (London: Macmillan Press, 1998).

Hallaq, W. B., *Authority, Continuity and Change in Islamic Law* (Cambridge: Cambridge University Press, 2001).

Hallaq, W. B., *A History of Islamic Legal Theories: An Introduction to Sunni usul al-fiqh* (Cambridge: Cambridge University Press, 1997).

Halliday, F., *Islam and the Myth of Confrontation* (London: I.B. Tauris, 2003).

Halperin, S., *War and Social Change in Modern Europe: The Great Transformation Revisited* (Cambridge: Cambridge University Press, 2004).

Hamidullah, M., *Muslim Conduct of State*, 5th ed. (Lahore: Ashraf Press, 1968).

Harvey, P., *Hybrids of Modernity: Anthropology, the Nation State and the Universal Exhibition* (London: Routledge, 1996).

Hasan, M., *Moderate or Militant Images of India's Muslims* (Oxford: Oxford University Press, 2009).

Hawting, G. R., *The First Dynasty of Islam: The Umayyad Caliphate AD 661–750*, 2nd Ed. (London: Routledge, 2000).

Hawting, G. R., *The Idea of Idolatry and the Emergence of Islam: From Polemic to History* (Cambridge: Cambridge University Press, 1999).

Henkin, L., *How Nations Behave,* 2nd ed. (New York: Columbia University Press, 1979).
Hillenbrand, C., *The Crusades: Islamic Perspectives* (New York: Routledge, 2000).
Hillgarth, J. N., *Christianity and Paganism, 350–370: The Conversion of Western Europe* (Philadelphia: University of Pennsylvania Press, 1986).
Hinsley, F. H., *Power and the Pursuit of Peace: Theory and Practice in the History of Relations between States* (Cambridge: Cambridge University Press, 1963).
Hitti, P. K., *The Arabs: A Short History* (Washington: Regnery Publishing, 1996).
Hitti, P. K., *History of the Arabs: From the Earliest Times to the Present* (London: Macmillan, 1956).
Hourani, A., *A History of the Arab Peoples* (London: Faber and Faber Limited, 2005).
Hsiung, C., *Anarchy & Order: The Interplay of Politics and Law in International Relations* (London: Lynne Rienner Publishers, 1997).
Hunter, F. R., *Egypt under the Khedives 1805–1879: From Household Government to Modern* (Cairo: The American University in Cairo Press, 1984).
Hunter, S., *The Future of Islam and the West: Clash of Civilizations or Peaceful Coexistence?* (Westport: Praeger, 1998).
Hunter, S., *Iran's Foreign Policy in the Post-Soviet Era: Resisting the New International Order* (Santa Barbara: ABC-CLIO, 2010).
Huntington, S. P., *The Clash of Civilizations and the Remaking of World Order* (New York: Simon & Schuster, 1996).
Inalcik, H., *Osmanlilar: Futuhat, Imparatorluk, Avrupa ile Iliskiler* (Istanbul: Timas Yayinlari, 2010).
Islamoglu-Inan, H., *State and Peasant in the Ottoman Empire: Agrarian Power Relations and Regional Economic Development in Ottoman Anatolia during the Sixteenth Century* (Leiden: Brill, 1994).
Ishaq, I.; Guillaume, A. (trans.), *The Life of Muhammad: A Translation of Ibn Ishaq's Sirat Rasul Allah* (Oxford: Oxford University Press, 1955).
Israeli, R., *Islam in China: Religion, Ethnicity, Culture, and Politics* (Lanham: Lexington Books, 2002).
Jackson, R., *Fifty Key Figures in Islam* (New York: Routledge, 2009).
Jackson, S. A., *Islam and the Black American: Looking toward the Third Resurrection* (Oxford: Oxford University Press, 2005).
Johnson, J. T., *Ethics and the Use of Force: Just War in Historical Perspective* (Surrey: Ashgate Publishing, 2011).
Johnson, J. T., *The Holy War Idea in Western and Islamic Traditions* (University Park: The Pennsylvania State University Press, 2002).
Jusdanis, G., *The Necessary Nation* (Princeton: Princeton University Press, 2001).
Kadi, I. H., *Ottoman and Dutch Merchants in the Eighteenth Century: Competition and Cooperation in Ankara, Izmir and Amsterdam* (Leiden: Brill, 2012).
Kamali, M. H., *Principles of Islamic Jurisprudence* (Cambridge: The Islamic Texts Society, 1989).
Kamali, M. H., *Shari'ah Law: An Introduction* (Oxford: Oneworld Publications, 2008).
Kamrava, M., *The Modern Middle East: A Political History since the First World War* (Berkeley: University of California Press, 2011).
Karoubi, M. T., *Just or Unjust War? International Law and Unilateral Use of Armed Force by States at the Turn of the 20th Century* (Aldershot: Ashgate Publishing, 2005).
Karsh, E., *Islamic Imperialism: A History* (London: Yale University Press, 2007).
Kayadibi, S., *Istihsan: The Doctrine of Juristic Preference in Islamic Law* (Selangor: Islamic Book Trust, 2010).
Kelsay, J., *Arguing the Just War in Islam* (Cambridge, MA: Harvard University Press, 2007).
Kelsay, J., *Islam and War: A Study in Comparative Ethics* (Louisville: John Knox Press, 1993).

Kennedy, D., *Of War and Law* (Oxford: Princeton University Press, 2006).
Kennedy, H., *The Armies of the Caliphs: Military and Society in the Early Islamic State* (New York: Routledge, 2001).
Kennedy, H., *The Great Arab Conquests: How the Spread of Islam Changed the World We Live in* (London: Phoenix, 2008).
Kenney, J. T., *Muslim Rebels: Kharijites and the Politics of Extremism in Egypt* (Oxford: Oxford University Press, 2006).
Kepel, G., *Beyond Terror and Martyrdom: The Future of the Middle East* (Cambridge, MA: Harvard University Press, 2008).
Kepel, G., *Jihad: The Trail of Political Islam* (London: I.B. Tauris, 2004).
Khadduri, M., *The Islamic Conception of Justice* (Baltimore: The Johns Hopkins Press, 1984).
Khadduri, M., *The Islamic Law of Nations: Shaybani's Siyar* (Baltimore: The Johns Hopkins Press, 1966).
Khadduri, M., *War and Peace in the Law of Islam* (Baltimore: Johns Hopkins Press, 1955).
Khaldun, I., Dawood, N. J. (ed.); Rosenthal, F. (trans.), *The Muqaddimah: An Introduction to History* (Princeton: Princeton University Press, 2004).
Khan, I. A., *Authentication of Hadith: Redefining the Criteria* (London: The International Institute of Islamic Thought, 2010).
Khan, M. A., *Islamic Jihad: A Legacy of Forced Conversion, Imperialism, and Slavery* (New York: iUniverse, 2009).
Khan, M. A., *Jihad for Jerusalem: Identity and Strategy in International Relations* (Westport: Praeger, 2004).
Khan, M. W., *The Prophet of Peace: Teachings of the Prophet Muhammad* (New York: Penguin, 2009).
Khatab, S.; Bouma, G. D., *Democracy in Islam* (New York: Routledge, 2007).
Koh, J. M., *Suppressing Terrorist Financing and Money* (New York: Springer, 2006).
Korman, S., *The Right of Conquest: The Acquisition of Territory by Force in International Law and Practice* (Oxford: Clarendon Press, 1996).
Koylu, M., *Islam and its Quest for Peace: Jihad, Justice and Education* (Washington: The Council for Research in Values and Philosophy, 2003).
Krasner, S. D., *Sovereignty: Organised Hypocrisy* (Princeton: Princeton University Press, 1999).
Lapidus, I. M., *A History of Islamic Societies,* 2nd ed. (Cambridge: Cambridge University Press, 2002).
Lapidus, I. M., *Islamic Societies to the Nineteenth Century: A Global History* (Cambridge: Cambridge University Press, 2012).
Lassner, J., *Jews, Christians, and the Abode of Islam: Modern Scholarship, Medieval Realities* (Chicago: The University of Chicago Press, 2012).
Lauterpacht, H., *The Function of Law in the International Community* (Oxford: Oxford University Press, 2011).
Lewis, B., *The Arabs in History* (London: Hutchinson's University Library, 1950).
Lewis, B., *The Crisis of Islam: Holy War and Unholy Terror* (London: Phoenix Press, 2004).
Lewis, B., *The Emergence of Modern Turkey* (London: Oxford University Press, 1961).
Lewis, B., *From Babel to Dragomans: Interpreting the Middle East* (Oxford: Oxford University Press, 2004).
Lewis, B., *Islam: From the Prophet Muhammad to the Capture of Constantinople,* Vol. II (Oxford: Oxford University Press, 1974).
Lewis, B., *The Middle East: 2000 Years of History from the Rise of Christianity to the Present Day* (London: Phoenix Press, 2000).

Lewis, B., *The Multiple Identities of the Middle East* (New York: Schocken Books, 2001).
Lewis, B., *The Political Language of Islam* (Chicago: The University of Chicago Press, 1988).
Lewis, B., *Politics and War in Islam* (Princeton: Princeton University Press, 1975).
Lewis, B., *What Went Wrong? Western Impact and Middle Eastern Response* (London: Phoenix Press, 2002).
Lewis, B.; Churchill, B. E., *Islam: The Religion and the People* (Indianapolis: Wharton School Publishing, 2008).
Levitt, M.; Ross, D., *Hamas: Politics, Charity, and Terrorism in the Service of Jihad* (Virginia: Yale University Press, 2006).
Lindsay, J. E., *Daily Life in the Medieval Islamic World* (Westport: Greenwood Press, 2005).
Maalouf, A., *Les Croisades vues par les Arabes* (Paris: J.C. Lattès, 1986).
Marlowe, J., *A History of Modern Egypt and Anglo-Egyptian Relations: 1800–1953* (New York: Praeger, 1954).
Marranci, G., *Jihad: Beyond Islam* (New York: Berg, 2006).
Masters, B., *Christians and Jews in the Ottoman Arab World: The Roots of Sectarianism* (Cambridge: Cambridge University Press, 2001).
Mawdudi, A. A., *Human Rights in Islam* (Leicester: The Islamic Foundation, 2002).
Mayer, A. E., *Islam and Human Rights: Tradition and Politics,* 4th ed. (Oxford: Westview Press, 2007).
Mehmet, O., *Islamic Identity and Development: Studies of the Islamic Periphery* (London: Routledge, 1990).
Miller, F. D., *Nature, Justice and Rights in Aristotle's Politics* (Oxford: Clarendon Press, 1997).
Milton-Edwards, B., *Islamic Fundamentalism since 1945* (New York: Routledge, 2005).
Mitchell, J., *Martyrdom: A Very Short Introduction* (Oxford: Oxford University Press, 2012).
Mitchell, R. P., *The Society of the Muslim Brothers* (Oxford: Oxford University Press, 1969).
Morsink, J., *The Universal Declaration of Human Rights: Origins, Drafting, and Intent* (Philadelphia: University of Pennsylvania Press, 1999).
Moskowitz, M., *International Concern with Human Rights* (Leiden: Sijthoff International Publishing, 1974).
Muhaiyaddeen, M. R. B., *Islam and World Peace: Explanations of a SUFI* (Philadelphia: The Fellowship Press, 2004).
Nabulsi, K., *Traditions of War: Occupation, Resistance, and the Law* (Oxford: Oxford University Press, 2005).
Nafziger, G. F.; Walton, M. W., *Islam at War: A History* (Westport: Praeger Publishers, 2003).
Nasir, J. J., *Islamic Laws of Personal Status* (London: Kluwer Academic Publishers, 1986).
Nasr, S. V. R., *Mawdudi and the Making of Islamic Revivalism* (New York: Oxford University Press, 1996).
Naumkin, V. V., *Radical Islam in Central Asia: Between Pen and Rifle* (Oxford: Rowman & Littlefield Publishers, 2005).
Neff, S. C., *War and the Law of Nations: A General History* (New York: Cambridge University Press, 2005).
Neumann, P. R., *Old & New Terrorism* (Cambridge: Polity Press, 2009).
Noorani, A. G., *Islam & Jihad: Prejudice versus Reality* (London: Zed Books, 2002).
Nyazee, I. A. K., *Theories of Islamic Law: The Methodology of Ijtihad* (Islamabad: The Other Press, 1994).
O'Donovan, O., *The Just War Revisited* (Cambridge: Cambridge University Press, 2003).
Opwis, F. M. M., *Maslaha and the Purpose of the Law* (Leiden: Martinus Nijhoff Publishers, 2010).

Palmer, A., *The Decline and Fall of the Ottoman Empire* (New York: M. Evans, 1994).

Paupp, T. E., *Redefining Human Rights in the Struggle for Peace and Development* (Cambridge: Cambridge University Press, 2014).

Peters, F. E., *Muhammad and the Origins of Islam* (Albany: Sunny Press, 1994).

Peters, R., *Islam and Colonialism: The Doctrine of Jihad in Modern History* (The Hague: Mouton Publishers, 1979).

Peters, R., *Jihad in Classical and Modern Islam* (Princeton: Markus Wiener Publishers, 1996).

Pickthall, M. M., *The Glorious Qur'an* (New York: TTQ Inc., 2001).

Pictek, J. S., *Development and Principles of International Humanitarian Law* (Lancaster: Kluwer Academic Publishers, 1985).

Pipes, D., *Slave Soldiers and Islam: The Genesis of a Military System* (London: Yale University Press, 1981).

Piscatori, J. P., *Islam in a World of Nation-States* (Cambridge: Cambridge University Press, 1986).

Potholm, C. P., *Winning at War: Seven Keys to Military Victory Throughout History* (Plymouth: Rowman & Littlefield Publishers, 2010).

Quataert, Q., *The Ottoman Empire, 1700–1922* (Cambridge: Cambridge University Press, 2000).

Qutb, S., *Milestones* (USA: SIME E-Publishing, 2005).

Rahman, F., *Islam & Modernity: Transformation of an Intellectual Tradition* (Chicago: The University of Chicago Press, 1982).

Rahman, F., *Major Themes of the Qur'an*, 2nd ed. (Chicago: The University of the Chicago Press, 2009).

Ramadan, H. M., *Understanding Islamic Law: From Classical to Contemporary* (Oxford: AltaMira Press, 2006).

Ramadan, T., *In the Footsteps of the Prophet: Lessons from the Life of Muhammad* (Oxford: Oxford University Press, 2007).

Ramadan, T., *Islam and the Arab Awakening* (Oxford: Oxford University Press, 2012).

Ramadan, T., *The Messenger: The Meanings of the Life of Muhammad* (London: Penguin Books, 2007).

Ramadan, T., *Radical Reform: Islamic Ethics and Liberation* (Oxford: Oxford University Press, 2009).

Ramadan, T., *Western Muslims and the Future of Islam* (New York: Oxford University Press, 2004).

Rehman, J., *Islamic State Practices, International Law and the Threat from Terrorism: A Critique of the 'Clash of Civilisations' in the New World Order* (Oxford: Hart Publishing, 2005).

Reeves, M., *Muhammad in Europe: A Thousand Years of Western Myth-Making* (New York: New York University Press, 2000).

Reynolds, M. A., *Shattering Empires: The Clash and Collapse of the Ottoman and Russian Empires 1908–1918* (Cambridge: Cambridge University Press, 2011).

Rippin, A., *Muslims: Their Religious Beliefs and Practices*, 3rd ed. (New York: Routledge, 2005).

Rodin, D., *War and Self-defence* (Oxford: Clarendon Press, 2002).

Rodinson, M., *Muhammad: Prophet of Islam* (New York: Pantheon Books, 1980).

Rogan, E., *The Arabs: A History* (London: Penguin, 2010).

Rosenthal, E. I. J., *Political Thought in Medieval Islam: An Introductory Outline* (Cambridge: Cambridge University Press, 1958).

Roy, O.; Holoch, G. (trans.), *Secularism Confronts Islam* (New York: Columbia University Press, 2007).

Roy, O.; C. Volk (trans.), *The Failure of Political Islam* (Cambridge, MA: Harvard University Press, 1994).

Rumi, M. J. M.; Whinfield, E. H. (trans.), *The Masnavi-i Ma'navi of Rumi* (Charleston: The Forgotten Books, 2008).

Russell, F. H., *The Just War in the Middle Ages* (Cambridge: Cambridge University Press, 1975).

Ruthven, M., *Islam in the World*, 2nd ed. (Oxford: Oxford University Press, 2001).

Sachedina, A. A., *The Just Ruler in Shi'ite Islam: The Comprehensive Authority of the Jurist in Imamite Jurisprudence* (Oxford: Oxford University Press, 1988)

Saeed, A., *Islamic Thought: An Introduction* (New York: Routledge, 2006).

Safi, L., *Tensions and Transitions in the Muslim World* (Lanham: University of America Press, 2003).

Said, E. W., *Covering Islam: How the Media and the Experts Determine How We See the Rest of the World* (London: Vintage Books, 1997).

Said, E. W., *Orientalism* (London: Penguin Books, 2003).

Salmi, R. H.; Majul, C. A.; Tanham, G. K., *Islam and Conflict Resolution: Theories and Practices* (Lanham: University Press of America, 1998).

Sardar, Z., *The Future of Muslim Civilisation* (London: Croom Helm, 1979).

Sarris, P., *Empires of Faith: The Fall of Rome to the Rise of Islam, 500–700* (Oxford: Oxford University Press, 2011).

Sawma, G., *The Quran Misinterpreted, Mistranslated, and Misread: The Aramaic Language of the Quran* (New York: Adibooks, 2006).

Scales, P. C., *The Fall of the Caliphate of Cordoba: Berbers and Andalusis in Conflict* (Leiden: Brill, 1994).

Schacht, J., *An Introduction to Islamic Law* (Oxford: Clarendon Press, 1964).

Schacht, J., *An Introduction to Islamic Law* (Oxford: Oxford University Press, 1982).

Schacht, J., *The Origins of Muhammadan Jurisprudence* (Oxford: Oxford University Press, 1967).

Schimmel, A., *And Muhammad is His Messenger: The Veneration of the Prophet in Islamic Piety* (London: The University of North Carolina Press, 1985).

Schimmel, A., *Islam in the Indian Subcontinent* (Leiden: Brill, 1980).

Schoenbaum, T. J., *International Relations—The Path Not Taken: Using International Law to Promote World Peace and Security* (Cambridge: Cambridge University Press, 2006).

Schulze, R., *A Modern History of the Islamic World* (London: I.B. Tauris, 2000).

Searcy, K., *The Formation of the Sudanese Mahdist State—Ceremony and Symbols of Authority: 1882–1898* (Leiden: Brill, 2011).

Sebeos; Thomson, R. W. (trans.), *The Armenian History Attributed to Sebeos*, Vol. I (Liverpool: University of Liverpool, 1999).

Sedlar, J. W., *East Central Europe in the Middle Ages, 1000–1500*, Vol. III (Seattle: The University of Washington Press, 1994).

Shah, N. A., *Self-Defence in Islamic and International Law: Assessing Al-Qaeda and the Invasion of Iraq* (New York: Palgrave Macmillan, 2008).

Shapiro, M., *Courts: A Comparative and Political Analysis* (London: The University of Chicago Press, 1981).

Shaw, M. N., *International Law*, 6th ed. (Cambridge: Cambridge University Press, 2008).

Shirazi, I. M., *War, Peace and Non-Violence: An Islamic Perspective* (London: Fountain Books, 2001).

Siddiqi, M. Z., *Hadith Literature: Its Origin, Development & Special Features* (Cambridge: The Islamic Texts Society, 2008).

Smith, W. C., *On Understanding Islam: Selected Studies* (The Hague: Mouton Publishers, 1981).

Springer, D. R.; Regens, J. L.; Edger, D. N., *Islamic Radicalism and Global Jihad* (Washington DC: Georgetown University Press, 2009).

Stumpf, C. A., *The Grotian Theology of International Law: Hugo Grotius and the Moral Foundations of International Relations* (Berlin: Deutsche Nationalbibliothek, 2006).

Super, J. C.; Turley, B. K., *Religion in World History* (New York: Routledge, 2006).

Thorsen, D., *Exploration of Christian Theology* (Grand Rapids: Baker Academic, 2010).

Timani, H. S., *The Kharijites in Western Literature* (New York: Peter Lang Publishing, 2008).

Tolan, J.; Veinstein, G.; Laurens, H., *Europe and the Islamic World: A History* (Princeton: Princeton University Press, 2013).

Toprak, B., *Islam and Political Development in Turkey* (Leiden: Brill, 1981).

Turner, C., *Islam: The Basics* (New York: Routledge, 2006).

Unal, A., *The Quran with Annotated Interpretation in Modern English* (Izmir: Sistem Matbaacilik, 2006).

Unal, M. A., *Yuzyılda Harput Sancagı* (Ankara: Turk Tarih Kurumu, 1989).

Villiger, M. E., *Commentary on the 1969 Vienna Convention on the Law of Treaties* (Leiden: Bill, 2009).

Vitoria, F. D.; Nys, E. (ed.); Bate, J. P. (trans.), *De Indis et de Ivre Belli Reflectiones* (New York: Oceana Publications, 1963).

Vitoria, F. D.; Doyle, J. P. (trans.), *Reflection on Homicide & Commentary on Summa Theologiae Iia-Iiae Q. 64 (Thomas Aquinas)* (Milwaukee: Marquette University Press, 1997).

Vogel, F. E., *Islamic Law and the Legal System of Saudi: Studies of Saudi Arabia* (Leiden: Brill, 2000).

Waldock, H., *The Law of Nations: An Introduction to the International Law of Peace* (New York: Oxford University Press, 1963).

Walzer, M., *Arguing about War* (London: Yale University Press, 2004).

Watt, W. M., *Islam and Christianity Today* (London: Routledge, 1983).

Watt, W. M., *Islamic Fundamentalism and Modernity* (London: Routledge, 1988).

Watt, W. M., *Muhammad at Mecca* (Oxford: Oxford University Press, 1953).

Watt, W. M., *Muhammad at Medina* (Oxford: Oxford University Press, 1956).

Watt, W. M., *Muhammad: Prophet and Statesman* (Oxford: Oxford University Press, 1961).

Weeramantry, C. G., *Islamic Jurisprudence: An International Perspective* (New York: St. Martin's Press, 1988).

Weiss, B.G., *The Spirit of Islamic Law* (London: The University of Georgia Press, 2006).

Wessels, A., *A Modern Arabic Biography of Muhammad* (Leiden: Brill, 1972).

Yaran, C. S., *Understanding Islam* (Edinburgh: Dunedin Academic Press, 2007).

Yasuaki, O., *A Transcivilizational Perspective on International Law* (The Hague: Hague Academy of International Law, 2010).

Ye'or, B., *Islam and Dhimitude: Where Civilisations Collide* (Ontario: Associated University Press, 2002).

Yilmaz, I., *Muslim Laws, Politics and Society in Modern Nation States: Dynamic Legal Pluralisms in England, Turkey and Pakistan* (Aldershot: Ashgate Publishing, 2005).

Zawati, H. M., *Is Jihad a Just War: War, Peace, and Human Rights under Islamic and Public International Law* (New York: The Edwin Mellen Press, 2001).

Zeidan, D., *The Resurgence of Religion: A Comparative Study of Selected Themes in Christian and Islamic Fundamentalist Discourses* (Boston: Brill, 2003).

Zeitlin, I. M., *The Historical Muhammad* (London: Polity, 2008).

Ziadeh, N. A., *Sanusiyyah: A Study of a Revivalist Movement in Islam* (Leiden: Brill, 1968).

Zubaida, S., *Law and Power in the Islamic World* (London: I.B. Tauris, 2005).
Zuhur, S., *Islamic Rulings on Warfare* (Carlisle Barracks: Strategic Studies Institute, 2004).
Zurcher, E. J., *Turkey: A Modern History* (New York: I.B. Tauris, 2004).

II. Chapters From Edited Collections

Abdal-Haqq, I., 'Islamic Law: An Overview of Its Origin and Elements' in: H. M. Ramadan (ed.), *Understanding Islamic Law: From Classical to Contemporary* (Oxford: AltaMira Press, 2006) 1.

Adams, C. J., 'Mawdudi and the Islamic State' in: J. L. Esposito (ed.), *Voices of Resurgent Islam* (New York: Oxford University Press, 1983) 103.

Aghnides, N. P., 'Classification of Persons' in: A. G. Bostom (ed.), *The Legacy of Jihad: Islamic Holy War and the Fate of Non-Muslims* (New York: Prometheus Books, 2008) 303.

Aksakal, M., '"Holy War Made in Germany?" Ottoman Origins of the 1914 Jihad' in: H. Gulalp; G. Seufert (eds.), *Religion, Identity and Politics: Germany and Turkey in Interaction* (London: Routledge, 2013) 34.

Ali, S. S., 'Resurrecting *Siyar* through *Fatwas*? (Re)Constructing Islamic International Law in a Post-(Iraq) Invasion World' in: M. C. Bassiouni; A. Guellali (eds.), *Jihad and its Challenges to International and Domestic Law* (The Hague: Hague Academic Press, 2010) 107.

Ali, S. S., 'The Twain Doth Meet! A Preliminary Exploration of the Theory and Practice of *As-Siyar* and International Law in the Contemporary World' in: J. Rehman; S. C. Breau (eds.), *Religion, Human Rights and International Law* (Leiden: Martinus Nijhoff Publishers, 2007) 86.

Allain, J., 'Acculturation through the Middle Ages: The Islamic Law of Nations and its Place in the History of International Law' in: A. Orakhelashvili (ed.), *Research Handbook on the Theory and History of International Law* (Northampton, MA: Edward Elgar Publishing, 2011) 394.

Al-Qaradawi, Y., 'Islam and Democracy' in: R. L. Euben; M. Q. Zaman (eds.), *Princeton Readings in Islamic Thought: Texts and Contexts from al-Banna to bin Laden* (Princeton: Princeton, 2009) 230.

An-Na'im, A., 'Religious Freedom in Egypt under the Shadow of the Islamic *Dhimma* System' in: L. Swidler (ed.), *Religious Liberty and Human Rights in Nations and in Religions* (Philadelphia: Ecumenical Press, 1986) 50.

Arikan, Z., 'Cumhuriyet Ideolojisi ve 1536 Kapitulasyonlari' in: N. Abaci (ed.), *VIII. Uluslararasi Turkiye'nin Sosyal ve Ekonomic Tarihi Kongresi* (Morrisville: Lulu Press, 2006) 154.

Arzt, D. E., 'The Treatment of Religious Dissidents under Classical and Contemporary Islamic Law' in: J. Witte; J. D. Vyver (eds.), *Religious Human Rights in Global Perspective: Religious Perspectives*, Vol. I (The Hague: Kluwer Law International, 1996) 412.

Baderin, M. A., 'The Role of Islam in Human Rights and Development in Muslim States' in: J. Rehman; S. C. Breau (eds.), *Religion, Human Rights and International Law: A Critical Examination of Islamic State Practices* (Leiden: Martinus Nijhoff Publishers, 2007) 340.

Bantekas, I., 'Religion as a Source of International Law' in: J. Rehman; S. C. Breau (eds.), *Religion, Human Rights and International Law: A Critical Examination of Islamic State Practices* (Leiden: Martinus Nijhoff Publishers, 2007) 115.

Bassiouni, M. C., 'Introduction' in: M. C. Bassiouni; A. Guellali (eds.), *Jihad and its Challenges to International and Domestic Law* (The Hague: Hague Academic Press, 2010) 2.

Beeman, W. O., 'Iran's Islamic Republic' in: J. L. Esposito; E. E. Shahin (eds.), *The Oxford Handbook of Islam and Politics* (Oxford: Oxford University Press, 2013) 399.

Beinin, J.; Stork, J., 'On the Modernity, Historical Specificity, and International Context of Political Islam' in: J. Beinin; J. Stork (eds.), *Political Islam: Essays from Middle East Report* (London: I.B. Tauris, 1997) 3.

Berger, M. S., 'Jihad and Counter-Jihad: Western European Legal Responses to Islamic Militancy' in: M. C. Bassiouni; A. Guellali (eds.), *Jihad and its Challenges to International and Domestic Law* (The Hague: Hague Academic Press, 2010) 229.

Bostom, A. G., 'Jihad Conquests and the Imposition of Dhimmitude: A Survey' in: A. G. Bostom (ed.), *The Legacy of Jihad: Islamic Holy War and the Fate of Non-Muslims* (New York: Prometheus Books, 2008) 29.

Bosworth, C. E., 'The Formation of the Early Islamic Polity and Society: General Characteristics' in: M. A. Al-Bakhit; S. M. Cissoko (eds.), *History of Humanity: From the Seventh Century to the Sixteenth Century*, Vol. IV (New York: Routledge, 2000) 27.

Bramsen, D., 'Divine Law and Human Understanding: The Idea of Sharia in Saudi Arabia' in: J. S. Nielsen; L. Christoffersen (eds.), *Shari'a as Discourse: Legal Traditions and the Encounter with Europe* (Farnham: Ashgate Publishing, 2010) 157.

Brockopp, J. E., 'Introduction' in: J. E. Brockopp (ed.), *The Cambridge Companion to Muhammad* (New York: Cambridge University Press, 2010) 10.

Brook, Y.; Epstein, A., 'Just War Theory vs. American Self-Defence' in: E. Journo (ed.), *Winning the Unwinnable War: America's Self-Crippled Response to Islamic Totalitarianism* (Plymouth: Rowman & Littlefield, 2009) 81.

Brown, D., 'Martyrdom in Sunni Revivalist Thought' in: M. Cormack (ed.), *Sacrificing the Self: Perspectives on Martyrdom and Religion* (Oxford: Oxford University Press, 2001) 107.

Chehabi, H. E.; Mneimneh, H. I., 'Five Centuries of Lebanese-Iranian Encounters' in: H. E. Chehabi (ed.), *Distant Relations: Iran and Lebanon in the last 500 Years* (Oxford: The Centre for Lebanese Studies, 2006) 32.

Cornell, V. J., 'Fruit of the Tree of Knowledge: The Relationship between Faith and Practice in Islam' in: J. L. Esposito (ed.), *The Oxford History of Islam* (Oxford: Oxford University Press, 1999) 63.

Dawisha, A., 'Islam in Foreign Policy: Some Methodological Issues' in: A. Dawisha (ed.), *Islam in Foreign Policy* (Cambridge: Cambridge University Press, 1983) 1.

Donner, F. M., 'The Sources of Islamic Conceptions of War' in: J. Kelsay; J. T. Johnson (eds.), *Just War and Jihad: Historical and Theoretical Perspectives on War and Peace in Western and Islamic Traditions* (New York: Greenwood Press, 1991) 31.

Dumont, P., 'The Origins of Kemalist Ideology' in: J. M. Landau (ed.), *Ataturk and the Modernization of Turkey* (Leiden: Brill, 1984) 26.

Engeland-Nourai, A. V., 'The Challenge of Fragmentation of International Humanitarian Law' in: M. C. Bassiouni; A. Guellali (eds.), *Jihad and its Challenges to International and Domestic Law* (The Hague: Hague Academic Press, 2010) 153.

Esposito, J. L., 'Trailblazers of the Islamic Resurgence' in: Y. Y. Haddad; J. O. Voll; J. L. Esposito; K. Moore; D. Sawan (eds.), *The Contemporary Islamic Revival: A Critical Survey and Bibliography* (Westport: Greenwood Publishing, 1991) 37.

Evans, M., 'Moral Theory and the Idea of a Just War' in: M. Evans (ed.), *Just War Theory: A Reappraisal* (Edinburgh: Edinburgh University Press, 2005) 1.

Falk, R., 'False Universalism and the Geopolitics of Exclusion: The Case of Islam' in: J. Allain (ed.), *Unlocking the Middle East: The Writings of Richard Falk* (Gloucestershire: Apris Books, 2003) 50.

Faraj, M. A. S., 'The Neglected Duty' in: R. L. Euben; M. Q. Zaman (eds.), *Princeton Readings in Islamic Thought: Texts and Contexts from al-Banna to bin Laden* (Princeton: Princeton, 2009) 327.

Frymer-Kensky, T., 'Biblical Voices on Chosenness' in: R. Jospe; T. G. Madsen; S. Ward (eds.), *Covenant and Chosenness in Judaism and Mormonism* (Cranbury: Fairleigh Dickinson University Press, 2001) 23.

Greaves, R., 'Iranian Relations with Great Britain and British India, 1798–1921' in: P. Avery; G. R. G. Hambly; C. Melville (eds.), *The Cambridge History of Iran: From Nadir Shah to the Islamic Republic*, Vol. VII (Cambridge: Cambridge University Press, 1991) 374.

Griffel, F., 'Introduction' in: A. Amanat; F. Griffel (eds.), *Islamic Law in the Contemporary Context* (Stanford: Stanford University Press, 2007) 2.

Guellali, A., 'Understanding the Discourses on Jihad in Islam' in: M. C. Bassiouni; A. Guellali (eds.), *Jihad and its Challenges to International and Domestic Law* (The Hague: Hague Academic Press, 2010) 59.

Guran, S., 'Administrative Law' in: T. Ansay; D. Wallace (eds.), *Introduction to Turkish Law* (The Hague: Kluwer Law International, 2005) 53.

Guriz, A., 'Sources of Turkish Law' in: T. Ansay; D. Wallace (eds.), *Introduction to Turkish Law* (The Hague: Kluwer Law International, 2005) 9.

Haddad, Y. Y., 'Sayyid Qutb: Ideologue of Islamic Revival' in: J. L. Esposito (ed.), *Voices of Resurgent Islam* (New York: Oxford University Press, 1983) 84.

Hambly, G. G. R., 'The Pahlavi Autocracy: Riza Shah, 1921–1941' in: P. Avery; G. G. R. Hambly; C. Melville (eds.), *The Cambridge History of Iran*, Vol. VII (Cambridge: Cambridge University Press, 1991) 239.

Hasan, S., 'Islamic Jurisprudence: Sources and Traditions Creating Diversity in Human Relationships' in: S. Hasan (ed.), *The Muslim World in the 21st Century: Space, Power, and Human Development* (London: Springer, 2012) 25.

Hashmi, S. H., 'Interpreting the Islamic Ethics of War and Peace' in: T. Nardin (ed.), *The Ethics of War and Peace: Religious and Secular Perspectives* (Princeton: Princeton University Press, 1996) 146.

Hashmi, S. H., 'Islamic Ethics in International Society,' in: S. H. Hashmi (ed.), *Islamic Political Ethics: Civil Society, Pluralism, and Conflict* (Princeton: Princeton University Press, 2002) 148.

Hashmi, S. H., 'Is There an Islamic Ethic of Humanitarian Intervention' in: M. A. Baderin (ed.), *International Law and Islamic Law* (Aldershot: Ashgate, 2008) 122.

Hashmi, S. H., 'Jihad and the Geneva Conventions: The Impact of International Law on Islamic Theory' in: S. H. Hashmi (ed.), *Just Wars, Holy Wars, and Jihads: Christian, Jewish, and Muslim Encounters and Exchanges* (Oxford: Oxford University Press, 2012) 325.

Hashmi, S. H., 'Saving and Taking Life in War' in: J. E. Brockopp (ed.), *Islamic Ethics of Life: Abortion, War, and Euthanasia* (Columbia: The University of South Carolina Press, 2003) 144.

Hashmi, S. H., 'War and Peace' in: S. H. Hashmi (ed.), *Islamic Political Ethics: Civil Society, Pluralism, and Conflict* (Princeton: Princeton University Press, 2002) 206.

Haykel, B., 'On the Nature of Salafi Thought and Action' in: R. Meijer (ed.), *Global Salafism: Islam's New Religious Movement* (New York: Columbia University Press, 2009) 33.

Hidemitsu, K., 'Mobility of Non-Muslims in Mid-Nineteenth-Century Aleppo' in: K. Hidemitsu (ed.), *The Influence of Human Mobility in Muslim Societies* (New York: Routledge, 2009) 117.

Inalcik, H., 'The Heyday and Decline of the Ottoman Empire' in: P. M. Holt; A. K. S. Lambton; B. Lewis (eds.), *The Cambridge History of Islam* (Cambridge: Cambridge University Press, 1970) 330.

Jankowski, J., 'Egypt and Early Arab Nationalism, 1908–1922' in: R. Khalidi; L. Anderson; M. Muslih; R. S. Simon (eds.), *The Origins of Arab Nationalism* (New York: Columbia University Press, 1991) 257.

Jansen, M., 'Terrorism is a Response to Western Hypocrisy' in: P. A. Winters (ed.), *Islam: Opposing Viewpoints* (San Diego: Greenhaven Press, Inc., 1995) 168.

Johnson, J. T., 'Introduction' in: J. T. Johnson; J. Kelsay (eds.), *Cross, Crescent, and Sword* (London: Greenwood Press, 1990) xvi.

Kamali, M. H., 'Jihad and the Interpretation of the Qur'an: Contextualising Islamic Tradition' in: M. C. Bassiouni; A. Guellali (eds.), *Jihad and its Challenges to International and Domestic Law* (The Hague: Hague Academic Press, 2010) 39.

Karpat, K. H., 'Modern Turkey' in: P. M. Holt; A. K. S. Lambton; B. Lewis (eds.), *Cambridge History of Islam* (Cambridge: Cambridge University Press, 1992) 527.

Khadduri, M., 'International Law' in: M. Khadduri; H. J. Lienbesny (eds.), *Law in the Middle East*, Vol. I (Washington DC: Middle East Institute, 1955) 349.

Khan, M., 'Reason and Individual Reasoning' in: J. J. Donohue; J. L. Esposito (eds.), *Islam in Transition: Muslim Perspectives*, 2nd ed. (Oxford: Oxford University Press, 2007) 501.

Kocak, M., 'Islam and National Law in Turkey' in: J. M. Otto (ed.), *Sharia Incorporated: A Comparative Overview of the Legal Systems of Twelve Muslim Countries in Past and Present* (Leiden: Leiden University Press, 2010) 231.

Krisch, N., 'More Equal than the Rest? Hierarchy, Equality and US Predominance in International Law' in: M. Byers; G. Nolte (eds.), *United States Hegemony and the Foundations of International Law* (Cambridge: Cambridge University Press, 2003) 150.

Lacroix, S., 'Ayman al-Zawahiri, Veteran of Jihad' in: G. Kepel; J. P. Milelli (eds.); P. Ghazaleh (trans.), *Al Qaeda in its Own Words* (Cambridge, MA: Harvard University Press, 2008) 150.

Lahoud, N., 'The Pitfalls of Jihad as an Individual Duty (*Fard 'Ayn*)' in: M. C. Bassiouni; A. Guellali (eds.), *Jihad and its Challenges to International and Domestic Law* (The Hague: Hague Academic Press, 2010) 87.

Lapidus, I. M., 'Sultanates and Gunpowder Empires: The Middle East' in: J. L. Esposito (ed.), *The Oxford History of Islam* (Oxford: Oxford University Press, 1999) 347.

Lentner, H. H., 'Politics, Power and States in Globalization' in: H. Goverde; P. G. Cerny; M. Haugaard; H. H. Lentner (eds.), *Power in Contemporary Politics: Theories, Practices, Globalizations* (London: Sage Publications, 2000) 198.

Lewis, B., 'Politics and War' in: J. Schacht; C. E. Bosworth (eds.), *The Legacy of Islam* (London: Oxford University Press, 1974) 165.

Liebesny, H. J., 'The Development of Western Judicial Privileges' in: M. Khadduri; H. J. Liebesny (eds.), *Law in the Middle East*, Vol. I (Washington DC: Middle East Institute, 1955) 316.

Little, D., '"Holy War" Appeals and Western Christianity: A Reconsideration of Bainton's Approach' in: J. Kelsay; J. T. Johnson (eds.), *Just War and Jihad: Historical and Theoretical Perspectives on War and Peace in Western and Islamic Traditions* (New York: Greenwood Press, 1991) 121.

Mahmud, M., 'Islam vs. Marxism and Capitalism' in: J. J. Donohue; J. Esposito (eds.), *Islam in Transition: Muslim Perspectives*, 2nd ed. (Oxford: Oxford University Press, 2007) 129.

Martin, R. C., 'The Religious Foundations of War, Peace and Statecraft in Islam' in: J. Kelsay; J. T. Johnson (eds.), *Just War and Jihad: Historical and Theoretical Perspectives on War and Peace in Western and Islamic Traditions* (New York: Greenwood Press, 1991) 91.

Mayer, A. E., 'War and Peace in the Islamic Tradition and International Law' in: J. Kelsay; J. T. Johnson (eds.), *Just War and Jihad: Historical and Theoretical Perspectives on War and Peace in Western and Islamic Traditions* (New York: Greenwood Press, 1991) 195.

Metzemaekers, L., 'How Counter-Developmental is Muslim Fundamentalism?' in: C. A. O. Nieuwenhuijze (ed.), *Development Regardless of Culture?* (Leiden: Brill, 1984) 54.

Mir, M., 'The Sura as a Unity: A Twentieth Century Development in Quran Exegesis' in: G. R. Hawting; A. A. Shareef (eds.), *Approaches to the Quran* (New York: Routledge, 1993) 218.

Mirza, S. K., 'An Exegesis on *Jihad* in Islam' in: K. E. Shienbaum; J. Hasan (eds.), *Beyond Jihad: Critical Voices from Inside Islam* (Bethesda: Academica Press, 2006) 77.

Moosa, E., 'Colonialism and Islamic Law' in: M. K. Masud; A. Salvatore; M. Bruinessen (eds.) *Islam and Modernity: Key Issues and Debates* (Edinburgh: Edinburgh University Press, 2009) 158.

Moussalli, A. S., 'An Islamic Model for Political Conflict Resolution: *Tahkim* (Arbitration)' in: P. Salem (ed.) *Conflict Resolution in the Arab World: Selected Essays* (Beirut: American University of Beirut Press, 1997) 44.

Neff, S. C., 'A Short History of International Law' in: M. D. Evans (ed.), *International Law*, 2nd ed. (New York: Oxford University Press, 2006) 29.

Onar, S. S., 'The Majalla' in: M. Khadduri; H. J. Liebesny (eds.), *Law in the Middle East*, Vol. I (Washington DC: Middle East Institute, 1955) 293.

Raja, M. A., 'Muslim Modernity: Poetics, Politics, and Metaphysics' in: G. Marranci (ed.), *Muslim Societies and the Challenge of Secularization: An Interdisciplinary Approach* (London: Springer, 2010) 99.

Rajaee, F., 'Conclusion: Why "Alone"' in: T. Juneau; S. Razavi (eds.), *Iranian Foreign Policy since 2001* (New York: Routledge, 2013) 208.

Rex, J., 'Islam in the United Kingdom' in: S. T. Hunter (ed.), *Islam, Europe's Second Religion: The New Social, Cultural, and Political Landscape* (Westport, CT: Praeger, 2002) 70.

Rudolph, H., 'The Ottoman Empire and the Institutionalization of European Diplomacy, 1500–1700' in: M. L. Frick; A. T. Muller (eds.), *Islam and International Law: Engaging Self-Centrism from a Plurality of Perspectives* (Leiden: Brill, 2013) 161.

Sachedina, A. A., 'The Development of *Jihad* in Islamic Revelation and History' in: J. T. Johnson; J. Kelsay (eds.), *Cross, Crescent, and Sword* (London: Greenwood Press, 1990) 35.

Sahliyeh, E., 'Islam and Human Rights' in: D. P. Forsythe; P. C. McMahon (eds.), *Human Rights and Diversity: Area Studies Revisited* (Lincoln: University of Nebraska Press, 2003) 262.

Schulz, M., 'The Guarantees of Humanity: The Concert of Europe and the Origins of the Russo-Ottoman War of 1877' in: B. Simms; D. J. B. Trim (eds.), *Humanitarian Intervention: A History* (Cambridge: Cambridge University Press, 2011) 184.

Serjeant, R. B., 'Early Arabic Prose' in: A. F. L. Beeston; T. M. Johnstone; R. B. Serjeant; G. R. Smith (eds.), *Arabic Literature to the End of the Umayyad Period* (Cambridge: Cambridge University Press, 1983) 141.

Shaltut, M., 'The Koran and Fighting' in: R. Peters (ed.), *Jihad in Classical and Modern Islam* (Princeton: Markus Wiener Publishers, 1996) 79.

Stern, D., 'Sacred Text and Canon' in: A. A. Cohen; P. Mendes-Flohr (eds.), *20th Century Jewish Religious Thought* (Philadelphia: The Jewish Publication Society, 1987) 841.

Stoll, O., 'The Religions of the Armies' in: P. Erdkamp (ed.), *A Companion to the Roman Army* (Sussex: Wiley Publishing, 2007) 451.

Strawson, J., 'Holy War in the Media: Images of *Jihad*' in: S. Chermak; F. Y. Bailey; M. Brown (eds.), *Media Representations of September 11* (Westport: Praeger, 2003) 17.

Syed, M.; College, B., '*Jihad* in Classical Islamic Legal and Moral Thought' in: J. Neusner; B. D. Chilton; R. E. Tully (eds.), *Just War in Religion and Politics* (Lanham: University Press of America, 2013) 145.

Szabó, K. T., 'Self-Defense Arguments in Jihad and Western International Law' in: M. C. Bassiouni; A. Guellali (eds.), *Jihad and its Challenges to International and Domestic Law* (The Hague: Hague Academic Press, 2010) 209.

Voll, J. O., 'Two Renewal and Reform in Islamic History: Tajdid and Islah' in: J. L. Esposito (ed.), *Voices of Resurgent Islam* (New York: Oxford University Press, 1983) 38.

Waardenburg, J., 'The Early Period: 610–650' in: J. Waardenburg (ed.), *Muslim Perceptions of Other Religions: A Historical Survey* (New York: Oxford University Press, 1999) 3.

Warde, I., 'Global Politics, Islamic Finance and Islamist Politics Before and After 11 September 2001' in: C. M. Henry; R. Wilson (eds.), *The Politics of Islamic Finance* (Edinburgh: Edinburgh University Press, 2004) 37.

Zaman, M. R., 'Islamic Perspectives on Territorial Boundaries and Autonomy' in: S.H. Hashmi (ed.), *Islamic Political Ethics: Civil Society, Pluralism, and Conflict* (Princeton: Princeton University Press, 2002) 79.

Zawati, H. M., '*Jus in Bello:* Civilians' Fundamental Rights under Islamic and Public International Law' in: M. C. Bassiouni; A. Guellali (eds.), *Jihad and its Challenges to International and Domestic Law* (The Hague: Hague Academic Press, 2010) 167.

Ziegler, K. H., 'The Peace Treaties of the Ottoman Empire with European Christian Powers' in: R. Lesaffer (ed.), *Peace Treaties and International Law in European History: From the Late Middle Ages to World War One* (Cambridge: Cambridge University Press, 2004) 345.

Zubaida, S., 'Is Iran an Islamic State?' in: J. Beinin; J. Stork (eds.), *Political Islam: Essays from Middle East Report* (London: I.B. Tauris Publishers, 1997) 103.

III. Articles

Abo-Kazleh, M., 'Rethinking International Relations Theory in Islam: Toward a More Adequate Approach' (2006) 5 *Turkish Journal of International Relations,* 4.

AbuSulayman, A., 'Al-Dhimmah and Related Concepts in Historical Perspective' (1988) 9 *Institute of Muslim Minority Affairs,* 8.

Ali, S. S.; Rehman, J., 'The Concept of *Jihad* in Islamic International Law' (2005) 10 *Journal of Conflict & Security Law,* 321.

Al-Qazwini, I. S. M., 'Just War: An Islamic Perspective' (2004) 9 *Nexus,* 79.

Al-Zuhili, S., 'Islam and International Law' (2005) 87 *International Review of the Red Cross,* 269.

Anghie, A., 'Finding the Peripheries: Sovereignty and Colonialism in Nineteenth-Century International Law' (1999) 40 *Harvard International Law Journal,* 1.

An-Na'im, A., 'Islam and International Law: Toward a Positive Mutual Engagement to Realise Shared Ideals' (2004) 98 *American Society of International Law Proceedings,* 159.

An-Na'im, A., 'Islamic Law, International Relations, and Human Rights: Challenge and Response' (1987) 20 *Cornell International Law Journal,* 317.

An-Na'im, A., 'The Rights of Women and International Law in the Muslim Context' (1988) 9 *Whittier Law Review,* 491.

Arzt, D. E., 'The Application of International Human Rights Law in Islamic States' (1990) 12 *Human Rights Quarterly,* 202.

Badr, G. M., 'A Survey of Islamic International Law' (1982) 12 *American Society of International Law,* 56.

Baran, Z., 'Fighting the War of Ideas' (2005) 84 *Foreign Affairs*, 6.

Bassiouni, M. C., 'Evolving Approaches to Jihad: From Self-Defence to Revolutionary and Regime-Change Political Violence' (2008) 8 *Chicago Journal of International Law*, 119.

Bassiouni, M. C., 'Protection of Diplomats under Islamic Law' (1980) 74 *American Journal of International Law*, 609.

Bennoune, K., 'As-Salamu Alaykum? Humanitarian Law in Islamic Jurisprudence' (1994) 15 *Michigan Journal of International Law*, 605.

Brunnée, J.; Toope, S. J., 'Slouching Towards New "Just" Wars: The Hegemon after September 11th' (2004) 18 *International Relations*, 405.

Bsoul, L. A., 'Historical Evolution of Islamic Law of Nations/Siyar: Between Memory and Desire' (2008) 17 *Domes*, 48.

Bukay, D., 'Peace of Jihad? Abrogation in Islam' (2007) 14 *Middle East Quarterly*, 3.

Calverley, E. E., 'Mohammad, Seal of the Prophets?' (1936) 26 *The Muslim World*, 79.

Cockayne, J., 'Islam and International Humanitarian Law: From a Clash to a Conversation between Civilisations' (2002) 84 *International Review of the Red Cross*, 597.

Dayem, M. A.; Ayub, F., 'In the Path of Allah: Evolving Interpretations of Jihad and its Modern Challenges' (2009) 7 *UCLA Journal of Islamic and Near Eastern Law*, 67.

Dinstein, Y., 'Comments on War' (2004) 27 *Harvard Journal of Law & Public Policy*, 877.

El-Ayouty, Y., 'International Terrorism under the Law' (1999) 5 *ILSA Journal of International & Comparative Law*, 485.

Elbe, J. V., 'The Evolution of the Concept of the Just War in International Law' (1939) 33 *The American Journal of International Law*, 665.

Elshtain, J. B., 'Just War and Humanitarian Intervention' (2001) 17 *American University International Law Review*, 1.

Ereksoussi, M. K., 'Le Coran et les Conventions Humanitaries' (1960) 503 *Revue Internationale de la Croix-Rouge*, 641.

Euben, R. L., 'Killing (for) Politics: *Jihad*, Martyrdom, and Political Action' (2002) 30 *Political Theory*, 4.

Ford, C. A., 'Siyar-ization and its Discontents: International Law and Islam's Constitutional Crisis' (1995) 30 *Texas International Law Journal*, 499.

Goolam, N. M., '*Ijtihad* and its Significance for Islamic Legal Interpretation' (2006) *Michigan State Law Review*, 1443.

Green, L. C., 'Cicero and Clausewitz or Quincy Wright: The Interplay of Law and War' (1999) 9 *Journal of Legal Studies*, 59.

Hallaq, W. B., 'From *Fatwas* to *Furu*: Growth and Change in Islamic Substantive Law' (1994) 1 *Islamic Law and Society*, 29.

Hallaq, W. B., 'On the Authoritativeness of Sunni Consensus' (1986) 18 *International Journal of Middle East Studies*, 427.

Hallaq, W. B., 'On the Origins of the Controversy about the Existence of Mujtahids and the Gate of Ijtihad' (1986) 63 *Studia Islamica*, 129.

Hallaq, W. B., 'Was the Gate of Ijtihad Closed?' (1984) 16 *International Journal of Middle East Studies*, 3.

Hassan, F. A., 'The Sources of Islamic Law' (1982) 76 *American Society of International Law Proceedings*, 65.

Huart, C., 'Le Droit de La Guerre' (1907) 2 *Revue du Monde Musulman*, 331.

Huntington, S. P., 'The Clash of Civilizations?' (1993) 72 *Foreign Affairs*, 3.

Jackson, S. A., 'Jihad and the Modern World' (2002) 7 *Journal of Islamic Law and Culture,* 1.
Kamali, M. H., 'Methodological Issues in Islamic Jurisprudence' (1996) 11 *Arab Law Quarterly,* 3.
Kaye, D., 'Adjudicating Self-Defense: Discretion, Perception, and the Resort to Force in International Law' (2005) 44 *Columbia Journal of Transnational Law,* 134.
Kelsay, J., 'Religion, Morality, and the Governance of War: The Case of Classical Islam' (1990) 18 *Journal of Religious Ethics,* 123.
Khadduri, M., 'Islam and the Modern Law of Nations' (1956) 50 *The American Journal of International Law,* 358.
Khadduri, M., 'The *Maslaha* (Public Interest) and *Illa* (Cause) in Islamic Law' (1980) 12 *New York University Journal of International Law and Politics,* 213.
Khadduri, M., 'Nature and Sources of Islamic Law' (1953) 22 *The George Washington Law Review,* 3.
Khan, A., 'The Reopening of the Islamic Code: The Second Era of Ijtihad' (2003) 1 *University of St. Thomas Law Journal,* 341.
Kunz, J. L., 'Bellum Justum and Bellum Legale' (1951) 45 *The American Journal of International Law,* 528.
Laghmani, S., 'Les Écoles Juridiques du Sunnisme' (2003) 104 *Pouvoirs,* 21.
Lewis, B., 'The Roots of Muslim Rage' (1990) 266 *The Atlantic Monthly,* 47.
MacEoin, D., 'Suicide Bombing as Worship Dimensions of Jihad' (2009) *Middle East Quarterly,* 15.
Mahmoudi, S., 'The Islamic Perception of the Use of Force in the Contemporary World' (2005) 7 *Journal of the History of International Law,* 55.
Mertus, J., 'Reconsidering the Legality of Humanitarian Intervention: Lessons from Kosovo' (2000) 41 *William and Mary Law Review,* 1751.
Mohammad, N., 'The Doctrine of *Jihad*: An Introduction' (1985) 3 *Journal of Law and Religion,* 381.
Mohammed, N., 'Principles of Islamic Contract Law' (1988) 6 *Journal of Law and Religion,* 115.
Murphy, C. F., 'The Grotian Vision of World Order' (1982) 76 *American Journal of International Law,* 477.
Napoleoni, L., 'Modern Jihad: The Islamist Crusade' (2003) 23 *Sais Review,* 53.
Nawaz, M. K., 'The Concept of Human Rights in Islamic Law' (1965) 11 *Howard Law Journal,* 325.
Parvin, M.; Sommer, M., 'Dar al-Islam: The Evolution of Muslim Territoriality and its Implications for Conflict Resolution in the Middle East' (1980) 11 *International Journal of Middle East Studies,* 1.
Potter, P. B., 'As Determined by the United States' (1946) 40 *American Journal of International Law,* 792.
Raab, D., 'Armed Attack after the *Oil Platforms* Case' (2004) 17 *Leiden Journal of International Law,* 719.
Rehman, J., 'Islam, "War on Terror" and the Future of Muslim Minorities in the United Kingdom: Dilemmas of Multiculturalism in the Aftermath of the London Bombings' (2007) 29 *Human Rights Quarterly,* 831.
Renard, J., 'Al-Jihad Al-Akbar: Notes on a Theme in Islamic Spirituality' (1988) 78 *The Muslim World,* 225.
Ritchie, A. D., 'The Ethics of Pacifism' (1940) 15 *Philosophy,* 227.

Said, J., 'Law, Religion and the Prophetic Method of Social Change' (2001) 15 *Journal of Law and Religion*, 83.

Schacht, J., 'Islamic Law in Contemporary States' (1959) 8 *American Journal of Comparative Law*, 133.

Schachter, O., 'Self-Defence and the Rule of Law' (1989) 83 *American Journal of International Law*, 259.

Schroeder, E., 'Kosovo Crisis: Humanitarian Imperative versus International Law' (2004) 28 *Fletcher Forum of World Affairs*, 181.

Scott, J. B., 'The Legal Nature of International Law' (1905) 5 *Columbia Law Review*, 124.

Shaw, A., 'Revival of the Just War Doctrine' (1976) 3 *Auckland University Law Review*, 156.

Silverman, A. L., 'Just War, *Jihad*, and Terrorism: A Comparison of Western and Islamic Norms for the Use of Political Violence' (2002) 44 *Journal of Church & State*, 73.

Simon, D. W., 'US Foreign Policy and the World of Islam' (1995) 3 *Willamette Bulletin of International Law & Policy*, 69.

Thayer, L. E., 'The Capitulations of the Ottoman Empire and the Question of their Abrogation as its Affects the United States' (1923) 17 *American Journal of International Law*, 207.

Weightman, M. A., 'Self-Defense in International Law' (1951) 37 *Virginia Law Review*, 1095.

Weiss, B. G., 'Interpretation in Islamic Law: The Theory of Ijtihad' (1978) 26 *The American Journal of Comparative Law*, 199.

Whalen, J. F., 'In Search of *Jihad*: Toward a Policy of Constructive Islamic Engagement' (1998) 5 *Brown Journal of World Affairs*, 279.

Willis, J. R., 'Jihad Fi Sabil Allah—Its Doctrinal Basis in Islam and Some Aspects of its Evolution in Nineteenth-Century West Africa' (1967) 3 *Journal of African History*, 395.

Wright, Q., 'The Meaning of the Pact of Paris' (1933) 27 *American Journal of International Law*, 39.

Index